Visions of Faith

VISIONS *of* FAITH

An Anthology of Reflections

Compiled by William Sykes

The Bible Reading Fellowship

Compilation and introductions
copyright © William Sykes 1996

The author asserts the moral right
to be identified as the author of this work

Published by
The Bible Reading Fellowship
Peter's Way
Sandy Lane West
Oxford OX4 5HG
ISBN 0 7459 3098 0
Albatross Books Pty Ltd
PO Box 320, Sutherland
NSW 2232, Australia
ISBN 0 7324 0904 7

First edition 1996

Acknowledgments

Unless otherwise stated, Scripture is taken from
The Revised Standard Version of the Bible,
copyright © 1946, 1952, 1971 by the Division of
Christian Education of the National Council of the
Churches of Christ in the USA.

Extracts are reproduced by permission of the
publishers, or, in some cases, by permission of
the holders of the rights of reproduction.

Extracts from the Authorized Bible (The King
James Bible) the rights in which are invested in
the Crown, are reproduced by permission of the
Crown's patentee, Cambridge University Press.

New English Bible © 1970 by permission of
Oxford and Cambridge University Presses.

Every effort has been made to trace and contact
copyright owners. If there are any inadvertent
omissions in the acknowledgments we apologize
to those concerned.

A catalogue record for this book is available
from the British Library

Printed and bound in Great Britain
by Arrowsmith Limited, Bristol

Contents

Acceptance	15	Humanism	110	Renunciation	206
Action	18	Image of God	113	Repentance	209
Adversity	21	Incarnation	115	Resurrection	211
Anxiety	23	Inner life	118	Revelation	214
Atheism	26	Intercession	121	Saints	219
Authority	28	Jesus Christ	124	Salvation	221
Belief	32	Judgment	128	Sanctification	224
Bible	34	Kingdom of		Science and	
Brotherhood	37	God	131	religion	226
Charity	40	Knowledge	134	Secular	230
Christianity	43	Man	138	Selfishness	232
Church	46	Meditation	141	Service	235
Commitment	49	Miracles	145	Sin	237
Community	51	Mission	147	Society	241
Conversion	53	Morals	150	Sons of God	243
Creation	56	Mystics &		Soul	246
Cross	59	mysticism	153	Suffering	248
Death	63	New creation	157	Temptation	253
Discipleship	66	Other faiths	161	Thanksgiving	255
Doubt	68	Pain	164	Time	258
Dying to self	70	Paradise	167	Transformation	260
Eternal life	74	Penitence	169	Trinity	263
Evil	77	Philosophy	172	Trust	266
Faith	80	Politics	174	Truth	268
Finding God	83	Power	177	Unity	273
Forgiveness	86	Prayer	180	Vocation	276
Free will &		Preaching	183	The way	279
determinism	89	Pride	186	Wholeness	281
God	92	Prophets	188	Will	285
Grief	95	Providence	191	Work	287
Guidance	99	Purpose	193	Worldliness	290
Heaven	102	Reconciliation	198	Worship	293
Hell	104	Redemption	200		
Holy Spirit	106	Religion	202		

Preface
A READER'S VIEW

Steve Sheppard teaches law in Michigan in the United States. He was at University College, Oxford, pursuing his D. Phil. from 1989 to 1992. He has written prefaces for *Visions of Hope, Visions of Love* and *Visions of Glory.* This is what he has now written about *Visions of Faith...*

Bill Sykes is a man one might underestimate, if only at first glance. A rather soft-spoken fellow with the type of quirky grin that disarms and suggests the proximate existence of a cup of tea, he seems not at all the tenacious scholar exposed in these pages. Then again, his trundling past the cynical halls of Oxford, his ministering in the most dubious wards of London, and his scrambling through the thickest Asian jungles with the Gurkhas have clearly taught him the fine art of camouflage. This point of camouflage will not be lost on the reader of *Visions of Faith,* this book collecting reflections on a host of seemingly random topics, but under which lurks an industrious soul and teacher. The reader, lulled, may be duped completely by Bill's plain-spoken descriptions and well-chosen readings before realizing that nothing less than a full description of Christian life is built upon these foundations. And, as we shall see, it is a description upon which each reader is challenged to build.

Some readers will not be surprised. *Visions of Faith* is here being reissued, some years after its all-too-fast exit from print, and the kernel of its original success is present in this modified edition. *Visions of Faith* is the fourth of the quintet of Bill's *Visions* projects to be published currently.

I have been pleased to watch these books mature from, nearly, their earliest days, when they were no more than vast binders of notes under the couch of his rooms in college. I would, with several of my most skeptical friends, descend upon the Chaplain's Rooms for an hour each week of term. We were an unlikely mob for one of his many 'reflection groups', but that was our purpose, even if only we thought it was clandestine.

We'd settle in Bill's bottomless upholstery, cradling tea and coffee, and ponder a list of topics. We could, of course, choose something like Judgment, Faith, or Worship, and often we did. (Though there was somewhat more interest in Sin and Evil, at least in the Springtime.) In any event, one hapless soul would eventually admit to a topic of choice, and we would knuckle down to reading it, that is reading an entry that is now a *Visions* topic. Each entry takes about twenty minutes to read, a few minutes more if there are particularly good biscuits.

With Bill's light goading the conversation started, the student on the hot seat inventing a quick lie to explain why the topic was chosen. Some of the talks that followed could be commonplace, but often they were much more. Catalysed by just a few vents to the steam from Bill, the discourse would sometimes rise to a nearly thrilling pitch. I found myself, and still find myself, remembering those talks with a sense that there may really have been inspiration.

I left Oxford to continue my studies and to labour at my doctoral work, which is perhaps nearly complete. In the years that have followed, Bill has finally turned his notebooks over to a press. *Visions of Love* was published first, followed in quick succession by *Hope* and *Glory*, and now *Faith*. The final volume will be *Visions of Grace*. Each book is a unique part of a whole, and each is enough to stand easily alone as a testament to Bill's project.

Patience, they say, is a virtue (a point well made in the selections under that title in *Visions of Love*, also available from you-know-who), and the long wait of Bill Sykes' fans is here rewarded. For the lucky reader who has just found this unique collection, *Visions of Faith* may augur a lifelong consultation with Sykes' books.

Steve Sheppard

HOW A SCHOOLMASTER USES AN ANTHOLOGY
OF REFLECTIONS

Robert Aldred is a housemaster at St Edward's School, a boys' boarding school in Oxford. A few years ago his wife, Alison, was the nurse at University College, and working closely in that capacity with the chaplain of the college, Bill Sykes. Through that contact Robert discovered Bill Sykes' first anthology, the original *Visions of Faith* (now out of print), and from the moment he read it he realized what an invaluable resource it was. He has been using it for various groups in the school ever since and I asked him how.

'I use it in just one way,' he told me. 'We have copies of the book for the boys. We had a set of about forty at one stage, but over the years they have diminished. It is a very stimulating book, and sometimes a boy will say "Can I borrow it?" And he will take it away for a while and then bring it back—but not always!

'What I do is to give them just one section of quotations to look at in one period, which usually lasts for forty minutes. They stay in the classroom and I ask them just to go through the quotations, to think about them, and to make notes. Then the following week they come back and we discuss them. I use the book two or three times a year, and I try to choose subjects which the boys themselves are interested in pursuing.

'Basically, I use the same method that Bill uses himself, in order to get people to think about whatever subject it is, and to meditate upon it. I actually use the word meditate, and I say to them, "To meditate means to chew it over and to thrash it through, to ask yourself whether you agree with it, and to ask yourself: *What is it actually saying? What does it mean by this phrase, and that phrase?*' I find that it raises the intellectual level of discussion to a much more serious one.

'Quite often a group will tend to treat things at the level where they are, which can be rather shallow. But I have found that this book forces them to go to a level which is more mature and more demanding, and there is a greater level of seriousness in the discussion. This year I have got four groups. Three of them are fine, but one is rather hard work, because of the level of input (or the lack of it) from the various members. There is a group within the group who are somewhat immature, and they tend to be flippant and a bit silly. But using Bill's book has forced them to be more thoughtful.

'It is enormously stimulating, and it provides a broad spectrum of types of writing. To give you an example, I wanted to do something with the sixth form on marriage and sexuality, and when I was looking through those sections I found this marvellous quotation from *The Prophet*, by Kahlil Gibran:

But let there be spaces in your togetherness,
and let the winds of heaven dance between you.

'Brilliant! First of all I found it strange to see that juxtaposed against the Christian view of marriage. But then I thought, "Well, there's nothing much wrong with that!" And it made me realize how good it was to read people who were writing from all backgrounds, and from all walks of life and all the Church traditions. It's an enlarging experience.

'It is interesting how the pupils invariably pick out that passage from *The Prophet*. And when we are looking at the theme of suffering they almost always pick out the passage by Margaret Fishback Powers (and often known as 'Footprints'):

One night a man had a dream. He dreamt he was walking along the beach with his Lord. Across the sky flashed scenes from his life. For each scene he noticed two sets of footprints in the sand, one belonging to him, the other to the Lord. When the last scene in his life flashed before him he looked back at the footprints on the sand. He noticed that many times along the path of his life there was only one set of footprints. He also noticed that it happened at the very lowest and saddest times of his life. This really bothered him, and he questioned the Lord about it. 'Lord, you said that, once I decided to follow you, you would walk with me all the way. But I've noticed that during the most difficult times in my life there is only one set of footprints. I don't understand why, in times when I needed you most, you would leave me.' The Lord replied, 'My precious child, I love you and would never leave you during your trials and sufferings; when you see only one set of footprints, it was then that I carried you.'

The Reverend Shelagh Brown
Bible Reading Fellowship

The story behind *Visions of Faith*
HOW IT CAME INTO BEING AND HOW TO USE IT

A priest who lost his faith

What happens when a priest thinks he has lost his faith? I was thirty years old and, faced with this situation, saw three options: leave the Church; stay put in the Church and go through the motions; or stand my ground and fight. I had one thing on my side in making the choice—fresh memories from being a Gurkha officer. I had to fight.

Where he started the fight to find it

I started anew in the book of Genesis. In the story of the creation of man, God is depicted as fashioning and shaping man in his own image. He breathed into man and man became a living being. I was fascinated by this simple story. I took it to mean that God breathed something of his own nature into man, giving a divine potential for life.

Then I turned to the Gospels and found 'something of God in man' worked out in the man—Jesus Christ. He found the Father in the depths of himself. He tried to explain this to the disciples: 'Do you not believe that I am in the Father and the Father in me? . . . the Father who dwells in me does his works' (John 14:10). As I struggled with what these words meant, I began to understand Jesus as the image of the invisible God.

Starting to see the way of faith

This understanding brought me a new insight. Jesus discovered not only the presence of 'the Father' in himself, but also discovered that this presence is love, not just an abstraction but for people individually: 'As the Father loved me, so have I loved you; abide in my love' (John 15:9). This is the basis for the two great commandments: 'You shall love the Lord your God with all your heart . . . and you shall love your neighbour as yourself' (Matthew 22:37–39). He made this simpler: 'A new commandment I give to you, that you love one another; even as I have loved you' (John 13:34). Living in love, he lived in faith, and faith prevailed to the end of his life, to his death on the cross: 'Father, into thy hands I commit my spirit!' The vision of faith was beginning to take shape.

I went back to the Epistles. Paul discovered that what Christ had experienced in his life, we can all experience in some measure. Some time after his conversion on the Damascus road, Paul wrote: 'It is no longer I who live, but Christ who lives in me . . .' (Galatians 2:20). 'In him the whole fullness of deity dwells bodily, and you have come to fullness of life in him' (Colossians 2:9–10). I knew this meant much to me, that the whole power of the Trinity could be found in each of us as well as such attributes as life, light, truth, joy, love—and faith. I found to my delight that Paul had discovered the enormity of this faith and expressed it concisely in his Epistle to the Ephesians: 'For this reason I bow my knees before the Father, from whom every family in heaven and on earth is named, that according to the riches of his glory he may grant you to be strenthened with might through his Spirit in the inner man, and that Christ may dwell in your hearts through faith; that you, being rooted and grounded in love, may have power to comprehend with all the saints what is the breadth and length and height and depth, and to know the love of Christ which surpasses all knowledge, that you may be filled with all the fulness of God' (Ephesians 3:14–19). He summarized this in his epistle to the Galatians: 'For in Christ Jesus you are all sons of God, through faith' (Galatians 3:26). I was excited by this, but still felt that I was missing some part of his vision for me.

Dust and divinity
Then something in Genesis clicked into place: *that which was fashioned and shaped in the image and likeness of God was taken from the dust of the earth.* I saw then that in addition to being born with a 'divine' potential, we are still earthy and creaturely. This was no news to me, but now I saw that if either side was repressed or allowed too much sway the consequences would be negative and destructive.

But how could I make such a balance? I went back again to the Gospels. What do we find in the life of Christ? An integration of the divine and the earthy, the godly and the creaturely—'very God and very Man'—a perfect combination of the divine and the human. I now began to understand why he was called 'the second Adam'. By his life, death, and resurrection he had pioneered a way of integrating both sides of his nature, and so became the prototype of a new humanity. The vision of faith underlying this anthology finally made sense.

In many people over many years
Granted this vision of faith, I thought I might find evidence of it in the experience of men and women in the last two thousand years. I started searching for signs of this vision in the thoughts and words of others. First, I sought it in the recorded experience of saints and theologians. Secondly, from poets, novelists, playwrights, musicians and artists. Thirdly, of philosophers, scientists, statesmen, historians, politicians, economists and psychologists.

The material found has been set out in ninety-six topics. These contain many aspects of faith, and their opposites—with some related topics.

How to grow in this vision

The aim of this anthology is to provide a means to grow in this vision of faith. This is done primarily through the practice of reflection. Hence the subtitle, *An Anthology of Reflections.*

The *Concise Oxford Dictionary* defines 'reflection' as to 'go back in thought, meditate, or consult with oneself, remind oneself, or consider'. Reflection indicates a way of thinking with the mind, the imagination, intuition and feelings. It includes 'lateral thinking' and 'vertical thinking'—thinking which takes into account the spiritual dimension. A good description comes from the Collect for the Second Sunday in Advent (a prayer for the study of the Scriptures) '... Grant that we may in such wise hear them, read, mark, learn and inwardly digest them.' Reflection can have a devotional aspect, and merge into meditation and contemplation. I hope *Visions of Faith* can be used in many ways—as a book to dip into from time to time—as a bedside book—as a guide in time of need—as an aid in keeping a journal—as a personal book of devotion.

How to run a reflection group

As chaplain and fellow of an Oxford college, I have used the material for 'reflection groups'. These have been very popular, and in term-time at least thirty groups of up to five students meet each week.

I have been asked to describe in detail how these groups function. We meet for an hour a week at a mutually convenient time. We begin with a cup of tea, coffee or hot chocolate and briefly catch up on news. A list of topics is circulated and after two or three minutes a topic is chosen by consensus. Each topic consists of an introduction and some twenty quotations, two from the Old Testament, two from the New Testament, and the remaining sixteen from a wide variety of sources. Each person in the group is then given a copy of this material and the reflection group gets under way.

We then have about half an hour of silence. We look through the quotations thinking them through, and working out what they mean to us individually. Some of our participants are not used to being quiet and find silence difficult at first, so I make available a clipboard, pen and paper. We have found that writing down thoughts and insights has eased this period of silence and been a useful way of developing ideas.

As convenor of the group, I use this half- hour period to go through the quotations in the same way as the others but, in addition, to formulate some questions. These can be useful for stimulating discussion in the second half of the reflection group.

At the half-way stage, I ask if everyone has completed the material. I then ask, 'Was there any particular reason for choosing this topic?' Someone usually comes forward with a reason. My next question is: 'Did you find anything helpful?' The person who has chosen the topic responds, and then the other members of the group join in. Having reflected on the same material, conversation comes fairly easily. As convenor, my role is mainly to listen and make sure everyone has an opportunity to contribute. Sometimes the questions formulated by me earlier are a help; often they are not needed. The group ends promptly on the hour. (Time is precious in an eight-week term.)

How a reflection group begins
I usually start a new group with one person. Before long he or she usually suggests a person to join. Sometimes the addition is actually uninterested in religion but a good thinker. Sometimes it is someone committed to a particular creed, often not that of the first in the group. The two of them then invite a third member and so on. So the groups are based on trust and friendship, not orthodoxy. In the groups we have Roman Catholics, Methodists, members of the Church of England, the United Reformed Church, and the Christian Union, and the occasional Jew, Hindu, Muslim, Buddhist, atheist and agnostic.

Sometimes a group doesn't grow. Some people are shy, and are not ready for the group experience. Others want to go forward slowly. A few need individual attention. Some function quite happily in twos and threes. I reckon four or five is the best working number. Trust can still be maintained, and everyone can fully participate. Above this number, communication tends to break down.

I see *Visions of Faith* as a skeleton (or framework) of faith—and I leave it to the individual to put upon it (or clothe it with) his or her own flesh and blood.

Bill Sykes

ACCEPTANCE

'Acceptance'—favourable reception, approval, belief, toleration.

Whilst an undergraduate I had the great privilege of being the interpreter of the Oxford University Expedition to Nepal, 1963. We had gone there in the long vacation, to collect blood samples for the Lister Institute in London. This came under the auspices of the World Health Organization who were doing a world-wide survey of blood groupings. So far they had no data on Nepal. Our project was to be part of this wider programme.

We spent two months busily collecting our data, and having completed our project, went on a trek on the slopes of Annapurna. After a three-day climb we set up camp midway between two villages, at an altitude of 10,000 feet. Here the views of the mountains were spectacular.

One evening, we went up to the village of Ghanpokhara and came across a Gurkha pensioner, milking his cow. He greeted us cheerfully, and then slapped his wooden leg and said, 'Libya, 6th June, 1942.' We immediately understood what had happened, and were impressed with his carefree attitude to life. Later, when we came to leave the area, he bravely tackled the steep and rugged path down to our camp to bid us farewell. Here was someone who epitomized 'acceptance'. He had come to terms with the loss of his leg, without a trace of bitterness, and was living a full and active life. He had learnt one of the great secrets of life, turning to good use, a major set-back. We shall never forget him. His quiet courage had introduced us to 'acceptance'.

The beloved of the Lord, he dwells in safety by him; he encompasses him all the day long, and makes his dwelling between his shoulders.

Deuteronomy 33:12

Every man also to whom God has given wealth and possessions and power to enjoy them, and to accept his lot and find enjoyment in his toil—this is the gift of God. For he will not much remember the days of his life because God keeps him occupied with joy in his heart.

Ecclesiastes 5:19-20

But to all who received him, who believed in his name, he gave power to become children of God.

John 1:12

And we also thank God constantly for this, that when you received the word of God which you heard from us, you accepted it not as the word of men but as what it really is, the word of God, which is at work in you believers.

1 Thessalonians 2:13

Accept the fact that you are accepted!

Paul Tillich, The Shaking of the Foundations, SCM Press, 1949, page 162

He who is in a state of rebellion cannot receive grace, to use the phrase of which the Church is so fond—so rightly fond, I dare say—for in life as in art the mood of rebellion closes up the channels of the soul, and shuts out the airs of heaven.

Oscar Wilde, 'De Profundis', in The Works of Oscar Wilde, edited by G.F. Maine, William Collins Sons and Co., 1948, page 866

Our innate desire is to have something for ourselves, of ourselves. Often enough what lies behind 'favours' and a preoccupation with them is a deep desire for assurance. We feel these things authenticate our spiritual life. They do not. Nothing we experience in the spiritual life is itself any guarantee.

We have no guarantee except God's love and fidelity. He does not want us to have any but this. We turn from him when we make much of such things, when we crave them and welcome them. Too easily they induce spiritual pride simply because we read in them signs of great spirituality. We must be convinced they are no such sign.

The true signs of the Spirit are very different: an ever-growing selflessness in daily living, self-disregard in all spheres, humility, service, devotedness, and in our inmost heart a joy at being empty of all, poor, abandoned to God as he appears at every moment and in whatever guise.

Ruth Burrows, in *The Watchful Heart*, edited by Elizabeth Ruth Obbard, Darton, Longman and Todd, 1988, page 16

There liveth no man on earth who may always have rest and peace without troubles and crosses, with whom things always go according to his will; there is always something to be suffered here, turn which way you will. And as soon as you are quit of one assault, perhaps two will come in its place. Wherefore yield thyself willingly to them, and seek only that true peace of the heart, which none can take away from thee, that thou mayest overcome all assaults.

Thus then, Christ meant that inward peace which can break through all assaults and crosses of oppression, suffering, misery, humiliation and what more there may be of the like, so that a man may be joyful and patient therein, like the beloved disciples and followers of Christ. Now he who will in love give his whole diligence and might thereto, will verily come to know true eternal peace which is God Himself, as far as it is possible to a creature; insomuch that what was bitter to him before, shall become sweet, and his heart shall remain unmoved among all changes...

Theologia Germanica, translated by Susanna Winkworth, Stuart and Watkins, 1966, page 53

Nekhlyudov called to mind how at Kuzminskoye he had started to reflect over his life, trying to decide what he should do and how he should do it, and remembered how tangled up he had become, unable to arrive at any decision because there were so many considerations connected with each problem. He now put the same problems to himself and was surprised how easy they were. Everything was simple now because he was not thinking of what would be the result for himself—he was not even interested in that—but only of what he ought to do. And, strange to say, he had no idea what to do for his own needs, but knew beyond any doubt what he had to do for others...

The black cloud had spread until the whole sky was dark. Now it was not sheet—but fork-lightning that flashed vivid, lighting up the yard and outlining the crumbling house with its tumble-down porches, while thunder growled overhead. The birds were all silent but the leaves began to rustle and the wind reached the porch where Nekhlyudov sat...

Nekhlyudov went into the house.

'No, no,' he thought, 'the reason for what happens in our lives, all that we do, the meaning of it, is incomprehensible and must remain incomprehensible to me. Why did I have aunts? Why did Nikolenka Irtenyev die, while I am still alive? Why should there be a Katusha? What about my lunacy? Why that war? Why my reckless life afterwards? To understand all that, to understand the Master's purpose is beyond me. But to do His will, inscribed in my conscience—is in my power, and this I know unquestioningly. And when I am obeying His will, there is no doubt that my soul is at peace.'

Leo Tolstoy, *Resurrection*, translated by Rosemary Edmonds, Penguin Books, 1981, page 296

We can get in touch with another person only by an attitude of unprejudiced objectivity. This may sound like a scientific precept, and may be confused with a purely intellectual and detached attitude of mind. But what I mean to convey is something quite different. It is a human quality—a kind of deep respect for facts and events and for the person who suffers from them—a respect for the secret of such a human life. The truly religious person has this attitude. He knows that God has brought all sorts of strange and inconceivable things to pass, and seeks in the most curious ways to enter a man's heart. He therefore senses in everything the unseen presence of the divine will. This is what I mean by 'unprejudiced objectivity.' It is a moral achievement on the part of the doctor, who ought not to let himself be repelled by illness and corruption. We cannot change anything unless we accept it. Condemnation does not liberate, it oppresses. I am the oppressor of the person I condemn, not his friend and fellow-sufferer. I do not in the least mean to say that we must never pass judgement in the cases of persons whom we desire to help and improve. But if the doctor wishes to help a human being he must be able to accept him as he is. And he can do this in reality only when he has already seen and accepted himself as he is.

Perhaps this sounds very simple, but simple things are always the most difficult. In actual life it requires the greatest discipline to be simple, and the acceptance of oneself is the essence of the moral problem and the epitome of a whole outlook upon life. That I feed the hungry, that I forgive an insult, that I love my enemy in the name of Christ—all these are undoubtedly great virtues. What I do unto the least of my brethren, that I do unto Christ. But what if I should discover that the least amongst them all, the poorest of all the beggars, the most impudent of all the offenders, the very enemy himself—that these are within me, and that I myself stand in need of the alms of my own kindness—that I myself am the enemy who must be loved—what then? As a rule, the Christian's attitude is then reversed; there is no longer any question of love or long-suffering; we say to the brother within us 'Raca', and condemn and rage against ourselves. We hide it from the world; we refuse to admit ever having met this least among the lowly in ourselves. Had it been God himself who drew near to us in this despicable form, we should have denied him a thousand times before a single cock crowed...

Neurosis is an inner cleavage—the state of being at war with oneself. Everything that accentuates this cleavage makes the patient worse, and everything that mitigates it tends to heal the patient. What drives people to war with themselves is the intuition or the knowledge that they consist of two persons in opposition to one another. The conflict may be between the sensual and the spiritual man, or between the ego and the shadow. It is what Faust means when he says: 'Two souls, alas, dwell in my breast apart'. A neurosis is a dissociation of personality.

Healing may be called a religious problem. In the sphere of social or national relations, the state of suffering may be civil war, and this state is to be cured by the Christian virtue of forgiveness for those who hate us. That which we try with the conviction of good Christians to apply to external situations, we must also apply to the inner state in the treatment of neurosis. This is why modern man has heard enough about guilt and sin. He is sorely enough beset by his own bad conscience, and wants rather to learn how he is to reconcile himself with his own nature—how he is to love the enemy in his own heart and call the wolf his brother...

It is well known that Freudian psychoanalysis is limited to the task of making conscious the shadow-side and the evil within us. It simply brings into action the civil war that was latent, and lets it go at that. The patient must deal with it as best he can. Freud has unfortunately overlooked the fact that man has never yet been able single-handed to hold his own against the powers of darkness—that is, of the unconscious. Man has always stood in need of the spiritual help which each individual's own religion held out to him. The opening up of the unconscious always means the outbreak of intense spiritual suffering; it is as when a flourishing civilization is abandoned to invading hordes of barbarians, or when fertile fields are exposed by the bursting of a dam to a raging torrent...

To-day this eruption of destructive forces has already taken place, and man suffers from it in spirit... We must first tread with the patient the path of his illness—the path of his mistake that sharpens his conflicts and increases his loneliness till it grows unbearable—hoping that from the psychic depths which cast up the powers of destruction the rescuing forces will come also... It is as though, at the culmination of the illness, the destructive powers were converted into healing forces... As the religious-minded person would say: guidance has come from God... To the patient it is nothing less than a revelation when, from the hidden depths of the psyche, something arises to confront him—something strange that is not the 'I' and is therefore beyond the reach of personal caprice. He has gained access to the sources of psychic life, and this marks the beginning of the cure...

Such experiences reward the sufferer for the pains of the labyrinthine way. From this point forward a light shines through his confusion; he can reconcile himself with the warfare within and so come to bridge the morbid split in his nature upon a higher level.

C.G. Jung, *Modern Man in Search of a Soul*, translated by W.S. Dell and Cary F. Baynes, Kegan Paul and Co., 1973, page 270

ACTION

'Action'—process of acting, exertion, of energy or influence, as men of action, thing done, act.

In *The Devils of Loudun*, Aldous Huxley comes out with this challenging sentence: 'A man of prayer can do more in a single year than another can accomplish in a whole lifetime.'

In retrospect, the early years of my life were taken up in action. I loved all sorts of sport—rugby, hockey, cricket, and golf—and played them to the full. In my late teens I was called up for National Service and spent two years in the army. I was keen to make the most of this, and so was commissioned into the Gurkhas, which meant a posting in Singapore and possible action in the jungles of 'Malaya'. After this I went to Balliol for three years, followed by an Expedition to Nepal, and then training at theological college. The emphasis of the four-year curacy at Bradford Cathedral was on 'action' and this included a six-month secondment in war-torn Nigeria. By the time I was thirty I was beginning to feel the strain and in need of taking stock. Fortunately about this time I came into contact with a monk—Father Simon Holden of the Community of the Resurrection. Little by little, Simon introduced me to the passive side of life, to the life of prayer, leading on to the practice of reflection, meditation and contemplation. The result has been the gradual emergence of a balance between the active life and the passive life, each feeding the other. I now know a little bit more about the meaning of Aldous Huxley's challenging sentence, though I have a long way to go before this is accomplished in my experience of life.

Whatever your hand finds to do, do it with your might.
Ecclesiastes 9:10

... but the people who know their God shall stand firm and take action.
Daniel 11:32

Truly, I say to you, as you did it to one of the least of these my brethren, you did it to me.
Matthew 25:40

... faith by itself, if it has no works, is dead.
James 2:17

What you theoretically know, vividly realize.
Francis Thompson, 'Shelley', in *The Works of Francis Thompson*, Burns and Oates, 1913, volume III, page 2

Perform every action as though it were your last.
Marcus Aurelius, *The Meditations of Marcus Aurelius*, translated by Jeremy Collier, Walter Scott, page 25

The end of man is an Action, and not a Thought, though it were the noblest?
Thomas Carlyle, *Sartor Resartus*, Ward, Lock and Co., page 108

Action springs not from thought, but from a readiness for responsibility.
Dietrich Bonhoeffer, *Letters and Papers from Prison*, William Collins Sons and Co., 1963, page 158

In our era, the road to holiness necessarily passes through the world of action.
Dag Hammarskjöld, *Markings*, translated by Leif Sjöberg and W.H. Auden, Faber and Faber, 1964, page 108

Christians are living in this sinful world and must bear its burden, they may not steal away from the battlefield.
Nicolas Berdyaev, *Christianity and Class War*, translated by Donald Attwater, Sheed and Ward, 1933, page 50

The worst of partialities is to withhold oneself, the worst ignorance is not to act, the worst lie is to steal away.

Charles Péguy, *Basic Verities*, translated by Ann and Julian Green, Kegan Paul, Trench, Trubner and Co., 1943, page 51

Enlarging insight depends on expansion due to exercise; vision on action, on acting up to the limit of what has been glimpsed.

Anon.

Why stand we here trembling around
Calling on God for help, and not ourselves, in whom God dwells
Stretching a hand to save the falling Man?

William Blake, 'Jerusalem', in *The Complete Writings of William Blake*, edited by Geoffrey Keynes, Oxford University Press, 1974, page 672

'Tis God gives skill,
But not without men's hands: He could not make
Antonio Stradivari's violins
Without Antonio.

George Eliot, 'Stradivarius', in *The Works of George Eliot*, Virtue and Co., 1913, volume XVIII, *Jubal and Other Poems*, page 218

It is an indelible principle of Eternal truth, that practice and exercise is the Life of all. Should God give you worlds, and laws, and treasures, and worlds upon worlds, and Himself also in the Divinest manner, if you will be lazy and not meditate, you lose all. The soul is made for action, and cannot rest till it be employed. Idleness is its rust. Unless it will up and think and taste and see, all is in vain. Worlds of beauty and treasure and felicity may be round it, and itself desolate. If therefore you would be happy, your life must be as full of operation as God of treasure. Your operation shall be treasure to Him, as His operation is delightful to you.

Thomas Traherne, *Centuries*, The Faith Press, 1969, page 217

Seen with the eyes of the social historian, this three years' activity as a social revolutionary is the life of Jesus in its impact upon human history. What makes it unique is the scope of the vision which it embodies, and his profound insight into the conditions demanded for its accomplishment. The teaching of Jesus is not something separable from his life; it is the expression of the understanding which grew out of his life. Theory and practice are there completely unified. The one interprets and expounds the other. It is the fusion of insight and action that makes the life of Jesus the religious life *par excellence*, though it is far from being the kind of life that nowadays would be so described.

John Macmurray, *Creative Society*, SCM Press, 1935, page 88

Two methods exist, of aiming at human improvement,—by adjusting circumstances without and by addressing the affections within; by creating facilities of position, or by developing force of character; by mechanism or by mind. The one is institutional and systematic, operating on a large scale; reaching individuals circuitously and at last; the other is personal and moral, the influence of soul on soul, life creating life, beginning in the regeneration of the individual and spreading thence over communities; the one, in short, reforming from the circumference to the centre, the other from the centre to the circumference. And in comparing these it is not difficult to show the superior triumphs of the latter, which was the method of Christ and Christianity.

James Martineau, *Endeavours after the Christian Life: Discourses*, Longmans, Green, Reader and Dyer, 1876, page 90

He would have urged all Christians to fulfil their duties as citizens in a world that still belongs to God despite its sin and shame. But equally firmly he would have declared that no scheme for social betterment, no international organization, no political or ecclesiastical reform can in themselves heal the wounds of humanity. In one way only men can be saved, by ridding their hearts of the selfishness that hides from them the knowledge of the love of God. Once that love can gain admittance, lighting up the whole universe as the sun breaks through the clouds at the end of a day of sodden rain, then the whole quality of life is changed and inevitably men will go out to help their fellow-men.

Florence Higham, said of F.D. Maurice, in *Frederick Denison Maurice*, SCM Press, 1947, page 126

Christians engaged actively in modern economic and social progress and in the struggle for justice and charity must be convinced that they have much to contribute to the prosperity of mankind and to world peace. Let them, as individuals and as group members, give a shining example to others. Endowed with the skill and experience so absolutely necessary for them, let them preserve a proper sense of values in their earthly activity in loyalty to Christ and his Gospel, in order that their lives, individual as well as social, may be inspired by the spirit of the Beatitudes, and in particular by the spirit of poverty.

Anyone who in obedience to Christ seeks first the kingdom of God will derive from it a stronger and purer love for helping all his brethren, and for accomplishing the task of justice under the inspiration of charity.

Vatican Council II, *The Conciliar and Post Conciliar Documents*, general editor, Austin Flannery, O.P., Fowler Wright Books, 1981, page 979

Meditation is neither a backward glance nor a timorous projection forward but rather combines the old and the new in the glory of the eternal present—the 'perpetual now'. It is this element in meditation that makes the meditator a truly contemporary person, fully open and alive to the ever-present creative power of God sustaining the universe in being from moment to moment.

The liberty to 'move with the times', to recognize the changing needs and circumstances of the community or society around us, is the fruit of stability at the centre of our being.

It often seems to many people that prayer is an introspective state and that the meditator is someone going into himself to the exclusion of the people and creation around him, that he is socially irrelevant. Nothing could be further from the truth.

Not only is the timeless contemplative vision the necessary basis for the contemporary action but it is the essential condition for a fully human response to life—to the richness, the unpredictability, the sheerly *given* quality of life.

John Main, OSB, *Letters from the Heart*, Crossroad, 1982, page 65

God made man in His own image. Whatever that means, it means that man is important to God and is responsible to God. The Word became flesh and dwelt among us. God came to earth in the person of a humble carpenter, and thereby sanctified the individual. This means that what the individual believes, *is*, and does, counts ... We cannot foresee the results of our actions. It is our responsibility, not our helplessness, which appals me ... As each ... goes out to industry ... or university or family life, (his) influence, for good or bad, will radiate across the centuries. An act of kindness may help to mould a Gandhi, our failures may be creating a new Hitler. The progress of mankind has always depended upon those who, seemingly isolated and powerless in their own day, have seen their vision and remained true to it. In the darkening corridors of time they preserved integral their vision of the daylight at the end. This is a matter not of calculation but of faith. Our work may be small and its results invisible to us. But we may rest assured it will come to fruition in God's good time.

John Ferguson, *The Enthronement of Love*, The Fellowship of Reconciliation, 1950, page 103

Reliance on God, of course, does not mean passivity. On the contrary, it liberates man for a clearly defined activity, 'the will of God' ... God wills that we act humanly, therefore intelligently. He wills that we act for His sake, for love of the truth, not out of concern for immediate material interest ...

We find ourselves more and more backed into a corner in which there seems to be no choice but that of a 'lesser evil', for the sake of some urgency, some imaginary or desperately hoped-for good. But an evil choice can never have wholly good consequences. When one chooses to do good irrespective of the consequences, it is a paradox that the consequences will ultimately be good.

We are not responsible for more than our own action, but for this we should take *complete responsibility*. Then the results will follow of themselves, in a manner we may not always be able to foresee.

But the point is we do not always have to foresee every possiblity.

We must recover our inner faith not only in God but in the good... in the power of the good to take care of itself and us as well.

Thomas Merton, *Conjectures of a Guilty Bystander*, Burns and Oates, 1968, page 117

ADVERSITY

'Adversity'—condition of adverse fortune, misfortune.

At one level, I was born into adversity. The Second World War was shortly to break out, and my early childhood memories were mainly to do with the war. I remember my parents had some friends—the Elly family. There was the time when 'Uncle' Harry died early in life and the grief that followed. Aunty Emily was then faced with bringing up her two sons, John and Frank, on her own. This was no easy task in post-war Britain. They lived in Dunkinfield, some distance away from our home in Huddersfield. Occasionally they would come over for the day and we would play in the garden.

Life picked up; we went to school; and the years sped by. I was well into my teens before I met John and Frank again. They both came over with Aunty Emily on a fleeting visit. This was the last time I was to see them. Some years later John was killed in a motorway crash, and Frank suffered a similar fate shortly afterwards in a water-skiing accident. Poor Aunty Emily was badly smitten by these cruel blows. Worse was to follow. During the next few years she became crippled with rheumatoid arthritis. For most people this would have been the last straw, yet she faced up to this latest affliction with courage and dignity. I still have a very clear picture of her in my mind's eye. Her face looked as though she had been refined 'by fire', and was marked with a certain serenity and beauty. She had learned through her experience to face adversity creatively. She rarely complained about her lot in life, and was not given to self-pity. She lived a day at a time—and in the best possible way.

The Lord is a stronghold for the oppressed, a stronghold in times of trouble.

Psalm 9:9

Gold is tried in the fire, and acceptable men in the furnace of adversity.

Ecclesiasticus 2:5 (AV)

I have said this to you, that in me you may have peace. In the world you have tribulation; but be of good cheer, I have overcome the world.

John 16:33

Rejoice in your hope, be patient in tribulation, be constant in prayer.

Romans 12:12

Adversity introduces a man to himself.

Anon.

In prosperity, caution; in adversity, patience.

Dutch Proverb

Great and honest men take more courage in adversities and become stronger.

Irving Stone, *The Agony and the Ecstacy*, William Collins Sons and Co., 1961, page 550

Prosperity doth best discover vice, but adversity doth best discover virtue.

Francis Bacon, *The Moral and Historical Works of Lord Bacon*, Henry G. Bohn, 1852, page 14

He knows not his own strength, that hath not met Adversity. Heaven prepares *good men* with *crosses.*

Ben Jonson, 'Explorata: or, Discoveries', in C. H. Herford, Percy and Evelyn Simpson, editors, *Ben Jonson*, volume VIII, *The Poems, The Prose Works*, Oxford at the Clarendon Press, 1947, page 563

He that wrestles with us strengthens our nerves, and sharpens our skill. Our antagonist is our helper.

Edmund Burke, *Reflections on the Revolution in France*, edited by Conor Cruise O'Brien, Penguin Books, 1969, page 278

Sweet are the uses of adversity,
Which like the toad, ugly and venomous,
Wears yet a precious jewel in his head.

William Shakespeare, *As You Like It*, Act II. sc.i. l.12

Adversity not only draws people together but brings forth that beautiful inward friendship, just as the cold winter forms ice-figures on the window-panes which the warmth of the sun effaces.

Søren Kierkegaard, in *The Journals of Søren Kierkegaard*, a selection edited and translated by Alexander Dru, Oxford University Press, 1938, page 20

In prosperous times I have sometimes felt my fancy and powers of language flag, but adversity is to me at least a tonic and bracer; the fountain is awakened from its inmost recesses, as if the spirit of affliction had troubled it in his passage.

Sir Walter Scott, *Sir Walter Scott's Journal, 1825–1832*, T. Nelson and Sons, 1926, volume I, page 99

Now let us thank th'eternal pow'r: convinc'd,
That heav'n but tries our virtue by affliction:
That oft' the cloud which wraps the present hour,
Serves but to brighten all our future days!

John Brown, *Barbarossa*, 1755, page 56

Let us be patient! These severe afflictions
Not from the ground arise,
But oftentimes celestial benedictions
Assume this dark disguise.

Henry Wadsworth Longfellow, *By the Fireside*, 'Resignation', in *The Poetical Works of Longfellow*, Oxford University Press, 1913, page 185

Then, welcome each rebuff
That turns earth's smoothness rough,
Each sting that bids not sit nor stand, but go!
Be our joys three-parts pain!
Strive, and hold cheap the strain;
Learn, nor account the pang; dare, never grudge the throe!

Robert Browning, *Dramatis Personae*, 'Rabbi Ben Ezra', in *The Poetical Works of Robert Browning*, volume I, Smith, Elder and Co., 1899, page 581

It is a good thing that we have to face difficulties and opposition from time to time, because this brings us back to ourselves; it makes us realize that we are exiles and cannot pin our hopes on anything in this world.

It is a good thing that we are maligned now and again, and are misjudged and disliked even when we mean and do well. This sort of thing is often a great help in achieving humility, and it keeps us from groundless self-satisfaction for we are more ready to listen for God's assuring voice within, when those around believe the worst of us and treat us with contempt. That is why a man should build his life on God, for then he will not need to look for human consolation.

Thomas à Kempis, *The Imitation of Christ*, translated by Betty I. Knott, William Collins Sons and Co., 1979, page 52

St John of the Cross tells us that the desert is an excellent training ground, a teacher of discipline. The Book of Exodus illustrates this point.

The desert offers little satisfaction to the senses: there we learn quickly that God alone suffices and so we attain true wisdom. In silence, solitude and detachment we experience our weakness. We are without support, hungry and desolate.

Like Hagar we can cry aloud to God and like Elijah cast ourselves down exhausted and discouraged; but we also become aware of a Presence which fills the desert, ever watchful, ever tender.

So does God answer our childlike cry and show us to a fountain of living water at which to quench our thirst; so does he feed us with living bread to strengthen and comfort us on our lonely journey.

Ruth Burrows, in *The Watchful Heart*, edited by Elizabeth Ruth Obbard, Darton, Longman and Todd, 1988, page 17

No one ever told me that grief felt so like fear. I am not afraid, but the sensation is like being afraid. The same fluttering in the stomach, the same restlessness, the yawning. I keep on swallowing.

At other times it feels like being mildly drunk, or concussed. There is a sort of invisible blanket between the world and me. I find it hard to take in what anyone says. Or perhaps, hard to want to take it in. It is so uninteresting. Yet I want the others to be about me. I dread the moments when the house is empty. If only they would talk to one another and not to me…

And grief still feels like fear. Perhaps, more strictly, like suspense. Or like waiting; just hanging about waiting for something to happen. It gives life a permanently provisional feeling. It doesn't seem worth starting anything. I can't settle down. I yawn, I fidget, I smoke too much. Up till this I always had too little time. Now there is nothing but time. Almost pure time, empty successiveness…

I think I am beginning to understand why grief feels like suspense. It comes from the frustration of so many impulses that had become habitual. Thought after thought, feeling after feeling, action after action, had H. for their object. Now their target is gone. I keep on through habit fitting an arrow to the string; then I remember and have to lay the bow down. So many roads lead thought to H. I set out on one of them. But now there's an impassable frontier-post across it. So many roads once; now so many *culs de sac*…

Tonight all the hells of young grief have opened again; the mad words, the bitter resentment, the fluttering in the stomach, the nightmare unreality, the wallowed-in tears. For in grief nothing 'stays put'. One keeps on emerging from a phase, but it always recurs. Round and round. Everything repeats. Am I going in circles, or dare I hope I am on a spiral?

But if a spiral, am I going up or down it?…

Sorrow, however, turns out to be not a state but a process. It needs not a map but a history, and if I don't stop writing that history at some quite arbitrary point, there's no reason why I should ever stop. There is something new to be chronicled every day. Grief is like a long valley, a winding valley where any bend may reveal a totally new landscape. As I've already noted, not every bend does. Sometimes the surprise is the opposite one; you are presented with exactly the same sort of country you thought you had left behind miles ago. That is when you wonder whether the valley isn't a circular trench. But it isn't. There are partial recurrences, but the sequence doesn't repeat.

C.S. Lewis, *A Grief Observed*, Faber and Faber, 1961, page 7

ANXIETY

'Anxiety'—uneasiness, concern, solicitous desire (for a thing, to do).

When I was young I went through several periods of anxiety. A close friend recommended a book to me by Dale Carnegie. The title of this book was *How to Stop Worrying and Start Living*. I found it helpful and can still remember one of his illustrations. He observed far too may people lived in the future and were caught up in fears and anxieties. He drew our attention to the design of a modern liner. Many of these were now equipped with heavy steel partition doors. If a liner was holed and in danger of sinking, the doors could seal off the damaged part and enable the liner to stay afloat. He suggested we discipline ourselves to live 'in watertight compartments' and concentrate on living a day at a time. This struck a chord with me. Another book I found helpful was *The Power of Positive Thinking* by Norman Vincent Peale. I used to have a problem with anxiety in taking exams. In time set aside for revision fear would set in and I would almost talk myself into failure. Having read this book, I suddenly realized it was possible to adopt a more positive approach and gently talk myself in to passing exams. Later I found 'positive thinking' a valuable help in all areas of life and a great antidote to anxiety.

Somewhere in my reading I have picked up the phrase 'wise forethought' and this has become my motto as regards facing anxiety. Allied to this is finding a time in the day for silent reflection, and quietly thinking out solutions to possible anxieties in the future. A part of the weekend can also be used for this purpose.

Fear not, for I am with you, be not dismayed, for I am your God; I will strengthen you, I will help you, I will uphold you with my victorious right hand.

Isaiah 41:10

Envy and wrath shorten the life, and carefulness bringeth age before the time.

Ecclesiasticus 30:24 (AV)

Do not be anxious about your life, what you shall eat or what you shall drink, nor about your body, what you shall put on. Is not life more than food, and the body more than clothing? Look at the birds of the air: they neither sow nor reap nor gather into barns, and yet your heavenly Father feeds them. Are you not of more value than they? And which of you by being anxious can add one cubit to his span of life? And why are you anxious about clothing? Consider the lilies of the field, how they grow; they neither toil nor spin; yet I tell you, even Solomon in all his glory was not arrayed like one of these. But if God so clothes the grass of the field, which today is alive and tomorrow is thrown into the oven, will he not much more clothe you, O men of little faith? Therefore do not be anxious, saying, 'What shall we eat?' or 'What shall we drink?' or 'What shall we wear?' For the Gentiles seek all these things; and your heavenly Father knows that you need them all. But seek first his kingdom and his righteousness, and all these things shall be yours as well. Therefore do not be anxious about tomorrow, for tomorrow will be anxious for itself. Let the day's own trouble be sufficient for the day.

Matthew 6:25–34

Humble yourselves therefore under the mighty hand of God, that in due time he may exalt you. Cast all your anxieties on him, for he cares about you.

1 Peter 5:6–7

He has not learned the lesson of life who does not every day surmount a fear.

Ralph Waldo Emerson, *The Works of Ralph Waldo Emerson*, volume III, *Society and Solitude: Letters and Social Aims Addresses*, edited by George Sampson, George Bell and Sons, 1906, page 147

This bewilderment—this confusion as to who we are and what we should do—is the most painful thing about anxiety. But the positive and hopeful side is that just as anxiety destroys our self-awareness, so awareness of ourselves can destroy anxiety. That is to say, the stronger our consciousness of ourselves, the more we can take a stand against and overcome anxiety.

Rollo May, *Man's Search For Himself*, George Allen and Unwin Ltd., 1953, page 44

Many people seem to think that worry is an expression of virtuous concern. On the contrary it is a subtle sin for it amounts to a distrust of God—his love, his will, his grace.

Moreover, it makes one confused in mind and unable to think clearly. We should take any quiet forethought possible, and then trust God to guide and strengthen us to meet each duty, difficulty or emergency, as and when it comes.

George Appleton, *Journey for a Soul*, William Collins Sons and Co., 1976, page 113

Look at life carelessly. The only things worth being disappointed in or worrying about are in ourselves, not in externals. Take life as it comes and do what lies straight in front of you. It's only real carelessness about one's own will, and absolute hope and confidence in God's, that can teach one to believe that whatever is, is best. Don't you think this is the key to happiness in an apparently spoilt and disappointing life?

Edward Wilson, in George Seaver, *Edward Wilson of the Antarctic*, John Murray, 1935, page 56

'Anxiety and misgiving,' wrote Fénèlon, 'proceed solely from love of self. The love of God accomplishes all things quietly and completely; it is not anxious or uncertain. The spirit of God rests continually in quietness. Perfect love casteth out fear. It is in forgetfulness of self that we find peace. Happy is he who yields himself completely, unconsciously, and finally to God. Listen to the inward whisper of His Spirit and follow it—that is enough; but to listen one must be silent, and to follow one must yield.'

Lilian Whiting, *The Life Radiant*, Gay and Bird, 1904, page 320

Most of our conflicts and difficulties come from trying to deal with the spiritual and practical aspects of our life separately instead of realising them as parts of one whole. If our practical life is centred on our own interests, cluttered up by possessions, distracted by ambitions, passions, wants and worries, beset by a sense of our own rights and importance, or anxieties for our own future, or longings for our own success, we need not expect that our spiritual life will be a contrast to all this. The soul's house is not built on such a convenient plan: there are few sound-proof partitions in it. Only when the conviction—not merely the idea—that the demand of the Spirit, however inconvenient, comes first and IS first, rules the whole of it, will those objection-able noises die down which have a way of penetrating into the nicely furnished little oratory, and drowning all the quieter voices by their din. For a spiritual life is simply a life in which all that we do comes from the centre, where we are anchored in God: a life soaked through and through by a sense of His reality and claim, and self-given to the great movement of His will.

Evelyn Underhill, *The Spiritual Life*, Harper and Row, 1936, page 37

A great many worries can be diminished by realising the unimportance of the matter which is causing the anxiety. I have done in my time a considerable amount of public speaking; at first every audience terrified me, and nervousness made me speak very badly; I dreaded the ordeal so much that I always hoped I might break my leg before I had to make a speech, and when it was over I was exhausted from the nervous strain. Gradually I taught myself to feel that it did not matter whether I spoke well or ill, the universe would remain much the same in either case. I found that the less I cared whether I spoke well or badly, the less badly I spoke, and gradually the nervous strain diminished almost to vanishing point. A great deal of nervous fatigue can be dealt with in this way. Our doings are not so important as we naturally suppose; our successes and failures do not after all matter very much. Even great sorrows can be survived; troubles which seem as if they must put an end to happiness for life fade with the lapse of time until it becomes almost impossible to remember their poignancy. But over and above these self-centred considerations is the fact that one's ego is no very large part of the world. The man who can centre his thoughts and hopes upon something transcending self can find a certain peace in the ordinary troubles of life which is impossible to the pure egoist.

Bertrand Russell, *The Conquest of Happiness*, George Allen and Unwin, 1984, page 56

ATHEISM

'Atheism'—disbelief in the existence of a God; godlessness.

Some friends invited me to lunch. Before the meal began we had a drink and sat down to lunch. After a few minutes they showed me their latest acquisition—a 'Magic Eye' book. They opened the book and showed me a complex picture made up of attractive colours, lines and circles. At first I could make nothing of it. They then instructed me to shut my eyes, and bring the picture close to my eyes. Next I was told to open my eyes, look at the picture, and gradually withdraw it. To my great surprise and delight I saw the outline of a fairly large rabbit emerging out of the picture. The rabbit had been there all the time, but I had looked at the picture from one angle, and missed out on the crucial angle for spotting that rabbit. I was excited by this experience, and felt my eyes had almost been opened to the existence of another dimension.

Some time prior to this an undergraduate had invited an atheist friend to a reflection group. In our second meeting the friend chose the topic 'atheism'. During our period of silent reflection on the assembled material, I felt a little apprehensive as to what might come out in the discussion which was to follow. Indeed, when the time came, some searching questions were asked. However, in this session, our atheist friend had something equivalent to a 'Magic Eye' experience. It was as though his eyes had been opened to the spiritual dimension, and from then onwards he experienced a greatly enriched life, viewed from a different perspective.

The fool says in his heart, 'There is no God.'
Psalm 53:1

The hope of the ungodly is like dust that is blown away with the wind.
Wisdom of Solomon 5:14 (AV)

He who is of God hears the words of God; the reason why you do not hear them is that you are not of God.
John 8:47

Remember that you were at that time separated from Christ, alienated from the commonwealth of Israel, and strangers to the covenants of promise, having no hope and without God in the world.
Ephesians 2:12

The fearful Unbelief is unbelief in yourself.
Thomas Carlyle, *Sartor Resartus*, Ward, Lock and Co., page 113

Atheism is rather in the lip than in the heart of man.
Francis Bacon, *The Moral and Historical Works of Lord Bacon*, Henry G. Bohn, 1852, page 46

The three great apostles and supporters of practical atheism are Wealth, Health, and Power.
C.C. Colton, *Lacon*, William Tegg, 1866, page 23

Christianity founds hospitals, and atheists are cured in them, never knowing that they owe their cure to Christ.
William Temple, *Readings in St. John's Gospel*, First and Second Series, Macmillan and Co., 1947, page 109

Some are Atheists by Neglect; others are so by Affectation: they, that think there is no God, at some times; do not think so, at all times.
Benjamin Whichcote, *Moral and Religious Aphorisms*, century I, number 1, Elkin Mathews and Marrot, 1930, page 1

The atheist who is moved by love is moved by the spirit of God; an atheist who lives by love is saved by his faith in the God whose existence (under that name) he denies.

William Temple, *Nature, Man and God*, Macmillan and Co., 1934, page 416

My atheism, like that of Spinoza, is true piety towards the universe and denies only gods fashioned by men in their own image, to be servants of their human interests.

George Santayana, *Soliloquies in England and Later Soliloquies*, Constable and Company, 1922, page 246

To every soul, even to one ignorant of the name of God, even one reared in atheism, grace offers... that Reality of absolute goodness, which merits all our love and is able to save our life.

Jacques Maritain, *True Humanism*, translated by M.R. Adamson, Geoffrey Bles: The Centenary Press, 1938, page 56

They that deny a God destroy a man's nobility; for certainly man is of kin to the beasts by his body; and, if he be not of kin to God by his spirit, he is a base and ignoble creature. It destroys likewise magnanimity, and the raising of human nature.

Francis Bacon, *The Moral and Historical Works of Lord Bacon*, Henry G. Bohn, 1892, page 48

The growth of Christian experience over the centuries can be interpreted as some sort of conversation of faith, where people have learned to trust that the world has a meaning, and so have found one. Now you can say this is all fantasy but the non-believer is then left with some rather difficult questions when he looks at the oddity of existence.

John Habgood, in Gerald Priestland, *Priestland's Progress*, BBC Worldwide, 1982, page 49

One cannot escape the feeling that what modern atheism is revolting against is, in part at least, the objectified God, conceived by the atheists, as by many Christians, as an immensely magnified human person, with whom men can talk on equal terms and arraign His government of the world. But that... is not God, but an idol and, in so far as modern atheism destroys that idol, it is doing a service to true religion.

J.H. Oldham, *Life is Commitment*, SCM Press, 1953, page 47

Forth from his dark and lonely hiding-place,
(Portentous sight!) the owlet Atheism,
Sailing on obscene wings athwart the noon,
Drops his blue-fringed lids, and holds them close,
And hooting at the glorious sun in Heaven,
Cries out, 'Where is it?'

Samuel Taylor Coleridge, 'Fears in Solitude', in *Coleridge, Poetical Works*, edited by Ernest Hartley Coleridge, Oxford University Press, 1978, page 259

Not many years ago when I was an atheist, if anyone had asked me, 'Why do you not believe in God?' my reply would have run something like this: 'Look at the universe we live in. By far the greatest part of it consists of empty space, completely dark and unimaginably cold. The bodies which move in this space are so few and so small in comparison with the space itself that even if every one of them were known to be crowded as full as it could hold with perfectly happy creatures, it would still be difficult to believe that life and happiness were more than a bye-product to the power that made the universe... History is largely a record of crime, war, disease, and terror, with just sufficient happiness interposed to give them, while it lasts, an agonised apprehension of losing it, and, when it is lost, the poignant misery of remembering. Every now and then they improve their condition a little and what we call a civilisation appears. But all civilisations pass away and, even while they remain, inflict peculiar sufferings of their own probably sufficient to outweigh what alleviations they may have brought to the normal pains of man... If you ask me to believe that this is the work of a benevolent and omnipotent spirit, I reply that all the evidence points in the opposite direction. Either there is no spirit behind the universe, or else a spirit indifferent to good and evil, or else an evil spirit.' There was one question which I never dreamed of raising. I never noticed that the very strength and facility of the pessimists' case at once poses us a problem. If the universe is so bad, or even half so bad, how on earth did human beings ever come to attribute it to the activity of a wise and good Creator?

C.S. Lewis, The Problem of Pain, The Centenary Press, 1941, page 1

Godlessness justifies itself on various grounds, scientific-positivistic, moral or social. In the second half of the nineteenth century a heavy stratum of both European and Russian intelligentsia convinced themselves that science had demonstrated that there was no God, that belief in God could not be combined with the existence of science. It must be said that this is the most naïve and the feeblest of all the arguments of atheism. It was based on the belief that science is supreme not only over all knowledge, but over the whole of human life. Men thought that science had the answer to every question. In the twentieth-century positive science, specially physics and chemistry, have made colossal advances, but there is no longer the belief that science can solve all problems. Such a remarkable scholar as Eddington, astronomer and physicist, expresses his recognition of the results of science in these words: 'something unknown does something unknown.' The very existence of material, in which the earlier science believed so firmly, is now subject to doubt, consciously or unconsciously. Everything in the principal basis of science has become doubtful... True science, always conscious of its limitations, can say nothing about God, positive or negative: it can neither prove nor disprove the existence of God. The problem of God's existence belongs in quite another sphere than that of science, which is concerned with the knowledge of the world of nature. The arguments of atheism based on the natural sciences are just as feeble as the arguments for God's existence, based on these same natural sciences. And Christian apologetics that refute the arguments of natural sciences against faith in God are very feeble and out-moded. We may ignore completely the arguments of natural science. But the Christian consciousness should be freed from all connection with the out-moded natural history with which it was linked in the past. Biblical natural history is the knowledge of humanity in its childhood; we cannot now consider it of serious importance. What is really important, is the possibility of a conflict between Christianity and the science of history. Historical knowledge may offer serious difficulties for the Christian faith in so far as this faith is to be based on the facts of history... And only the worship of God in spirit and in truth rises above the difficulties connected with the science of history.

Nicolas Berdyaev, Christian Existentialism, edited and translated by Donald A. Lowrie, George Allen and Unwin, 1965, page 218

AUTHORITY

'Authority'—power, right to enforce obedience; person having authority; personal influence, especially over opinion; weight of testimony; a book, quotation, considered to settle the question; person whose opinion is accepted, especially an expert in (on) a subject.

My first real brush with authority came in the army. I had been called up for basic training with the Devon and Dorsets and was stationed at Topsham Barracks, Exeter. Shortly after arrival I was hauled up before the Regimental Sergeant Major for a minor misdemeanour. I started to explain... '*Silence when you speak to me*,' he retorted—and he then proceeded to give me a thorough dressing-down. A few months later, at Mons Officer Cadet School, I came across another 'authority figure'—a Drill-Sergeant from the Irish Guards. He was fearsome in appearance, and his handle-bar moustache somehow enhanced his authority. He wasted no time in letting us know exactly where we stood. 'I calls you Sir, you calls me Sir; the only difference is—*you mean it!*'

So much for institutional authority. With National Service behind me I was discovering a different kind of authority. This had more to do with personal influence, coming through character and personality. If someone was to ask what was authoritative for me now I would have to say my experience of God, checked by the canon of scripture. This would be closely backed up with 2,000 years of Christian experience and scholarship.

The God of Israel has spoken, the Rock of Israel has said to me: When one rules justly over men, ruling in the fear of God, he dawns on them like the morning light, like the sun shining forth upon a cloudless morning, like rain that makes grass to sprout from the earth.

2 Samuel 23:3–4

Where there is no prophecy the people cast off restraint.

Proverbs 29:18

All authority in heaven and on earth has been given to me.

Matthew 28:18

And they were astonished at his teaching, for he taught them as one who had authority, and not as the scribes.

Mark 1:22

The spiritual authority of the Gospel for those who accept it is secured by the fact that it is transmitted in a form which perpetually calls for private judgement.

William Temple, *Nature, Man and God*, Macmillan and Co., 1934, page 351

The spiritual authority of God Himself consists, not in His having the power to create and to destroy, but in His being the appropriate object of worship and love.

William Temple, *Nature, Man and God*, Macmillan and Co., 1934, page 349

The Gospel stories are not to be treated as something sacred, as a final authority, but as the means whereby we can come in touch with the living Christ who is the same yesterday, to-day, and for ever.

William Temple, *Basic Convictions*, Hamish Hamilton, 1937, page 46

There is no authority short of God. Look up to him, expect his teachings. And though clouds of uncertainty may come, never let them make you turn your eyes away in discouragement, or think that on the earth you can find that guidance which is not a thing of earth, but which must come to us from heaven.

Phillips Brooks, *Series of Miscellaneous Illustrated Cards*, 1902, page 16

There is only one authority in this field, and that is the authority which truth itself possesses when it is perceived to be true by the individual concerned; or, in other words, when it authenticates itself . . . It is I who finally decide to submit to the authority.

Leslie D. Weatherhead, *The Christian Agnostic*, Hodder and Stoughton, 1965, page 21

Therefore, lest the political community be ruined while everyone follows his own opinion, an authority is needed to guide the energies of all towards the common good—not mechanically or despotically, but by acting above all as a moral force based on freedom and a sense of responsibility.

Vatican Council II, *The Conciliar and Post Conciliar Documents*, general editor, Austin Flannery, O.P., Fowler Wright Books, 1981, page 981

The spiritual authority of God is that which He exercises by displaying not His power, but His character. Holiness, not omnipotence, is the spring of His spiritual authority. In such a vision as that of Isaiah there is awe-inspiring majesty but what leaps to the prophet's consciousness is not the sense of his powerlessness before the Almighty, but the sense of his uncleanness before the All-Holy.

William Temple, *Nature, Man and God*, Macmillan and Co., 1934, page 348

In Jesus' eyes, human authority has a very lowly place: limited, without grandeur or fine titles, with no advantages whatever for the ones holding authority but only for those at whose service they are.

If we hold any sort of authority, either as an individual or as a group, we must avoid laying unnecessary burdens on those concerned. God never does this. His disciples must recognize this and refuse to offer cult or incense to any human authority.

Jesus wants every one of his disciples to be wholly detached from desire for human recognition, praise, status, popularity. If we want these things (as opposed to merely liking them) then we cut ourselves off from Jesus who wanted nothing but the Father's glory.

Only our grasp that we have a Father in heaven and a supreme Master in Jesus can enable us to live in our simple dignity without craving for false esteem.

Ruth Burrows, in *The Watchful Heart*, edited by Elizabeth Ruth Obbard, Darton, Longman and Todd, 1988, page 53

Thus, his whole life long, the man of today is exposed to influences which are bent on robbing him of all confidence in his own thinking. The spirit of spiritual dependence to which he is called on to surrender is in everything that he hears or reads; it is in the people whom he meets every day; it is in the parties and associations which have claimed him as their own; it pervades all the circumstances of his life.

From every side and in the most varied ways it is dinned into him that the truths and convictions which he needs for life must be taken by him from the associations which have rights over him. The spirit of the age never lets him come to himself. Over and over again convictions are forced upon him in the same way as, by means of the electric advertisements which flare in the streets of every large town, any company which has sufficient capital to get itself securely established, exercises pressure on him at every step he takes to induce him to buy their boot polish or their soup tablets. By the spirit of the age, then, the man of today is forced into scepticism about his own thinking, in order to make him receptive to truth which comes to him from authority. To all this constant influence he cannot make the resistance that is desirable because he is an overworked and distracted being without power to concentrate. Moreover, the manifold material trammels which are his lot work upon his mentality in such a way that he comes at last to believe himself unqualified even to make any claim to thoughts of his own.

Albert Schweitzer, *My Life and Thought*, translated by C.T. Campion, George Allen and Unwin, 1966, page 255

It is useful to divide authority into external and internal authority. External authority is that attaching to a person as an official or to an office as an office. When someone obeys a policeman who asks him not to park his car in a certain place it is not the intrinsic conviction of the policeman's words that counts but his holding office as a guardian of the law. Internal authority is the authority residing in convincing argument or weighty moral or spiritual example or experience. If a woman buys a product advertised on television, for instance, it is the authority of the words and actions of the advertiser which has moved her. The authority of a bishop is an example of external, and the authority of a writer or a saint is that of internal, authority.

In the New Testament almost all authority is internal. The ultimate authority (which is the word of God) is expressed through preaching or through miraculous occurrences, or found in meditation or prayer or inspired vision and dream or in reading the (OT) scripture. Even the twelve apostles do not hold authority because they have been invested with an office, but because they are in a position to witness to what Christ did in the days of his flesh and to his appearances as risen Lord. But as the church gradually became a fixed and relatively uniform institution, official, external, authority inevitably came to play a greater and greater part... By the end of the Middle Ages the church was supported by a vast system of external authority.

But the advent of the Reformation with its emphasis upon the response of the individual in faith to the demand of the word of God, and the divisions of the church which resulted from it, assisted by the many impulses created by the Renaissance towards individualism and the rejection of established authority in metaphysics and theology, gradually brought about an entire change of attitude in the minds of Christians. Today the pendulum of opinion has swung to the other extreme. Internal authority is now widely regarded as the only authority in matters religious...

Judged by modern conceptions of authority, then, the authority of scripture will not be that of an inerrant oracle delivering equal truth in all its parts nor the authority of the church that of an autonomous institution under no responsibility to refer to the sources of its doctrine, but the Bible will be considered as the unique witness to the acts of God in history by which he makes himself known to all men and demands their response, and the church as the organ chosen by God to point to the Bible, to preach it, teach it, and to order its life by the light of the Bible. The authority of the Bible does not lie in the book itself but in the subject to which it witnesses, and the authority of the church lies ultimately in the Word of God whom it obeys and whose witness it finds in the Bible... In the barest terms, the church, and the church alone, had authority to offer to everybody the opportunity of being convinced by the authority of the Bible. But once this position is understood, it must be pointed out that it is impossible and indeed disastrous to attempt to exclude external authority altogether. Every organization claiming to be the church, or to have any association with the church, or to represent the church, even partially or locally, must wield administrative and executive authority in some form and must claim in some sense to wield it in the name of Christ. Again, the collective experience of the church, either in forming and holding to fundamental dogmas of the Christian faith tested by centuries of discussion and worship, or in learning moral and spiritual wisdom through a continuous history of prayer, worship and practice, still forms a very impressive argument not easily overthrown when rightly understood and handled.

Two more forms of authority must be mentioned. One is the authority of scholarship. To this, fluctuating and subjective though it be, the church and its theologians must pay full and respectful attention, without elevating it to a position of ultimate authority. The development of historical, literary and linguistic studies in the last two centuries has made this essential. The other is the authority of religious experience. In one sense this must be decisive for every individual, because the personal, existential nature of Christian belief in God implies prayer and worship. And properly handled (e.g. by P.T. Forsyth or F. von Hügel), this aspect of Christian truth can become a strong argument. But it never can stand alone because of its subjective nature. If religious experience is our sole authority then the experience of a Joseph Smith, a Bernadette Soubirous or a Mrs Eddy is as authoritative as that of an Augustine or of a John of the Cross. The authority of religious experience must be supported and balanced by that of scripture and tradition. Authority for the Christian is a combination or harmony of several forms of authority, all fused in faith.

R.P.C. Hanson, in *A New Dictionary of Christian Theology*, edited by Alan Richardson and John Bowden, SCM Press, 1983, page 58

BELIEF

'Belief'—trust or confidence (in); acceptance of the Christian theology; thing believed, religion, opinion, intuition.

On a Monday evening we used to have a study group for the Youth Fellowship of Bradford Cathedral. About a dozen of us would meet in my room in the Clergy House, and tackle a different topic every week. At the end of each session we would relax over a cup of coffee and biscuits. I remember one of these study groups in which we tackled 'Belief'. Various obstacles to belief were mentioned. Firstly, there were natural catastrophes such as earthquakes in which many thousands of lives were lost. How could a loving God allow this to happen? Secondly, there was cancer, again raising questions about the existence and nature of 'a loving and almighty God'? How could he permit such suffering to continue on a massive scale unabated? Thirdly, there were the two World Wars. These conflicts had for many people spelled out the end of belief in God. Fourthly, there was the sheer complexity and confusion of modern life, which for many people made belief in a personal God untenable. Someone also questioned whether belief in God made any difference to our lives anyway.

One of the members of the group, a staff nurse, cut us all short. 'Well,' she said, 'I don't know about you lot, but I *have* to believe.' She went on to explain that for her, belief in God was essential—for her sense of identity and her work on the wards. She gave us much to think about that evening.

Blessed are the men whose strength is in thee, in whose heart are the highways to Zion.

Psalm 84:5

For thus said the Lord God, the Holy One of Israel, 'In returning and rest you shall be saved; in quietness and in trust shall be your strength.'

Isaiah 30:15

I believe; help my unbelief!

Mark 9:24

Have you believed because you have seen me? Blessed are those who have not seen and yet believe.

John 20:29

There are three sources of belief: reason, custom, inspiration.

Blaise Pascal, *Pensées,* translated by W.F. Trotter, Random House Inc., 1941, page 87

Believe that life *is* worth living, and your belief will help create the fact.

William James, *The Will to Believe,* Longmans, Green and Co., 1904, page 62

Belief consists in accepting the affirmations of the soul;
unbelief, in denying them.

Ralph Waldo Emerson, in *The Works of Ralph Waldo Emerson,* volume I, *Essays and Representative Men,* edited by George Sampson, George Bell and Sons, 1906, page 453

That gracious Child, that thorn-crowned Man!
He lived while we believed.

Matthew Arnold, 'Obermann Once More', in *The Poems of Matthew Arnold*, edited by Kenneth Allott, Longmans, Green and Co., 1965, page 526

It is your own assent to yourself, and the constant voice of your own reason, and not of others, that should make you believe.

Blaise Pascal, *Pensées*, translated by W.F. Trotter, Random House Inc., 1941, page 91

So, once again, you chose for yourself—and opened the door to chaos. The chaos you become whenever God's hand does not rest upon your head.

Dag Hammarskjöld, *Markings*, translated by Leif Sjöberg and W.H. Auden, Faber and Faber, 1964, page 95

We all know people who tell us they cannot believe what cannot be proved. Of course it is not true. Of course they do in fact believe a great deal that they cannot prove—concerning the trustworthiness of their friends, for example.

William Temple, *The Hope of a New World*, SCM Press, 1940, page 107

Strong Son of God, immortal Love,
Whom we, that have not seen thy face,
By faith, and faith alone, embrace.
  Believing where we cannot prove.

Alfred, Lord Tennyson, *In Memoriam A.H.H.*, in *The Poems of Tennyson*, edited by Christopher Ricks, Longmans, Green and Co., 1969, page 861

We have only to believe. And the more threatening and irreducible reality appears, the more firmly and desperately must we believe. Then, little by little, we shall see the universal horror unbend, and then smile upon us, and then take us in its more than human arms.

Pierre Teilhard de Chardin, *Le Milieu Divin*, William Collins Sons and Co., 1960, page 129

There is nothing that so sanctifies the heart of man, that keeps us in such habitual love, prayer and delight in God: nothing that so kills all the roots of evil in our nature, that so renews and perfects all our virtues, that fills us with so much love, goodness, and good wishes to every creature as this faith that God is always present in us with His light and Holy Spirit.

William Law, *Selected Mystical Writings of William Law*, edited by Stephen Hobhouse, Rockliff, 1948, page 32

The existence of God is fully credible only if evil is being transmuted into good; and that cannot—demonstrably cannot—finally be accomplished unless God the Supreme Good becomes the apparent good to every man... The Supreme Good can only be my apparent good and so dominate all my Self if it both is, and, in a form quickening my sympathy, manifestly displays itself as, utterly selfless love.

William Temple, *Nature, Man and God*, Macmillan and Co., 1934, page 519

I believe in one God, the creator of the universe. That he governs it by his Providence. That he ought to be worshipped. That the most acceptable service we can render to him is doing good to his other children. That the soul of man is immortal, and will be treated with justice in another life respecting its conduct in this. These I take to be the fundamental points in all sound religion, and I regard them as you do in whatever sect I meet with them. As to Jesus of Nazareth, my opinion of whom you particularly desire, I think the system of morals and his religion as he left them to us, the best the world saw or is like to see.

Benjamin Franklin, *The Private Correspondence of B. Franklin 1753–1790*, printed for Henry Colburn, 1817, page 131

In Chapter 5 of Paul's letter to the Romans he writes about what God has accomplished in the person of His Son, Jesus: Therefore, now that we have been justified through faith, let us continue at peace with God through our Lord, Jesus Christ, through whom we have been allowed to enter the sphere of God's grace, where we now stand. Let us exalt in the hope of the divine splendour that is to be ours... because God's love has flooded our inmost heart through the Holy Spirit He has given us (Romans 5:1–5).

Just think about this language for a moment and consider the quite staggering claim it is making. 'We have been allowed to enter the sphere of God's grace, where we now stand.' 'God's love has flooded our inmost heart through the Holy Spirit He has given us.' St Paul was no mere theorist. He was a passionate announcer of a real event that he was trying to make all men realize, and his words were urgent indicators of this event, as a reality shared by all men. His great conviction is, that the central reality of our Christian faith is the sending of the Spirit of Jesus; indeed our faith is a living faith precisely because the living Spirit of God dwells within us, giving new life to our mortal bodies.

John Main OSB, *Word into Silence*, Darton, Longman and Todd, 1980, page 2

Faith has to be something more than an assent of the mind. It is also a grasp, a contact, a communion of wills...

By faith one not only assents to propositions revealed by God... but one assents to God Himself. One *receives* God. One says 'yes' not merely to a statement *about* God, but to the Invisible, Infinite God Himself...

Faith is not just one moment of the spiritual life, not just a step to something else. It is that acceptance of God which is the very climate of all spiritual living. It is the beginning of communion... I do not mean merely that now all our thoughts are couched in certain fideist or pietistic formulas, but rather that faith gives a dimension of simplicity and *depth* to all our apprehensions and to all our experiences.

What is this dimension of depth? It is the incorporation of the unknown and of the unconscious into our daily life. Faith brings together the known and the unknown so that they overlap; or, rather, so that we are *aware* of their overlapping...

Faith incorporates the unknown into our everyday life in a living, dynamic and actual manner.

Thomas Merton, *New Seeds of Contemplation*, Burns and Oates, 1962, page 99

BIBLE

'Bible'—the Scriptures of the Old and New Testament, a copy of them, a particular edition of them; authoritative textbook.

In 1968 I was sent to Nigeria for six months, to stand in for a priest who was coming home to England on long leave. At that time a fierce civil war was being fought in the Eastern region. Fortunately for me my destination was Ibadan (in the West) some 300 miles from the battle zone. Even so, I soon became aware I was working in a country at war with itself. A feature of this war was military road blocks. Any person leaving or entering the city in a car or other vehicle was subject to these routine checks. Sometimes there were difficulties. To cut these down to a minimum, I made a practice of removing my sunglasses as I drove up, so that the soldiers could make eye contact with me. On one occasion I was waiting my turn in the queue, sunglasses in my hand, close to the open window. One of the soldiers passing by suddenly grabbed them with the words, 'Huh, I want these.' I was infuriated. Our instructions were never argue with armed soldiers, but before I could stop myself I had snatched back my sunglasses. The situation took a turn for the worse and began to look ugly. Swiftly I seized some biblical tracts from the dashboard and thrust these into the soldier's hands, saying, 'Here, have some of these instead.' This somehow did the trick. Much to my relief he went off quite happily reading through the tracts. The Bible was certainly crucially important to me on that particular occasion.

Thy word is a lamp to my feet and a light to my path.

Psalm 119:105

Seek and read from the book of the Lord.
Isaiah 34:16

Heaven and earth will pass away, but my words will not pass away.
Mark 13:31

For whatever was written in former days was written for our instruction, that by steadfastness and by the encouragement of the scriptures we might have hope.
Romans 15:4

If you knew the whole Bible off by heart and all the expositions of scholars, what good would it do you without the love and grace of God.
Thomas à Kempis, *The Imitation of Christ*, translated by Betty I. Knott, William Collins Sons and Co., 1979, page 37

I have sometimes seen more in a line of the Bible then I could well tell how to stand under, and yet at another time the whole Bible hath been to me as drie as a stick.
John Bunyan, *Grace Abounding and The Pilgrim's Progress*, edited by Roger Sharrock, Oxford University Press, 1966, page 104

When thou readest God's Word, then in everything that thou readest, constantly to say to thyself, 'It is I that am addressed, to me this is spoken.'
Søren Kierkegaard, *For Self-Examination and Judge For Yourselves*, translated by Walter Lowrie, Princeton University Press, 1968, page 61

That they might feel something *nearer* to them than the Scriptures, to wit, the *Word in the Heart*, from whence all Holy Scripture came, which is *Christ within them, the Hope of their Glory*.
William Penn, *A Collection of the Works of William Law*, volume II, 1726, page 782

You may learn the whole Bible by heart and speak to any point in divinity according to text and letter, and yet *know* nothing of God or of spiritual life.
Rufus M. Jones, *Spiritual Reformers in the 16th and 17th Centuries*, Macmillan and Co., 1914, page 245

After the sacred volumes of God and the Scriptures, study, in the second place, that great volume of the works and creatures of God, strenuously, and before all books, which ought to be only regarded as commentaries.
Francis Bacon, 'To Trinity College, Cambridge' in *Letters and Remains of the Lord Chancellor Bacon*, collected by Robert Stephens, 1734, page 184

But herein is the Bible itself greatly wronged. It nowhere lays claim to be regarded as *the* Word, *the* Way, *the* Truth. The Bible leads us to Jesus, the inexhaustible, the ever unfolding Revelation of God. It is Christ, 'in whom are hid all the treasures of wisdom and knowledge,' not the Bible, save as leading to him.
George Macdonald, *Unspoken Sermons*, First Series, Alexander Strahan, 1867, page 52

Now concerning the Holy Scriptures, we do believe that they were given forth by the Holy Spirit of God through the holy men of God, who spoke, as the Scriptures of Truth saith, 'As they were moved by the Holy Ghost' (2 Peter 1:21); and that they are to be read, and believed, and fulfilled, and he that fulfils them is Christ; and they are 'profitable for doctrine, that the man of God may be perfect, thoroughly furnished unto all good works' (2 Timothy 3:16, 17) and are able to make us wise to salvation through faith in Christ Jesus.
George Fox, *The Journal of George Fox*, a revised edition by John L. Nickalls, Cambridge University Press, 1952, page 604

In determining the intention of the sacred writers, attention must be paid, *inter alia*, to 'literary forms for the fact is that truth is differently presented and expressed in the various types of historical writing, in prophetical and poetical texts,' and in other forms of literary expression.

Hence the exegete must look for that meaning which the sacred writer, in a determined situation and given the circumstances of his time and culture, intended to express, and did in fact express, through the medium of a contemporary literary form.

Vatican Council II, *The Conciliar and Post Conciliar Documents*, general editor, Austin Flannery, O.P., Fowler Wright Books Ltd., 1981, page 757

At Christmas I managed to get hold of a Greek Testament, and every morning, after I had cleaned my cell and polished my tins, I read a little of the Gospels, a dozen verses taken by chance anywhere. It is a delightful way of opening the day. Every one, even in a turbulent, ill-disciplined life, should do the same. Endless repetition, in and out of season, has spoiled for us the freshness, the naïvete, the simple romantic charm of the Gospels. We hear them read far too often and far too badly, and all repetition is anti-spiritual. When one returns to the Greek, it is like going into a garden of lilies out of some narrow and dark house.

Oscar Wilde, *De Profundis*, in *The Works of Oscar Wilde*, edited by G.F. Maine, William Collins Sons and Co., 1948, page 874

If we come closer to the inner heart of Bible reading we are not just stuffing our minds with information; we are letting God feed us through his word, and this means letting the scriptures speak to imagination, conscience, feeling, and will, as well as to the mind.

As we read, and read slowly, we pause and let the truth of God come home to us. Our imagination is moved to *wonder*, our conscience is pricked to *penitence*, our feelings are moved to *love*, our will is stirred to *resolve*, and our mind to whatever *understanding* we can muster.

In that way we quietly let the passage of scripture come home to us, mould us, and be our food and drink.

Michael Ramsey, *Through the Year with Michael Ramsey*, edited by Margaret Duggan, Hodder and Stoughton, 1975, page 158

I believe my early morning readings are the secret of my own happiness in life. Read chiefly the N.T., and in it chiefly the Gospels, and of them chiefly St. John's, and write out what you think each verse means in your own words as you read it, and in between each morning's readings put down shortly what has happened to you—I mean a sort of diary, only make it a mixture of self-examination and your prayers. Write out a short prayer or a short thanksgiving for anything that happens out of the way, no matter whether it has pleased you or not; for having once given your life and your will to God as a reasonable offering, *everything* that happens to you is sanctioned by Him because He allows only such things to happen to you, when once you have put your life in His hands, as can do you some good. Nine times out of ten you will be able to see. The tenth perhaps you won't—just make a note of it and ask God to show you. Only be quite sure that you have not given up your will to Him merely in so many words, but in reality, and then you will have every reason to take things exactly as they happen to come and find a blessing in the worst of them. God lives in and with those who get into this habit of thought, only it takes some perseverance to get out of the way of grumbling and impatience. I have been at it for some eight years now and I haven't succeeded yet, but it's worth sticking to.

Edward Wilson, George Seaver, *The Faith of Edward Wilson*, John Murray, 1949, page 14

The early Christians' understanding of Jesus was close to the heart of their spirituality, not only narrowly in terms of their form of prayer but in the wider sense of their manner of approach to God. From this point of view, the Gospels, each taken as a whole, may be seen as expressions of spirituality. It has become customary to read them as doctrinal or religious documents, each representing a particular viewpoint current in the early church. But... doctrine and spirituality are not much distinguished at this time, and these four outlooks may be viewed appropriately as 'spiritualities'. It is indeed neither fanciful nor unhelpful to see in the various Gospels, in rudimentary form, spiritual outlooks which have subsequently become both more firmly distinguished and of central significance in Christian history. Thus (to give the barest outline of a sketch), Matthew, with his sense of Christian life thoroughly mapped out by both old law and new, yet infused with the presence of Christ, is not different in essence from that form of Christian discipleship which centres on steady and willing obedience to a monastic rule or its like. Mark's dismissal of the Jewish Law in favour of the central demand of the kingdom has his heirs in those who set the gospel continually against all other forces, which seem always to be its rivals rather than its helpers. Luke's piety, centred on Jesus and Christian fellowship, and with a strong sense of the continuity of both from Israel of old, speaks to those for whom wide, tolerant acceptance of all reasonable aids to the gospel seems legitimate, provided the religious centrality of Jesus is maintained. John's more obviously structured and comprehensive picture of Jesus' significance as the expression of God's being and purpose may be seen as the first of those whose spirituality must always seek integration with the concerns of the intellect, while still centred on Jesus as the clue to the disclosure of God's mind and as the way to union with the Father.

J.L. Houlden, in *A Dictionary of Christian Spirituality*, edited by Gordon S. Wakefield, SCM Press, 1983, page 50

BROTHERHOOD

'Brotherhood'—fraternal tie; companionship; community of feeling.

In the early 1970s I visited Russia and spent a long weekend in Moscow with a group of friends. It was winter-time and Moscow looked most attractive in the snow. We visited Red Square and saw Lenin's tomb. We witnessed the changing of the guard, and found the goose-stepping of the soldiers awesome. We explored the Kremlin and admired the biggest bell in the world. We attended a service in the cathedral and were surprised to find it full. We were fascinated by the Metro, with its precision timing, reputedly superior to the Swiss. We ate in local restaurants, and enjoyed observing the local clientele at play.

As most of the group could speak Russian, we eventually abandoned the official tour and went off on our own. A female member of our party had previously spent a year at Moscow State University, and wanted to see her former lecturer again. Once contacted we were invited to dinner at her apartment on the outskirts of Moscow. After a frightening journey, with the bus skidding on the ice, we eventually found her apartment and were given a royal reception. After enthusiastic greetings, we were sat down to a huge candlelit feast. The vodka flowed. The lecturer was overjoyed to see her former student again and expressed her delight to us all. We were treated to a night never to be forgotten. When we remember this happened at the height of the Cold War, I wonder if 'brotherhood' succeeded, where power politics had failed. Perhaps the events of the last twenty years have proved this to be true.

And if your brother becomes poor, and cannot maintain himself with you, you shall maintain him; as a stranger and a sojourner he shall live with you. Take no interest from him or increase, but fear your God; that your brother may live beside you.

Leviticus 25:35–36

Have we not all one father? Has not one God created us?

Malachi 2:10

For you have one teacher, and you are all brethren.

Matthew 23:8

For he who sanctifies and those who are sanctified have all one origin. That is why he is not ashamed to call them brethren.

Hebrews 2:11

Of a truth, men are mystically united: a mystic bond of brotherhood makes all men one.

Thomas Carlyle, 'Goethe's Works,' in *The Works of Thomas Carlyle*, volume II, *Critical and Miscellaneous Essays*, Chapman and Hall, 1899, page 388

Those who love not their fellow-beings, live unfruitful lives,
and prepare for their old age a miserable grave.

Percy Bysshe Shelley, 'Alastor', in *The Poetical Works of Percy Bysshe Shelley*, volume 1, edited by H. Buxton Forman, George Bell & Sons, 1892, page 141,

Whoever degrades another degrades me,
And whatever is done or said returns at last to me.

Walt Whitman, 'Song of Myself', in *The Complete Poems*, edited by Francis Murphy, Penguin Books, 1982, page 86

Every experience proves that the real problem of our existence lies in the fact that we ought to love one another, but do not.

Reinhold Niebuhr, *Christian Realism and Political Problems*, Faber and Faber, 1953, page 106

No man can be perfectly free till all are free; no one can be perfectly moral till all are moral; no one can be perfectly happy till all are happy.

Herbert Spencer, *Social Statics*, Williams and Norgate, 1892, page 268

It is easy enough to be friendly to one's friends. But to befriend the one who regards himself as your enemy, is the quintessence of true religion. The other is mere business.

Mohandas K. Gandhi, *Non-Violence in Peace & War*, volume II, Navajivan Publishing House, 1949, page 249

We are beginning to discover that our problem is worldwide, and no one people of the earth can work out its salvation by detaching itself from others. Either we shall be saved together or drawn together into destruction.

Rabindranath Tagore, *Letters to a Friend*, George Allen and Unwin, 1928, page 133

What I inveigh against is a cursed spirit of intolerance, conceived in distrust and bred in ignorance, that makes the mental attitude perennially antagonistic, even bitterly antagonistic, to everything foreign, that subordinates everywhere the race to the nation, forgetting the higher claims of brotherhood.

Sir William Osler, *Aphorisms from His Bedside Teachings and Writings*, collected by Robert Bennett Bean, edited by William Bennett Bean, Charles C. Thomas, 1962, page 84

Only when man succeeds in developing his reason and love further than he has done so far, only when he can build a world based on human solidarity and justice, only when he can feel rooted in the experience of universal brotherliness, will he have found a new, human form of rootedness, will he have transformed his world into a truly human home.

Erich Fromm, *The Sane Society*, Routledge and Kegan Paul, 1956, page 60

No man is an Iland, intire of it selfe; every man is a peece of the Continent, a part of the maine; if a Clod bee washed away by the Sea, Europe is the lesse, as well as if a Promontorie were, as well as if a Mannor of thy friends or of thine owne were; any mans death diminishes me, because I am involved in Mankinde; And therefore never send to know for whom the bell tolls; It tolls for thee.

John Donne, 'Devotions,' XVII, in *Complete Poetry and Selected Prose*, edited by John Hayward, The Nonesuch Press, 1929, page 538

We human beings are not isolated individuals in God's sight; we are his dear family, of whom Jesus is the first-born and head.

Love is our supreme and only law, the love which Jesus revealed, and our destiny lies in intimate fellowship with the Father even in this life, expanding into perfect fulfilment when 'the Kingdom of God comes'.

Those of the family, privileged to know its blessedness, who bear the name of Christ, rejoicing in the re-creation he brings, are sent out to be the Light of the World. They know, each of them, that they are called to the fullness of love and holiness following the poor, humble, cross-bearing Jesus.

Living in the world they must bear responsibility for it, working for the welfare of others in whatever way they can.

Their faith in the Risen One enables them to combat evil confidently wherever it is met, for contrary to all appearances the victory of the Risen Lord dominates the world. Each task well done, each talent developed, each advance in the mastery of the world's energies, each effort to improve the human condition, all are contributing to God's great design: the resurrection and transformation of the human race.

Ruth Burrows, in *The Watchful Heart*, edited by Elizabeth Ruth Obbard, Darton, Longman and Todd, 1988, page 1

The Fellowship of those who bear the Mark of Pain. Who are the members of this Fellowship? Those who have learnt by experience what physical pain and bodily anguish mean, belong together all the world over; they are united by a secret bond. One and all they know the horrors of suffering to which man can be exposed, and one and all they know the longing to be free from pain. He who has been delivered from pain must not think he is now free again, and at liberty to take life up just as it was before, entirely forgetful of the past. He is now a 'man whose eyes are open' with regard to pain and anguish, and he must help to overcome those two enemies (so far as human power can control them) and to bring to others the deliverance which he has himself enjoyed. The man who, with a doctor's help, has been pulled through a severe illness, must aid in providing a helper such as he had himself, for those who otherwise could not have one. He who has been saved by an operation from death or torturing pain, must do his part to make it possible for the kindly anaesthetic and the helpful knife to begin their work, where death and torturing pain still rule unhindered. The mother who owes it to medical aid that her child still belongs to her, and not to the cold earth, must help, so that the poor mother who has never seen a doctor may be spared what she has been spared. Where a man's death agony might have been terrible, but could fortunately be made tolerable by a doctor's skill, those who stood around his deathbed must help, that others, too, may enjoy that same consolation when they lose their dear ones.

Such is the Fellowship of those who bear the Mark of Pain.

Albert Schweitzer, *On the Edge of the Primeval Forest*, translated by C.T. Campion, A. and C. Black, 1953, page 116

CHARITY

'Charity'—Christian love of fellow men, kindness, natural affection.

When I was a part-time hospital chaplain, I used to go visiting on the wards of Bradford Royal Infirmary. Each patient, if they were not too ill, would get a short visit of about ten minutes. Often they would talk in affectionate terms of the people on the ward. 'It's marvellous in here, you know, padre. It's just like it was in the war. Everyone is so kind, and they'll do anything for you. There's a real spirit of companionship here.' The nurses, in particular, were singled out for praise, for their care and loving kindness.

I remember one occasion when there was a pay dispute. The men on the ward were indignant at the low pay of nurses. Somehow they managed to trap me in the day room at the far end of the ward and refused to let me go until I had written a letter to the Prime Minister. Physical struggle was inappropriate in those circumstances so I sat down and wrote a brief letter to the then Prime Minister, Harold Wilson. I suspect he never saw the letter, but I think I'm right in recalling nurses' pay went up shortly afterwards, though by a smaller percentage than the men were demanding. Still, I like to think my action made a contribution to the cause of charity in the ward. One man decided to respond by teasing me. A patient in the opposite bed, asked me to get something from his bottom locker. When I was fully stretched, I heard a great broad Yorkshire voice boom round the ward. 'That's what I like to see, a vicar doing some work.' The patients roared with laughter, and we experienced that other facet of charity, natural affection.

Blessed is he who considers the poor!

Psalm 41:1

Do not withhold good from those to whom it is due, when it is in your power to do it.

Proverbs 3:27

Thus, when you give alms, sound no trumpet before you, as the hypocrites do in the synagogues and in the streets, that they may be praised by men. Truly, I say to you, they have received their reward. But when you give alms, do not let your left hand know what your right hand is doing, so that your alms may be in secret; and your Father who sees in secret will reward you.

Matthew 6:2-4

But if any one has the world's goods and sees his brother in need, yet closes his heart against him, how does God's love abide in him?

1 John 3:17

Charity is a virtue of the heart, not of the hands.

Joseph Addison, *The Works of Joseph Addison*, volume IV, edited and published by Henry G. Bohn, 1856, page 321

Did universal charity prevail, earth would be a heaven, and hell a fable.

C.C. Colton, *Lacon*, William Tegg, 1866, page 39

Charity and personal force are the only investments worth any thing.

Walt Whitman, 'Song of Prudence', in *The Complete Poems*, edited by Francis Murphy, Penguin Books, 1982, page 396

For this I think (is) charity, to love God for himselfe, and our neighbour for God.

Sir Thomas Browne, *The Works of Sir Thomas Browne*, volume I, *Religio Medici*, edited by Geoffrey Keynes, Cambridge University Press, 1964, page 92

No sound ought to be heard in the church but the healing voice of Christian charity.

Edmund Burke, *Reflections on the Revolution in France*, edited by Conor Cruise O'Brien, Penguin Books, 1969, page 94

To do him any wrong was to beget
A kindness from him, for his heart was rich,
Of such fine mould, that if you sow'd therein
The seed of Hate, it blossom'd Charity.

Alfred, Lord Tennyson, *Queen Mary, A Drama*, IV. i, Henry S. King and Co., 1875, page 188

God is love, and he that has learnt to live in the Spirit of love has learnt to live and dwell in God. Love was the beginner of all the works of God, and from eternity to eternity nothing can come from God but a variety of wonders and works of love over all nature and creature.

William Law, *Selected Mystical Writings of William Law*, edited by Stephen Hobhouse, Rockliff, 1948, page 182

Now Scripture enjoins nothing except charity and condemns nothing except lust, and in that way informs the practices of men ... I mean by charity that affection of the mind which aims at the enjoyment of God for His own sake and of one's self and one's neighbour for God's sake. By lust I mean that affection of the mind which aims at the enjoyment of one's self and one's neighbour without reference to God ... Now in proportion as the dominion of lust is pulled down, in the same proportion that of charity is built up.

St. Augustine, *An Augustine Synthesis*, arranged by Erich Przywara, SJ, Sheed and Ward, 1945, page 347

Charity is God's way of loving; it is God's love itself.
   It is a person who is called Holy Spirit.
   It is the love which unites the Father with the Son.
   It is the love which penetrated us at Pentecost.
   We are baptized no longer in water, but in the fire of the Holy Spirit—that is, in love.
   He who possesses the Holy Spirit and listens to Him understands everything; he who does not possess Him and does not listen understands nothing.
   Light and darkness in our spirits are formed by this Spirit. When he came down upon the chaos this Spirit created the universe.
   When he covered Mary of Nazareth with His shadow, the flesh of the woman became the flesh of the Son of God.

Carlo Carretto, *The God Who Comes*, translated by Rose Mary Hancock, Darton, Longman and Todd, 1974, page 197

We call it charity when men gave away what they did not want themselves in order to patch up evils and ameliorate bad conditions which their greed, slackness, or stupidity have helped to create. This is not charity, and it is blasphemy to call it by that splendid name. We call it charity when we give a poor devil half a crown to get shut of him and rid ourselves of the sight of his misery, that is blasphemy too. Real charity is not easy, it is always hard, it means that we must be ready to take time, trouble, and infinite pains to create life. The business man who seeks to give good value for money, who prides himself on his fellow workers in the business, and whose aim is to see that by efficiency, and energy his business produces and sustains fine life, he is the charitable man. Our faith is that God is Charity—that His charity is so great that he spares Himself no suffering and no agony in order to create in the world fine life. We are meant to be like Him.

G.A. Studdert Kennedy, *The New Man in Christ*, edited by the Dean of Worcester, Hodder and Stoughton, 1932, page 230

God is love, or rather Charity; generous, out-flowing, self-giving love, *Agape*. When all the qualities which human thought attributes to Reality are set aside, this remains. Charity is the colour of the Divine personality, the spectrum of Holiness. We believe that the tendency to give, to share, to cherish, is the mainspring of the universe, ultimate cause of all that is, and reveals the Nature of God: and therefore that when we are most generous we are most living and most real... To enter the Divine order then, achieve the full life for which we are made, means entering an existence which only has meaning as the channel and expression of an infinite, self-spending love... When we look out towards this Love that moves the stars and stirs in the child's heart, and claims our total allegiance and remember that this alone is Reality and we are only real so far as we conform to its demands, we see our human situation from a fresh angle; and perceive that it is both more humble and dependent, and more splendid, than we had dreamed. We are surrounded and penetrated by great spiritual forces, of which we hardly know anything. Yet the outward events of our life cannot be understood, except in their relation to that unseen and intensely living world, the Infinite Charity which penetrates and supports us, the God whom we resist and yet for whom we thirst; who is ever at work, transforming the self-centred desire of the natural creature into the wide-spreading, outpouring love of the citizen of Heaven.

Evelyn Underhill, *The School of Charity*, Longmans, Green and Co., 1956, page 10

Once I asked Blessed François how one may best become perfect. 'You must love God with your whole heart,' he answered, 'and your neighbour as yourself.'

'I did not ask in what perfection consists,' I replied, 'but how to attain it?'

'Charity,' he repeated, 'is both the means and the end, the one and only way by which we can attain that perfection which in truth is charity itself. It was St. Paul who said: 'I will show you a more excellent way'; and then he elaborates more fully upon charity. It is the one way to God, the only truth, the only life of the soul, for it carries us out of the death of sin into the life of grace. It nourishes faith and hope. And just as the soul is the life of the body, so charity is the life of the soul.'

'I am aware of that,' I said, 'But I want to know *how* one is to love God with one's whole heart and one's neighbour as oneself?'

Again he answered the same: 'We must love God with our whole heart and our neighbour as ourselves.'

'I am still just where I was,' I rejoined. 'Tell me how I may acquire such love.'

'The best way, the shortest and easiest way of loving God with one's whole heart—is simply to love Him wholly and heartily!'

This is the only answer he would give.

Finally, however, François said: 'There are many others who would also like me to tell them of techniques and methods and secret ways of attaining perfection. Yet I can only tell them that the sole secret is a hearty love of God and the only method of acquiring that love is by loving. You learn to speak by speaking, to study by studying, to run by running, to work by working. All those who wish to learn in any other way only deceive themselves. If you really want to love God, go on and love Him more and more. Never look back. Move forward constantly. Begin as a humble apprentice and the very power of love will draw you on to become a master in the art. Those who have made most progress will constantly press ahead, never for a moment thinking that they have reached the goal. For charity should continue to increase in us until we draw our last breath.'

Jean Pierre Camus, *The Spirit of St. François de Sales*, edited and translated by C.F. Kelley, Harper and Brothers, 1952, page 1

CHRISTIANITY

*'Christianity'—the Christian faith, doctrines of Christ and his
apostles; a Christian religious system; being a Christian, Christian
quality of character.*

I have found Kenneth Kirk's classic book, *The Vision of God*, very helpful. In this book he wrote: 'Christianity... had come into the world with a double purpose, to offer people the vision of God and to call them to the pursuit of that vision.' *Visions of Faith* is an attempt to offer people a vision of God. At the heart and centre of this vision is the person of Jesus Christ. In the first instance there is the Christ of history, in whom we discern the presence of the Father, the Holy Spirit, and divine attributes, such as life, light, joy, hope and love. In the second instance there is the resurrected Christ, the Christ who comes to us today through the Holy Spirit, a 'presence' experienced in the depths of our being, and discerned around us. Out of corporate experience the Christian faith has evolved—'the doctrines of Christ and his apostles; a Christian religious system; being a Christian; and the Christian quality of character' as in the definition above.

The 'call and pursuit' of this vision of God comes through the practice of reflection. In silence we ponder and mull over the contents of *Visions of Faith*, opening ourselves to receive something of God's grace. This practice requires the use of our minds and feelings, though the crucial element is always the Holy Spirit. The contents of this book offer a vision of God, and provide a means to pursue a vibrant Christianity.

Afterward he appeared to the eleven themselves as they sat at table; and he upbraided them for their unbelief and hardness of heart, because they had not believed those who saw him after he had risen. And he said to them, 'Go into all the world and preach the gospel to the whole creation.'

Mark 16:14–15

For I am not ashamed of the gospel: it is the power of God for salvation to every one who has faith.

Romans 1:16

For if I preach the gospel, that gives me no ground for boasting. For necessity is laid upon me. Woe to me if I do not preach the gospel!

1 Corinthians 9:16

Beloved, being very eager to write to you of our common salvation, I found it necessary to write appealing to you to contend for the faith which was once for all delivered to the saints.

Jude 3

Christianity is the highest perfection of humanity.

Samuel Johnson, *Boswell's Life of Johnson*, volume II, edited by G.B. Hill, revised by L.F. Powell, Oxford at the Clarendon Press, 1934, page 27

I still & shall to Eternity Embrace Christianity and Adore Him who is the Express image of God.

William Blake, 'The Letters', number 23, in *The Complete Writings of William Blake*, edited by Geoffrey Keynes, Oxford University Press, 1974, page 815,

The true religion of Christ is written in the soul and Spirit of man, by the Spirit of God; and the believer is the only book, in which God himself writes his New Testament.

William Dell, *Select Works of William Dell*, printed for John Kendall, 1773, page 438

For what is now called the Christian religion existed even among the ancients and was not lacking from the beginning of the human race until 'Christ came in the flesh.' From that time, true religion, which already existed, began to be called Christian.

St. Augustine, *The Retractions*, translated by Sister Mary Inez Bogan, The Catholic University of America Press, Inc., 1968, page 52

Christianity is not primarily a system of ideas divinely communicated, nor a way of life divinely enjoined or guided, nor a method of worship divinely taught. It is primarily a self-revelation of God in a historical Person, and in that Person's life, death and resurrection.

William Temple, *Nature, Man and God*, Macmillan and Co., 1934, page 436

We may be suspicious of the clergy and refuse to have anything to do with catechisms, and yet love the Holy and the Just, who came to save and not to curse. Jesus will always supply us with the best criticism of Christianity, and when Christianity has passed away the religion of Jesus will in all probability survive. After Jesus as God we shall come back to faith in the God of Jesus.

Henri Frédéric Amiel, *Amiel's Journal*, translated by Mrs Humphry Ward, Macmillan and Co., 1918, page 140

Christianity can never be merely a pleasant or consoling religion. It is a stern business. It is concerned with the salvation through sacrifice and love of a world in which, as we can all see now, evil and cruelty are rampant. Its supreme symbol is the Crucifix—the total and loving self-giving of man to the redeeming purposes of God.

Evelyn Underhill, *The Fruits of the Spirit*, Longmans, Green and Co., 1949, page 71

Christ's teaching is better than all the teaching of the saints, and any man who has the Spirit will find *the hidden manna* there. It so happens that many people hear the Gospel frequently and yet feel little desire, and this is because they do not have the Spirit of Christ. Anyone who wishes to understand and to savour the words of Christ to the full must try to make his whole life conform to the pattern of Christ.

Thomas à Kempis, *The Imitation of Christ*, translated by Betty I. Knott, William Collins Sons and Co., 1979, page 37

It is not easy to take the principles of Christianity and to deduce how a Christian should behave in a concrete case in order to be, without any doubt, a Christian. For Christianity is not a philosophical problem composed of lifeless abstract principles. It is, on the contrary, of its very principles that every individual can always be under the living providence of the living God in every particular case—and then there is nothing to deduce, for God is freedom.

Theodor Haecker, *The Journal in the Night*, translated by Alexander Dru, The Harvill Press, 1950, page 80

The claim of Christianity is simply the claim of Christ Himself: 'I am come that you may have life and have it more abundantly.' He set Himself to teach us what full living means, to show us how to become really alive. 'I am the way,' He said, 'the truth and the life'. Those who heard Him and watched Him got tremendously excited about Him. Christ was a revolutionary. He had a secret which altered people's lives, that put spring and energy and youth and joy into them, the joy of living.

R.L. Smith, in *Man's Dilemma and God's Answer*, Broadcast Talks, SCM Press, 1944, page 70

In one fundamental sense ... it seems to me that Christianity alone attacks the seat of evil in the kind of world we have been considering, and has a solvent for the intellectual predicaments which arise in such a world. It addresses itself precisely to that crust of self-righteousness which, by the nature of its teaching, it has to dissolve before it can do anything else with a man. The more human beings are lacking in imagination, the more we shall find that their self-righteousness hardens, so that it is just the thick-skinned who are more sure of being right than anybody else.

Herbert Butterfield, *Christianity and History*, G. Bell and Sons, 1949, page 41

Christianity in its origin was essentially a rich and vivid consciousness of God, rising to a perfect experience of union with God in mind, and heart, and soul. It was a personal exhibition of the Divine in the human, the Eternal in the midst of time. The direct impact and power of Christ's life on His followers is the most extraordinary thing in the Gospels—it, and not any portents, caused the realization that He was Divine. Christ always taught His disciples to expect a personal experience of God like His own, though less in degree. Thus Christianity is, in its very heart, a mystical religion. The first Church was a mystical fellowship, in which each member had received the Holy Ghost. In St. Paul the mystical element is very strong. Christ's 'method of inwardness,' His directions as to prayer, His idealism and attitude towards wealth, towards death; His emphasis on love—all His teaching implied, we may say, a mystical view of life.

W.R. Inge, *The Awakening of the Soul*, edited by Prebendary A.F. Judd, A.R. Mowbray and Co., 1959, page 29

Christianity... does not consist in the mere knowing of history and applying the history-knowledge to ourselves, saying: 'Christ died for us; He hath paid the ransom for us, so that we need do nothing but comfort ourselves therewith and steadfastly believe that it is so.' The 'doctors' and 'the wise world' and 'the makers of opinion' will have it that Christ suffered on the Cross for all our sins, and that we can be justified and acquitted of all our transgressions by what He did for us, but it is no true, safe way for the soul. To stake faith upon a history that once was, to look for 'satisfaction' through the sufferings which Christ endured before we were born is to be 'the child of an assumed grace,' is to possess a mere external and historical faith that leaves the dim, weak soul where it was before.

Rufus M. Jones, *Spiritual Reformers in the 16th and 17th Centuries*, Macmillan and Co., 1914, page 192

Let us never forget what it means that the revelation of which the Church is 'repository and trustee' is not a book but a person. It is this which makes Christianity compatible with progress, and indeed a constant source of progress; it is this which fits it for universality. For here we have no code of rules that can only be obeyed in the circumstances of their origin, no scheme of thought which can only be understood in the terms in which it was first conceived, but a Person to whom we can be loyal in all circumstances whatever, with that infinite flexibility and delicacy of adjustment which are compatible with a loyalty that remains absolute and unalterable. Here we see God self-revealed, and we must admit to our minds no thought or image of God that is not a reflection in us of His personality.

William Temple, *Thoughts On Some Problems Of The Day*, Macmillan and Co., 1931, page 28

Let us frankly recognize the true import and the true challenge of the Christian message. The whole gospel kerygma becomes impertinent and laughable if there is an easy answer to everything in a few external gestures and pious intentions. Christianity is a religion for men who are aware that there is a deep wound, a fissure of sin that strikes down to the very heart of man's being. They have tasted the sickness that is present in the inmost heart of man estranged from his God by guilt, suspicion and covert hatred. If that sickness is an illusion, then there is no need for the Cross, the sacraments and the Church... then there is no need to preach Christ any more, and there is no need either of liturgy or of meditation.

It is precisely the function of dread to break down this glass house of false interiority and to deliver man from it... Without dread... man would remain content with himself and with his 'inner life' in meditation, in liturgy or in both.

Without dread, the Christian cannot be delivered from the smug self-assurance of the devout ones who know all the answers.

Thomas Merton, *Contemplative Prayer*, Darton, Longman and Todd, 1973, page 134

The fundamental principle of Christianity is simple to state. Christ said, The time is fulfilled, and the Kingdom of God is at hand. Christianity is no more and no less than the advent of the Kingdom of God. Some people extract 'God' from the Kingdom of God to construct a philosophy upon, while others seize on 'Kingdom' to carry out a social movement. The latter choice has resulted in social theories and political parties. Thomas Aquinas, on the other hand, emphasized the idea of God. As that system gradually declined, it became an individualistic religion, in which God was separated from the daily life of mankind.

True Christianity, however, is not an individualistic religion, but a superindividualistic one. While it is a social movement, it involves the co-operation between God and men. This point should be made clear.

The idea of the Kingdom of God was not clear even to the disciples. That was why Jesus was finally crucified. Judas Iscariot exchanged the Kingdom of God for a 'Kingdom' movement, leaving out 'God.' Seeing that Jesus would not become a king, Judas betrayed him.

Peter, on the contrary, excluded all but God, and forgot the element of love to which he should have bent his energies. Even in the Bible we find places where the idea of the Kingdom of God is sundered and dim. We must consider the meaning of the Kingdom of God in its totality and clarity.

Toyohiko Kagawa, *Meditations*, number 15, translated by Jiro Takenaka, Harper and Brothers, 1950

CHURCH

'Church'—building for public Christian worship; body of all Christians, organized Christian society, clergy or clerical profession.

One of my favourite churches is the Barn Chapel in the grounds of Micklepage House, near Maplehurst, West Sussex. The Chapel is old, small and quaint, with hay covering the earthen floor. One Christmas I discovered ten overseas students who were unable to return to their homes for the vacation, so I invited them to spend Christmas with me at Micklepage House. The party was made up of three Canadians, two Africans, an American, an Australian, an Anglo-Indian, an Englishman (whose parents lived overseas), and myself. Early on Christmas Eve, it snowed heavily. The Africans were amazed as they had never seen snow before. More logs were piled on the sitting-room fire to keep the house warm.

Just before midnight we made our way through the snow to the Barn Chapel. We took the unprecedented risk of lighting the Chapel with candles. This created a wonderful atmosphere. Sitting in the hay we began our informal celebration of Midnight Communion, interspersed with carols, including, of course, the Sussex Carol. I think we all experienced something of Christmas 'in the stable' during the service, and this was enhanced by the presence of our international representatives. There was something special about our time spent together at Micklepage. I sometimes wonder what happened to the participants, dispersed now in several different parts of the world.

How lovely is thy dwelling place, O Lord of hosts!...
Blessed are those who dwell in thy house, ever singing thy praise!...
For a day in thy courts is better than a thousand elsewhere.

Psalm 84:1, 4, 10

Unless the Lord builds the house, those who build it labour in vain.

Psalm 127:1

And I tell you, you are Peter, and on this rock I will build my church, and the powers of death shall not prevail against it.

Matthew 16:18

And they devoted themselves to the apostles' teaching and fellowship, to the breaking of bread and the prayers.

Acts 2:42

Religion that is not embedded in the common life too soon degenerates into religiosity, and an inward-looking Church is a dying Church.

F.R. Barry, *Christian Ethics and Secular Society*, Hodder and Stoughton, 1966, page 117

It is the Church of the saints and martyrs and prophets, who have been the lights of the world in their several generations, that has the demand upon your allegiance—not the Church which has been corrupted by wealth and worldly power. But the true Church is embedded in the existing Churches—you will not find it elsewhere.

Alec R. Vidler, *God's Demand And Man's Response*, John Hermitage, The Unicorn Press, 1938, page 102

To be of no church is dangerous. Religion, of which the rewards are distant, and which is animated only by Faith and Hope, will glide by degrees out of the mind unless it be invigorated and reimpressed by external ordinances, by stated calls to worship, and the salutary influence of example.

Samuel Johnson, in G.B. Hill, editor, *Lives of the English Poets*, volume I, *Milton*, Oxford at the Clarendon Press, 1905, page 155

The Church is the community of the Spirit, not as having a monopoly of the Spirit, but as having been called into existence by God and entrusted with the word and the sacraments. In the Church there should be going on in a concentrated way the work of the Spirit, which in a diffuse way is going on throughout creation. When the Church is truly the Church it is introducing a new dimension into the social situation, thus giving hope for an eventual transformation.

George Appleton, *Journey for a Soul*, William Collins Sons and Co., 1976, page 166

If it seems to you that the Church as organised has somehow lost sense of proportion, remember that only through the Church has the Gospel ever reached you, and that only through the Church can it reach the ages far ahead. And you will do more to the cause of Christ by bringing what reality you can into its life than you can ever render by staying outside and doing what seems possible to you, or you and your few friends, in isolation.

William Temple, *Christian Faith and Life*, SCM Press, 1931, reissued 1963, page 131

Modern man tends to see himself either as an anonymous part of the pattern unfolded to him daily in the newspapers and on the television or, more insidiously, as the impartial observer, the universal journalist or commentator.

The immediate task for the contemporary Christian is to see and experience ourselves as the Church. If the Church is failing to respond to the deep religious needs of our contemporaries it is because we, its people and ministers, fail in our personal response to Christ.

Our effectiveness in trying to turn back the tide of fear and hatred in the world depends upon our own insertion into the mystery of Christ.

John Main OSB, in *The Joy of Being*, selected by Clare Hallward, Darton, Longman and Todd, 1989, page 7

Meanwhile, the special work assigned to the Church of England would seem to be the development of a *Johannine* Christianity, which shall be both Catholic and Evangelical without being either Roman or Protestant. It has been abundantly proved that neither Romanism nor Protestantism, regarded as alternatives, possesses enough of the truth to satisfy the religious needs of the present day. But is it not probable that, as the theology of the Fourth Gospel acted as a reconciling principle between the opposing sections in the early Church, so it may be found to contain the teaching which is most needed by both parties in our own communion? In St. John and St. Paul we find all the principles of a sound and sober Christian Mysticism; and it is to these 'fresh springs' of the spiritual life that we must turn, if the Church is to renew her youth.

W.R. Inge, *Christian Mysticism*, Methuen and Co., 1899, page 324

When we build a church or set apart a place of worship we do something which reaches far beyond the obvious significance of the fact. The whole world which God created has become a place where men have sinned; the devil has been at work, a fight is going on constantly; there is no place on this earth which has not been soiled by blood, suffering or sin. When we choose a minute part of it, calling upon the power of God himself, in rites which convey his grace, to bless it, when we cleanse it from the presence of the evil spirit and set it apart to be God's foothold on earth, we reconquer for God a small part of this desecrated world. We may say that this is a place where the kingdom of God reveals itself and manifests itself with power. When we come to church we should be aware that we are entering upon sacred ground, a place which belongs to God, and we should behave accordingly.

Anthony Bloom, *Living Prayer*, Darton, Longman and Todd, 1966, page 67

When I see a little church environed with trees, how many things are there which mine eye discerneth not. The labour of them which in ancient ages builded it; the conversion of a kingdom of God from paganism, its protection by laws, its subjection to kings, its relation to bishops, its usefulness and convenience for the entertainment of Christians, the divine service, the office of ministry, solemn assemblies, praises and thanksgivings, for the sake of which it was permitted, is governed, standeth and flourisheth.

Perhaps when I look upon it, it is desolate and empty almost like a heap of stones, none of these things appearing to the eyes which nevertheless are the spiritual beauties which adorn and clothe it. The uses, relations, services and ends being the spiritual and invisible things that make any material to be of worth.

He who cannot see the invisible cannot enjoy nor value temples. But he that seeth them may esteem them all to be his own and wonder at the divine bounty for giving them so richly.

Thomas Traherne, in *Landscapes of Glory*, edited by A.M. Allchin, Darton, Longman and Todd, 1989, page 21

What do I mean by saying that Christianity is unthinkable apart from the Church? In the first place, if Christianity is the revelation of the depths of the personal and of love as the ultimate meaning of the universe, it can find expression only in a community. Love can exist only between persons. It demands community. Christ is not Christ without the community of love which He founded. In contrast with all other forms of association which exist for particular, limited purposes, the Church is the association which unites persons with persons, inclusive of all ages—the tiniest infants are admitted by baptism—all occupations, all classes, all races.

The Church is indispensable, secondly, as the society which has to do with men's ultimate concern. Our ultimate concern is about our fundamental being and the meaning of our life and destiny. Other associations have to do with men's immediate concerns in their temporal existence. If one admits that men have an ultimate concern, distinct from the endless variety of their immediate interests, and if one believes or hopes that the universe is not indifferent to that ultimate concern, then there must be an association in which that ultimate concern finds expression in religious worship. Take away the Church with its centres of worship, and life becomes wholly this-worldly and loses immeasurably in depth.

Thirdly, the Church is necessary because Christianity is essentially the proclamation, not of a demand, but of fulfilment. It is not the insistence on love as an ideal to be striven after, but the joyful news that God is love and that we know this because His love has been manifested in history. Grace and truth came by Jesus Christ. The Church is the witness to that revelation and the continuing embodiment of that new life. Take away the Church and Christianity itself disappears. It is a delusion to suppose that we can cut out twenty centuries of lived experience and establish a direct relation between ourselves and the historic Jesus. As historical criticism has proved, we can never reach back to Him behind the witness which His disciples bear to Him. He continues to live in the memory, experience and lives of His disciples. Jesus confronts us today not merely as an individual who lived and acted in Palestine in the first thirty years of our era, but as the source of all the influences that have emanated from Him through the centuries. If we relate ourselves to Him, it is as those who stand in the living stream of tradition and are caught up and borne forward by it.

Fourthly, the coming of this new being and life, when it is apprehended by the mind, is found to imply certain conceptions about God, the world and man, that is to say a theology. The Church is the guardian of the new message and proclamation, and has to see that they are preserved in their purity and power and protected against error, misrepresentation and emasculation. These considerations seem to me conclusive and unanswerable.

J.H. Oldham, *Life Is Commitment*, SCM Press, 1953, page 79

COMMITMENT

'Commitment'—act of committing or being committed; dedication or obligation to particular action or cause, etc.

I can remember my initial act of commitment very clearly. The occasion was a Sunday morning in Oxford during my first year as an undergraduate. I went along to a church service, little knowing what lay in store for me that day. The preacher was Cuthbert Bardsley, the then Bishop of Coventry. I remember very little of the sermon, but what impressed me was the man himself. Here was someone vitally alive and radiant, living the Christian life in the power of the Spirit. This was the quality of life I had unconsciously been looking for. At the end of the service I went forward, along with a few others, to take a step of commitment. The bishop spoke to us gently, and invited us to commit our lives to the person of Jesus Christ. After a short pause in which we each made our commitment, he prayed for us and gave us his blessing. I remember feeling at the time a vital step had been taken in life, and was now looking forward to the future with a mixture of feelings, of awe and excitement, and of fear and trepidation.

Following the initial step of commitment, I was invited to join a 'beginners' group' and started Bible reading and learning how to pray. Two years later I was extremely fortunate in being invited to join a small group to explore the Christian faith in depth. The experience of this group was invaluable. This was the start of *Visions of Faith*, the practice of reflection, and reflection groups—a vital resource for those who have recently taken a step of commitment.

You shall fear the Lord your God; you shall serve him and cleave to him, and by his name you shall swear. He is your praise; he is your God.

Deuteronomy 10:20–21

Take good care to observe the commandment and the law which Moses the servant of the Lord commanded you, to love the Lord your God, and to walk in all his ways, and to keep his commandments, and to cleave to him, and to serve him with all your heart and with all your soul.

Joshua 22:5

And every one who has left houses or brothers or sisters or father or mother or children or lands, for my name's sake, will receive a hundredfold, and inherit eternal life.

Matthew 19:29

After this he went out, and saw a tax collector, named Levi, sitting at the tax office; and he said to him, 'Follow me.' And he left everything, and rose and followed him.

Luke 5:27

The choice is always ours. Then let me choose
The longest art, the hard Promethean way
Cherishingly to tend and feed and fan
That inward fire, whose small precarious flame,
Kindled or quenched creates
The noble or the ignoble men we are,
The worlds we live in and the very fates,
Our bright or muddy star.

Aldous Huxley, in *The Choice is Always Ours*, edited by Dorothy Berkley Phillips, Harper and Row, 1960, *Orion*, page 39

We stand by Jesus in verbal affirmation and in liturgical ceremony, but each of us has to examine how far our actual commitment squares with what we profess.

We are committed—up to a point; we follow him—up to a point; but we have not yet cast ourselves absolutely, irrevocably, onto his side.

Think about it: those seemingly small but pernicious criticisms, those quick retorts expressive more of indignation and aggrieved pride than of pure love, the allowing of resentful thoughts and feelings, playing with mistrust, depression, discouragement, instead of a loyal rejection of such things.

God's grace is always flowing plentifully. Each morning there are special outpourings. Let us determine that today will see an end of our equivocation and the beginning of an unswerving discipleship.

Let us go to die with him.

Ruth Burrows, in *The Watchful Heart*, edited by Elibabeth Ruth Obbard, Darton, Longman and Todd, 1988, page 23

Of the many half-truths floating about in sermons and articles today I know few so misleading as this: 'Religion is life.' It is misleading just because it is not obviously false. It contains important truths. For one thing, it says this: Religion, wherever it exists, spreads over the whole of life. One cannot take it up as one takes up golf—by giving it a couple of afternoons a week. That kind of amateur religion is not religion. Religion is either the whole of one's life, or else it is not religion, no matter how much fuss is made over it. This is true, and dangerously true. 'Religion is life,' so understood, cuts with condemnation. To all those who want religion, but want it 'in its place,' that is, apart from their business, their politics, their luxuries or their conveniences, or anything else, this says, 'My good friend, what you call your 'religion' is something or other, but you had better find its name and call it by its name; don't call it religion.'

Religion can never be lived except with one's whole life, and what cannot be humanly lived is not religion or any concern of religion. So far 'religion is life' makes sense. But how much farther? Does it hint at the all-important fact that religion is not any kind of life, but a difficult and exacting way to which many are called but few chosen? Does it suggest just what it is that marks off religion from all the other kinds of lives that have been lived and can be lived—the life of the dilettante or of the egotist or the cynic or the romantic, or of the healthy cabbage? Jesus told Nicodemus, 'You must be born again.' He told the rich young ruler, 'Sell all you have,' and the disciples, 'He who would save his life must lose it.' Could you have guessed any of these things from 'religion is life?' Where is the way of the cross, the demand for decision, the necessity for absolute loyalty? Something slips between the fingers of this plausible generality and this something is commitment.

Commitment is all-important in our understanding of religion because it expresses clearly, as 'life' does not, this fact: Religion is a relationship. This may sound like a truism. Yet even a truism is significant when it is denied. Every kind of subjectivism is such a denial. Nothing is so attractive to the tired sophisticate as the call to leave awhile the world that is too much with him and retreat to a place of stillness within his own soul. That there is such a place is an exciting discovery, and so is the art of finding it, steering safely to it, and avoiding the dangerous turmoils of the world of outer fact or the world of the inner self, both full of confusion and strife. To explore this middle ground of introspection and reverie, and flavour its precarious peace, is an engrossing adventure, especially when it is dignified with the name of religion. To such religious romanticism the word 'commitment' brings a rude corrective. It reminds one inescapably of the essential thing in religion—God. It is easy to forget God when one is most concerned about one's inner experiences. It is not so easy to forget Him when one is concerned about commitment. One can give oneself only to something which is there, which can be observed, understood and obeyed; to something which makes demands and holds out promises and obligations. It warns against subjectivity. One's own subjectivity can hide God from one just as much as the pressure of work or the hypocrisies of polite society.

If one is not clear about God, one will always tend to shy away toward something more accessible, like one's own conscious states. To talk about commitment brings one face to face with the question of God, so that one cannot dodge it... God is that within and beyond the universe which expresses the greatest good which now is and ever can be: the direction of life against death, the direction of unity against discord, the direction of creation and increasing growth against destruction and decay. God is the power of good in all its various forms: in the order and structure of inorganic matter, in the process of growth and sensitivity in the realm of life, in the conditions of intelligence, cooperation, appreciation and creative love on the human level.

This cosmic reach in our description of God must not distract our attention from the specific human focus within which our experiences of the good are most intense and most decisive. It is here most of all that we know God as a daily fact. We have tried the ways of ambition, of self-aggrandizement, of aggressive opportunism, and we have seen the kind of flimsy success to which they lead, we have tasted the bitter poisons they generate, we have known the conflict, the disgust, the inner division, the outer isolation that follow in their wake. We have also tried in some small measure the other way, and known that every man and woman must have love; that there is no life or peace without love; only strife, waste, madness, destruction, death. There is that in life which makes it necessary that men should find the way of truth, of understanding, of justice, or else destroy themselves and each other. You have not seen it? You cannot move a step but you stumble into it; it is in the structure of your world; you cannot live a day or an hour without saying either yes or no to it, without finding life through it or death without it.

Even a faint glimpse of this reality brings you back to yourself. Whither do you move? With it or without it? The alternatives are simple—terrifyingly simple and clear. To compromise in this matter is to decide; to waver is to decide; to postpone and evade decision is to decide; to hide the matter is to decide. There is no escape. You must say yes, or no. There are a thousand ways of saying no; one way of saying yes; and no way of saying anything else.

Gregory Vlastos, *The Religious Way and The Religious Person in the World Today*, National Board of the Young Women's Christian Association of the U.S.A., 1934

COMMUNITY

'Community'—a body of people living in the same locality; a body of people having religion in common.

When I was chaplain to University College London, I was allowed to have an assistant chaplain—Father Simon Holden, C.R.—a monk and a member of the Community of the Resurrection, Mirfield. We worked together for five years and I was extremely fortunate in having him as a colleague. I remember there was an occasion early on in our relationship when I got something wrong with Simon. I had written a letter to him and had addressed it to 'Father Simon Holden'. Shortly afterwards he tackled me, and said: 'Bill, I know it's only a small point, but it is very important to me. When you write to me in future could you please add 'C.R.' after my name. He went on to explain. 'I'm very proud of belonging to the Community of the Resurrection. From it I get my sense of identity, my way of life, and the manner in which I relate to other members of the community. A belief in the resurrection, and of living in the power of the resurrection is central for our community. To this end we find it helpful to have 'C.R.' added after our names. It acts as a constant reminder of what we stand for.'

I took his point and was careful to add 'C.R.' to his name, in all future correspondence. In turn this acts as a timely reminder that a belief in the resurrection of Christ was the 'original gospel' and living in the power of the resurrection, through the Holy Spirit, the hallmark of a Christian community.

For you are a people holy to the Lord your God, and the Lord has chosen you to be a people for his own possession, out of all the peoples that are on the face of the earth.

Deuteronomy 14:2

But he who is joined with all the living has hope.

Ecclesiastes 9:4

Let no one seek his own good, but the good of his neighbour.

1 Corinthians 10:24

But you are a chosen race, a royal priesthood, a holy nation, God's own people, that you may declare the wonderful deeds of him who called you out of darkness into his marvellous light. Once you were no people but now you are God's people; once you had not received mercy but now you have received mercy.

1 Peter 2:9–10

I am a part of all that I have met.

Alfred, Lord Tennyson, *Ulysses*, in *The Poems of Tennyson*, edited by Christopher Ricks, Longmans, Green and Co., 1969, page 563

The community stagnates without the impulse of the individual. The impulse dies away without the sympathy of the community.

William James, *The Will To Believe*, Longmans, Green and Co., 1904, page 232

All are but parts of one stupendous whole,
Whose body Nature is, and God the soul.

Alexander Pope, *An Essay on Man*, epistle I, Cassell and Company, 1905, page 23

Life is the one universal soul, which by virtue of the enlivening BREATH, and the informing WORD, all organized bodies have in common, each *after its kind.*

Samuel Taylor Coleridge, 'Aids to Reflection' in *Coleridge, Select Poetry & Prose*, edited by Stephen Potter, The Nonesuch Press, page 449

We don't live alone. We are members of one body. We are responsible for each other. And I tell you that the time will soon come when, if men will not learn that lesson, then they will be taught it in fire and blood and anguish.

J.B. Priestley, *An Inspector Calls*, Act III, William Heinemann Ltd., 1947, page 57

We cannot imagine a human being living from birth without any contact with fellow-men. Without other people we could not achieve worthwhile self-consciousness. Human personality cannot develop in isolation. Human society cannot function without understanding, communication and co-operation between people. I *am* only through relationship with others.

George Appleton, *Journey for a Soul*, William Collins Sons and Co., 1976, page 26

The individual, if left alone from birth, would remain primitive and beastlike in his thoughts and feelings to a degree that we can hardly conceive. The individual is what he is and has the significance that he has not so much in virtue of his individuality, but rather as a member of a great human community, which directs his material and spiritual existence from the cradle to the grave.

Albert Einstein, *Ideas and Opinions*, Souvenir Press (Educational & Academic), 1973, page 13

No amount of philosophical theories are worth much compared with a simple picture of home life. It is these common relations of life which are most awful and sacred. The highest life we know is, I think I may say with reverence, family life—life of Father and Son; family life on earth is a faint picture of something better in heaven. We shall be surprised some day to find that, while we have been searching for the noble and divine, we have it all the while at home.

Forbes Robinson, *Letters to his Friends*, SCM Press, 1938, page 60

I want you to form the nucleus of a new community which shall start a new life amongst us—a life in which the only riches is integrity of character. So that each one may fulfil his own nature and deep desires to the utmost, but wherein the ultimate satisfaction and joy is in the completeness of us all as one. Let us be good all together, instead of just in the privacy of our chambers, let us know that the intrinsic part of all of us is the best part, the believing part, the passionate, generous part. We can all come croppers, but what does it matter. We can laugh at each other, and dislike each other, but the good remains, and we know it. And the new community shall be established upon the known, eternal good part in us . . . I hold this the most sacred duty—the gathering together of a number of people who shall so agree to live by the best they know, that they shall be *free* to live by the *best* they know. The ideal, the religion, must now be *lived, practised.*

D.H. Lawrence, *The Letters of D.H. Lawrence*, volume II, edited by George J. Zytaruk and James T. Boulton, Cambridge University Press, 1981, page 271

CONVERSION

'Conversion'—converting or being converted, especially in belief or religion; bringing over (to an opinion, party, faith, etc.); turning sinners to God.

Nigeria is a colourful country. A typical bus or lorry has a brightly painted proverb fixed on the front, rather like an enlarged number-plate, usually fixed above the driver's cabin. I recall an incident one hot afternoon. I was driving my car and vaguely aware of a lorry coming towards me from the opposite direction. The driver must have nodded off, and I was suddenly aware of the lorry heading straight for me. I had no option but to get out of the way, and off the road as quickly as possible. As I hit the ditch, I took a hasty glance at the lorry. The words of the proverb caught my eye. Ironically the message was—'God First!'

Looking back over the early part of my life I realized I had been selfish and self-centred, and my proverb would probably have read 'Self First!' In my early twenties I went through a conversion experience. This led to a radical change of priorities. From then onwards I tried to put 'God First.' Initially I expected life to change overnight. This has not been my experience. In the struggle which ensued I have come to value the words and experience of William of St Thierry. 'But this work may not be accomplished in one moment of conversion; it is not the work of one day, but of much time, much sweat, much labour, according to the grace of God that pitieth and the zeal of man that willeth and runneth.'

I now believe conversion is the work of a lifetime.

Restore to me the joy of thy salvation, and uphold me with a willing spirit. Then I will teach transgressors thy ways, and sinners with return to thee.

Psalm 51:12–13

When I think of thy ways, I turn my feet to thy testimonies; I hasten and do not delay to keep thy commandments.

Psalm 119:59–60

... I have prayed for you that your faith may not fail; and when you have turned again, strengthen your brethren.

Luke 22:32

... for you know how, like a father with his children, we exhorted each one of you and encouraged you and charged you, to lead a life worthy of God, who calls you into his own kindgom and glory.

1 Thessalonians 2:11–12

Suddenly I heard the words of Christ and I understood them, and life and death ceased to seem to me evil, and instead of despair I experienced happiness and the joy of life undisturbed by death.

Leo Tolstoy, *A Confession and What I Believe*, translated by Aylmer Maude, Humphrey Milford, Oxford University Press, 1921, page 105

There may have been a neurotic element in the make-up of Saul of Tarsus, John Bunyan and George Fox, and this may account for some features in the story of the conversion of each. But in all three examples, the man is re-made psychologically, morally and intellectually by his vision. This does not happen to the drug addict.

H.G. Wood, *Belief and Unbelief Since 1850*, Cambridge University Press, 1955, page 84

The life of communion which the conversion sets going, the humble and arduous year by year acceptance and using every experience in supernatural regard: this it is which gradually converts the penitent into the saint, as a real garden is made, not by sticking in plants, but by long and unremitting cultivation of the soil.

Evelyn Underhill, *Man and The Supernatural*, Methuen and Co., 1927, page 220

Five years ago I came to believe in Christ's teaching, and my life suddenly changed; I ceased to desire what I had previously desired, and began to desire what I formerly did not want. What had previously seemed to me good seemed evil, and what had seemed evil seemed good. It happened to me as it happens to a man who goes out on some business and on the way suddenly decides that the business is unnecessary and returns home. All that was on his right is now on his left, and all that was on his left is now on his right.

Leo Tolstoy, *A Confession and What I Believe*, translated by Aylmer Maude, Humphrey Milford, Oxford University Press, 1921, page 103

Give Me the greedy heart and the little creeping treasons,
Give Me the proud heart and the blind, obstinate eyes (to Caiaphas);
Give me the shallow heart, and the vain lust, and the folly (to Herod);
Give me the coward heart and the spiritless refusals (to Pilate);
Give me the confused self that you can do nothing with; I can do something.

Dorothy L. Sayers, *The Just Vengeance*, Victor Gollancz, 1946, page 68

Everyone who lives in this deplorable exile of ours knows that he cannot be filled with a love of eternity, or anointed with the sweet oil of heaven, unless he be truly converted to God. Before he can experience even a little of God's love he must really be turned to him, and, in mind at least, be wholly turned from every earthly thing. The turning indeed is a matter of daily ordered love, so that, first, he loves what he ought to love and not what he ought not, and, second, his love kindles more towards the former than to the latter.

Richard Rolle, *The Fire of Love*, translated by Clifton Wolters, Penguin Books, 1981, page 48

What is quite certain is that the self cannot by any effort of its own lift itself off its own self as centre and resystematise itself about God as its centre. Such radical conversion must be the act of God, and that too by some process other than the gradual self-purification of a self-centred soul assisted by the ever-present influence of God diffused through nature, including human nature. It cannot be a process only of enlightenment. Nothing can suffice but a redemptive act. Something impinging upon the self from without must deliver it from the freedom which is perfect bondage to the bondage which is its only perfect freedom.

William Temple, *Nature, Man and God*, Macmillan and Co., 1934, page 397

While I silently ponder on that change wrought in me, I find no language equal to convey to another a clear idea of it. I looked upon the works of God in this visible creation, and an awfulness covered me. My heart was tender and often contrite, and universal love to my fellow-creatures increased in me. This will be understood by such as have trodden the same path. Some glances of real beauty may be seen in their faces, who dwell in true meekness. There is a harmony in the sound of that voice to which divine love gives utterance, and some appearance of right order in their temper and conduct, whose passions are regulated yet these do not fully show forth that inward life to those who have not felt it; this... new name is only known rightly by such as receive it.

John Woolman, *The Journal of John Woolman*, Edward Marsh, 1857, page 8

I think that, like most other converts, I faced the problem of the 'religiousness' and came to terms with it. God was not for me a working hypothesis, to fill in gaps left open by a scientific world view. Nor was He a God enthroned somewhere in outer space. Nor did I ever feel any particular 'need' for superficial religious routines merely to keep myself happy. I would even say that, like most modern men, I have not been much moved by the concept of 'getting into heaven' after muddling through this present life. On the contrary, my conversion to Catholicism began with a realization of the presence of God *in this present life*, in the world and in myself, and that my task as a Christian is to live in full and vital awareness of this ground of my being and of the world's being. Acts and forms of worship help one to do this, and the Church, with her liturgy and sacraments, give us the essential means of grace. Yet God can work without these means if He so wills. When I entered the Church I came seeking God, the living God, and not just 'the consolations of religion.'

Thomas Merton, *Conjectures of a Guilty Bystander*, Burns and Oates, 1968, page 312

We see that we cannot partake deeply of the life of God unless we change profoundly. It is therefore essential that we should go to God in order that he should transform and change us, and that is why, to begin with we should ask for conversion.

Conversion in Latin means a turn, a change in the direction of things. The Greek word *metanoia* means a change of mind.

Conversion means that instead of spending our lives in looking in all directions, we should follow one direction only. It is turning away from a great many things which we value solely because they were pleasant or expedient for us. The first impact of conversion is to modify our sense of values: God being at the centre of all, everything acquires a new position and a new depth. All that is God's, all that belongs to him, is positive and real. Everything that is outside him has no value or meaning. But it is not a change of mind alone that we can call conversion. We can change our minds and go no farther; what must follow is an act of will and unless our will comes into motion and is redirected Godwards, there is no conversion; at most there is only an incipient, still dormant and inactive change in us.

Anthony Bloom, *Living Prayer*, Darton, Longman and Todd, 1966, page 65

During the two years just before and after I was twenty I had two experiences which led to religious conversion. The first occurred when I was waiting at a bus stop on a wet afternoon. It was opposite the Odeon cinema, outside the station, and I was surrounded by people, shops, cars. A friend was with me. All of a sudden, for no apparent reason, everything looked different. Everything I could see shone, vibrated, throbbed with joy and with meaning. I knew that it had done this all along, and would go on doing it, but that usually I couldn't see it. It was all over in a minute or two. I climbed on to the bus, saying nothing to my friend—it seemed impossible to explain—and sat stunned with astonishment and happiness.

The second experience occurred some months later. I left my office at lunch-time, stopped at a small Greek café in Fleet Street to buy some rolls and fruit, and walked up Chancery Lane. It was an August day, quite warm but cloudy, with the sun glaringly, painfully bright, behind the clouds. I had a strong sense that something was about to happen. I sat on a seat in the garden of Lincoln's Inn waiting for whatever it was to occur. The sun behind the clouds grew brighter and brighter, the clouds assumed a shape which fascinated me, and between one moment and the next, although no word had been uttered, I felt myself spoken to. I was aware of being regarded by love, of being wholly accepted, accused, forgiven, all at once. The joy of it was the greatest I had ever known in my life. I felt I had been born for this moment and had marked time till it occurred.

Monica Furlong, *Travelling In*, Hodder and Stoughton, 1971, page 26

CREATION

'Creation'—all that has been made; the bringing into being of the world.

Four years ago three of us went off to Australia to a wedding of one of our former post-graduates from University College, Oxford. The flight involved a brief visit to Kuala Lumpur, and the beauty of the dawn in our approach to the coast of Australia was awe-inspiring. Once in Sydney we went on a boat-trip round the harbour and were fascinated by the Harbour Bridge and the Opera House. The aquarium in Darling Harbour introduced us to marine life, and we saw for the first time, a real live shark. After a day or two sight-seeing, the wedding took place, and after the reception, we flew up to Brisbane to stay with some more Australian friends. Here we went to a park, and saw koala bears and kangaroos, as well as a wide variety of other animals and parrots. Another flight took us to the town of Gladstone, and from there we set out on a long boat-trip to a part of the Great Barrier Reef, called Wistari Reef. Here a wooden platform had been anchored. Excitedly we put on wet suits and flippers, and went snorkelling. The sight was well worth the long journey. We marvelled at the many different varieties of brightly coloured tropical fish. After the swim we went out in glass-bottomed boats and gazed at these species at leisure. Later in the day we saw turtles, and were royally entertained by a school of dolphins frollicking nearby. Looking back over this trip, we were privileged to witness some of the wonders of creation, and were much refreshed by our brief time 'down-under'.

Thou art the Lord, thou alone; thou hast made heaven, the heaven of heavens, with all their host, the earth and all that is on it, the seas and all that is in them; and thou preservest all of them; and the host of heaven worships thee.

Nehemiah 9:6

Bless the Lord, O my soul! O Lord my God, thou art very great! Thou art clothed with honour and majesty, who coverest thyself with light as with a garment, who hast stretched out the heavens like a tent, who hast laid the beams of thy chambers on the waters, who makest the clouds thy chariot, who ridest on the wings of the wind, who makest the winds thy messengers, fire and flame thy ministers.

Psalm 104:1-4

... that you should turn from these vain things to a living God who made the heaven and the earth and the sea and all that is in them. In past generations he allowed all the nations to walk in their own ways; yet he did not leave himself without witness, for he did good and gave you from heaven rains and fruitful seasons, satisfying your hearts with food and gladness.

Acts 14:15-17

Worthy art thou, our Lord and God, to receive glory and honour and power, for thou didst create all things, and by thy will they existed and were created.

Revelation 4:11

All creatures are living in the hand of God; the senses perceive only the action of the creature, but faith sees the action of God in everything.

Jean Pierre de Caussade, SJ, *Self-Abandonment to Divine Providence*, edited by Father John Joyce, SJ, Burns and Oates, 1962, page 18

Any child knows that the earth was not made in six days. But not everyone knows that God made the world through his Spirit and man in his own image.

Dietrich Bonhoeffer, 'Letters, Lectures and Notes 1928–1936,' in *The Collected Works of Dietrich Bonhoeffer*, volume I, *No Rusty Swords*, edited by Edwin H. Robertson, translated by Edwin H. Robertson and John Bowden, William Collins Sons and Co., 1965, page 143

Two things fill the mind with ever new and increasing admiration and awe, the oftener and the more steadily they are reflected on: the starry heavens above me and the moral law within me.

Immanuel Kant, *Critique of Practical Reason*, translated and edited by Lewis White Beck, The University of Chicago Press, 1949, page 258

The essence of the doctrine of Creation is not that God inaugurated the existence of the world at a particular moment of time, but that it owes its existence—not only its beginning—to His volitional activity.

William Temple, *Nature, Man and God*, Macmillan and Co., 1934, page 301

Flower in the crannied wall,
I pluck you out of the crannies,
I hold you here, root and all, in my hand,
Little flower—but *if* I could understand
What you are, root and all, and all in all,
I should know what God and man is.

Alfred, Lord Tennyson, 'Flower in the crannied wall', in *The Poems of Tennyson*, edited by Christopher Ricks, Longmans, Green and Co., 1969, page 1193

Every man, in the course of his life, must not only show himself obedient and docile. By his fidelity he must *build*—starting with the most natural territory of his own self—a work... into which something enters from all the elements of the earth. He *makes his own soul* throughout all his earthly days and at the same time he collaborates in another work, which infinitely transcends... the perspectives of his individual achievement: the completing of the world.

Pierre Teilhard de Chardin, *Le Milieu Divin*, William Collins Sons and Co., 1960, page 32

God is *in* the world, or nowhere, creating continually in us and around us. This creative principle is everywhere, in animate and so-called inanimate matter, in the ether, water, earth, human hearts. But this creation is a continuing process, and 'the process is itself the actuality,' since no sooner do you arrive than you start on a fresh journey. In so far as man partakes of this creative process does he partake of the divine, of God, and that participation is his immortality, reducing the question of whether his individuality survives death of the body to the estate of an irrelevancy. His true destiny as co-creator in the universe is his dignity and his grandeur.

Alfred North Whitehead, *Dialogues of Alfred North Whitehead*, as recorded by Lucien Price, Max Reinhardt, 1954, page 366

For I have learned
To look on nature, not as in the hour
Of thoughtless youth; but hearing oftentimes
The still, sad music of humanity,
Nor harsh nor grating, though of ample power
To chasten and subdue. And I have felt
A presence that disturbs me with the joy
Of elevated thoughts; a sense sublime
Of something far more deeply interfused,
Whose dwelling is the light of setting suns,
And the round ocean and the living air,
And the blue sky, and in the mind of man:
A motion and a spirit, that impels
All thinking things, all objects of all thought,
And rolls through all things.

William Wordsworth, 'Lines composed a few miles above Tintern Abbey', in *The Poetical Works of William Wordsworth*, volume II, edited by E. de Selincourt, Oxford at the Clarendon Press, 1944, page 261

If only our hearts were always tender and our souls fresh when we look at creation. What a source of joy it would be on our pilgrimage!

We can pass by and see, or we can pass by and not see; it depends on us.

Creation is like a message written on things, a story told in symbol, a source of conversation for our souls.

But we have to learn how to read, listen and converse.

We are in constant danger of our hearts turning into stone, either with old age or with the petrifaction of sin: and then it is goodbye to our hymn, goodbye to our conversation!

We become the deaf mutes of the Gospel, and in that case only Jesus can cure us.

Loving nature, conversing with nature, is not something extraneous to our love for God; it is part of it, an essential ingredient.

God speaks to us, teaches us, gives us His first revelation, in the symbols of the created world. Later we shall receive the revelation in word and later still a direct personal revelation from God, but things still continue to reveal God, as God himself intended, and we cannot forget it.

Not to look at nature, not to love it to the full, is to refuse to read a document God has specifically composed for us in His love.

Carlo Carretto, *Love is for Living*, translated by Jeremy Moiser, Darton, Longman and Todd, 1976, page 84

The spacious firmament on high,
With all the blue ethereal sky,
And spangled heavens, a shining frame,
Their great Original proclaim:
The unwearied sun from day to day
Does his Creator's power display,
And publishes to every land
The work of an Almighty hand.
Soon as the evening shades prevail,
The moon takes up the wondrous tale,
And nightly to the listening earth
Repeats the story of her birth:
Whilst all the stars that round her burn,
And all the planets, in their turn,
Confirm the tidings as they roll,
And spread the truth from pole to pole.
What though, in solemn silence, all
Move round the dark terrestrial ball?
What though nor real voice nor sound
Amid their radiant orbs be found?
In reason's ear they all rejoice,
And utter forth a glorious voice,
For ever singing, as they shine,
'The hand that made us is Divine.'

Joseph Addison, *The Works of Joseph Addison*, volume III, edited and published by Henry G. Bohn, 1856, page 485

Sometimes I look about me with a feeling of complete dismay. In the confusion that afflicts the world today, I see a disrespect for the very values of life. Beauty is all about us, but how many are blind to it! They look at the wonder of this earth—and seem to see nothing. People move hectically but give little thought to where they are going. They seek excitement for its mere sake, as if they were lost and desperate. They take little pleasure in the natural and quiet and simple things of life.

Each second we live is a new and unique moment of the universe, a moment that never was before and will never be again. And what do we teach our children in School? We teach them that two and two make four, and that Paris is the capital of France. When will we also teach them what they are? We should say to each one of them: Do you know what you are? You are a marvel. You are unique. In all of the world there is no other child exactly like you. In the millions of years that have passed there never has been another child like you. And look at your body— what a wonder it is! Your legs, your arms, your cunning fingers, the way you move! You may become a Shakespeare, a Michelangelo, a Beethoven. You have the capacity for anything. Yes, you are a marvel. And when you grow up, can you then harm another who is, like you, a marvel? You must cherish one another. You must work—we all must work—to make the world worthy of its children...

The love of one's country is a natural thing. But why should love stop at the border? Our family is one—each of us has a duty to his brothers. We are all leaves of a tree, and the tree is humanity.

Pablo Casals, *Joys and Sorrows: Reflections by Pablo Casals*, as told to Albert E. Kahn, Macdonald and Co., 1970, page 295

What we have to find is a metaphysical landscape, a way of seeing the world, which shall justify the saint, the artist and the scientist, and give each his full rights. Not a doctrine of watertight compartments, an opposition of 'appearance' to 'reality'. Rather, a doctrine of the indwelling of this visible world by an invisible, yet truly existent, world of spirit which, while infinitely transcending, yet everywhere supports and permeates the natural scene. Even to say this, is to blur the true issue by resort to the deceptive spatial language which colours and controls our thoughts, and translate the dynamic and spiritual into static and intellectual terms. The first demand we must make of such a diagram is, that it shall at least safeguard, though it can never represent, all the best that man has learned to apprehend of the distinct and rich reality of God... For that which above all a genuine theism requires of our human ways of thinking, is the acknowledgement of two sorts or stages of reality, which can never be washed down into one: of a two-foldness that goes right through man's experience, and cannot without impoverishment be resolved. We may call these two sorts of reality, this two-foldness, by various names—Supernature and Nature, Eternity and Time, God and the World, Infinite and Finite, Creator and Creature. These terms do but emphasize one or another aspect of a total fact too great for us to grasp, without infringing the central truth of its mysterious duality: for 'God', as Plotinus says, 'never was the All. That would make Him dependent on His universe'.

Evelyn Underhill, *Man and The Supernatural*, Methuen and Co., 1927, page 54

CROSS

'Cross'—stake (usually with traverse bar) used by the ancients for crucifixion, especially that on which Christ was crucified; Christian religion; trial, affliction, annoyance.

I was in the middle of my curacy at Bradford Cathedral. The Boy's Brigade Captain invited me to join their annual summer camp on the shores of Lake Windermere. The Provost thought this was a good idea, so I packed my bags and spent a week under canvas.

On the third evening I went down to the lakeside and looked across to the other side. We were camped at the widest part of the lake. I was joined by one of our tough lads from Bradford, who suggested in a rather jocular way: 'Let's swim across it tomorrow.' 'Sure,' I replied jokingly, 'let's give it a go.' Unfortunately he was being serious, and before I knew what was happening, was committed to the venture. To make matters worse, I discovered that evening he was a very good swimmer.

We hired two rowing boats, one to accompany each swimmer. At the appointed hour we took to the chilly waters of the lake. Shortly after we set off I fixed my eyes on the outline of a tree on the other side of the lake, shaped like a 'cross'. Whenever I was feeling tired and exhausted and there was a danger of cramp setting in, I concentrated on that 'cross'. Little by little the 'cross' came fully in to sight and it took us an hour and a half to complete the crossing.

There is no accounting for some forms of suffering, but in Christ's cross we learn that God has entered the human scene, and that even he suffers from time to time.

Then Jesus told his disciples, 'If any man would come after me, let him deny himself and take up his cross and follow me. For whoever would save his life will lose it, and whoever loses his life for my sake will find it.

Matthew 16:24–25

This was why the Jews sought all the more to kill him, because he not only broke the sabbath but also called God his own Father, making himself equal with God.

John 5:18

For Jews demand signs and Greeks seek wisdom, but we preach Christ crucified, a stumbling block to Jews and folly to Gentiles, but to those who are called, both Jews and Greeks, Christ the power of God and the wisdom of God.

1 Corinthians 1:22–24

I have been crucified with Christ; it is no longer I who live, but Christ who lives in me; and the life I now live in the flesh I live by faith in the Son of God, who loved me and gave himself for me.

Galatians 2:20

No Cross, No Crown.

William Penn, title of pamphlet, 1669

The cross is 'I' crossed out.

Anon.

The way to God is the way of the Cross. Christ Himself is the pattern and His way of Life is the typical way for all who would find God.

Rufus M. Jones, *Spiritual Reformers in the 16th and 17th Centuries*, Macmillan and Co., 1914, page 250

The Way of the Cross winds through our towns and cities, our hospitals and factories, and through our battlefields; it takes the road of poverty and suffering in every form. It is in front of these new Stations of the Cross that we must stop and meditate and pray to the suffering Christ for strength to love him enough to act.

Michel Quoist, *Prayers of Life*, translated by Anne Marie de Commaile and Agnes Mitchell Forsyth, Gill and Macmillan, 1963, page 5

(How could Christ die for our sins?) This is the hardest thing for people to realise intellectually. You can tell them about it, but I believe the experience of Christ's death, the freedom from sin, can only be experienced personally. You can hear about it and know about it, but I think this is the gap across which a person has to leap by experience or by faith.

George Reindorp, in Gerald Priestland, *Priestland's Progress*, BBC Worldwide, 1982, page 79

THE CROSS IS NOT a) the angry Father appeasing his wrath by taking it out of his loving Son; b) the Son standing in my place to take the punishment I ought to have. THE CROSS IS God accepting in his own person the worst evil of the world he has created and, by accepting the worst that men can do, assuring us that all men, however bad, are accepted by his love.

Hugh Montefiore, *My Confirmation Notebook*, SPCK, 1983, page 28

After all, the fundamental idea both of St. John and of St. Paul is simply that the death of Christ, the culminating act in a life of self-sacrifice, is the supreme manifestation of Christ's love, and therefore of the love of the Father whom He reveals; and that the contemplation of that life and death gives other men the power, as nothing else has done, to overcome temptation and to lead lives of love like His.

Hastings Rashdall, *The Idea of Atonement in Christian Theology*, Macmillan and Co., 1920, page 184

We Christians often use the words 'Christ died to save us from our sins.' He shows us the limitless measure of God's love and that draws our hearts to him. He makes known to us God's forgiveness, not only in his teaching, but by the fact of his own forgiveness of those who brought him to the cross. There is something more which it is difficult to describe—he works within us, assuring us of God's forgiveness, changing our hearts towards sin and selfishness, and sharing his risen life so that sin, though it may attack us, need find no entry.

George Appleton, *Journey for a Soul*, William Collins Sons and Co., 1976, page 178

The Cross is the glory of God because self-sacrifice is the expression of love. That glory would be complete in itself even if it had no consequences. But in fact what is revealed in the Cross is not only the perfection of the divine love, but its triumph. For by its sacrifice the divine love wins those who can appreciate it out of their selfishness which is spiritual death into loving fellowship with itself which is true life.

William Temple, *Readings in St. John's Gospel*, First and Second Series, Macmillan and Co., 1947, page 308

The Cross was not a transaction. It was the culmination of this mighty Love, for 'here on the cross hung God and man'—God's Love springing forth in a soul strong enough to show it in its full scope. But let no person think that he can 'cover himself with the purple mantle of Christ's sufferings and death,' and so win his salvation: 'Thou thyself,' he says, 'must go through Christ's whole journey, and enter wholly into His process.'

Rufus M. Jones, *Spiritual Reformers in the 16th and 17th Centuries*, Macmillan and Co., 1914, page 194

You can say that Christ died for our sins. You may say the Father has forgiven us because Christ has done for us what we ought to have done. You may say that we are washed in the blood of the Lamb. You may say that Christ has defeated death. They are all true. If any of them does not appeal to you, leave it alone and get on with the formula that does. And, whatever you do, do not start quarrelling with other people because they use a different formula from yours.

C.S. Lewis, *Mere Christianity*, William Collins Sons and Co., 1961, page 153

I simply argue that the Cross be raised again at the centre of the market place as well as on the steeple of the church. I am recovering the claim that Jesus was not crucified in a Cathedral between two candles, but on a Cross between two thieves; on the town garbage heap; at a crossroad so cosmopolitan that they had to write his title in Hebrew and in Latin and in Greek (or shall we say in English, in Bantu and in Afrikaans?); at the kind of place where cynics talk smut, and thieves curse, and soldiers gamble. Because that is where He died. And that is what He died about. And that is where churchmen should be and what churchmen should be about.

George F. Macleod, *Only One Way Left*, The Iona Community, 1956, page 38

'There cannot be a God of love,' men say, 'because if there were, and He looked upon this world, His heart would break.' The Church points to the Cross and says, 'His heart does break.'
   'It is God who has made the world,' men say, 'it is He who is responsible and it is He who should bear the load.'
   The Church points to the Cross and says, 'He does bear it.' 'God is beyond men's comprehension, and it is blasphemy to say you know Him;' and the Church answers, 'We do not know Him perfectly but we worship the majesty we see.'

William Temple, *The Preacher's Theme To-day*, SPCK, 1936, page 62

The great message of the *Cross* stands or falls with the divinity of Christ. Is it not the truth that all the rivals of Christianity fail just here? All the religious philosophies of antiquity, it seems to me, shrink, in the last resort, from grasping the nettle of suffering quite firmly. They all want to make us invulnerable, somehow. There must always be a back-door of escape if the ills of life become too overpowering. Either defiant resistence, or suicide, or complete detachment, is recommended. By some means or other, the man himself must be rescued from circumstance, he must provide himself with a magic impenetrable armour. And *therefore*, the sting of pain is never drawn. The good news of Christianity is that suffering is itself divine. It is not foreign to the experience of God Himself. 'In all their afflictions He was afflicted.' 'Surely He hath borne our griefs and carried our sorrows.' 'If thou be the Son of God,' said His enemies, 'come down from the Cross.' No; not while any man remains unredeemed. The divine suffering is not an episode, but a revelation. It is the necessary form which divine love takes, when it is brought into contact with evil. To overcome evil with good means to suffer unjustly and willingly.

W.R. Inge, *Speculum Animae*, Longmans, Green and Co., 1911, page 22

I think the traditional accounts of Atonement and Redemption have tended to start with an assumption about the Creation and Fall. They see Creation as something that was perfect at the beginning, which men then spoiled with their sins, and which at some point in history had to be restored to proper relationship by something dramatic. Now seeing the Creation and Fall as a story (I'll avoid the word myth), I believe in Creation as something continuous that is going on all the time. So I see Redemption as something that is going on all the time, as the fundamental character of God's creative activity. And I see the Cross as focussing this truth of God's reconciling love working for the harmony of His Creation...

Crucifixion seems to me to show that the way this reconciliation may be achieved is by breaking the continual process of revenge. And Resurrection expresses the confidence that this is the way the world is ultimately built. It is a long-term process, and it does not do away with the fact that very often this is the way of disaster for those who practise it. But it does express the conviction that in the long run this is the only way human violence and self-destruction can be overcome.

Maurice Wiles, in Gerald Priestland, *Priestland's Progress*, BBC Worldwide, 1982, page 87

Sometimes we can feel as if life is too hard, or just too uninteresting and drab. It can seem that the obstacles within ourselves are mountainous and insuperable. Jesus' own unwavering faith must be ours. Everything is possible to him who believes, was his humble boast.

When everything seemed to be going wrong for him, when the 'no' of human hearts had congealed into hard rock which threatened to grind him down, he was certain that the Father could and would remove the hard mass and drown it forever. He died in hope, not in hopes realized.

The picture of him asleep in a violent storm when others were frantic and angered by his seeming indifference reveals his inmost heart in its perfect trust.

If we would be his friends we must live like that. A friend of Jesus dares all and never says such and such is too hard. If God asks something, then it is possible of accomplishment. His friends evade nothing, be it trying situations, uncongenial people, difficult duties. They take each day as it comes with its pleasures and joys, its disagreeable things and pains. They shoulder their cross and go with Jesus.

The significance of the cross is not suffering but obedience—doing the Father's will regardless of whether it is easy or hard.

Ruth Burrows, in *The Watchful Heart*, edited by Elizabeth Ruth Obbard, Darton, Longman and Todd, 1988, page 46

DEATH

'Death'—dying, end of life, ceasing to be, annihilation, want of spiritual life.

In 1972, I went on an expedition to the Asia part of Turkey with three students. We set off by car across Europe, and had a near-death experience en route from Vienna to Budapest. At the time we were travelling at sixty miles an hour on a busy road. Suddenly, without warning, we had a blow-out, and our heavily laden car went out of control. We then did a complete circle in the midst of three lane traffic, and shot off backwards down an embankment on the opposite side of the road. Fortunately we didn't hit any other vehicles in transit, but ended up in a shocked and bewildered state. The only casualty, apart from the tyre, was the exhaust pipe. Later that day, over the evening meal, we each admitted there was a time when we thought the end had come.

This experience made me think about death, and brought about some fundamental changes in my attitude to life. Firstly, I'm very thankful to be alive, and now look upon each day as being extremely valuable. Secondly, I have examined carefully how I spend my time and have cut out uncreative activities. Thirdly, I have come to regard nature, people, friendships and the spiritual life, as being supremely important. I try to live a full life now, so that I will have no regrets later on, and see death as an entrance to a greater life in the future.

To a certain extent I have come to terms with death, but I still go through agonies when young people die, particularly those I have known in my work.

Naked I came from my mother's womb, and naked shall I return; the Lord gave, and the Lord has taken away; blessed be the name of the Lord.
Job 1:21

But the souls of the righteous are in the hand of God, and there shall no torment touch them. In the sight of the unwise they seemed to die; and their departure is taken for misery. And their going from us to be utter destruction: but they are in peace. For though they be punished in the sight of men, yet is their hope full of immortality. And having been a little chastised, they shall be greatly rewarded: for God proved them, and found them worthy for himself.
The Wisdom of Solomon 3:1–5 (AV)

And as for the resurrection of the dead, have you not read what was said to you by God, 'I am the God of Abraham, and the God of Isaac, and the God of Jacob'? He is not God of the dead, but of the living.
Matthew 22:31–32

For this perishable nature must put on the imperishable, and this mortal nature must put on immortality.
1 Corinthians 15:53

A good life has a peaceful death.
French Proverb

As a well-spent day brings happy sleep, so life well used brings happy death.

Leonardo da Vinci, *The Notebooks of Leonardo da Vinci*, edited by Edward McCurdy, volume 1, Jonathan Cape, 1977, page 65

I came from God, and I'm going back to God, and I won't have any gaps of death in the middle of my life.

George Macdonald, *Mary Marston*, volume III, Sampson Low, Marston, Searle, and Rivington, 1881, page 317

To die is poignantly bitter, but the idea of having to die without having lived is unbearable.

Erich Fromm, *Man For Himself*, Routledge and Kegan Paul, 1975, page 162

Do not seek death. Death will find you. But seek the road which makes death a fulfilment.

Dag Hammarskjöld, *Markings*, translated by Leif Sjöberg and W.H. Auden, Faber and Faber, 1964, page 136

The only religious way to think of death is as part and parcel of life; to regard it, with the understanding and with the emotions, as the inviolable condition of life.

Thomas Mann, *The Magic Mountain*, translated by H.T. Lowe-Porter, Penguin Books, 1983, page 200

What do I dread most? The answer nearly always is having to face this or that ordeal alone. It is being cut off. It is not the ordeal itself; it is the being with it on my own. Death is one such ordeal. Not the moment or the pain, but the being out of reach.

Hubert van Zeller, *Considerations*, Sheed and Ward, 1974, page 19

On the day when death will knock at thy door what wilt thou offer to him? Oh, I will set before my guest the full vessel of my life—I will never let him go with empty hands.

All the sweet vintage of all my autumn days and summer nights, all the earnings and gleanings of my busy life will I place before him at the close of my days when death will knock at my door.

Rabindranath Tagore, *Gitanjali*, Macmillan and Co., 1971, page 83

Our attitude to all men would be Christian if we regarded them as though they were dying, and determined our relation to them in the light of death, both of their death and our own. A person who is dying calls forth a special kind of feeling. Our attitude to him is at once softened and lifted on to a higher plane. We then can feel compassion for people whom we did not love. But every man is dying, I too am dying and must never forget about death.

Nicolas Berdyaev, *The Destiny of Man*, translated by Natalie Duddington, Geoffrey Bles: The Centenary Press, 1937, page 156

The Lord does not promise that anyone who keeps His word shall avoid the physical incident called death; but that if his mind is turned towards that word it will not pay any attention to death: death will be to it irrelevant. It may truly be said that such a man will not 'experience' death, because, though it will happen to him, it will matter to him no more than the fall of a leaf from a tree under which he might be reading a book.

William Temple, *Readings in St. John's Gospel*, First and Second Series, Macmillan and Co., 1947, page 147

The birth of a human being is pregnant with meaning; then why is this not true of death also? Twenty years or more of a young man's life are spent in preparation for the full unfolding of his individual existence; why then should he not spend twenty years or more preparing for his end? . . .

I am convinced that it is hygienic—if I may use the word—to discover in death a goal towards which one can strive, and that shrinking away from it is something unhealthy and abnormal which robs the second half of life of its purpose.

C.G. Jung, *Psychological Reflections*, selected and edited by Jolande Jacobi, Routledge and Kegan Paul, 1953, page 287

God must, in some way or other, make room for Himself, hollowing us out and emptying us, if He is finally to penetrate into us. And in order to assimilate us in Him, He must break the molecules of our being so as to re-cast and re-model us. The function of death is to provide the necessary entrance into our inmost selves. It will make us undergo the required dissociation. It will put us into the state organically needed if the divine fire is to descend upon us.

And in that way its fatal power to decompose and dissolve will be harnessed to the most sublime operations of life. What was by nature empty and void, a return to bits and pieces, can, in any human existence, become fullness and unity in God.

Pierre Teilhard de Chardin, *Le Milieu Divin*, William Collins Sons and Co, 1960, page 68

If we would become wise we must learn that we have here no abiding city (Hebrews 13:14).

To have life in focus we must have death in our field of vision. Within this vision we see life as preparation for death and death as preparation for life.

If we are to meet our own death with hope it must be a hope built not on theory or on belief alone but on experience. We must know from experience that *death is an event in life*, an essential part of any life which is lived as a perpetually expanding and self-transcending mystery.

Only the experience of the continuous death of the ego can lead us into this hope, into an ever-deepening contact with the power of life itself.

Only our own death to self-centredness can really persuade us of death as the connecting link in the chain of perpetual expansion, and as the way to fullness of life.

John Main OSB, in *The Joy of Being*, selected by Clare Hallward, Darton, Longman and Todd, 1989, page 19

For dying is an art, which has to be learned in the practice of life by allowing it to dissolve our assertive will and refine our perceptions, until we come to feel habitually the mystery of death in each new-born moment and to see with wonder in all around us that mutual embrace of light and shadow, of idea and substance in which life and death unite. This is the art to which those who are growing old should in particular devote themselves, thus helping to form the new body or bodies within them in which they are soon to live. Yet an assent to death is as much a grace of ardent youth, though unconscious then, as it is of an old age fulfilled in wisdom and under-standing. In fact the whole of our life, with its physical and mental changes and its continual demands upon us to adapt to new circumstances and pressures from within and without, is a testing of our capacity to maintain and consciously deepen the union between living and dying by which we are created and can ourselves create.

Hugh L'Anson Fausset, *Fruits of Silence*, Abelard-Schuman, 1963, page 215

To accept death as an act of love is not easy, and I believe that this was the climax of Christ's achievement in his travail towards love.

And it is for us to imitate him, even in our weakness.

Real death is separation from God, and this is unbearable; real death is faithlessness, hopelessness, lovelessness.

We all know what pain and sadness are, for we have all experienced them and are all immersed in them...

Real death is emptiness, darkness, desolation, despair, hatred, destruction. So... Christ agreed to enter into this death, into this separation, so as to identify himself with all who were in separation, and to save them.

When he had touched the depths of their despair, he announced hope with his resurrection.

When he was immersed in their darkness, he made the brightness of truth burst forth with his resurrection.

When engulfed in the abyss of their lovelessness he showed them the infinite joy of love with his resurrection.

By rising from the dead Christ made all things new.

By rising from the dead he opened new heavens.

By rising from the dead he opened new life.

Carlo Carretto, *Blessed Are You Who Believed*, translated by Barbara Wall, Burns and Oates, 1982, page 52

DISCIPLESHIP

*'Discipleship'—one who attends upon another for the purpose of
learning from him/her—includes practice as well as theory;
learning by doing.*

When I first went to Bradford Cathedral as a curate I had a brief chat with one of my senior colleagues. I was keen to find out how best to operate in this new environment. His advice was; observe the Provost closely and learn all you can from him. He likened this to an apprenticeship, in which one learned from an experienced old hand. At theological college the emphasis had been mainly on theory, on the academic side of things. In that rarefied atmosphere we had studied the Bible, doctrine, Church history, ethics and worship. Now the time had come for practical application, under the watchful eye of the Provost.

I soon received my marching orders. I was required to preach and teach in the Cathedral and take my part in leading the worship. From time to time I was asked to lead Bible studies. He gave me the task of visiting the occupants of high-rise flats in the parish. As a part-time hospital chaplain I was to go on the wards of Bradford Royal Infirmary and visit a hundred patients each week. He delegated to me the running of the youth fellowship. The Bishop in turn appointed me to be chaplain of a secular youth club, situated near the rugby league statium at Odsal. Lastly I was gently broken into taking baptisms, weddings and funerals. Looking back over that four year curacy, the 'apprenticeship' was in reality a valuable period of discipleship. Theory and practice were carefully brought together.

And you shall speak to him and put the words in his mouth; and I will be with your mouth and with his mouth, and will teach you what you shall do.

Exodus 4:15

Blessed is he whom thou dost choose and bring near, to dwell in thy courts! We shall be satisfied with the goodness of thy house, thy holy temple!

Psalm 65:4

A disciple is not above his teacher, nor a servant above his master; it is enough for the disciple to be like his teacher, and the servant like his master.

Matthew 10:24–25

Therefore every scribe who has been trained for the kingdom of heaven is like a householder who brings out of his treasure what is new and what is old.

Matthew 13:52

There are two words used a great deal by Jesus in the Gospels. One is 'Come' and the other is 'Go'. It's no use coming unless you go, and it's no use going unless you come.

Anon.

When we fail in our discipleship it is always for one of two reasons; either we are not trying to be loyal, or else we are trying in our own strength and find that it is not enough.

William Temple, *Readings in St. John's Gospel*, First and Second Series, Macmillan and Co., 1947, page 225

There is a kind of Church-worker for whom our age even more urgently calls, and on whom the life and example of Christ set more immediately the seal of discipleship—the man who, to the glory of God and for the good of his fellows, does honest work of the everyday sort.

Archibald C. Craig, *University Sermons*, James Clarke and Co., 1937, page 147

To him who obeys, and thus opens the doors of his heart to receive the eternal gift, God gives the spirit of his Son, the spirit of himself, to be in him, and lead him to the understanding of all

---

truth; that the true disciple shall thus always know what he ought to do, though not necessarily what another ought to do.

George Macdonald, *Unspoken Sermons*, Third Series, Longmans, Green and Co., 1889, page 155

He prepared His disciples for a change after the critical moment was passed; with the Cross and Resurrection His Kingdom would have come with power, and they were no longer to be apart from the world, bringing to it *ab extra* the divine act of redemption which is itself the revelation of God, but were to carry its power into the world as leaven that should leaven the whole lump.

William Temple, *Citizen And Churchman*, Eyre and Spottiswoode, 1941, page 65

On one occasion three would-be disciples came to Jesus and offered their discipleship with reservations or delays. He warned them that discipleship involved hardship, with total, immediate and life-long commitment (Luke 9:57–62). When we begin to follow we shall soon realize that more is needed, and if we are honest enough or rash enough to ask 'What do I still lack?' he will unerringly put his finger on the one thing we are least ready to surrender.

George Appleton, *Journey for a Soul*, William Collins Sons and Co., 1976, page 188

Every disciple knows that the aim of his life is to grow like his Lord. To achieve this he will study the earliest records of the divine life lived among men. He will want to get back behind the words to their meaning, behind the actions to the mind and character which inspired those actions. He will be eager to enter into intimate touch with him who promised to be with men and to live within the inmost being of each man. So with the outer study and the inner communion he will come to understand and acquire something of the mind of Christ.

George Appleton, *Journey for a Soul*, William Collins Sons and Co., 1976, page 157

Spiritual discipline . . . is a road, a way in which we open ourselves to Christ, to the grace of God. This is all discipline, all we can do. It is God who in response to this ascetical endeavour will give us his grace and fulfil us. We have a tendency to think that what we are to aim at is a high, deep, mystical life. This is not what we should aim at. A mystical life is a gift from God; in itself it is not an achievement of ours and even less is it an expression of our devotion to God. What we must aim at in response to the love of God declared, manifest in Christ, is to become true disciples by bringing ourselves as a sacrifice to God; on our part it is the ascetical endeavour which is the summit of our loyalty, allegiance and love. We must offer this to God and he will fulfil all things as he has promised. 'My child, give me thy heart; I shall fulfil all things.'

Anthony Bloom, *Meditations on a Theme*, A.R. Mowbray & Co., 1972, page 20

Doing the will of God is a discipline in the best sense of the word. It is also a test of our loyalty, of our fidelity to Christ. It is by doing in every detail, at every moment, to the utmost of our power, as perfectly as we can, with the greatest moral integrity, using our intelligence, our imagination, our will, our skill, our experience, that we can gradually learn to be strictly, earnestly obedient to the Lord God. Unless we do this our discipleship is an illusion and all our life of discipline, when it is a set of self-imposed rules in which we delight, which makes us proud and self-satisfied, leaves us nowhere, because the essential momentum of our discipleship is the ability in this process of silence and listening to reject our self, to allow the Lord Christ to be our mind, our will and our heart. Unless we renounce ourselves and accept his life in place of our life, unless we aim at what St Paul defines as 'it is no longer I but Christ who lives in me', we shall never be either disciplined or disciples.

Anthony Bloom, *Meditations on a Theme*, A.R. Mowbray and Co., 1972, page 18

. . . discipleship begins with silence and listening. When we listen to someone, we think we are silent because we do not speak; but our minds continue to work, our emotions react, our will responds for or against what we hear, we may even go further than this, with thoughts and feelings buzzing in our heads which are quite unrelated to what is being said. This is not silence as it is implied in discipleship. The real silence towards which we must aim as a starting-point is a complete repose of mind and heart and will, the complete silence of all there is in us, including our body, so that we may be completely aware of the world we are receiving, completely alert and yet in complete repose. The silence I am speaking of is the silence of the sentry on duty at a critical moment; alert, immobile, poised and yet alive to every sound, every movement. This living silence is what discipleship requires first of all, and this is not achieved without effort. It requires from us a training of our attention, a training of our body, a training of our mind and our emotions so that they are kept in check, completely and perfectly.

Anthony Bloom, Meditations on a Theme, A.R. Mowbray and Co., 1972, page 15

The Christian who reads, in these verses (Luke 14:25–35), of the price of discipleship will see that, if he is to take the divine words seriously, he must learn not to be too much 'entangled in the affairs of this life', whether human affairs or relationships, or personal and material things. He must learn to think of these as things that he can do without, including life itself. No one knows what he may be called upon one day to face or to do in loyalty to his profession as a Christian disciple—especially in a world as dangerous and uncertain as that in which our lives are cast. The man who is bogged down by worldly ties and considerations will find obedience much harder if God should call him one day to some sacrificial act.

The price of discipleship, therefore, is to be willing to give up everything if occasion should demand it, and, in the meanwhile, to live as men 'looking for their Lord', with loins girt and lamps burning, ready for action when the word is given. Discipleship is, or may be, a very costly thing. It may cost us all we have. In this passage, therefore, Jesus introduces a fourth condition, and that is that we should not go into it except with our eyes wide open. He does this in the form of three little parables, those of the tower builder who carefully surveys his material; the warrior-king who closely considers his chances of success; and the salt, which, if it cannot last out, goes bad.

Jesus bids us count the cost of discipleship. Can we face it? Is it going to be too much for us? Dare we risk failure and be cast out?

'He that hath ears to hear let him hear.' Let him hear: let him ponder: let him decide.

J.R.H. Moorman, The Path To Glory, SPCK and Seabury Press, 1960, page 182

DOUBT

'Doubt'—feeling of uncertainty about something, undecided state of mind, inclination to disbelieve; uncertain state of things, lack of full proof or clear indication.

At theological college we had a quiet day. It was taken by the then Archbishop of York, Stuart Blanch. He was giving us some advice about coping with doubt, and told us of a recent experience. It was summertime. In the evening he was taking his dog for a walk in his grounds, and they came across a hedgehog in the middle of the lawn. The dog had never seen a hedgehog before and joyfully bounded up to explore. The hedgehog, sensing danger, curled itself into a ball, and the dog got its nose badly pricked. With a great howl of pain the dog tucked its tail between its legs and headed off for the security of the bushes. From time to time he would cautiously emerge, sniff the air in the direction of the hedgehog, making sure he kept at a safe distance. The next evening the archbishop told us he went for another walk round the garden with his dog, and the hedgehog was again in the middle of the lawn. This time the dog was more circumspect. He approached the hedgehog slowly, stopping six feet in front of it, observing it carefully. After a while he turned on his heels, tail high, and bounded off to the bushes, intent on exploring the delights of the garden. The archbishop made the point the dog was unable to understand the hedgehog but reached the conclusion he could still enjoy life, not knowing all the answers. He wondered if this had something to tell us about living creatively with doubt. Better still he might have added: 'Feed your faith and your doubts will starve to death.'

And among these nations you shall find no ease, and there shall be no rest for the sole of your foot; but the Lord will give you there a trembling heart, and failing eyes, and a languishing soul; your life shall hang in doubt before you; night and day you shall be in dread, and have no assurance of your life.

Deuteronomy 28:65–66

And I applied my mind to know wisdom and to know madness and folly. I perceived that this also is but a striving after wind. For in much wisdom is much vexation, and he who increases knowledge increases sorrow.

Ecclesiastes 1:17–18

So the other disciples told him, 'We have seen the Lord.' But he said to them, 'Unless I see in his hands the print of the nails, and place my finger in the mark of the nails, and place my hand in his side, I will not believe.'

John 20:25

Draw near to God and he will draw near to you. Cleanse your hands, you sinners, and purify your hearts, you men of double mind.

James 4:8

Feed your faith, and your doubts will starve to death.

Anon.

Modest doubt is call'd
The beacon of the wise.

William Shakespeare, *Troilus and Cressida*, II. ii. 15

There lives more faith in honest doubt,
Believe me, than in half the creeds.

Alfred, Lord Tennyson, 'In Memoriam A.H.H.', in *The Poems of Tennyson*, edited by Christopher Ricks, Longmans, Green and Co., 1969, page 948

If Christ has grappled our hearts to Himself at all, then it were surely wise to trust His certainties and not our own doubts, however persistent.

Herbert H. Farmer, *The Healing Cross*, Nisbet and Co., 1938, page 208

If a man will begin with certainties, he shall end in doubts; but if he will be content to begin with doubts, he shall end in certainties.

Francis Bacon, *The Advancement of Learning*, Cassell and Company, 1905, page 38

You call for faith:
I show you doubt, to prove that faith exists.
The more of doubt, the stronger faith, I say,
If faith o'ercomes doubt.

Robert Browning, *Men and Women*, 'Bishop Blougram's Apology', in *The Poetical Works of Robert Browning*, volume I, Smith, Elder and Co., 1899, page 536

For nothing worthy proving can be proven,
Nor yet disproven: wherefore thou be wise,
Cleave ever to the sunnier side of doubt,
And cling to Faith beyond the forms of Faith!

Alfred, Lord Tennyson, 'The Ancient Sage', in *The Poems of Tennyson*, edited by Christopher Ricks, Longmans, Green and Co., 1969, page 1351

There is an increasing number of people to whom everything they are doing seems futile. They are still under the spell of the slogans which preach faith in the secular paradise of success and glamour. But doubt, the fertile condition of all progress, has begun to beset them and has made them ready to ask what their real self-interest as human beings is.

Erich Fromm, *Man For Himself*, Routledge and Kegan Paul, 1975, page 140

And your doubt can become a good quality if you train it. It must become *aware*, it must become criticism. Ask it, whenever it wants to spoil something for you, *why* something is ugly, demand proofs from it, test it, and you will perhaps find it helpless and nonplussed, perhaps also aggressive. But do not give way, demand arguments and conduct yourself thus carefully and consistently every single time, and the day will dawn when it will become, instead of a subverter, one of your best workmen,—perhaps the cleverest of all who are building at your life.

Rainer Maria Rilke, *Letters to a Young Poet*, translated by Reginald Snell, Sidgwick and Jackson, 1945, page 42

This power of self-surrender is not gained except through the experience of that dread which afflicts us when we taste the awful dereliction of the soul closed in upon itself.

... the full maturity of the spiritual life cannot be reached unless we first pass through the dread, anguish, trouble and fear that necessarily accompany the inner crisis of 'spiritual death' in which we finally abandon our attachment to our exterior self and surrender completely to Christ. But when this surrender has been truly made, there is no longer any place for fear and dread. There can be no longer any doubt or hesitation in the mind of one who is completely and finally resolved to seek nothing and do nothing but what is willed for him by God's love. Then, as St Benedict says 'Perfect love casts out dread,' and dread itself is turned into love, confidence and hope.

The purpose of the dark night, as St John of the Cross shows, is not simply to punish and afflict the heart of man, but to liberate, to purify and to enlighten in perfect love. The way that leads through dread goes not to despair, but to perfect joy, not to hell, but to heaven.

Thomas Merton, *Contemplative Prayer*, Darton, Longman and Todd, 1973, page 136

Doubt and perplexity will often be the lot of travellers on this life's journey. Beyond the questions arising in our daily thought and conduct are those greater difficulties which seem to stop our progress and to render existence an insoluble riddle. Doubt has many sources. It may be true that some could find the origin of their doubts in an unwillingness to face their moral condition and obey the demands of duty. But at the present day, doubt frequently arises from a sense that received dogmas do not correspond with the facts of life or with the moral values which our truest insight reveals. In other cases there may be not so much perplexity and doubt as an exhilarating spirit of inquiry and exploration driving a man forward on the quest for truth for himself and all men. We strongly deprecate the attitude of mind, still too often current, which brands as unbelief that criticism of accepted ideas without which progress is impossible. We may often attain to a fuller understanding of the truth that God intends for us through doubts of the orthodoxy of the past. For true faith is not a passive acceptance of authority, but is an inner assurance of truth, asking, seeking, knocking until the door is opened. The enjoyment of idle questionings may indeed become an excuse for living a poor and careless life, but the genuine seeker is obeying the very call of God within him.

Christian faith and practice in the experience of the Society of Friends, London Yearly Meeting of the Religious Society of Friends, 1972, number 119, 1911; 1925

DYING TO SELF

'Dying to Self—a dying to the supremacy of the ego in order to live for God.

A good illustration of 'dying to self' is the life of Albert Schweitzer. Here was a man of enormous intellect, who had completed four doctorates (in theology, philosophy, music and medicine) before he had reached his mid-thirties. In spite of all this study, he was well-known as a brilliant organist, with an established reputation in the concert halls of Europe.

Some thought he would devote his life to academia and become a brilliant lecturer. Others felt he might concentrate on music, and become the greatest organist of his day. They were all wrong. With calm deliberation he died to the supremacy of the ego. He was to be a medical missionary in Lambarene, a remote area of West Africa, healing the sick.

Many of us know the outcome of his life. He used his considerable skills to build a hospital (later replacing this with another building) and performed complicated operations under difficult and primitive conditions. Thousands of patients came under his care at Lambarene in his many years in West Africa. In spite of a busy and active life as a doctor, he managed to keep his organ playing going, and turned out to be an influential and a prolific writer on theological topics. Here was a man who had set 'self' aside in order to serve humanity, and in losing his life, found it at a deeper level, and greatly enriched the lives of others.

Remember, O Lord, in David's favour, all the hardships he endured; how he swore to the Lord and vowed to the Mighty One of Jacob, 'I will not enter my house or get into my bed; I will not give sleep to my eyes or slumber to my eyelids, until I find a place for the Lord, a dwelling place for the Mighty One of Jacob.'

Psalm 132:1-5

It is good for a man that he bear the yoke in his youth.
Lamentations 3:27

The kingdom of heaven is like treasure hidden in a field, which a man found and covered up; then in his joy he goes and sells all that he has and buys that field. Again, the kingdom of heaven is like a merchant in search of fine pearls, who, on finding one pearl of great value, went and sold all that he had and bought it.

Matthew 13:44-46

If any one purifies himself from what is ignoble, then he will be a vessel for noble use, consecrated and useful to the master of the house, ready for any good work.

2 Timothy 2:21

It is the crushed grape that yields the wine.

Anon.

A man there was, though some did count him mad,
The more he cast away the more he had.

John Bunyan, *The Pilgrim's Progress*, J.M. Dent and Sons, 1964, page 263

All the activity of man in the works of self-denial has no good in itself, but is only to open an entrance for the one only Good, the light of God, to operate upon us.

William Law, *Selected Mystical Writings of William Law*, edited by Stephen Hobhouse, Rockliff, 1948, page 99

We must learn to detach ourselves from all that is capable of being lost, to bind ourselves absolutely only to what is absolute and eternal.

Henri Frédéric Amiel, *Amiel's Journal*, translated by Mrs Humphry Ward, Macmillan and Co., 1918, page 1

Know, that when thou learnest to lose thy self,
Thou wilt reach the Beloved.
There is no other secret to be revealed,
And more than this is not known to me.

Al-Ansari, *The Persian Mystics*, translated by Sardar Sir Jogendra Sing, John Murray, 1939, page 40

Batter my heart, three person'd God; for, you
As yet but knocke, breathe, shine, and seeke to mend;

That I may rise, and stand, o'erthrowe mee, 'and bend
Your force, to breake, blowe, burn and make me new.

John Donne, 'Divine Poems, Holy Sonnets' xiv, in *Poetical Works,* edited by Sir Herbert Grierson, Oxford University Press, page 299

In all your doing and thinking you should act on the assumption that you are going to die today... Try to live in such a way now that when the hour of death comes you may feel joy, not fear. Learn to die to the world now, so that you may begin to live with Christ then.

Thomas à Kempis, *The Imitation of Christ,* translated by Betty I. Knott, William Collins Sons and Co., 1979, page 72

Except the seed die... It has to die in order to liberate the energy it bears within it so that with this energy new forms may be developed. So we have to die in order to liberate a *tied up* energy, in order to possess an energy which is free and capable of understanding the true relationship of things.

Simone Weil, *Gravity and Grace,* Routledge and Kegan Paul, 1972, page 30

'Our kingdom go' is the necessary and unavoidable corollary of 'Thy Kingdom come.' For the more there is of self, the less there is of God. The divine eternal fullness of life can be gained only by those who have deliberately lost the partial, separative life of craving and self-interest, of egocentric thinking, feeling, wishing and acting.

Aldous Huxley, *The Perennial Philosophy,* Chatto and Windus, 1974, page 113

Therefore we should make ourselves poor, that we may fundamentally die, and in this dying be made alive again. Therefore Christ said, 'Unless the grain of corn fall into the ground and die it cannot bring forth fruit. But if it die it bringeth forth much fruit.' So also is it in truth. Whoso wisheth to have all the fruit of life must suffer all manner of death... And whoso doth not entirely die cannot either fully live.

John Tauler, *The Following of Christ,* translated by J.R. Morell, Burns and Oates, 1886, page 175

The proper good of a creature is to surrender itself to its Creator—to enact intellectually, volitionally, and emotionally, that relationship which is given in the mere fact of its being a creature... In the world as we now know it, the problem is how to recover this self-surrender. We are not merely imperfect creatures who must be improved: we are, as Newman said, rebels who must lay down our arms... to surrender a self-will inflamed and swollen with years of usurpation is a kind of death... Hence the necessity to die daily: however often we think we have broken the rebellious self we shall still find it alive.

C.S. Lewis, *The Problem of Pain,* The Centenary Press, 1941, page 78

The only ultimate tragedy is a life that has not opened to eternal life.

In the Christian vision, death is not the all-important moment in our life. The supreme all-important moment in any life is the moment of full openness to Jesus. We have to take practical steps to put ourselves into readiness.

Anyone who meditates in faith knows that the journey within takes us out of ourselves. Saying the mantra is learning to die and to accept the eternal gift of our being in one and the same act.

Our being passes through various stages of life, through many deaths, but we can never slip out of *being*. God never withdraws the immortal gift of life he has given to us. This is the essential preparation we need *in experience* to face our own death without fear, without false consolation, with open minds and open hearts.

All death is death to limitation. If we can die to self we rise to an infinite liberty of love. This way of dying to the ego, the first death, is what we call prayer.

John Main OSB, in *The Joy of Being,* selected by Clare Hallward, Darton, Longman and Todd, 1989, page 20

There is, of course, a negative element or aspect in all genuine religion. No person can grow rich in spiritual experience or can gain an intimate acquaintance with a God of purity and truth without negating the easy ways of instinct, the low pursuits of life which end in self, the habits of thought and action which limit and hamper the realization of the diviner posssibilities of the whole nature. Sometimes the eye that hinders must be plucked out or the right hand cut off and thrust away for the sake of a freer pursuit of the soul's kingdom. There is, too, a still deeper principle of negativity involved in the very fibre of personal life itself. No one can advance without surrender, no one can have gains without losses, no one can reach great goals without giving up many things in themselves desirable. There is 'a rivalry of mes' which no person can ever escape, for in order to choose and achieve one typical self another possible self must be sternly sacrificed. In a very real sense it remains forever true that we must die to live, we must die to the narrow self in order to be raised to the wider and richer self.

Rufus M. Jones, *Spiritual Reformers in the 16th and 17th Centuries*, Macmillan and Co., 1914, page xxv

ETERNAL LIFE

'Eternal life'—existing always, without end or usually beginning;
a quality and value of life; endless life after death; being eternal.

I once had the good fortune to meet George Appleton in his home in Oxford, where he had settled down in retirement. His writings had always appealed to me; that is why there are so many of them in *Visions of Faith.* After my brief visit I came to value them even more.

I have found his second contribution in this section particularly helpful. He describes eternal life as 'a quality of life, the kind of life which Jesus had, human life permeated by the grace and love of God'. I feel he gets right to the heart of the matter in these few words. If we want to know more about this quality of life we can go to the Gospels, and focus our attention on the life of Jesus. In the pages of the Gospels we can see for ourselves a human life permeated by the grace and love of God. As we read, we might become aware of this grace and love of God welling up inside us, and experience eternal life for ourselves. George Appleton comes out with this further truth at the end of his quotation. He concludes: 'Jesus taught his disciples they could have eternal life now, the perfection of which will come in the dimension beyond death.' One of the great joys of Christianity is to experience moments of eternal life in this present life, in the here and now, and thus have an assurance of eternal life in the future.

> ... and lead me in the way everlasting!
> Psalm 139:24

> I will make you majestic for ever, a joy from age to age.
> Isaiah 60:15

For God so loved the world that he gave his only Son, that whoever believes in him should not perish but have eternal life.
John 3:16

Truly, truly, I say to you, he who hears my word and believes him who sent me, has eternal life.
John 5:24

We feel and know that we are eternal.
Spinoza, *Spinoza's Ethics and De Intellectus Emendatione,* J.M. Dent and Sons, 1955, page 214

To have the sense of the eternal in life is a short flight for the soul. To have had it, is the soul's vitality.
George Meredith, *Diana of the Crossways,* Archibald Constable and Company, 1909, page 11

But felt through all this fleshly dresse
Bright *shoots* of everlastingnesse.
Henry Vaughan, 'Silex Scintillans,' in *The Works of Henry Vaughan,* edited by L.C. Martin, Oxford at the Clarendon Press, 1957, page 419

Every creative act of ours in relation to other people—an act of love, of pity, of help, of peacemaking—not merely has a future but is eternal.

Nicolas Berdyaev, *The Destiny of Man*, translated by Natalie Duddington, Geoffrey Bles: The Centenary Press, 1937, page 189

Eternal life is the life of God, and to have eternal life is to share the life of God. Here we are at the very heart of the matter. Eternal life is nothing less than God's life.

William Barclay, *The Plain Man Looks at the Apostles' Creed*, William Collins Sons and Co., 1967, page 374

It is eternity now. I am in the midst of it. It is about me in the sunshine; I am in it, as the butterfly floats in the light-laden air. Nothing has to come: it is now. Now is eternity; now is the immortal life.

Richard Jefferies, *The Story of My Heart*, Duckworth and Co., 1923, page 30

If a man once knows the Spirit within him, the source of all his aspiration after holiness, as indeed the Spirit of Jesus Christ, and if he knows this Spirit of Jesus Christ within himself as none other than the Spirit of the Eternal and Almighty God, what more can he want? *This is the eternal life.*

William Temple, *Readings in St. John's Gospel*, First and Second Series, Macmillan and Co., 1947, page 310

The eternal life is not the future life; it is life in harmony with the true order of things,—life in God. We must learn to look upon time as a movement of eternity, as an undulation in the ocean of being. To live, so as to keep this consciousness of ours in perpetual relation with the eternal, is to be wise; to live, so as to personify and embody the eternal, is to be religious.

Henri Frédéric Amiel, *Amiel's Journal*, translated by Mrs Humphry Ward, Macmillan & Co., 1918, page 96

Religion, in its fullest development, essentially requires, not only this our little span of earthly years, but a life beyond. Neither an Eternal Life that is already fully achieved here below, nor an Eternal Life already to be begun and known solely in the beyond, satisfies these requirements. Only an Eternal Life already begun and truly known in part here, though fully to be achieved and completely to be understood hereafter, corresponds to the deepest longings of man's spirit as touched by the prevenient Spirit, God.

Friedrich von Hügel, *Eternal Life*, T. and T. Clarke, 1913, page 396

Jesus did not promise to men simply life after death, but a quality of life now. He promised us eternal life, the sharing of God's life, participation in his own risen life. He said that he had come to give men abundant life—sufficient to keep the body in health and strength, to illuminate and guide the mind, to bring peace to the heart. If we have that life within us now, we shall not worry about our last migration into the spiritual world, for we shall know a good deal about it already.

George Appleton, *Journey for a Soul*, William Collins Sons and Co., 1976, page 212

Eternal life is not just everlasting life, a continuation of what goes on at present, for that might not be too joyful for many people. It is a quality of life, the kind of life which Jesus had, human life permeated by the grace and love of God, and so invulnerable to physical death. Jesus taught his disciples that they could have eternal life now, just as in the teaching of the Buddha the sphere of bliss and blessing which he called Nirvana can be enjoyed now. The perfection of both will come in the dimension beyond death.

George Appleton, *Journey for a Soul*, William Collins Sons and Co., 1976, page 213

Wherever man wakes to consciousness and knowing himself in his basic intuitive consciousness as open to the transcendent mystery of existence, the power of the Spirit in him is drawing him to eternal life.

The Church is man become conscious of his destiny as a son of God. In the biblical perspective Adam is man created in the image and likeness of God and called to be a son of God.

When Adam sins he fails to respond to the spirit and falls back on his limited time-bound nature. The upward evolution from matter through life and consciousness to eternal life in the spirit is checked, but at the same time the mystery of redemption begins. A new power of the spirit enters creation and begins to draw man back into the life of the spirit.

In this sense the Church is present in humanity from the beginning of history.

Bede Griffiths OSB, in *The Universal Christ*, edited by Peter Spink, Darton, Longman and Todd, 1990, page 15

Side by side with Paul's achievement as a thinker must be set his achievement as a man. Having a personality at once simple and profound, he avoids an abstract and unnatural ideal of perfection, and makes perfection consist in the complete adjustment of spiritual with natural reality. So long as the earthly world with all its circumstances still subsists, what we have to do is so to live in it in the spirit of unworldliness that truth and peace already make their influence felt in it. That is the ideal of Paul's ethic, to live with the eyes fixed upon eternity, while standing firmly upon the solid ground of reality. He gives to the enthusiastic conception of the Good a practical direction, without thereby robbing it of its originality and power.

He proves the truth of his ethic by his way of living it. Alike in suffering and in action he shows himself a human being, who by the Spirit of Christ has been purified and led up to a higher humanity. Though his work lies in the world, he ventures to live the unworldly life, and to rely only on the power which is at his disposal, because of that which he, in the Spirit of Christ, has inwardly become.

Albert Schweitzer, *The Mysticism of Paul the Apostle*, translated by William Montgomery, A. & C. Black, 1931, page 333

Our hearts tell us of a higher form of existence, in which the doom of death is not merely deferred but abolished. This eternal world we here see through a glass darkly: at best we can apprehend but the outskirts of God's ways, and hear a small whisper of His voice; but our conviction is that, though our earthly house be dissolved (as dissolved it must be), we have a home not made with hands, eternal in the heavens. In this hope we may include all creation and trust that in some way neither more nor less incomprehensible than the deliverance which we expect for ourselves, all God's creatures, according to their several capacities, may be set free from the bondage of corruption and participate in the final triumph over death and sin. Most firmly do I believe that this faith in immortality, though formless and inpalpable as the air we breathe, and incapable of definite presentation except under inadequate and self-contradictory symbols, is nevertheless enthroned in the centre of our being, and that those who have steadily set their affections on things above, and lived the risen life even on earth, receive in themselves an assurance which robs death of its sting, and is an earnest of a final victory over the grave.

W.R. Inge, *Christian Mysticism*, Methuen and Co., 1899, page 328

The corn was orient and immortal wheat, which never should be reaped, nor was ever sown. I thought it had stood from everlasting to everlasting. The dust and stones of the street were as precious as gold: the gates were at first the end of the world. The green trees when I saw them first through one of the gates transported and ravished me, their sweetness and unusual beauty made my heart to leap, and almost mad with ecstasy, they were such strange and wonderful things. The Men! O what venerable and reverend creatures did the aged seem! Immortal Cherubims! And young men glittering and sparkling Angels, and maids strange seraphic pieces of life and beauty! Boys and girls tumbling in the street, and playing, were moving jewels. I knew not that they were born or should die; But all things abided eternally as they were in their proper places. Eternity was manifest in the Light of the Day, and something infinite behind everything appeared: which talked with my expectation and moved my desire. The city seemed to stand in Eden, or to be built in Heaven. The streets were mine, the temple was mine, the people were mine... and so the sun and moon and stars, and all the World was mine; and I the only spectator and enjoyer of it.

Thomas Traherne, *Centuries*, edited by Bertram Dobell, J. and A.E. Dobell, 1950, page 152

EVIL

'Evil'—morally bad, wicked; harmful, tending to harm; evil thing,
wickedness.

When I was in my late thirties I went on a mid-service clergy course at St George's House, Windsor. For several weeks twenty-five of us were freed from normal duties, and given an opportunity to re-train. Whilst there I wanted to investigate the nature of 'evil' so undertook a private study in my spare time. As it turned out Morris West's book, *The Shoes of the Fisherman*, provided me with the vital clue. In that book he wrote that the mystery of evil is the deepest one of all. He believed it to be the mystery of the primal creative act, when God called into existence the human soul, made in his own image, and presented it with the terrifying choice of centring itself on itself, or of centring itself upon him without which it could not subsist at all. In humility he acknowledged the mystery renews itself daily in him, as it does in every man born of woman.

His insight fitted in perfectly with my understanding of the Genesis story of the creation of man. In that story God is depicted as fashioning and shaping man in his own image and likeness and the last thing he does is breathe into man and man becomes a living being. The other truth in this story, often overlooked, is that that which was fashioned and shaped in the image and likeness of God was taken from the dust of the earth. This means part of man's basic nature is earthy and creaturely, and in this lies the potential source of all evil. When we centre ourselves on ourselves, and not on God, we are in grave danger of activating evil.

Do you not know this from of old, since man was placed upon the earth, that the exulting of the wicked is short, and the joy of the godless but for a moment?

Job 20:4–5

Depart from evil, and do good; seek peace, and pursue it. The eyes of the Lord are toward the righteous, and his ears toward their cry.

Psalm 34:14–15

For I do not do the good I want, but the evil I do not want is what I do.

Romans 7:19

... but test everything; hold fast what is good, abstain from every form of evil.

1 Thessalonians 5:21–22

The only thing necessary for the triumph of evil is for good men to do nothing.

Attributed to Edmund Burke

Wickedness is always easier than virtue; for it takes the short cut to every thing.

Samuel Johnson, in *Boswell's Life of Johnson*, volume V, edited by G.B. Hill, revised by L.F. Powell, Oxford at the Clarendon Press, 1950, page 218

It is the evil that lies in ourselves that is ever least tolerant of the evil that dwells within others.

Maurice Maeterlinck, *Wisdom and Destiny*, translated by Alfred Sutro, George Allen, 1898, page 342

A belief in a supernatural source of evil is not necessary; men alone are quite capable of every wickedness.

Joseph Conrad, *Under Western Eyes*, J.M. Dent and Sons, 1923, page 151

There is some soul of goodness in things evil,
Would men observingly distil it out.

William Shakespeare, *Henry V*, IV. i. 4

He who passively accepts evil is as much involved in it as he who helps to perpetrate it. He who accepts evil without protesting against it is really operating with it.

Martin Luther King, *Stride Toward Freedom*, Harper and Row, Publishers, 1958, page 51

There is no explanation for evil. It must be looked upon as a necessary part of the order of the universe. To ignore it is childish; to bewail it senseless.

W. Somerset Maugham, *The Summing Up*, Bernhard Tauchnitz, 1938, page 225

Every minute you are thinking of evil, you might have been thinking of good instead. Refuse to pander to a morbid interest in your own misdeeds. Pick yourself up, be sorry, shake yourself, and go on again.

Evelyn Underhill, *The Letters of Evelyn Underhill*, edited by Charles Williams, Longmans, Green and Co., 1947, page 72

Must I do all the evil I can, before I learn to shun it? Is it not enough to know the evil to shun it? If not, we should be sincere enough to admit that we love evil too well to give it up.

Mohandas K. Gandhi, *Non-Violence in Peace & War*, volume II, Navajivan Publishing House, 1949, page 74

The germs of all things are in every heart, and the greatest criminals as well as the greatest heroes are but different modes of ourselves. Only evil grows of itself, while for goodness we want effort and courage.

Henri Frédéric Amiel, *Amiel's Journal*, translated by Mrs Humphry Ward, Macmillan and Co., 1918, page 101

The mystery of evil is the deepest one of all. It is the mystery of the primal creative act, when God called into existence the human soul, made in His own image, and presented it with the terrifying choice, to centre itself upon itself, or to centre itself upon Him without whom it could not subsist at all ... The mystery renews itself daily in me, as it does in every man born of woman.

Morris West, *The Shoes of the Fisherman*, William Heinemann, 1963, page 302

I much prefer absolute silence about things which with the best will in the world I do not understand, to the semi, forced explanations that leave a bitter taste in my mind.

It is so easy to say God permits evil—and what evil—in order to bring good out of it. I confess that while I understand that, it has never *entirely* satisfied me. And so I prefer to be silent in the abyss of my ignorance, and to pray.

Theodor Haecker, *Journal in the Night*, translated by Alexander Dru, The Harvill Press, 1950, page 195

Hatred of evil destroys the spiritual world of man just as much as hatred of the good, which does not mean to say that our attitude towards evil must not be ruthless nor that there can be any question of a truce with it. Hence our attitude to evil must be twofold: we must be tolerant of it as the Creator is tolerant, and we must mercilessly struggle against it. True spirituality consists in believing in the power of good rather than that of ill, in God rather than Satan.

Nicolas Berdyaev, *Freedom and the Spirit*, translated by Olivier Fielding Clarke, Geoffrey Bles: The Centenary Press, 1935, page 182; and *The Destiny of Man*, translated by Natalie Duddington, Geoffrey Bles: The Centenary Press, 1937, page 190

At all times, all too many Christians have behaved as though the devil were a First Principle, on the same footing as God.

They have paid more attention to evil and the problem of its eradications than to good and the methods by which individual goodness may be deepened, and the sum of goodness increased. The effects which follow too constant and intense a concentration upon evil are always disastrous. Those who crusade, not *for* God in themselves, but *against* the devil in others, never succeed in making the world better, but leave it either as it was, or sometimes even perceptibly worse than it was, before the crusade began. By thinking primarily of evil we tend, however excellent our intentions, to create occasions for evil to manifest itself.

Aldous Huxley, *The Devils of Loudun*, Penguin Books, 1973, page 175

The further I advance into solitude the more clearly I see the goodness of all things.

In order to live happily in solitude I must have a compassionate knowledge of the goodness of other men, a reverent knowledge of the goodness of all creation and a humble knowledge of the goodness of my own body and of my own soul.

How can I live in solitude if I do not see everywhere the goodness of God, my Creator and Redeemer and the Father of all good?

What is it that has made me evil and hateful to myself? It is my own folly, my own darkness, which have divided me, by sin, against the light which God has placed in my soul to be the reflection of His goodness and the witness of His mercy.

Shall I drive evil out of my soul by wrestling with my own darkness? This is not what God has planned for me.

It is sufficient to turn away from my darkness to His light. I do not have to run away from myself; it is sufficient that I find myself, not as I have made myself, by my own stupidity, but as He has made me in His wisdom and remade me in His infinite mercy.

Thomas Merton, *Spiritual Direction and Meditation*, Burns and Oates, 1961, page 115

FAITH

*'Faith'—strong belief, especially in the Christian faith;
things believed; loyalty, trustworthiness.*

When I was ordained, I had a fear about the future. I felt I would be keen and enthusiastic for the first twelve years of ministry, and then would end up just going through the motions. I was wrong on both counts. My faith came to a grinding halt after only four years, and I refused to go through the motions. A new way beckoned forward through the discovery of *The Choice is Always Ours*—an anthology compiled by Dorothy Berkley Phillips. This remarkable book opened up to me a vision of faith of enormous dimensions. At first I had to be content with a skeleton of faith, but for the last twenty years I have been collecting material and putting flesh and blood on it. As described elsewhere, this vision of faith is founded on the Bible and the writings of many theologians, but includes the insights from poets, novelists, playwrights, philosophers, historians, scientists, politicians, economists, statesmen, psychologists, artists and musicians.

Side by side with the evolution of this vision of faith has been the practice of a simple form of meditation, making use of mind and heart, as well as instinct, intuition and imagination. In reflection we mull over and think about the contents of *Visions of Faith*. After thirty years of ministry I am still keen and enthusiastic about faith, and so far have not had to resort to going through the motions.

Believe in the Lord your God, and you will be established; believe his prophets, and you will succeed.

2 Chronicles 20:20

Behold, he whose soul is not upright in him shall fail, but the righteous shall live by his faith.

Habakkuk 2:4

... for in Christ Jesus you are all sons of God, through faith.

Galatians 3:26

Therefore, since we are surrounded by so great a cloud of witnesses, let us also lay aside every weight, and sin which clings so closely, and let us run with perseverance the race that is set before us, looking to Jesus the pioneer and perfecter of our faith.

Hebrews 12:1–2

Reason saw not till *Faith* sprung the Light.

John Dryden, 'Religio Laici', in *The Poems of John Dryden*, volume I, edited by James Kinsley, Oxford at the Clarendon Press, 1958, page 313

Faith is kept alive in us, and gathers strength, from practice more than from speculation.

Joseph Addison, *The Works of Joseph Addison*, volume III, edited and published by Henry G. Bohn, 1856, page 484

Relying on God has to begin all over again every day as if nothing had yet been done.

C.S. Lewis, *Letters of C.S. Lewis*, edited by W.H. Lewis, Geoffrey Bles, 1966, page 220

Faith is a kind of winged intellect. The great workmen of history have been men who believed like giants.

Charles H. Parkhurst, *The Pattern in the Mount and Other Sermons*, R.D. Dickinson, 1890, page 57

It is neither *necessary*, nor indeed *possible*, to understand any matter of Faith; farther than it is Revealed.

Benjamin Whichcote, *Moral and Religious Aphorisms*, century XII, number 1168, Elkin, Mathews and Marrot, 1930, page 136

Nothing in life is more wonderful than faith—the one great moving force which we can neither weigh in the balance nor test in the crucible.

Sir William Osler, *Aphorisms from his Bedside Teachings and Writings*, collected by Robert Bennett Bean, edited by William Bennett Bean, Charles C. Thomas, 1961, page 102

The only faith that wears well and holds its colour in all weathers is that which is woven of conviction and set with the sharp mordant of experience.

J.R. Lowell, *My Study Windows*, George Routledge and Sons, 1905, page 142

Faith is a certitude without proofs... Faith is a sentiment, for it is a hope; it is an instinct, for it precedes all outward instruction.

Henri Frédéric Amiel, *Amiel's Journal*, translated by Mrs. Humphry Ward, Macmillan and Co., 1918, page 192

Religious faith does not consist in supposing that there is a God; it consists in personal trust in God rising to personal fellowship with God.

William Temple, *Basic Convictions*, Hamish Hamilton, 1937, page 16

It is faith that is expected of you and honest living, not profound understanding and deep knowledge of the mysteries of God.

Thomas à Kempis, *The Imitation of Christ*, translated by Betty I. Knott, William Collins Sons and Co., 1979, page 249

One in whom persuasion and belief
Had ripened into faith, and faith become
A passionate intuition.

William Wordsworth, *The Excursion*, iv. 1294, in *The Poetical Works of William Wordsworth*, volume V, edited by E. de Selincourt and Helen Darbishire, Oxford at the Clarendon Press, 1959, page 150

That man is perfect in faith who can come to God in the utter dearth of his feelings and his desires, without a glow or an inspiration, with the weight of low thoughts, failures, neglects, and wandering forgetfulness, and say to him, 'Thou art my refuge, because thou art my home.'

George Macdonald, *Unspoken Sermons*, First Series, Alexander Strahan, 1867, page 25

The creeds are not objects of faith; they are expressions of a faith of which Christ is the object, and in regard to all such personal relationship there is scope for at least a great width of intellectual movement as we seek more and more perfectly to understand and to interpret the character with which we are confronted.

William Temple, *The Preacher's Theme To-day*, SPCK, 1936, page 31

Faith is an act of self-consecration, in which the will, the intellect, and the affections all have their place. It is the resolve to live as if certain things were true, in the confident assurance that they are true, and that we shall one day find out for ourselves that they are true. The process of verification begins as soon as we have honestly set out to climb. We ourselves change, and the world changes to our sight. The landscape opens out more and more as we get further up the hill.

W.R. Inge, *Personal Life and the Life of Devotion*, Longmans, Green and Co., 1924, page 45

Faith is not knowledge or certainty. It is often contrasted with reason, but the true contrast is with the evidence of the senses. Faith is a kind of spiritual sight, an in-seeing into realities. It always wants to get beyond the superficial surface of things, into the spiritual behind the material. It wants to go beyond the outside symptoms into the causes of them. It consists of following knowledge and reason as far as they will take us, and then going beyond, in the same direction. There is a risk about faith, which can only be tested by taking the leap when the sure path comes to an end.

George Appleton, *Journey for a Soul*, William Collins Sons and Co., 1976, page 118

Faith enables us to get free from:
The domination of place and time, for it gives the additional dimension of the spiritual and the eternal.
The domination of happenings, for we are not at the mercy of circumstances, but can draw upon the inexhaustible wisdom and grace of God.
The domination of the written word, for we do not identify it with the inerrant word of God, but test it by the incarnate word.
The domination of theology, for men's thoughts about God change, and our theories, however good, are seen to be imperfect.
The domination of puritanism, for we see that truth and love must be decisive about action.
The domination of conscience, for conscience constantly needs educating from our growing knowledge of God.

George Appleton, *Journey for a Soul*, William Collins Sons and Co., 1976, page 182

Faith is a state of the mind and the soul... The language of religion is a set of formulas which register a basic spiritual experience. It must not be regarded as describing in terms to be defined by philosophy, the reality which is accessible to our senses and which we can analyse with the tools of logic. I was late in understanding what this meant. When I finally reached that point, the beliefs in which I was once brought up and which, in fact, had given my life direction even while my intellect still challenged their validity, were recognised by me as mine in their own right and by my free choice... The explanation of how man should live a life of active social service in full harmony with himself as a member of the community of the spirit, I found in the writings of those great medieval mystics for whom 'self-surrender' had been the way to self-realisation, and who in 'singleness of mind' and 'inwardness' had found strength to say Yes to every demand which the needs of their neighbours made them face, and to say Yes also to every fate life had in store for them... Love—that much misused and misinterpreted word—for them meant simply an over-flowing of the strength with which they felt themselves filled when living in true self-oblivion. And this love found natural expression in an unhesitant fulfilment of duty and an unreserved acceptance of life, whatever it brought them personally of toil, suffering—or happiness.

Dag Hammarskjöld, *Markings*, translated by Leif Sjöberg and W.H. Auden, Faber and Faber, 1964, page 10

This approach of Faith, this appreciation of the nature of God as He has been unveiled in the ethical processes of history, especially in the Person of Christ, and in His expanding conquest of the world, must always be one of the great factors of spiritual religion...
Once at least there shone through the thin veil of matter a personal Life which brought another kind of world than this world of natural law and utilitarian aims full into light. There broke through here in the face of Jesus Christ a revelation of Purpose in the universe so far beyond the vague trend of purpose dimly felt in slowly evolving life that it is possible here to catch an illuminating vision of what the goal of the long drama may be—the unveiling of sons of God. Here the discovery can be made that the deepest Reality towards which Reason points, and which the mystical experience *feels*, is no vague Something Beyond, but a living, loving Some One, dealing with us as Person with person. In Him there comes to focus in a Life that we can love and appreciate a personal character which impresses us as being absolutely good, and as being in its inexhaustible depth of Love and Grace worthy to be taken as the revelation of the true nature of the God whom all human hearts long for. And finally through this personal revelation of God in Christ there has come to us a clear insight that pain and suffering and tragedy can be taken up into a self-chosen Life and absorbed without spoiling its immense joy, and that precisely through suffering-love, joyously accepted, a Person expressing in the world the heart of God may become the moral and spiritual Saviour of others...

Nowhere else in the universe—above us or within us—has the moral significance of life come so full into sight, or the reality of actual divine fellowship, whether in our aspirations or in our failures, been raised to such a pitch of practical certainty as in the personal life and death and resurrection and steady historical triumph of Jesus Christ...

He shows the moral supremacy, even in this imperfect empirical world, of the perfectly good will, and He impresses those who *see* Him—see Him, I mean, with eyes that can penetrate through the temporal to the eternal and find His real nature—as being the supreme personal unveiling of God... strong enough in His infinite Grace and divine self-giving to convince us of the eternal co-operation of God with our struggling humanity, and to settle our Faith in the essential Saviourhood of God. He who sees *that* in Christ has found a real way to God and discovered a genuine way of salvation. It is the way of Faith, but Faith in no airy and unsubstantial road, no capricious leap. There is no kind of aimful living conceivable that does not involve faith in something trans-subjective—faith in something not given in present empirical experience. Even in our most elementary life-adjustments there is something operative in us which far underlies our conscious perceiving and the logic of our conclusions. We are moved, not alone by what we clearly picture and coldly analyse, but by deep-lying instincts which defy analysis, by background and foreground fringes of consciousness, by immanent and penetrative intelligence which cannot be brought to definite focus, by the vast reservoirs of accumulated wisdom through which we *feel* the way to go, though we can pictorially envisage no 'spotted trees' that mark the trail.

This religious and saving Faith, through which the soul discovers God and makes the supreme life-adjustment to Him, is profoundly moral and, in the best sense of the word, rational. It does not begin with an assumption, blind or otherwise, as to Christ's metaphysical nature, it does not depend upon the adoption of systematically formulated doctrines; it becomes operative through the discovery of a personal Life, historically lived—and continued through the centuries as a transforming Spirit—rich enough in its experience to exhibit the infinite significance of life, inwardly deep enough in its spiritual resources to reveal the character of God, and strong enough in sympathy, in tenderness, in patience, and in self-giving love to beget forever trust and confidence and love on the part of all who thus find Him.

The God whom we learn to know in Christ—the God historically revealed—is no vague first Cause, no abstract Reality, no all-negating Absolute. He is a concrete Person, whose traits of character are intensely moral and spiritual. His will is no fateful swing of mechanical law; it is a morally good will which works patiently and forever toward a harmonized world, a Kingdom of God. The central trait of His character is Love. He does not *become* Father. He is not reconciled to us by persuasive offerings and sacrifices. He is inherently and by essential disposition Father and the God of all Grace. He is not remote and absentee—making a world 'in the beginning,' and leaving it to run by law, or only occasionally interrupting its normal processes—He is immanent Spirit, working always,—the God of beauty and organizing purpose. He is Life and Light and Truth, an Immanuel God who can and does show Himself in a personal Incarnation, and so exhibits the course and goal of the race.

Rufus M. Jones, *Spiritual Reformers in the 16th and 17th Centuries*, Macmillan and Co., 1914, page xli

FINDING GOD

'Finding God'—the search, discovery and coming to a personal knowledge of God.

Of all the authors in *Visions of Faith*, one of the most brilliant is William Law. Originally a Fellow of Emmanuel College, Cambridge, he went on to write one of the greatest religious treatises in the English language—*A Serious Call to a Devout and Holy Life*. In this topic we have included an important passage from another of his influential books, *The Spirit of Prayer*. In the passage he encourages us to find God by searching the deepest and most central part of our souls. There, we are told, we shall discover the Light and Spirit of God, and so come to a personal knowledge of God. This approach rings true to my own experience.

Early in life, I discerned something of God the Creator in the creation. Several years later, in the Gospels and in the lives of certain Christians, I discovered something of the person of Jesus Christ. In my early twenties I read the book *Margaret* and experienced something of the Holy Spirit. However these manifestations were mainly seen to be outside myself, and so lacked conviction. What ultimately proved to be decisive was the search suggested by William Law which led to the discovery of the light and Spirit of God within me, and so to a personal knowledge of God.

Reflecting on the material in *Visions of Faith* may help us to find God. The best thing we can do is put ourselves in a position where God can find us, and be exposed to what has been called 'the gift of faith'.

Oh, that I knew where I might find him, that I might come even to his seat!
Job 23:3

For he will be found of them that tempt him not; he sheweth himself unto such as do not distrust him.
Wisdom of Solomon 1:2 (AV)

Seek, and you will find.
Matthew 7:7

For whoever would draw near to God must believe that he exists and that he rewards those who seek him.
Hebrews 11:6

People are generally better persuaded by the reasons which they have themselves discovered than by those which have come into the mind of others.
Blaise Pascal, *Pensées*, translated by W.F. Trotter, Random House, 1941, page 7

Console thyself, thou wouldst not seek Me, if thou hadst not found me.
Blaise Pascal, *Pensées*, translated by W.R. Trotter, Random House, 1941, page 177

Humble recognition of what your nature is will lead more surely to God than profound searching for knowledge.
Thomas à Kempis, *The Imitation of Christ*, translated by Betty I. Knott, William Collins Sons and Co., 1979, page 41

Thy hand be on the latch to open the door at his first knock.
Shouldst thou open the door and not see him, do not say he did not knock, but understand that he is there, and wants thee to go out to him. It may be he has something for thee to do for him. Go and do it, and perhaps thou wilt return with a new prayer, to find a new window in thy soul.
George Macdonald, *Unspoken Sermons*, Third Series, Longmans, Green and Co., 1889, page 227

Especially four ways among the many in which the human creature experiences the fact of God, and God is self-disclosed to men, stand out before us.
First, in History we find the Supernatural penetrating Process and revealed through it.
Next, in Incarnation—and, depending from this, in the fact of sanctity—we find the Supernatural penetrating Personality and revealed through it.
Thirdly, in Sacraments and Symbols we find the Supernatural penetrating created Things, and revealed to the soul through the channels of sense.
Last, in Prayer we find the Supernatural in immediate contact with created spirit; self-revealed and self-active within the Individual Soul.
Evelyn Underhill, *Man And The Supernatural*, Methuen and Co., 1927, page 90

For this turning to the Light and Spirit of God within Thee, is thy *only true* turning unto God, there is no other way of finding Him but in that Place where he dwelleth in Thee. For though

God be everywhere present, yet He is only present to Thee in the deepest, and most central Part of thy Soul. Thy natural *Senses* cannot possess God, or unite Thee to Him, nay thy inward Faculties of *Understanding, Will,* and *Memory,* can only reach after God, but cannot be the *Place* of his Habitation in Thee. But there is a *Root,* or *Depth* in Thee, from whence all these Faculties come forth, as Lines from a *Centre,* or as Branches from the Body of the Tree. This Depth is called the *Centre,* the *Fund* or *Bottom* of the Soul. This Depth is the *Unity,* the *Eternity,* I had almost said, the *Infinity* of thy Soul for it is so infinite, that nothing can satisfy it, or give it any Rest, but the infinity of God.

William Law, *The Spirit of Prayer,* edited by Sidney Spencer, James Clarke and Co., 1969, page 44

We say we want faith, but we don't want to open our purses to the poor. We claim we are looking for Christ, but we make no effort to change our lives, even though we can see how mistaken they are.

I feel we must give the lie to the man who says, 'I'm looking for God, but I can't find him!' Let him try to do everything in the truth, free from the demon of pride and the suffocating density of egoism. Let every trace of racism be rooted out, let every man be welcomed as a brother, and... you will see, you will see!

Live *love.* Act *truth.* Honour *life.* And it will be God within you whom you live, act, and honour. God will not come to you because you have been 'good'. He was already there. He has always been coming and always is coming. But now you can see Him because you have purified your eyes, softened your heart, and stooped down.

Remember! He was already there, He was already there, He was already there. The only difficulty was that you were unable to see Him.

Carlo Carretto, *The God Who Comes,* translated by Rose Mary Hancock, Darton, Longman and Todd, 1974, page 10

How many of us feel a secret longing to find God and this usually accompanied by the perception that we are confronted by an impenetrable barrier—we cannot find Him. We waste too much time looking for Him in impossible directions and by impossible means. He is not to be found by merely studying lengthy arguments, brilliant explanations of theological statements, or controversies upon the meaning of obscure dogmas. He is not even to be found through organising charity concerts and social reforms, however useful. We shall find Him through a self stripped bare of all other interests and pretentions—stripped bare of everything but a humble and passionately seeking heart. He says to the soul, 'Long for Me, and I will show Myself. Desire Me with a great desire and I will be found'... the hound of God must have in his heart no plan of his own. It is hard for the heart to say, 'I have no wishes of my own; I have no interests, no plans, no ambitions, no schemes, no desires, no love, no will. Thy desire is my desire. Thy love is my all. I am empty of all things, that I may be a channel for the stream of Thy will.'

Anon.

In ancient times the love of the beauty of the world had a very important place in men's thoughts and surrounded the whole of life with marvellous poetry. This was the case in every nation in China, in India, and in Greece...

The example of Saint Francis shows how great a place the beauty of the world can have in Christian thought. Not only in his actual poem perfect poetry, but all his life was perfect poetry in action. His very choice of places for solitary retreats or for the foundations of his convents was in itself the most beautiful poetry in action. Vagabondage and poverty were poetry with him; he stripped himself naked in order to have immediate contact with the beauty of the world...

Today one might think that the white races had almost lost all feeling for the beauty of the world, and that they had taken upon them the task of making it disappear from all the continents where they have penetrated with their armies, their trade and their religion. As Christ said to the Pharisees:

'Woe to you for ye have taken away the key of knowledge; ye entered not in yourselves and they that were entering in ye hindered.' (Luke 11:52).

And yet at the present time, in the countries of the white races, the beauty of the world is almost the only way by which we can allow God to penetrate us, for we are still further removed from the other two. Real love and respect for religious practices are rare even among those who are most assiduous in observing them, and are practically never to be found in others. Most people do not even conceive them to be possible. As regards the supernatural purpose of affliction, compassion and gratitude are not only rare but have become almost unintelligible for almost everyone today. The very idea of them has almost disappeared; the very meaning of the words has been debased. On the other hand a sense of beauty, although mutilated, distorted and soiled, remains rooted in the heart of man as a powerful incentive. It is present in all the preoccupations of secular life. If it were made true and pure it would sweep all secular life in a body to the feet of God, it would make the total incarnation of the faith possible. Moreover, speaking generally, the beauty of the world is the commonest, easiest and most natural way of approach.

Simone Weil, *Waiting on God*, translated by Emma Craufurd, William Collins Sons and Co., 1974, page 115

FORGIVENESS

'Forgiveness'—act of forgiving; state of being forgiven.

I enjoy reading the mystical poets, especially the works of George Herbert. Some words from his poem 'The Church Porch' have been crucial to me in forming a practice of forgiveness. The specific lines are as follows:

'Summe up at night, what thou hast done by day . . .
Dresse and undresse thy soul: mark the decay
And the growth of it.'

As a youth I was taught to say my prayers. This included a time for confession and absolution. At the end of the day, before going to sleep, I would briefly go over the events of the day, and work out where I had gone wrong—'in thought, word, deed and omission'. Often I would feel ashamed at what was unravelled, but at least was able to get it off my chest. Soon I noticed an underlying pattern. Many things which go wrong start in our thoughts, lead on to words, and issue forth in deeds. This practice of forgiveness acted as a check on my thought-life and led to changes in behaviour. Going over the day and noting what I had omitted to do also brought out an element of shame, but proved to be valuable from a practical point of view. At the end of this short period of self-examination, I would quietly accept God's forgiveness and move on to the Lord's Prayer.

I remember reading the story of a young girl. She was dying of an unknown disease. The doctors and consultants were baffled. Suddenly she recovered. Apparently she had been able to forgive someone. Forgiveness is more important than we tend to think.

Blessed is he whose transgression is forgiven, whose sin is covered.

Psalm 32:1

Help us, O God of our salvation, for the glory of thy name; deliver us, and forgive our sins, for thy name's sake!

Psalm 79:9

Father, forgive them; for they know not what they do.

Luke 23:34

And be kind to one another, tenderhearted, forgiving one another, as God in Christ forgave you.

Ephesians 4:32

Forgive us our sins as we forgive those who sin against us.

Lord's Prayer—ASB

The one final and utter failure of the church would be its ceasing to be able to bring sinners assurance of forgiveness.

Leonard Hodgson, *The Doctrine of the Atonement*, Nisbet and Co., 1951, page 150

The brave know only how to forgive... but a coward never forgave. It is not in his nature.

Laurence Sterne, *Sermons of Laurence Sterne*, 1779, page 153

'I can forgive, but I cannot forget,' is only another way of saying, '*I will not forgive.*'

Henry Ward Beecher, *Life Thoughts*, Alexander Strahan and Co., 1859, page 67

A wise man will make haste to forgive, because he knows the true value of time, and will not suffer it to pass away in unnecessary pain.

Samuel Johnson, 'The Rambler', in *The Yale Edition of the Works of Samuel Johnson*, volume V, edited by W.J. Bate and Albrecht B. Strauss, Yale University Press, 1969, page 208

There is not one Moral Virtue that Jesus Inculcated but Plato & Cicero did Inculcate before him; what then did Christ Inculcate? Forgiveness of Sins. This alone is the Gospel, & this is the Life & Immortality brought to light by Jesus.

William Blake, 'The Everlasting Gospel', supplementary passages, in *The Complete Writings of William Blake*, edited by Geoffrey Keynes, Oxford University Press, 1974, page 757

If we are to love others as we love ourselves, then we must learn to love the little self which so often needs to be forgiven for doing the things we do not want to do and saying the things we do not want to say.

Rebecca Beard, *Everyman's Search*, Arthur James, 1951, page 122

To ask that one's own higher self should forgive one's own trespasses is the hardest prayer to answer that we can ever offer up. If we can breathe this prayer, and find it truly answered in a harmony of exalted comprehension and acceptance, then we shall have learnt what forgiveness is. There is no other way to learn forgiveness.

Havelock Ellis, *Selected Essays*, J.M. Dent and Sons, 1936, page 324

If forgiveness meant letting off the criminal it would be a violation of the love-commandment. We have no right to be turning other people's cheeks, leaving other people's children to be raped or lonely old ladies to be beaten up, allowing thieves and murderers to run loose. But in Christian theology, forgiveness does not mean being let off the consequences. Forgiveness means reconciliation.

F.R. Barry, *Christian Ethics and Secular Society*, Hodder and Stoughton, 1966, page 240

Forgiveness is the answer to the child's dream of a miracle by which what is broken is made whole again, what is soiled is again made clean. The dream explains why we need to be forgiven, and why we must forgive. In the presence of God, nothing stands between Him and us—we *are* forgiven. But we *cannot* feel his presence if anything is allowed to stand between ourselves and others.

Dag Hammarskjöld, *Markings*, translated by Leif Sjöberg & W.H. Auden, Faber and Faber, 1964, page 110

Forgiveness breaks the chain of causality because he who 'forgives' you—out of love—takes upon himself the consequences of what *you* have done. Forgiveness, therefore, always entails a sacrifice. The price you must pay for your own liberation through another's sacrifice, is that you in turn must be willing to liberate in the same way, irrespective of the consequences to yourself.

Dag Hammarskjöld, *Markings*, translated by Leif Sjöberg & W.H. Auden, Faber and Faber, 1964, page 163

The Christian who has heard his word of pardon from the lips of Christ upon the Cross is never in danger of supposing that God does not mind. He minds, like that. And so, as St. Paul says, Christ as set forth upon the Cross shows the righteousness of God in the very act of forgiveness.

This is part—I know not whether it be the whole, but this is part—at least of that which Christian tradition has stood for in its insistence that the mere appeal of love to our souls is not sufficient as an account of the Atonement—that there must also be in a true sense a propitiation toward God.

William Temple, The Preacher's Theme To-day, SPCK, 1936, page 58

What is the Christian method of correction? Not retributive, nor deterrent, nor even reformative punishment, but the conversion of the offender's heart and will by the readiness of his victim to suffer at his hands. That is the Christian method of meeting wrong-doing; it is revealed in the Passion of Christ to be the nature of God, and it is the point in God's purification which is singled out for us to imitate: 'Love your enemies and pray for them that persecute you that ye may be the sons of your Father which is in Heaven for He maketh His sun to rise on the evil and the good, and sendeth rain on the just and unjust... ye therefore shall be perfect as your heavenly Father is perfect.' There is the Christian principle beyond all doubt. The good man will not be given to taking care that the bad man is punished, but he will convert the bad man by consenting to suffer, at his hands.

William Temple, The Kingdom of God, Macmillan and Co., 1912, page 80

Judgement would hold nothing but terror for us if we had no sure hope of forgiveness. And the gift of forgiveness itself is implicit in God's and people's love. Yet it is not enough to be granted forgiveness, we must be prepared to receive it, to accept it...

We must consent to be forgiven by an act of daring faith and generous hope, to welcome the gift humbly, as a miracle which love alone, love human and divine, can work, and forever be grateful for its gratuity, its restoring, healing, reintegrating power...

We must never confuse forgiving with forgetting, or imagine that these two things go together. Not only do they not belong together, but they are mutually exclusive. To wipe out the past has little to do with constructive, imaginative, fruitful forgiveness; the only thing that must go, be erased from the past, is its venom; the bitterness, the resentment, the estrangement; but not the memory.

Anthony Bloom, Meditations on a Theme, A.R. Mowbray and Sons, 1972, page 104

Jesus says that our Father will not forgive us unless we forgive each other from our hearts. It is not that he will not but that he cannot. An unforgiving heart is closed to receiving the rivers of Christ's redemptive love.

'Do not judge', because you simply cannot know the truth about someone else's motives. Only God can know the mysterious depth of the human heart. When we judge, what we are actually saying is that if *I* did or said so and so it would be because I was angry, jealous, etc. But we presume to add, *they* do this therefore *they* are angry, jealous, etc. They mean to hurt me.

By making a habit based on Jesus' teaching (but also on common sense and experience) of reflecting that we simply *cannot know* another's motives, we are forced into blind trust in our neighbours, and that is wonderful.

I am convinced that this resolution, consistently practised, produces a pure, constant, tender love for all.

What greater blessing could we wish for, and what better way to ensure our openness to Jesus so that he can use us as channels of his love.

Ruth Burrows, in The Watchful Heart, edited by Elizabeth Ruth Obbard, Darton, Longman and Todd, 1986, page 51

Why do I forgive anyone? Ordinary ethics say, because I feel sympathy with him. They allow men to seem to themselves, when they pardon others, frightfully good, and allow them to practise a style of pardoning which is not free from humiliation of the other. They thus make forgiveness a sweetened triumph of self-devotion.

The ethic of Reverence for Life does away with this unpurified view. All acts of forbearance and of pardon are for it acts forced from one by veracity toward oneself. I must practise unlimited forgiveness because, if I did not, I should be wanting in veracity to myself, for it would be acting as if I myself were not guilty in the same way as the other has been guilty towards me. Because my life is so liberally spotted with falsehood, I must forgive falsehood which has been practised upon me because I myself have been in so many cases wanting in love, and guilty of hatred, slander, deceit, or arrogance, I must pardon any want of love, and all hatred, slander, deceit, or arrogance which have been directed against myself. I must forgive quietly and without drawing attention to it; in fact, I do not really pardon at all, for I do not let things develop to any such act of judgement. Nor is this any eccentric proceeding; it is only a necessary widening and refinement of ordinary ethics.

The struggle against the evil that is in mankind we have to carry on not by judging others, but by judging ourselves. Struggle with oneself and veracity towards oneself are the means by which we work upon others. We quietly draw them into our efforts after the deep spiritual self-assertion which springs out of reverence for one's own life. Power makes no noise. It is there, and works. True ethics begin where the use of language ceases.

The innermost element then, in activist ethics, even if it appears as self-devotion, comes from the compulsion to veracity towards oneself, and obtains therein its true value; the whole ethic of being other than the world flows pure only when it comes from this source. It is not from kindness to others that I am tender-hearted, peaceable, forbearing, and friendly, but because by such behaviour I prove my own deepest self-assertion to be true. Reverence for Life which I apply to my own existence, and Reverence for Life which keeps me in a temper of devotion to other existence than mine, interpenetrate each other.

Albert Schweitzer, in George Seaver, *Albert Schweitzer: Christian Revolutionary*, James Clarke and Co., 1944, page 91

FREE WILL & DETERMINISM

'Free will and Determinism'—power of directing our own actions without constraint by necessity or fate, and the theory that human action is not free but determined by motives regarded as external forces acting on the will.

At school we had a teacher who had a 'passion' for handwriting. His own particular style was a work of art, and he was determined we should all write like him. I went along with this as I rather liked his style, and wanted to emulate him. So I would sit in the front row of his class and watch his instructions. In spare time I would practise writing and develop my style. I was secretly pleased with the results. However, as time became more pressing with the approach of 'O' and 'A' Levels, style became less important and gave way to speed. It was then I noticed I was writing exactly like my father. Was I now becoming a victim of determinism?

For me the key to an understanding of free will and determinism comes out in this section in the words of Carl Jung. In his book *Modern Man in Search of a Soul*, he wrote that we moderns are faced with the necessity of rediscovering the life of the spirit, and must experience it anew for ourselves. He went on to state that this is the only way in which we can break the spell that binds us to the cycle of biological events.

Jung is spot on here. Even Jesus was baptized, and in the wilderness broke the spell that bound him to the cycle of biological events, freeing him to live a balanced life, both human and divine.

I have chosen the way of faithfulness, I set thy ordinances before me.

Psalm 119:30

If thou wilt, to keep the commandments, and to perform acceptable faithfulness. He hath set fire and water before thee: stretch forth thy hand unto whether thou wilt.

Ecclesiasticus 15:15–16 (AV)

So if the Son makes you free, you will be free indeed.

John 8:36

For this reason the Father loves me, because I lay down my life, that I may take it again. No one takes it from me, but I lay it down of my own accord. I have power to lay it down, and I have power to take it again; this charge I have received from my Father.

John 10:17–18

We moderns are faced with the necessity of rediscovering the life of the spirit; we must experience it anew for ourselves. It is the only way in which we can break the spell that binds us to the cycle of biological events.

C.G. Jung, *Modern Man in Search of a Soul*, translated by W.S. Dell and Cary F. Baynes, Kegan Paul, Trench, Trubner and Co., 1933, page 140

The important thing to grasp is that while we are born in a determined condition, we do have the freedom to acquire insight, maturity, responsibility to make something of the materials entrusted to us. That's where redemption as new freedom leads us into the communion of saints, where we realise our full stature.

John Bowker, in Gerald Priestland, *Priestland's Progress*, BBC Worldwide, 1982, page 65

Man is a passion which brings a will into play, which works an intelligence,—and thus the organs which seem to be in the service of intelligence, are in reality only the agents of passion. For all the commoner sorts of being, determinism is true: inward liberty exists only as an exception and as the result of self-conquest. And even he who has tasted liberty is only free intermittently and by moments. True liberty, then, is not a continuous state: it is not an indefeasible and invariable quality. We are free only so far as we are not dupes of ourselves, our pretexts, our instincts, our temperament. We are freed by energy and the critical spirit—that is to say, by detachment of soul, by self-government. So that we are enslaved, but susceptible of freedom; we are bound, but capable of shaking off our bonds. The soul is caged, but it has power to flutter within its cage.

Henri Frédéric Amiel, *Amiel's Journal*, translated by Mrs Humphry Ward, Macmillan and Co., 1918, page 285

We are faced with the determined everyday world where processes are going on in time, and the future seems inexorable. Man is burdened and bound. He both strives toward freedom and fears it. The paradox of liberation lies in the fact that to maintain freedom and struggle from freedom, it is somehow necessary to be free, to have freedom in oneself. He who is a slave to the depths of his being does not know the word freedom and hence cannot struggle for it. The ancient taboos surround man on every side, cramp his moral life. And to liberate himself from their power, man must first feel himself inwardly free, and only then can he struggle externally for freedom. The inward conquest of enslavement is the basic task of moral living. And this means conquest of enslavement to the past as well as to the future, conquest of enslavement to the external world and enslavement to oneself, to one's lower self. To arouse man's creative energy means inward liberation, and this is accompanied by a sense of freedom. Creativity is the way of liberation.

Nicolas Berdyaev, *Christian Existentialism*, selected and translated by Donald A. Lowrie, George Allen and Unwin, 1965, page 142

Until man appeared, evolution strove only, from an observer's point of view, to manufacture an organ, the brain, in a body capable of assuring its protection. All the ancestors of man were but irresponsible actors playing an imposed part in a play which they did not understand, or try to understand. Man continues to play his part but wants to comprehend the play.

He becomes capable of perfecting himself, and he is even the only one capable of doing this. But in order to improve himself he must be free, since *his contribution to evolution will depend on the use he makes of his liberty.*

This transformation of man into an active, responsible individual is the new event which, more than any other, characterizes man. Of course the ancient mechanism of evolution, natural selection, will again enter into play. But, instead of depending as formerly on the slow action of biological laws and of chance, natural selection now depends on *conscience*, a manifestation of cerebral activity based on freedom which becomes, in each of us, the means put at our disposal to advance. According to the degree of evolution we have reached we will choose to progress or regress. Our choice will indicate precisely the state of perfection we have attained.

Lecomte du Noüy, *Human Destiny*, Longmans, Green and Co., 1947, page 226

It must be freely admitted that, in this experimental world, to which God has given the risky privilege of free-will, there are inevitable 'ills and accidents'. Moreover, the cumulative effect over the centuries of millions of individuals' choosing to please themselves rather than the Designer of 'the whole show' has infected the whole planet. That is what the theologians mean when they call this a 'sinful' world. This naturally means that, so far as this world is concerned, the tough, insensitive, and selfish, will frequently appear to get away with it, while the weak and sensitive will often suffer.

Once we admit the possibilities of free-will we can see that injustices and grievances are inevitable. (As Christ once said: 'It must needs be that offences come.') We may not agree with the risk that God took in giving Man the power to choose—we might even have preferred God to have made a race of robots who were unfailingly good and cheerful and kind...

The people who feel that God is a Disappointment have not understood the terms on which we inhabit this planet. They are wanting a world in which good is rewarded and evil is punished— as in a well-run kindergarten. They want to see the good man prosper invariably, and the evil man suffer invariably, here and now. There is, of course, nothing wrong with their sense of justice. But they misunderstand the conditions of this present temporary life in which God witholds His Hand, in order, so to speak, to allow room for His plan of freewill to work itself out.

J.B. Phillips, *Your God Is Too Small*, Epworth Press, 1952, page 44

The world is tired of individualism (which economic-dominated minds call by its economic symptom, capitalism). Many men are so desperate that they will use violence to rid themselves of individualism, though it itself is the product of violence, and grows with violence. They are like men adrift and dying of thirst who in their madness drink sea-water. The compulsory economic communism is based on hate. The psychological (communism) on love, on the steadily expanding power which grows by giving. Because consciousness and the psyche are more fundamental than the means of life, it will always be the emotion and motive, and not the rationalisation, or the supposed aim, that will govern and shape the actual achievement. If the psychology is right, then the right economics, the only economics bearable to a happy, just, social and charitic nature, will follow. If a man realises how he must and how he may lose his individuality, he will not thereafter cling to greed which can prevent his deliverance and ruin his happiness. Men can work with any economic system if they have the right psychology, but the right psychology will undoubtedly result in a system in which economics are simplified beyond our individualistic recognition.

This, then, it would seem, is the future of religion, and one neither other-worldly nor distant. Men may enter on their happiness when they will, and they should not hesitate, for the old order is over anyhow. Man may be far more happy than any but the saints have so far been, or far more wretched than it is possible for a man to be and not to become a beast. Which he will choose to be no one can say. He may see the choice, make the effort and attain the new life. Or he may drift, persuade himself out of sloth that the crisis is still distant, that things are well enough, and that they will last his time. But it is certain that here in our day the middle path ends... Nationalism and individualism are outraged by the integration of the world; they must cut these tendrils and rootlets that are binding the world together, or they will be obliterated... At the same time physical science puts at their disposal forces that can really tear in pieces these connections and rupture every artery of the world's economic life... Everyone may destroy, and so none may escape.

Here therefore, and here alone, in the advance of religion there seems to lie to our hand the solution of the aeonic conflict of the individual, and with that solution, at the same stroke (for this is but its other side), the salvation of civilisation. Here lies the reconciliation of the individual's intense passion to survive and the race's apparently disregardful continuance. Here is the door passing through which the individual returns to society, society becomes the race, the race is reunited with life, and life is one with the universe.

Gerald Heard, *Social Substance of Religion*, George Allen and Unwin, 1931, page 312

GOD

'God'—Supreme Being, Creator and Ruler of the universe, often the Lord God, Almighty God, God the Father, Son, Holy Ghost, Persons of the Trinity.

There was a time when I used to go to art classes. On one occasion we were given the task of drawing God. I found this impossible. Half an hour after the start of the class I was still faced with a blank sheet of paper. The art teacher noticed my dilemma and appeared at my side. 'Why don't you draw something like this?' Effortlessly he sketched out the figure of an elderly man with a long white flowing beard, seated on a throne, high in the sky amongst the clouds. All things considered this was pretty good. He had attempted the impossible and tried to put down on paper a representation of God as 'Supreme Being, Creator and Ruler of the universe, the Lord God, the Almighty God.' I was not convinced. If someone came to me now and said 'show me God' I would direct them to this particular topic and encourage them to mull over the contents of 'God'. It is just possible one person's experience or observation might speak directly to them and ring true. As an alternative I would direct them to scripture and encourage them to look out for 'God the Father, God the Son and God the Holy Ghost'. This actually happened to me once in College. One of our Japanese students came to see me and wanted me to show him God. I first of all put before him my material to no avail. Eventually he found him—in God the Son, in the Gospels.

Be still, and know that I am God.
Psalm 46:10

... that men may know, from the rising of the sun and from the west, that there is none besides me; I am the Lord, and there is no other. I form light and create darkness, I make weal and create woe, I am the Lord, who do all these things.
Isaiah 45:6–7

Let not your hearts be troubled; believe in God, believe also in me.
John 14:1

God is love, and he who abides in love abides in God, and God abides in him.
1 John 4:16

God isn't a think; He's a feel.
Joyce Grenfell, *In Pleasant Places*, Macmillan General Books, 1983, page 161

God is not an optional extra, He's an absolute must.
A girl of fourteen

God! Thou art love! I build my faith on that.
Robert Browning, 'Paracelsus V', in *The Poetical Works of Robert Browning*, volume 1, Smith, Elder, and Co., 1899, page 61

The Divine Essence itself is Love and Wisdom.
Emanuel Swedenborg, *The Divine Love and Wisdom*, J.M. Dent and Sons, 1914, page 12

God shall be my hope,
My stay, my guide, and lantern to my feet.

William Shakespeare, King Henry VI, Part II, II. iii. 24

From thee, great God, we spring, to thee we tend,
Path, motive, guide, original and end.

Samuel Johnson, 'Motto for The Rambler,' in The Yale Edition of the Works of Samuel Johnson, volume III, edited by W.J. Bate and Albrecht B. Strauss, Yale University Press, 1969, page 36

The Father is our ground and origin, in which we begin our being and our life.

John of Ruysbroeck, The Adornment of the Spiritual Marriage, translated by C.A. Wynschenk Dom, edited by Evelyn Underhill, John M. Watkins, 1951, page 173

None but God can satisfy the longings of an immortal soul;
that, as the heart was made for Him, so He only can fill it.

Richard Chevenix Trench, Notes on the Parables of our Lord, Pickering and Inglis, 1953, page 400

I will tell you, Scholar, I have heard a grave Divine say, that God has two dwellings; one in heaven, and the other in a meek and thankful heart.

Izaak Walton, The Complete Angler, Macmillan and Co., 1906, page 175

A voice is in the wind I do not know;
A meaning on the face of the high hills,
Whose utterance I cannot comprehend.
A something is behind them: that is God.

George Macdonald, Within And Without, Longman, Brown, Green, and Longmans, 1855, page 9

What is that light whose gentle beams now and again strike through to my heart, causing me to shudder in awe yet firing me with their warmth? I shudder to feel how different I am from it: yet in so far as I am like it, I am aglow with its fire.

St. Augustine, Confessions, translated by R.S. Pine-Coffin, Penguin Books, 1964, page 260

Every man, though he realizes that he was conceived by a bodily father in his mother's womb, is conscious also that he has within him a spirit that is free, intelligent, and independent of the body.
> That eternal spirit proceeding from the infinite, is the origin of all and is what we call God.

Leo Tolstoy, A Confession, The Gospel in Brief, and What I Believe, translated by Aylmer Maude, Oxford University Press, 1940, page 267

The Word 'God' is used in most cases as by no means a term of science or exact knowledge, but a term of poetry and eloquence, a term *thrown out*, so to speak, at a not fully grasped object of the speaker's consciousness, a *literary* term, in short; and mankind mean different things by it as their consciousness differs.

Matthew Arnold, 'Literature and Dogma', The Complete Prose Works of Matthew Arnold, volume VI, Dissent and Dogma, edited by R.H. Super, The University of Michigan Press, 1968, page 171

Thou must not think that God is a Being who is off in an upper heaven, or that when the soul departs it goes many hundred thousands miles aloft. It does not need to do that, for as soon as it has entered the innermost Birth it is in heaven already with God—*near and far in God is one thing*... There is only one 'place' to look for God and that is in one's own soul, there is only one 'region' in which to find heaven or hell, and that is in the nature and character of the person's own desire and will.

Rufus M. Jones, Spiritual Reformers in the 16th and 17th Centuries, Macmillan and Co., 1914, page 186

I regularly and repeatedly find the whole notion of God quite incomprehensible. Faith, I always believe, takes us to where the language bends and I'm jumping for analogy and metaphor. But in worship, in private meditation and in service, yes I do get a sense of the transcendent and the

holy, a presence that is more than the universe and yet personal and benevolent towards me—
I'm not sure if I know the meaning of the word love, but there's a very strong benevolence there.
And I think at that level I know God.

Stuart Miller, in Gerald Priestland, *Priestland's Progress*, BBC Worldwide, 1982, page 58

Why should I wish to see God better than this day?
    I see something of God each hour of the twenty-four, and each moment then,
In the faces of men and women I see God, and in my own face in the glass,
I find letters from God dropt in the street, and every one is sign'd by God's name,
And I leave them where they are, for I know that wheresoe'er I go,
Others will punctually come for ever and ever.

Walt Whitman, 'Song of Myself', in *The Complete Poems*, edited by Francis Murphy, Penguin Books, 1982, page 121

When Bishop Robinson was asked how he prayed 'to the ground of your being' he replied:
    'I do not pray to the ground of my being. I pray to God as Father. Prayer, for the Christian, is
the opening of oneself to that utterly gracious personal reality which Jesus could only address as
"Abba, Father!" I have no interest in a God conceived in some vaguely impersonal pantheistic
terms. The only God who meets my need as a Christian is "the God of Abraham, Isaac and
Jacob", the God and Father of our Lord Jesus Christ.'

John B. Coburn, in, *Spirituality For Today*, edited by Eric James, SCM Press, 1968, page 26

The word for 'Father', which the earliest Christians learnt from Jesus... was the intimate mode
of address from child to father... We must suppose that Jesus used it, by choice, because it is
the appropriate way of speaking about the personal life with God which was his concern... He
was aware that there were sophisticated types who could not take his teaching... 'I thank thee,
Father,' he is recorded to have said, 'for hiding these things from the learned and wise, and
revealing them to the simple...' And again, 'Unless you turn round and become like children,
you will never enter the kingdom of God...' This 'turning round' is a large part of what is meant
by 'repentance' in the gospels. It is learning to think of God as your Father and of yourself as his
child, quite simply.

C.H. Dodd, *The Founder of Christianity*, William Collins Sons and Co., 1979, page 72

God is both Mother and Father. The Oriental tradition has always recognized this.
    The biblical name for the spirit (*ruah*) is feminine and in the later Syriac tradition which
preserved the same name the Holy Spirit was spoken of as Mother. In the Old Testament there is
the tradition of feminine wisdom.
    It is possible to see in the Holy Spirit the feminine aspect of God in the Trinity. The source of
the Trinity is both Father and Mother. The Son or Word is the source of order in the universe.
The Holy Spirit is the feminine principle of receptivity, an infinite capacity for love which
receives perpetually the outflowing of love through the Son and returns it to its source in the
Father. In Christ, this perfect unity of male and female, this yin and yang, are brought together,
for 'in Christ there is neither male nor female...'

Bede Griffiths OSB, in *The Universal Christ*, edited by Peter Spink, Darton, Longman and Todd, 1990, page 8

Over the infinity of space and time, the infinitely more infinite love of God comes to possess us.
He comes at his own time. We have the power to consent to receive him or refuse. If we remain
deaf, he comes back again and again like a beggar, but also, like a beggar, one day he stops
coming. If we consent, God puts a little seed in us and he goes away again. The seed grows. A
day comes when the soul belongs to God, when it not only consents to love but when truly and
effectively it loves. Then in its turn it must cross the universe to go to God. The soul does not
love like a creature with created love. The love within it is divine, uncreated; for it is the love of
God for God which is passing through it. God alone is capable of loving God. We can only
consent to give up our own feelings so as to allow free passage in one soul for this love. We are
created for this consent, and for this alone.

Victor Gollancz, *More For Timothy*, Victor Gollancz, 1953, page 95

It is clearly necessary, from the beginning to the end of time, that God's way of revealing Himself to His creatures should be a *simple* way, which *all* those creatures may understand. Whether taught or untaught, whether of mean capacity or enlarged, it is necessary that communion with their Creator should be possible to all; and the admission to such communion must be rested, not on their having a knowledge of astronomy, but on their having a human soul. In order to render this communion possible, the Deity has stooped from His throne, and has not only, in the person of His Son, taken upon Him the veil of our human *flesh*, but, in the person of the Father, taken upon Him the veil of our human *thoughts*, and permitted *us*, by His own spoken authority, to conceive Him simply and clearly as a loving Father and Friend;—a being to be walked with and reasoned with; to be moved by our entreaties, angered by our rebellion, alienated by our coldness, pleased by our love, and glorified by our labour; and finally, to be beheld in immediate and active presence in all the powers and changes of creation. This conception of God, which is the child's, is evidently the only one which can be universal, and therefore the only one which *for us* can be true.

John Ruskin, *Modern Painters*, volume IV, George Allen and Sons, 1910, page 90

GRIEF

'Grief—deep or violent sorrow caused by love or trouble; keen or bitter regret or remorse.

In recent years both my parents have died, so I now know something of grief from the inside. I think this helps me to understand the feelings of those who have recently lost a loved one, and are going through a time of bereavement. As a college chaplain I have come across a special form of grief, caused by the untimely death of young people. This leaves me feeling dreadfully upset and sorrowful. Sometimes I feel guilty and regret not having cared enough for that person when alive. Often I experience a sense of injustice, and feel angry the young person in question never had a chance to find fulfilment in life. I also experience feelings of inadequacy in dealing with grief-stricken parents. There is no easy way to comfort them in these circumstances, apart from going into grief with them, and this is very painful and costly. Yet this is a crucial part of the grieving process, and often turns out to be a privilege in disguise.

Keeping busy and occupied helps us cope with grief, provided we don't overdo it. Talking about feelings with relatives and friends acts as a valuable safety-valve though in itself is not a cure. One of the best aids I've come across is a Cruse publication entitled *All in the End is Harvest*, edited by Agnes Whitaker. This contains the recorded experiences of those who have known grief at first hand, and help us in our time of sorrow. (Cruse is a national organization for the widowed and their children.)

For my life is spent with sorrow, and my years with sighing; my strength fails because of my misery, and my bones waste away.

Psalm 31:10

The Lord is near to the brokenhearted, and saves the crushed in spirit.

Psalm 34:18

Blessed are those who mourn, for they shall be comforted.

Matthew 5:4

Behold, the dwelling of God is with men. He will dwell with them; and they shall be his people, and God himself will be with them; he will wipe away every tear from their eyes, and death shall be no more, neither shall there be mourning nor crying nor pain any more, for the former things have passed away.

Revelation 21:3–4

Grief is itself a med'cine.

William Cowper, 'Charity', in *The Poetical Works of Cowper*, edited by H.S. Milford, Oxford University Press, 1950, page 79

See how Time makes all griefs decay.

Adelaide Anne Procter, 'Life in Death and Death in life', in *The Complete Works of Adelaide Anne Procter*, George Bell and Sons, 1905, page 169

Time and thinking tame the strongest grief.

English Proverb

In mourning let grief suffice as its highest expression.

Confucius, *The Analects of Confucius*, translated by William Edward Soothill, edited by Lady Hosie, Oxford University Press, 1937, page 213

Those who have known real grief seldom seem sad.

Benjamin Disraeli, *Endymion*, volume I, Longmans, Green, and Co., 1880, page 42

For grief once told brings somewhat back of peace.

William Morris, 'Prologue, The Wanderers', in *The Earthly Paradise*, volume I, Reeves and Turner, 1896, page 5

To weep is to make less the depth of grief.

William Shakespeare, *King Henry VI, Part III*, II. i. 85

It is dangerous to abandon oneself to the luxury of grief; it deprives one of courage, and even the wish for recovery.

Henri Frédéric Amiel, *Amiel's Journal*, translated by Mrs Humphry Ward, Macmillan and Co., 1918, page 192

You cannot prevent the birds of sorrow from flying over your head, but you can prevent them from building nests in your hair.

Chinese Proverb

Grief melts away
Like snow in May,
As if there were no such cold thing.

George Herbert, 'The Church, The Flower', in *The Works of George Herbert*, edited by F.E. Hutchinson, Oxford at the Clarendon Press, 1972, page 165

No bond
In closer union knits two human hearts
Than fellowship in grief.

Robert Southey, *Joan of Arc and Minor Poems*, George Routledge and Co., 1854, page 9

To spare oneself from grief at all cost can be achieved only at the price of total detachment, which excludes the ability to experience happiness.

Erich Fromm, *Man For Himself*, Routledge and Kegan Paul, 1975, page 190

That Man, who is from God sent forth,
Doth yet again to God return?—
Such ebb and flow must ever be,
Then wherefore should we mourn?

William Wordsworth, 'Lines on the Expected Dissolution of Mr. Fox', in *The Poetical Works of William Wordsworth*, volume IV, edited by E. de Selincourt and Helen Darbishire, Oxford at the Clarendon Press, 1958, page 267

Can I see another's woe,
And not be in sorrow too?
Can I see another's grief,
And not seek for kind relief?

William Blake, *Songs of Innocence*, 'On Another's Sorrow,' in *The Complete Writings of William Blake*, edited by Geoffrey Keynes, Oxford University Press, 1974, page 122

Oh! then indulge thy grief, nor fear to tell
The gentle source from whence thy sorrows flow!
Nor think it weakness when we love to feel,
Nor think it weakness what we feel to show.

William Cowper, 'To Delia: On her endeavouring to conceal her grief at parting', in *The Poetical Works of Cowper*, edited by H.S. Milford, Oxford University Press, 1950, page 278

I can only tell you what I have felt to be the only thing which makes life endurable at a time of real sorrow—God Himself. He comes unutterably near in trouble. In fact, one scarcely knows He exists until one loves or sorrows. There is no 'getting over' sorrow. I hate the idea. But there is a 'getting into' sorrow, and finding right in the heart of it the dearest thing of all human beings—the Man of Sorrows, a God.

Forbes Robinson, *Letters to his Friends*, SCM Press, 1938, page 68

Almighty God, who hast shown us in the life and teaching of Thy Son the true way of blessedness. Thou hast also shown us in His suffering and death that the path of love may lead to the Cross, and the reward of faithfulness may be a crown of thorns. Give us grace to learn these hard lessons. May we take up our cross and follow Christ, in the strength of patience and the constancy of faith; and see even in our darkest hour of trial and anguish the shining of the eternal light.

A prayer

I would maintain the sanctity of human joy and human grief. I bow in reverence before the emotions of every melted heart. We have a human right to our sorrow. To blame the deep grief which bereavement awakens, is to censure all strong human attachments. The more intense the delight in their presence, the more poignant the impression of their absence and you cannot destroy the anguish unless you forbid the joy. A morality which rebukes sorrow rebukes love. When the tears of bereavement have had their natural flow, they lead us again to life and love's generous joy.

James Martineau, *Endeavours after the Christian Life: Discourses*, Longmans, Green, Reader and Dyer, 1876, page 45

If we will but be still and *listen,* I think we shall hear these sad trials talking to us; saying as it were, 'You have known life and enjoyed it, you have tried and suffered from it; your tent has been pitched in pleasant places among those dear relations and tried friends, and now they are disappearing from around you. The stakes are loosened one by one, and the canvas is torn away, with no vestige left behind, and you want something which will *not* be taken away. You want something large enough to fill your heart, and imperishable enough to make it immortal like itself. That something is God.'

Samuel Palmer, 'Letter to a bereaved person', in Lord David Cecil, *Visionary and Dreamer*, Constable and Company, 1969, page 103

The bereaved have lost someone infinitely significant for whom there is no substitute. They have this urgent restless need to search and to find; their searching is natural in their loss, but it cannot succeed because the object they seek is a living person. The one they so desperately need to find, for whom they must search and search, is the one they know and love. They seek the living: their search is vain because the one they love is no longer alive...

To find oneself behaving unusually, irrationally, yet restless and frustrated if one tries to stop; not to know why one is doing what it seems one must do; to feel ashamed and foolish and unable to explain; to find no comfort or satisfaction from one's restless activity; this is a bewildering, frightening experience in an already distressing situation. 'Am I going mad?' is the question so often asked, and probably even more often feared and ashamedly unasked.

When something of this concept of loss-and-search is understood, mourners are often relieved and comforted to discover that behaviour which seemed inexplicable, uncontrollable, senseless and disturbing, is a normal universal bereavement experience. This will not ease the urgent need to search, but it goes some way towards relieving the bewilderment and distress. It may make, too, for more compassionate understanding from those around if they are able to recognize something of what lies behind this compulsive restlessness.

Elizabeth Collick, in *All in the End is Harvest*, edited by Agnes Whitaker, Darton, Longman and Todd, 1994, page 23

Healthy grief, dramatic and even traumatic as it may be, is a three-stage process. First, it is fully experiencing and expressing all the emotions and reactions to the loss. Second, it is completing and letting go of your attachment both to the deceased and to sorrow. Third, it is recovering and reinvesting anew in one's own life. Missing any of the steps in the grieving process may result in unhealthy or unsuccessful grief. Because these stages may take many months, unsuccessful grief may not show up until long after the loss. However, when even unsuccessful grief becomes evident, it can be explored and successfully resolved. Unsuccessful grief is usually reversible.

For us to complete every step of the grieving process requires awareness, courage, openness, self-support, and support from others. Because of the complexity of this process, many of us do not fully complete each necessary step. That is why unsuccessful or unhealthy grief is common. Further complicating our completion of the grieving process is the fact that our responses to loss are often automatic or unconscious, so that we may be unaware of what we are going through.

Since the grieving process is mostly learned, few of us experience healthy grief without first using more unsuitable means for coping with our pain and sorrow...

Unsuccessful grief is also the result of the misguided ideas of courage in our society. For example, courage is often seen as a capacity to be silent when in pain, to control tears at all costs, to function regardless of the depths of turmoil inside us, and to handle our wounds and sorrows privately and independently. Few of us are so superhuman. When we try to act according to these ideals, we usually deny our pain and never learn to cope with it. Since pain unexpressed does not dissolve spontaneously, we may suffer severe consequences from pretending to be superhuman...

It takes enormous courage to face pain directly and honestly, to sit in the midst of such uncomfortable feelings and reactions until we have expressed them and finished with them. It takes courage to be willing to experience fully the pain and anguish of grief and to face feelings at the time they occur rather than postponing the encounter.

Judy Tatelbaum, in *All in the End is Harvest*, edited by Agnes Whitaker, Darton, Longman and Todd, 1994, page 25

There are many bereaved people who have surmounted the bitterness of being alone, and some who have found rich opportunities in new activities and friendships. Although there is still much to be done in neighbourliness and the provision of help for the bereaved, it is possible in most areas in this country to find an organization or social group that is wanting to know and care for those who are lonely.

For some, loneliness, a-lone-ness, may be the opportunity to experience the quiet joy that can be found in solitude. There are productive activities that can only be practised on one's own. Some have learnt to play an instrument, which might have been an excruciating experience for a marriage partner. Others have passed time catching up on reading and have found it far more enjoyable now that they can read in depth and at leisure rather than in the spare minutes snatched from a busy day. Some have learnt a foreign language, perhaps through radio lessons, while others have used the media to indulge a new or revived interest in astronomy, heraldry, politics or one of a hundred other possible subjects. A number—perhaps a rather surprisingly large number—have turned their minds to meditation.

Two kinds of activity seem particularly to encourage healing of the spirit.

The first is any form of creativity. Striving to bring something original into being is a positive personal assertion that life is—after all—worthwhile. Even small creative achievement is balm to those who are weary of the pain of loss and death.

Some have taken up painting or pottery, embroidery, weaving, woodcarving, perhaps going to classes for the first time since they left school. Others have tried their skill with words, writing stories or articles, poetry, a novel or autobiography; they may have joined a local Writers' Circle where they will have found advice and encouragement...

Another sphere of activity, gentle or strenuous as one may choose, which seems to have a special healing quality, is one that brings people in touch with nature: country walks, fishing, gardening, collecting shells or pebbles along a quiet stretch of beach, propagating and caring for houseplants or a herb garden—the opportunities are many and varied. In the closeness to natural and living things—sun, sea, rain and wind, earth and seeds and grass, woods, trees and flowers, bees, birds, butterflies—in the sight and sound and feel of natural elements and growing things, many have found themselves refreshed and at peace.

It is a hopeful, gladdening experience to listen to those who are still rather sad at heart telling of their hobbies, and sharing the quiet joy and precious contentment that they have found in productive solitude.

Elizabeth Collick, in *All in the End is Harvest*, edited by Agnes Whitaker, Darton, Longman and Todd, 1994, page 132

GUIDANCE

'Guidance'—guiding, being guided, advice on problems.

In the early years of ministry, I was mainly guided by the words of Scripture, focusing in particular on Christ's teaching, and by prayer. I would take a passage from the Gospels and go over it carefully, writing down any insights in my journal which came to mind as I read the passage. In some ways this was the beginning of a listening form of prayer. I had learnt this simple technique from George Seaver's book, *Edward Wilson of the Antarctic*. Edward Wilson was the doctor on Scott's expedition to the Antarctic, and one of my heroes. He was a deeply committed Christian, and had carefully worked through the Gospels, trying to assimilate the essence of Christ's teaching and then putting it into practice. I found all this very helpful, particularly the keeping of a journal. Later on, when life became more complicated, I began to collect insights which have evolved during the last 2,000 years of Christian and religious experience. I wanted to bring these into play, alongside Scripture. The outcome has been *Visions of Faith, Hope, Love* and *Glory*. These books can be used as aids for guidance on practical and spiritual matters. With the practice of reflection, and the keeping of a journal, the technique for guidance remains a simple one. With the combination of Scripture and modern insights, there is enough basic material on guidance to take us in to the twenty-first century with confidence.

He leads the humble in what is right, and teaches the humble his way.

Psalm 25:9

... this is God, our God for ever and ever. He will be our guide for ever.

Psalm 48:14

When the Spirit of truth comes, he will guide you into all the truth; for he will not speak on his own authority, but whatever he hears he will speak, and he will declare to you the things that are to come.

John 16:13

May the Lord direct your hearts to the love of God and to the steadfastness of Christ.

2 Thessalonians 3:5

For a time will come when your innermost voice will speak to you, saying: 'This is *my* path; here I shall find peace. I will pursue this path, come what may.'

Grace Cooke, *Spiritual Unfoldment*, The White Eagle Publishing Trust, 1961, page 13

I give you the end of a golden string:
Only wind it into a ball,
It will lead you in at Heaven's Gate
Built in Jerusalem's wall.

William Blake, 'Epigrams, Verses, and Fragments from the Note-Book', in *The Complete Writings of William Blake*, edited by Geoffrey Keynes, Oxford University Press, 1974, page 551

Jesus promised that his Spirit would guide his disciples into all truth, both truth of mind and direction of life. There can be no hesitation in the choice between what is good and what is evil, what is loving and what is selfish, what is true and what is false. Sometimes, however, the choice is between two goods or between two paths neither of which is completely good. How do we seek the Spirit's guidance?

George Appleton, *Journey for a Soul*, William Collins Sons and Co., 1976, page 207

Discernment is to see beyond the veils imposed by the senses; to see things as they are.

Such capacity to see comes to those who operate from the deep centre within themselves. It implies detachment and freedom: detachment from the world of the senses and freedom from personal desire.

In India discernment or discrimination has always been central to an understanding of what constitutes spirituality, for to follow the spiritual path involves withdrawal from the 'unreal to the real'. So does the heart become open to divine wisdom.

Bede Griffiths OSB, in *The Universal Christ*, edited by Peter Spink, Darton, Longman and Todd, 1990, page 19

Conditions for being shown God's will:
Readiness to accept and do God's will without any conditions or reservations.
Reference to God of all the problems, attitudes, opportunities and decisions of our lives.
Readiness to receive insights from others but not let them decide for us.
Examination of any intuitions to discover any ulterior motives or reluctance.
Patient waiting upon God until a persistent feeling of oughtness comes.
Quiet putting into practice of the guidance received without dithering or looking back.

George Appleton, *Journey for a Soul*, William Collins Sons and Co., 1976, page 207

Let us, then, labour for an inward stillness,—
An inward stillness and an inward healing;
That perfect silence where the lips and heart
Are still, and we no longer entertain
Our own imperfect thoughts and vain opinions,
But God alone speaks in us, and we wait
In singleness of heart, that we may know
His will, and in the silence of our spirits,
That we may do His will, and do that only!

Henry Wadsworth Longfellow, *John Endicott*, in *The Poetical Works of Longfellow*, Humphrey Milford, Oxford University Press, 1913, page 571

Spiritual direction (is) the pastoral guidance of souls by counselling and prayer through the illumination, grace and power of God the Holy Spirit. Certain men and women have been given this 'gift' which enables them to act as guides and counsellors on the spiritual way. Devoted souls benefit greatly from this ministry.

Père Grou says in *The Hidden Life of the Soul*, 'He who really desires to give himself to God, should weigh well the advantages of having guidance from another, because the best and wisest men are blinded as to their own inward life, and the holiest and best fitted to direct others would not effect to direct themselves.'

The spiritual director is a physician of souls, one who seeks to diagnose the condition of the soul with its graces and ills, and to assist it into the way of growth. He is not primarily a judge, nor at any time a dictator. He is a spiritual father/mother concerned with the welfare of his/her children.

There is no authoritarianism in spiritual direction. It should not be followed blindly; guidance of every kind should be checked against conscience, holy scripture, church teaching, the dictates of common sense, and relevant circumstances. It is a sign of deterioration in spiritual direction if force of any kind is used.

Spiritual direction since the Reformation has combined the hearing of confessions with spiritual counsel. The father of this post-Reformation teaching is Francis de Sales, whose penitent Madame de Chantal always had opportunity for talk with her 'director'.

Reginald Somerset Ward, who began this form of spiritual direction in the Church of England during the 1914–1918 war, always allowed time for talk and discussion as well as for confession. The *prie-dieu* and one chair (for the priest), gave way to the *prie-dieu* and two chairs (one for the penitent and one for the priest). The whole transaction is considered to be 'under the seal', thus establishing confidence between priest and penitent. Since Vatican Council II the Roman Catholic Church has started to develop this same kind of counselling technique, priest and penitent in a room with table and chairs.

What is the relationship of psychiatry to spiritual direction? Today the two go 'hand in hand' when there is confidence between the clergy and doctors. When psychiatric aid is needed the penitent will consult the doctor and later re-establish relationship with the priest. Spiritual counsellors by their gifts, training, and insight, are able to know when to advise help from a psychiatrist. The seal of confession might appear to be at risk but this is not so because medical records concern areas of ill-health in body, mind and spirit, rather than sin. Doctors, like clergy, exercise discretion about their patients and their work...

Spiritual direction is not necessary for all souls but it is very desirable for some and it can be a great help to many others. Those whose prayer is mystical in character specially need it because their consciousness of God is such that without 'direction' they could become afraid, depressed and self-centred. Counselling helps them to find a spiritual equilibrium...

The most positive use of spiritual direction is in two specific areas: understanding ourselves in the light of God, and the growth in the life of faith and prayer. The counsellor helps the soul to see itself and through direction shows the way to fullness and joy. The arts of meditation, intercession, and contemplation have to be learned. The life of prayer has to be maintained and sustained over the years if maturity and insight are to come. These gifts of grace are not achieved by our own efforts. We learn to stay in the light and love of God so that he can achieve them in us.

N.W. Goodacre, in *A Dictionary of Christian Spirituality*, edited by Gordon S. Wakefield, SCM Press, 1983, page 114

HEAVEN

'Heaven'—place believed to be the abode of God and of the righteous after death; place or state of supreme bliss, delightful.

I remember calling in at the Porter's Lodge to see if there were any letters in my pigeon-hole. Bill, the head porter, was on duty, his moustache bristling. He wanted back two gowns he had lent me. 'Chaplain,' he said gruffly, 'if I don't get those two gowns back soon, I'm going to send you to your Maker.' 'Oh, Bill,' came the dry retort of an elderly Fellow in the depths of the Lodge, 'don't give the Reverend too much to hope for.' This tickled the head porter's sense of humour, especially as it was at my expense.

Many people tend to think of heaven as a place where God dwells, and where some of us may end up after death. I prefer to think of heaven as a state or condition we can experience here and now. I'm not alone in this. Oscar Wilde in his book *The Picture of Dorian Gray* wrote that each of us has heaven and hell in him. This fits in well with the underlying vision of this anthology. Following on the divine inbreathing of the Genesis story of the creation of man, when this is a living reality, we become aware of the presence of God in our lives and find this delightful. We experience moments of peace, wholeness and harmony. Alternatively when this is not a reality we experience the emptiness, frustration and loneliness of hell. John Main puts the challenge of heaven before us in this section—'The Kingdom of Heaven is among us and we must be open to it now.'

How lovely is thy dwelling place, O Lord of hosts! My soul longs, yea, faints for the courts of the Lord; my heart and my flesh sing for joy to the living God.

Psalm 84:1–2

Thus says the Lord: 'Heaven is my throne and the earth is my footstool; what is the house which you would build for me, and what is the place of my rest?'

Isaiah 66:1

… but lay up for yourselves treasures in heaven, where neither moth nor rust consumes and where thieves do not break in and steal. For where your treasure is, there will your heart be also.

Matthew 6:20–21

Blessed be the God and Father of our Lord Jesus Christ, who has blessed us in Christ with every spiritual blessing in the heavenly places. Ephesians 1:3

Heaven means to be one with God.

Frederick W. Farrar, *Eternal Hope*, Macmillan and Co., 1892, page 25

Heaven is nothing but Grace perfected, 'tis of the same nature of that you enjoy here when you are united by faith to Christ.

Rufus M. Jones, *Spiritual Reformers in the 16th and 17th Centuries*, Macmillan and Co., 1914, page 252

How good is the presence of God! Right in the depths, in the heaven of my soul, I find him, for he never abandons me. God in me and I in him—that is my whole life.

Elizabeth of Dijon, in Hans Urs von Balthasar, *Elizabeth of Dijon*, translated and adapted by A.V. Littledale, The Harvill Press, 1956, page 76

The Second Person of the Blessed Trinity was no less *in heaven* during the period of the earthly ministry than either before or after it. What we see as we watch the life of Jesus is the very life of heaven—indeed of God—in human expression.

William Temple, *Readings in St. John's Gospel*, First and Second Series, Macmillan and Co., 1947, page 47

The Kingdom of Heaven is among us and we must be open to it now. As St Peter says, we must be alive in the Spirit and become fully alive with the life of God. As Christians we must never settle for less.

Christian life is not a question of just getting through our lives; every word of the New Testament suggests to us that it is of supreme importance that we live our lives in a state of continuous expansion of heart and spirit, growing in love and becoming more firmly rooted in God.

Above all, know from your own heart, from your own experience, that you were created for infinite expansion of spirit. Every act of faith is a step into the infinite expansion of God.

John Main OSB, in *The Joy of Being*, selected by Clare Hallward, Darton, Longman and Todd, 1989, page 60

Heaven is the goal of man, and heaven gives the true perspective for our present life. Our belief in the goal of heaven goes with our belief in the infinite and eternal worth of every man, woman, and child created in God's own image, and reminds us that we are called to nothing less than the Christ-like perfection of the saints. In the Communion of Saints, which is the family of Jesus, the Lord of the dead and the living, we are one with the saints in every age, and in that oneness with them we hold fast to the truth which belongs to no one age because it is timeless.

In the Communion of Saints we are freed from the dominance of the contemporary, as well as of the past. We shall know 'the glorious liberty of the children of God.'

Michael Ramsey, *Through The Year With Michael Ramsey*, edited by Margaret Duggan, Hodder and Stoughton, 1975, page 253

The first hope of every Christian is the hope of heaven: the first, the nearest, the most relevant of his hopes. Does that surprise you? Is heaven a possibility too far away for immediate thought? No ... man exists in order to have the most intimate relation with God that is possible; a relationship of fellowship and indeed friendship mingled with awe and dependence. To give glory to God, in the biblical phrase, is to enjoy that fellowship, to come to reflect God's own character of outgoing love and humbly to have God and not one's self as the centre. There lies man's true status, true freedom, and true destiny ... Do not be afraid of looking towards heaven, for heaven is the meaning of our existence as created in God's likeness for fellowship with him. And the quest of heaven is very far from being a pious escapism, inasmuch as the essence of heaven is selfless love, the same love which drives you to go without your dinner to help a family which has no food at all.

Michael Ramsey, *Freedom, Faith and the Future*, SPCK, 1970, pages 37 and 41

But how may we think of heaven? ... In his work *The City of God* St Augustine told of heaven thus: 'We shall rest and we shall see, we shall see and we shall love, we shall love and we shall praise, in the end which is no end.'

Rest: we shall be freed from the busy and fussy activity in which we get in our own light and expose ourselves to our self-centredness. Resting, we shall find that we *see* in a new way, without the old hindrances. We shall see our neighbours as what they really are, creatures and children of God in whom is the divine image, and that image will become newly visible to us. We shall see ourselves too as God's infinitesimally small creatures: and we shall begin to see God himself in his beauty. Seeing, we shall *love*, for how shall we not love God in his beauty and how shall we not love all our neighbours in whom the image of God is now visible to us? *Praise* will be the last word, for all is of God and none is of our own achievement, and we shall know the depth of gratitude and adoration. St Augustine adds 'in the end which is no end'. It will be the end, for here is perfection and nothing can be more final. It will be no end, for within the resting, seeing, loving and praising there is an inexhaustible adventure of new and ceaseless discovery. Such is the heaven for which we were created.

Michael Ramsey, *Be Still and Know*, William Collins Sons and Co., 1982, page 122

The final state of the Christian mystic, then, is not annihilation in the Absolute. It is a condition wherein we dwell wholly in God, one life and truth with Him yet still 'feel God *and* ourselves,' as the lover feels his beloved, in a perfect union which depends for its joy on an invincible otherness. The soul, transfused and transfigured by the Divine Love as molten iron is by the fire, becomes, it is true, 'one simple blessedness with God' yet ever retains its individuality: one with God beyond itself, yet other than God within itself. The 'deified man' is fully human still, but spiritualised through and through not by the destruction of his personality, but by the taking up of his manhood into God. There he finds, not a static beatitude, but a Height, a Depth, a Breadth of which he is made part, yet to which he can never attain: for the creature, even at its highest, remains finite, and is conscious that Infinity perpetually eludes its grasp and leads it on. So heaven itself is discovered to be no mere passive fulfillment, but rather a forward-moving life: an ever new loving and tasting, new exploring and enjoying of the Infinite fulness of God that inexhaustible Object of our knowledge and delight. It is the eternal voyage of the adventurous soul on the vast and stormy sea of the Divine.

Evelyn Underhill, in John of Ruysbroeck, *The Adornment of the Spiritual Marriage*, translated by C.A. Wynschenk Dom, edited with an introduction and notes by Evelyn Underhill, John M. Watkins, 1951, page xxxi

I wish there be not, among some, such a light and poor esteem of heaven, as makes them more to seek after assurance of heaven only in the idea of it as a thing to come, than after heaven itself which, indeed, we can never well be assured of, until we find it rising up within ourselves, and glorifying our own souls. When true assurance comes, heaven itself will appear upon the horizon of our souls, like a morning light, chasing away all our dark and gloom doubtings before it. We shall not need then to light up our candles to seek for it in corners; no: it will display its own lustre and brightness so before us, that we may see it in its own light, and ourselves the true possessors of it. We may be too nice and vain in seeking for signs and tokens of Christ's spiritual appearances in the souls of men, as well as the Scribes and Pharisees were in seeking for them at His first appearance in the world. When He comes into us, let us expect till the works that He shall do within us testify of Him and be not over credulous, till we find that He doth those works there which none other could do. As for a true, well-grounded, assurance, say not so much, 'Who shall ascend up into heaven,' to fetch it down from thence? or, 'who shall descend into the deep,' to fetch it up from beneath? for in the growth of true, internal, goodness, and in the progress of true religion it will freely unfold itself within us. Stay till the grain of mustard-seed itself breaks forth from among the clods that buried it till, through the descent of the heavenly dew, it sprouts up, and discovers itself openly. This holy assurance is, indeed, the budding and blossoming of felicity in our own souls; it is the inward sense and feeling of the true life, spirit, sweetness, and beauty of grace, powerfully expressing its own energy within us.

John Smith the Platonist, *Select Discourses*, Cambridge at the University Press, 1859, page 449

HELL

'Hell'—abode of the dead; abode of condemned spirits; place, state of wickedness or misery.

The college plumber (deep into atheism) used to tease me. If I bumped into him, and the weather was bad, he would greet me cheerfully with the words, 'Him up there (nodding heavenwards) hasn't given us a very good day today, has he, sir?' This quip would come out half a dozen times a year, usually in winter, and I would respond in like manner. As it was, I enjoyed his company and pulling my leg was usually the prelude to a brief conversation. One summer's day we had a scorcher. I bumped into him. The hot sun was clearly an embarrassment to him, so he tried a different tack. 'It's so warm today sir, Him up there (nodding heavenwards) couldn't possibly have given us this one (i.e. God can't be that generous). I reckon him down there (nodding downwards) has given us this one. It's as hot as hell.' A brief mopping of the brow. 'Well, Les,' I said, keeping a deadpan face, 'I expect you'll know more about that than I do.' We both dissolved into laughter, and went on to enjoy the heat of the day.

As with heaven, most people think of hell as a place, or a state we might end up in when we die. Henry Ward Beecher is not far from the mark when he writes there are materials enough in every man's mind to make a hell there. Looking back over the last thirty years I have come across enough evidence to suggest life for many people is a living hell. There is a need for many of us to take this to heart, and to open our lives to the love and grace of God.

But the eyes of the wicked will fail; all way of escape will be lost to them, and their hope is to breathe their last.

Job 11:20

There is severe discipline for him who forsakes the way; he who hates reproof will die. Sheol and Abaddon lie open before the Lord, how much more the hearts of men!

Proverbs 15:10–11

Put on the whole armour of God, that you may be able to stand against the wiles of the devil. For we are not contending against flesh and blood, but against the principalities, against the powers, against the world rulers of this present darkness, against the spiritual hosts of wickedness in the heavenly places.

Ephesians 6:11–12

Be sober, be watchful. Your adversary the devil prowls around like a roaring lion, seeking some one to devour.

1 Peter 5:8

Hell is not to love any more, Madame.

George Bernanos, *The Diary of a Country Priest*, translated by Pamela Morris, Boriswood, 1937, page 177

The heart of man is the place the devill dwels in; I feel sometimes a hell within my selfe.

Sir Thomas Browne, *Religio Medici*, in *The Works of Sir Thomas Browne*, volume I, edited by Geoffrey Keynes, Cambridge University Press, 1964, page 62

The hell to be endured hereafter, of which theology tells, is no worse than the hell we make for ourselves in this world by habitually fashioning our characters in the wrong way.

William James, *The Principles of Psychology*, volume II, Macmillan and Co., 1890, page 127

On that hard Pagan world disgust
And secret loathing fell.
Deep weariness and sated lust
Made human life a hell.

Matthew Arnold, 'Obermann Once More' in *The Poems of Matthew Arnold*, edited by Kenneth Allott, Longmans, Green and Co., 1965, page 523

See here the whole truth in short. All sin, death, damnation, and hell is nothing else but this kingdom of self, or the various operations of self-love, self-esteem, and self-seeking which separate the soul from God and end in eternal death and hell.

William Law, *Selected Mystical Writings of William Law*, edited by Stephen Hobhouse, Rockliff, 1948, page 92

They (men) are not in hell because Father, Son and Holy Ghost are angry at them, and so cast them into punishment which their wrath had contrived for them; but they are in wrath and darkness because they have done to the light which infinitely flows forth from God as that man does to the light of the sun who puts out his own eyes.

William Law, *Selected Mystical Writings of William Law*, edited by Stephen Hobhouse, Rockliff, 1948, page 49

All misery arises out of *ourselves*. It is a gross mistake, and men are of dull and stupid spirits who think that the state which we call Hell is an incommodious place only; and that God by His sovereignty throws men therein. Hell arises out of a man's self. And Hell's fuel is the guilt of a man's conscience. It is possible that any should be so miserable as Hell makes a man and as there a man is miserable by his own condemning of himself.

Rufus M. Jones, *Spiritual Reformers in the 16th and 17th Centuries*, Macmillan and Co., 1914, page 302

It hath been said, that there is of nothing so much in hell as of self-will. The which is true, for there is nothing else there than self-will, and if there were no self-will, there would be no Devil and no hell. When it is said that Lucifer fell from Heaven, and turned away from God and the like, it meaneth nothing else than that he would have his own will, and would not be at one with the Eternal Will. So was it likewise with Adam in Paradise. And when we say Self-will, we mean, to will otherwise than as the One and Eternal Will of God willeth.

Theologia Germanica, translated by Susanna Winkworth, Stuart and Watkins, 1966, page 118

The one principle of hell is—'*I* am my own. *I* am my own king and my own subject. *I* am the centre from which go out my thoughts; *I* am the object and end of my thoughts; back upon *me* as the alpha and omega of life, my thoughts return. My own glory is, and ought to be, my chief care; my ambition, to gather the regards of men to the one centre, myself. My pleasure is *my* pleasure. My kingdom is—as many as I can bring to acknowledge my greatness over them. My judgement is the faultless rule of things. My right is—what I desire. The more I am all in all to myself, the greater I am. The less I acknowledge debt or obligation to another the more I close my eyes to the fact that I did not make myself; the more self-sufficiency I feel or imagine myself—the greater I am. I will be free with the freedom that consists in doing whatever I am inclined to do, from whatever quarter may come the inclination. To do my own will so long as I feel anything to be my will, is to be free, is to live.'

To all these principles of hell, or of this world—they are the same thing, and it matters nothing whether they are asserted or defended so long as they are acted upon—the Lord, the king, gives the direct lie.

George Macdonald, *Unspoken Sermons*, Third Series, Longmans, Green, and Co. 1889, page 102

HOLY SPIRIT

'Holy Spirit'—third Person of the Trinity, God as spiritually acting, sevenfold gift of the Spirit: counsel, wisdom, understanding, knowledge, fear (awe, reverence), might (power), and the spirit of the Lord.

In my early twenties, whilst reading the book *Margaret*, by James Davidson Ross, I became deeply convinced of the paramount importance of the Holy Spirit. In the next few days I became conscious of a persistent little voice inside me saying, 'Bill, if this is so important to you, shouldn't you be actively engaged in extending this life of the Holy Spirit to others?' I took this to be 'my call' to ordination. Robert Bridges, in *The Spirit of Man*, confirmed my conviction of the importance of the Holy Spirit and helped me to see possible ways forward. 'Spirituality,' he wrote, 'is the basis and foundation of human life... It must underlie everything. To put it briefly, man is a spiritual being, and the proper work of his mind is to interpret the world according to his higher nature, and to conquer the material aspects of the world and to bring them into subjection to the spirit.'

This led me to discern a loss of our spiritual roots, and raised the serious question as to whether we might ever restore them again as the basis of our society. *Visions of Faith* is an attempt to round up something of our spiritual heritage, and along with the practice of reflection, provides a way and means to restore our spiritual roots. Out of these we might once more experience the gifts of the Holy Spirit, outlined in the definition above.

And the Spirit of the Lord shall rest upon him, the spirit of wisdom and understanding, the spirit of counsel and might, the spirit of knowledge and the fear of the Lord.

Isaiah 11:2

I will put my Spirit within you, and you shall live.

Ezekiel 37:14

Now we have received not the spirit of the world, but the Spirit which is from God, that we might understand the gifts bestowed on us by God.

1 Corinthians 2:12

Do you not know that you are God's temple and that God's Spirit dwells in you?

1 Corinthians 3:16

Spiritual experience is the supreme reality in man's life: in it the divine is not proven, it is simply shown.

Nicolas Berdyaev, *Christian Existentialism*, selected and translated by Donald A. Lowrie, George Allen and Unwin, 1965, page 39

Holy Spirit... was hardly recognised as distinct from the Word until the Word was uttered in a new fullness of expression, as Christians believe, in the historical Person, Jesus of Nazareth. That fuller objective self-manifestation of the divine called forth a new potency of responsive aspiration to which, as an experienced fact, was given the name Holy Spirit.

William Temple, *Nature, Man and God*, Macmillan and Co., 1934, page 446

From the beginning, the Spirit of God has been understood as God in the midst of men, God present and active in the world, God in his closeness to us as a dynamic reality shaping the lives and histories of men. The Spirit, in this sense, is not something other than God, but God in that manner of the divine Being in which he comes closest, dwells with us, acts upon us.

John Macquarrie, *Paths in Spirituality*, second edition, SCM Press, 1992, page 42

O holy Jesus, all the joys thou givest us in thy birth, all the virtues thou givest us in thy resurrection, all the privileges and triumphs, gifts and places thou givest us in thy ascension, are locked up and sealed in this promise of the coming of the Spirit, kept back and concealed from us till the Holy Spirit unlock the same.

O shed abroad thy Spirit in our hearts, for in that doth the fulfilling of all thy promises consist.

Thomas Traherne, in *Landscapes of Glory*, edited by A.M. Allchin, Darton, Longman and Todd, 1989, page 33

He does not take the place of an absent Christ, or work in His stead; His mission is to bring Christ, to ensure His Presence.

Before Christ had been *with* them; now, through the agency of the Holy Ghost, He is to be *in* them; His Presence and action is central, not on the circumference as before. The descent of the Holy Ghost at Pentecost was a change in the manner of His working, a change which may be described as both an extension and an intensification.

Frank H. Hallock, *The Gifts of the Holy Spirit*, SPCK, 1936, page 7

My own attempt to understand the Holy Spirit has convinced me He is active in precisely those experiences that are very common—experiences of recognition, sudden insight, an influx of awareness when you wake up and become alive to something. It may be another person, or a scientific problem, and suddenly the penny drops. Every time a human being cries 'Ah! I see it now!', that's what I mean by the Holy Spirit.

John V. Taylor, in Gerald Priestland, *Priestland's Progress*, BBC Worldwide, 1982, page 108

It is a comfort to consider that the Holy Ghost did not descend this day (Pentecost) for the apostles only but for all men, so that if we be concentred all in one place, in unity, verity and concord, in one faith and one Church, he shall fill us with his gifts and give us utterance of them in our lives and conversation.

He that loves prayer so fervently that in prayer he feels the vehemence and fire of the Holy Ghost, dwells in an everlasting Whitsunday with God almighty.

Thomas Traherne, in *Landscapes of Glory*, edited by A.M. Allchin, Darton, Longman and Todd, 1989, page 37

I think the point of the Holy Spirit is this: a divine something in them, enabling their response to the divine above and about them. Now it is so today: if I believe in God and Jesus and want to respond to them—there is a divine something enabling me to do so. To put it as simply as possible: where is God? God is above us and around us and everywhere, the world's creator. Where is God? God is particularly revealed in Jesus, the very image of God. Where is God? God is within me, enabling me to respond to God above me and around me. Why a person? Because God is always personal, not impersonal, so I find myself saying not that there's an *It* within me— but just as there is a *He* to whom I am responding, so there is a He within me enabling me to make that response.

Michael Ramsey, in Gerald Priestland, *Priestland's Progress*, BBC Worldwide, 1982, page 111

The mysteries of life, of love, of truth, run like a deep stream within our own natures, and beneath all the outward surface appearances which we see. It is a deep stream from which comes life and, as we open ourselves to its reality, we sense the mystery of our own being, and know ourselves to be part of a mysterious immensity, a tiny but great part of it. In this awareness of mysterious reality, of ourselves, and of the world, we touch the fringes of the garment of Holy Being which we call God, the source and life of all that is. It is the Spirit of God to whom countless men and women have borne witness by their writings, but above all by their lives, and it is the origin and life force of our lives ...

So the life of the Spirit is seen to be OUR LIFE LIVED IN ACCORD WITH THE SPIRIT OF GOD WHICH IS OUR TRUE END AND HAPPINESS.

Herbert Waddams, *The Life of the Spirit*, The Faith Press, 1969, pages 18 and 21

The outpouring of His Holy Spirit is really the outpouring of His love, surrounding and penetrating your little soul with a peaceful, joyful delight in His creature: tolerant, peaceful, a love full of long-suffering and gentleness, working quietly, able to wait for results, faithful, devoted, without variableness or shadow of turning. Such is the charity of God ...

Love breaks down the barrier that shuts most of us from Heaven. That thought is too much for us really ... Yet it is the central truth of the spiritual life. And that loving, self-yielding to the Eternal Love—that willingness that God shall possess, indwell, fertilize, bring forth fruit of *His* Spirit in us instead of fruits of our spirit—is the secret of all Christian power and Christian peace.

Evelyn Underhill, *The Fruits of the Spirit*, Longmans, Green and Co., 1949, page 3

It was something more than a glorified Christ in the heavens in which they (the Apostles) believed. At the beginning John the Baptist had taught his disciples to expect from the Christ the baptism, not of water only as in his baptism, but of the Spirit. Before His death Jesus had sought to fill His disciples' minds with the expectation of this gift as the chief object of His coming. And that Spirit had come in sensible power upon them some ten days after Jesus had disappeared for the last time from their eyes, and after that first outpouring on the original group of brethren, He had come successively to all who had received baptism, normally through the laying-on of the hands of the apostles so that the reception could be looked back to as an event at a particular moment of their experience. And this Spirit was the Spirit of God, but also and therefore the Spirit of Jesus. Jesus was not to them merely a past example, or a remote Lord, but an inward presence and power. A mere example in past history becomes in experience a feebler and feebler power, all the more if the example is that of a genius, of a more than ordinary man. But the example of Jesus was something much more than a memory. For He who had taught them in the past how to live was alive in the heavenly places, and was working within them by His Spirit, moulding them inwardly in conformity with the pattern He had shown them outwardly.

Charles Gore, *The Philosophy of the Good Life*, John Murray, 1930, page 195

When we pray 'Come, Holy Ghost, our souls inspire', we had better know what we are about. He will not carry us to easy triumphs and gratifying successes; more probably He will set us to some task for God in the full intention that we shall fail, so that others, learning wisdom by our failure, may carry the good cause forward. He may take us through loneliness, desertion by friends, apparent desertion even by God; that was the way Christ went to the Father. He may drive us into the wilderness to be tempted of the devil. He may lead us from the mount of Transfiguration (if He ever lets us climb it) to the hill that is called the Place of a Skull. For if we invoke Him, it must be to help us in doing God's will, not ours. We cannot call upon the

'Creator Spirit, by whose aid
The world's Foundations first were laid'

in order to use omnipotence for the supply of our futile pleasures or the success of our futile plans. If we invoke Him, we must be ready for the glorious pain of being caught by His power out of our petty orbit into the eternal purposes of the Almighty, in whose onward sweep our lives are as a speck of dust. The soul that is filled with the Spirit must have become purged of all pride or love of ease, all self-complacence and self-reliance; but that soul has found the only real dignity, the only lasting joy. Come then, Great Spirit, come. Convict the world; and convict my timid soul.

William Temple, *Readings in St. John's Gospel*, First and Second Series, Macmillan and Co., 1947, page 288

The religion of the Spirit, that autonomous faith which rests upon experience and individual inspiration, has seldom had much of a chance in the world since the Christian revelation, in which it received its full and final credentials. We may call it the Platonic tradition, since the school of Plato ended by being completely dominant in the last age of classical antiquity. We may venture to call it the true heir of the original Gospel, while admitting that no direct Hellenic influence can be traced in our Lord's teaching. We may confidently call it Pauline and Johannine Christianity, though the theology of St. Paul is woven of many strands. We find it explicitly formulated by Clement and Origen, and we may appeal to one side of that strangely divided genius, Augustine. It lives on in the mystics, especially in the German mediaeval school, of which Eckhart is the greatest name. We find it again, with a new and exuberant life, in many of the Renaissance writers, so much so that our subject might as well be called the Renaissance tradition. Our own Renaissance poetry is steeped in Platonic thoughts. Later, during the civil troubles of the seventeenth century, it appears in a very pure and attractive form in the little group of Cambridge Platonists, Whichcote, Smith, Cudworth, and their friends. In the unmystical eighteenth century Jacob Böhme takes captive the manly and robust intellect of William Law, and inspires him to write some of the finest religious treatises in the English language. Meanwhile, the Quakers had the root of the matter in them, but they have only recently discovered their spiritual affinities with Plato. The tradition has never been extinct or we may say more truly that the fire which, in the words of Eunapius, 'still burns on the altars of Plotinus,' has a perennial power of rekindling itself when the conditions are favourable. But the repressive forces of tyranny and bigotry have prevented the religion of the Spirit from bearing its proper fruits. The luck of history, we may say, has hitherto been unfavourable to what I, at least, hold to be the growth of the divine seed. It has either fallen on the rock or by the wayside, or the thorns have grown up with it and choked it. The religion of the Spirit has an intrinsic survival value, which is quite different from the extrinsic survival value of the religion of authority. Authority may for a time diminish the number of dissentients by burning their bodies or their books but 'On ne tue pas des idées par coup de bâton.'

W.R. Inge, *The Platonic Tradition in English Religious Thought*, Longmans, Green and Co., 1926, page 27

HUMANISM

'Humanism'—any system of thought or action which is concerned with merely human interests, or with those of the human race in general.

I was listening to a homespun form of humanism. The speaker was a student in London. He felt the most important thing in life was to be 'a good chap'. According to him 'the good chap' had the following characteristics. He worked hard enough to keep his lecturers happy, but no more. He played some sport though not with any great enthusiasm as this might be an embarrassment to others. He was well informed on football and could talk *ad nauseam* about players and teams. He smoked a few fags, and had a pint or two each day. He was an authority on various brews of beer. Occasionally he would overindulge so he had something of interest to talk about. Yes, he'd tried drugs, but was playing it safe and was now on pot only. 'The good chap' was a great party man and successful in relationships with women. A sense of humour was crucial, with an ability to come out with the odd smutty joke. As regards dress, jeans were essential garb, preferably with a hole or two in them, giving the impression they had not been washed for several weeks. Religion? No chance. 'The good chap' only believed in things he could see, feel and touch, and would claim his viewpoint scientific—and therefore true. If pushed, his main belief would be do to others as you would have them do to you, with the suggestion that if everyone lived this way the world would be all right. This was his particular brand of humanism.

And I applied my mind to seek and to search out by wisdom all that is done under heaven.

Ecclesiastes 1:13

I searched with my mind how to cheer my body with wine—my mind still guiding me with wisdom—and how to lay hold on folly, till I might see what was good for the sons of men to do under heaven during the few days of their life. I made great works; I built houses and planted vineyards for myself; I made myself gardens and parks, and planted in them all kinds of fruit trees. I made myself pools from which to water the forest of growing trees... I also gathered for myself silver and gold and the treasures of kings and provinces; I got singers, both men and women, and many concubines, man's delight. So I became great and surpassed all who were before me...

Ecclesiastes 2:3–9

I am speaking in human terms, because of your natural limitations.

Romans 6:19

From now on, therefore, we regard no one from a human point of view; even though we once regarded Christ from a human point of view, we regard him thus no longer. Therefore, if any one is in Christ, he is a new creation; the old has passed away, behold, the new has come.

2 Corinthians 5:16–17

For at least half a century its predominant culture has been what is called Humanism, which consists, roughly speaking, in the acceptance of many Christian standards of life with a rejection or neglect of the only sources of power to attain them.

William Temple, *The Hope of a New World*, SCM Press, 1940, page 64

Humanism is a very old phenomenon which flowered wonderfully in the Greek world, and flowered again in the great scholars and writers of the Renaissance. And it has been flowering again in our own time. Humanism essentially means a great reverence for man, for man's dignity, and man's wonderful potentialities.

What is today called scientific humanism is a particular version of humanism, dominated by a faith in the sciences as able to make man competent to solve the problems of human existence, and capable of leading a happy and moral life in society. Now we, as Christians, are bound to criticise the theses of scientific humanism, because, on the one hand, it does not diagnose properly the depth of man's trouble—that man as a creature is estranged from God his Creator—nor does it look high enough to the real heights of man's potentiality, not just to be a competent, moral, intelligent citizen of this world, but to be a saint reigning with Christ in glory in heaven, with the wonderful glow of humility, and the beauty of saintliness. So we say that humanism does not see deep enough into the pit of man's predicament, nor high enough into the potentialities of man's glory.

Michael Ramsey, *Through the Year with Michael Ramsey*, edited by Margaret Duggan, Hodder and Stoughton, 1975, page 138

We are called to create a better world. But we are first of all called to a more immediate and exalted task: that of creating our own lives. In doing this, we act as co-workers with God. We take our place in the great work of mankind, since in effect the creation of our own destiny, in God, is impossible in pure isolation. Each one of us works out his own destiny in inseparable union with all those others with whom God has willed us to live. We share with one another the creative work of living in the world...

This active response, this fidelity to life itself and to God Who gives Himself to us through our daily contacts with the material world, is the first and most essential duty of man.

Christianity does not teach man to attain an inner ideal of divine tranquillity and stoic quiet by abstracting himself from material things. It teaches him to give himself to his brother and to his world in a service of love in which God will manifest his creative power through men on earth.

The centre of Christian humanism is the idea that God is love, not infinite power. Being Love, God has given himself without reservation to man so that He has become man... It is man, in Christ, who has the mission of not only making himself human but of becoming divine by the gift of the Spirit of Love.

Thomas Merton, *Loving and Living*, Sheldon Press, 1979, pages 149 and 177

I refer to the scientific humanist with great respect because as a Christian I share with him a great regard for man, for human dignity, for human worth, and human freedom. I believe that Christians and scientific humanists have much in common in their belief in the dignity of man and the service of mankind. But we part company on this. The scientific humanist believes that if the knowledge of the sciences develops as it should, and if all the sciences, duly developed, are applied to human affairs in the right way, then the human race can be made more progressive, better organised, more comfortable, more happy, and indeed more moral as well. The scientific humanist will reject religion and the religious dimension altogether, as being an unnecessary drag upon the rightful scientific progress which of itself can put the human race to rights. My criticism is this: the evidence seems to show that the human race can become increasingly advanced in the knowledge of the sciences and the application of the sciences to human affairs, but can still go on being proud and selfish and cruel and insensitive. The tragic thing is that in the century in which the sciences have made the most stupendous strides, we have also seen the most terrible reactions in mass hysterical cruelty and selfishness. The scientific humanist's diagnosis does not go deep enough. The trouble with man is not that he is not sufficiently progressive or scientifically enlightened, but that he is too deeply estranged from his Creator, and needs to be reconciled to his Creator in awe and humility—to be cured of his deep pride and selfishness.

Michael Ramsey, *Through the Year with Michael Ramsey*, edited by Margaret Duggan, Hodder and Stoughton, 1975, page 138

The Renaissance began with the affirmation of man's creative individuality; it has ended with its denial. Man without God is no longer man: that is the religious meaning of the internal dialectic of modern history, the history of the grandeur and of the dissipation of humanist illusions. Interiorly divided and drained of his spiritual strength, man becomes the slave of base and unhuman influences; his soul is darkened and alien spirits take possession of him. The elaboration of the humanist religion and the divinization of man and of humanity properly forbodes the end of Humanism. The flowering of the idea of humanity was possible only so long as man has a deep belief in and consciousness of principles above himself, was not altogether cut off from his divine roots. During the Renaissance he still had this belief and consciousness and was therefore not yet completely separated; throughout modern history the European has not totally repudiated his religious basis. It is thanks to that alone that the idea of humanity remained consistent with the spread of individualism and of creative activity. The humanism of Goethe had a religious foundation, he kept his faith in God.

The man who has lost God gives himself up to something formless and inhuman, prostrates himself before material necessity.

Nowadays there is none of that 'renaissential' play and inter-play of human powers which gave us Italian painting and Shakespeare and Goethe; instead unhuman forces, spirits unchained from the deep, crush man and becloud his image, beating upon him like waves from every side. It is they, not man, who have been set free. Man found his form and his identity under the action of religious principles and energies; the confusion in which he is losing them cannot be re-ordered by purely human efforts.

Nicolas Berdyaev, *The End of our Time*, translated by Donald Attwater, Sheed and Ward, 1933, page 54

IMAGE OF GOD

'Image of God'—man's original nature, made in the image and
likeness of God, fully worked out in the life of Christ.

In the second chapter of the book of Genesis we read the Lord God formed man of dust from the ground, and breathed in his nostrils the breath of life; and man became a living being. Initially the man of dust was earthy and creaturely, but once the Lord God breathed in his nostrils the breath of life, man had also a divine potential. Meister Eckhart is in no doubt of the enormity of this divine gift. He reckoned when God made man the innermost heart of the Godhead was put into man.

If we wish to see this fully worked out in a life we go to the Gospels, to the person of Jesus Christ. During his life Jesus discovered the innermost heart of the Godhead in himself, and described this in various ways—Father, Holy Spirit, life, light, truth, joy and love. At the same time he accepted the earthy and creaturely side of his nature, bringing about an inner integration, and so was described as 'very God and very Man'. St Paul was one of the first to acknowledge Jesus as the image of the invisible God and recognized the implications of this for us: 'Just as we have borne the image of the man of dust, so shall we also bear the image of the man of heaven.'

He went on to be more specific: 'But we all, with open face beholding as in a glass the glory of the Lord, are changed into the same image from glory to glory, even as by the Spirit of the Lord.' To allow this process to happen in us is to find the secret of life.

Then God said, 'Let us make man in our image, after our likeness...' So God created man in his own image, in the image of God he created him; male and female he created them.
Genesis 1:26–27

Can we find such a man as this, in whom is the Spirit of God?
Genesis 41:38

Just as we have borne the image of the man of dust, we shall also bear the image of the man of heaven.
1 Corinthians 15:49

He is the image of the invisible God, the first-born of all creation; for in him all things were created, in heaven and on earth, visible and invisible, whether thrones or dominions or principalities or authorities—all things were created through him and for him. He is before all things, and in him all things hold together.
Colossians 1:15–17

When God made man the innermost heart of the Godhead was put into man.
Meister Eckhart, in Franz Pfeiffer, *Meister Eckhart*, volume I, translated by C. de B. Evans, John M. Watkins, 1956, page 436

The Difference then of a good and a bad Man does not lie in this, that the one wills that which is good, and the other does not, but solely in this, that the one concurs with the living inspiring Spirit of God within him, and the other resists it, and is and can be *only chargeable* with Evil, because he resists it.
William Law, *The Spirit of Love*, edited by Sidney Spencer, James Clarke and Co., 1969, page 207

I have often said before that there is an agent in the soul, untouched by time and flesh, which proceeds out of the Spirit, and which remains forever in the Spirit and is completely spiritual. In this agent God is perpetually verdant and flowering with all the joy and glory that is in him. Here is joy so hearty, such inconceivably great joy that no one can ever fully tell it ... God glows and burns without ceasing, in all his fullness, sweetness, and rapture.

Meister Eckhart, *Meister Eckhart*, translated by Raymond B. Blakney, Harper and Row, Publishers, 1941, page 209

And now, O Lord, Heaven and Earth are infinitely more valuable than they were before, being all bought with Thy precious blood. And Thou, O Jesus, art a treasure unto me far greater than all those. At what rate or measure shall I esteem thee?

Thou hast restored me again to the friendship of God, to the enjoyment of the World, to the hope of Eternal Glory, to the love of Angels, Cherubims and Men. To the enjoyment and obedience of Thy Holy Laws, which alone are sweeter to me than the honey and the honey-comb, and more precious than thousands of gold and silver. Thou hast restored me above all to the Image of God ... O let Thy love be in me that Thy joy may be fulfilled in me for evermore.

Thomas Traherne, *Centuries*, edited by Bertram Dobell, P.J. and A.E. Dobell, 1950, page 50

You are a principal work, a fragment of God Himself, you have in yourself a part of Him. Why then are you ignorant of your high birth? Why do you not know whence you have come? Will you not remember, when you eat, who you are that eat, and whom you are feeding, and the same in your relations with women? When you take part in society, or training, or conversation, do you not know that it is God you are nourishing and training? You bear God about you ... and know it not. Do you think I speak of some external god of silver or gold? No, you bear Him about within you and are unaware that you are defiling Him with unclean thoughts and foul actions. If an image of God were present, you would not dare to do any of the things you do; yet when God Himself is present within you and sees and hears all things, you are not ashamed of thinking and acting thus: O slow to understand your nature, and estranged from God!

Epictetus, *The Stoic and Epicurean Philosophers*, edited by Witney J. Oates, Random House, 1940, page 295

There is something more in man than is apparent in his ordinary consciousness, something which frames ideals and thoughts, a finer spiritual presence, which makes him dissatisfied with mere earthly pursuits. The one doctrine that has the longest intellectual ancestry is the belief that the ordinary condition of man is not his ultimate being, that he has in him a deeper self, call it breath or ghost, soul or spirit. In each being dwells a light which no power can extinguish, an immortal spirit, benign and tolerant, the silent witness in his heart. The greatest thinkers of the world unite in asking us to know the self. Mencius declares: 'Who knows his own nature knows heaven.' St. Augustine writes: 'I, Lord, went wandering like a strayed sheep, seeking thee with anxious reasoning without, whilst thou wast within me ... I went round the streets and squares of the city of this world seeking thee, and I found thee not, because in vain I sought without for him who was within myself.' We make a detour round the universe to get back to the self. The oldest wisdom in the world tells us that we can consciously unite with the divine while in this body, for this is man really born. If he misses his destiny, Nature is not in a hurry; she will catch him some day and compel him to fulfil her secret purpose. Truth, beauty, peace, power, and wisdom are all attributes of a divine self which awaits our finding.

Sir Sarvepalli Radhakrishnan, *Eastern Religious and Western Thought*, Oxford University Press, 1940, page 25

There is a divine element, an innermost essence in us, in the very structure of the soul, which is the starting-point of all spiritual progress, the mark of man's dignity, the real source of all religious experience, and the eternal basis of the soul's salvation and joy. He names this inward endowment by many names. It is the Word of God, the Power of God, Spirit, Mind of Christ, Divine Activity, Divine Origin, the inward Light, the true Light, the Lamp of the soul. 'The Inward Light ... is nothing else than the Word of God, God Himself, by whom all things were made and by whom all men are enlightened.' It is, in Franck's thought, not a capricious, subjective impulse or vision, and it is not to be discovered in sudden ecstatic experiences nor, on the other hand, is the divine Word, for Franck, something purely objective and transcendent. It is rather a common ground and essence for God and man. It is God in His self-revealing activity; God in

His self-giving grace; God as the immanent ground of all that is permanently real, and at the same time this divine endowment forms the fundamental nature of man's soul—and is the original substance of our being. Consciousness of God and consciousness of self have one fundamental source in this deep where God and man are unsundered. 'No man can see or know himself unless he sees and knows, by the Light and Life that is in him, God the eternally true Light and Life; wherefore nobody can ever know God outside of himself, outside that region where he knows himself in the ground of himself... Man must seek, find, and know God through an interrelation—he must find God in himself and himself in God.' This deep ground of inner reality is in every person, so far as he is a person; it shines forth as a steady illumination in the soul, and, while everything else is transitory, this Word is eternal and has been the moral and spiritual guide of all peoples in all ages.

Rufus M. Jones, *Spiritual Reformers in the 16th and 17th Centuries*, Macmillan and Co., 1914, page 53

INCARNATION

'Incarnation'—embodiment in flesh, especially in human form; living type (of quality); the incarnation of God in Christ.

For sixteen years I have been going to Mürren, a village high up in the Swiss Alps, to take services at the 'English Church' during the Christmas season. One of the main services is Midnight Communion on Christmas Eve. In the short address I usually speak about the mystery of the Incarnation. At one level we are celebrating the historical birth of Jesus at Bethlehem. At another level we are celebrating God's birth into this world and putting on human flesh, in the person of Jesus Christ. The emphasis is on a birth which happened nearly 2,000 years ago. However, Incarnation is not just about an historical birth, but includes a birth at the present time. A way of understanding this comes through some important words of Angelus Silesius:

Christ could be born
a thousand times in Galilee—
But all in vain
until he is born in me.

Incarnation, seen through these words of Angelus Silesius, is also about the birth of God in us today. In fact, some of our popular carols emphasize this fact. Take, for instance, *O Little Town of Bethlehem*, and note a line from the final verse: '*Be born in us today*'. Christmas, and the Incarnation is essentially about rebirth, about the birth of Jesus Christ in us today, to enrich and transform our lives—something to rejoice about.

In the beginning was the Word, and the Word was with God, and the Word was God... And the Word became flesh and dwelt among us, full of grace and truth.

John 1:1, 14

All things have been delivered to me by my Father.

Matthew 11:27

He who has seen me has seen the Father.

John 14:9

If a man loves me, he will keep my word, and my Father will love him, and we will come to him and make our home with him.

John 14:23

The Word of God, Jesus Christ our Lord: Who for His immense love's sake was made that which we are, in order that He might perfect us to be what He is.

S. Irenaeus, *Five Books of S. Irenaeus Against Heresies*, translated by the Rev. John Keble, James Parker and Co., 1872, page 449

Christianity does mean getting down to actual ordinary life as the medium of the Incarnation, doesn't it, and our lessons in that get sterner, not more elegant as time goes on?

Evelyn Underhill, *The Letters of Evelyn Underhill*, edited by Charles Williams, Longmans, Green and Co., 1947, page 259

Christ could be born
a thousand times in Galilee—
but all vain
until He is born in me.

Angelus Silesius, *The Book of Angelus Silesius*, translated, drawn, and handwritten by Frederick Franck, Wildwood House, 1976, page 107

At this time... the renewal of Christianity depends solely on accepting the Incarnation in all its fulness. For without the realization of God's love for the world, we can love neither the world nor God.

Alan W. Watts, *Behold the Spirit*, John Murray, 1947, page 244

As it is, there is one road, and one only, well secured against all possibility of going astray and this road is provided by one who is himself both God and man. As God, he is the goal; as man, he is the way.

St. Augustine, *City of God*, translated by Henry Bettenson, edited by David Knowles, Penguin Books, 1972, page 431

'Man is the true Shekinah'—the visible presence, that is to say, of the divine. We are far too apt to limit and mechanize the great doctrine of the Incarnation which forms the centre of the Christian faith. Whatever it may mean, it means at least this—that in the conditions of the highest human life we have access, as nowhere else, to the inmost nature of the divine.

A.S. Pringle-Pattison, *The Idea of God*, Oxford University Press, 1920, page 157

Once the Creator Spirit became involved in matter and in developing life, once the spirit of man was created in the likeness of the divine Spirit, it would seem natural that he should become fully incarnate in a person, not only to manifest the divine life but also to be the prototype of human life. The union of the divine and human in Jesus speaks of the hope of man sharing in the divine life.

George Appleton, *Journey for a Soul*, William Collins Sons and Co., 1976, page 135

The Incarnation was not an isolated event, wonderful though it would have been if it was that and nothing more. It was the beginning of something new, perhaps rather the manifestation of something which had never been recognized, but which could now happen in a fully conscious and effective way. The Spirit of God, incarnate fully and supremely in Jesus, wishes to indwell every man, not only as an immanent force, but as an invited, personal guest.

George Appleton, *Journey for a Soul*, William Collins Sons and Co., 1976, page 138

For a Person came, and lived and loved, and did and taught, and died and rose again, and lives on by His Power and His Spirit for ever within us and amongst us, so unspeakably rich and yet so simple, so sublime and yet so homely, so divinely above us precisely in being so divinely near,—that His character and teaching require, for an ever fuller yet never complete understanding, the varying study, and different experiments and applications, embodiments and unrollings of all the races and civilizations, of all the individual and corporate, the simultaneous and successive experiences of the human race to the end of time.

Friedrich von Hügel, *The Mystical Element of Religion*, volume I, J.M. Dent and Co., 1909, page 26

There is one secret, the greatest of all—a secret which no previous religion dared, even in enigma, to allege fully—which is stated with the utmost distinctness by Our Lord and the Church though this very distinctness seems to act as a thick veil, hiding the disc of the revelation as that of the Sun is hidden by its rays, and causing the eyes of men to avert themselves habitually from that one centre of all seeing. I mean the doctrine of the Incarnation, regarded not as an historical event which occurred two thousand years ago, but as an event which is renewed in the body of every one who is in the way to the fulfilment of his original destiny.

Coventry Patmore, 'Homo' in *The Rod, The Root, and the Flower*, The Grey Walls Press, 1950, page 124

So when God became incarnate as man his meaningfulness as God came into its own. The self-giving, the becoming-man, the suffering love were not additions to the divine experience or mere incidents in the divine history. In becoming man, God revealed the meaning of what it is to be God... The glory is seen in the becoming-man because it is a glory 'beyond' and eternal.

So, too, in Jesus the human race finds its own true meaning. Men rejected Jesus because they preferred the glory of man to the glory of God, as St John draws out in his gospel...

Man's true glory is the reflection in him of the divine glory, the self-giving love seen in Jesus.

Thus it is in Jesus that we see man becoming his true self, in that giving away of self which happens when man is possessed by God. The meaning of what it is to be man appears when man is the place where deity fulfils himself, and the glory of the one is the glory of the other. The phrase 'the Man for others' is an illuminating one, but it is not the whole story, for God created man not only for others but for God.

Michael Ramsey, *God, Christ and the World*, SCM Press, 1969, page 100

The Incarnation is a proclamation that 'the All-great is the All-loving too'—a doctrine which few, I think, accept who do not believe in the Incarnation of the Son of God in Christ.

And if, with the Church of the Creeds and Fathers, we accept something like the Logos-doctrine already held by St. Paul and briefly summarised by St. John, we have the most inspiring thought that the laws of the universe, in their deepest meaning, are the expression of the character of the creating and sustaining Word who became flesh and tabernacled among us in the person of Jesus of Nazareth. I need not dwell on the consecration of the whole of nature which follows from this belief; on the final repudiation of that unfortunate dualism between the natural and supernatural which has introduced chaos into both spheres, natural and spiritual alike; on the sanction which it gives to the pursuits of poetry, art, and science, as being each, in their different ways, a priestly and prophetic office, revealing to us the God whom we know in our hearts as the Good, under His other attributes of the True and the Beautiful. The world is good, for God the Word made it but it can be made better, for He came to redeem it. And His redeeming, transforming work did not come to an end when He left the earth; we are living under the dispensation which then began, a dispensation of progressive enlightenment and steady realisation of a great purpose—the achievement of a theophany in redeemed humanity itself.

W.R. Inge, *Speculum Animae*, Longmans, Green and Co., 1911, page 19

The Incarnation was to him the centre of all history, the blossoming of Humanity. The Life which followed the Incarnation was the explanation of the life of God, and the only solution of the problem of the life of man. He did not speak much of loving Christ; his love was fitly mingled with that veneration which makes love perfect; his voice was solemn, and he paused before he spoke His name in common talk; for what that Name meant had become the central thought of his intellect, and the deep realisation of his spirit. He had spent a world of study, of reverent meditation, of adoring contemplation on the gospel history. Nothing comes forward more vividly in his letters than the way in which he had entered into the human life of Christ. To that everything is referred—by that everything is explained. The gossip of a drawing-room, the tendencies of the time, the religious questions of the day, especially the Sabbath question, the loneliness and the difficulties of his work, were not so much argued upon or combated, as at once and instinctively brought to the test of a Life which was lived out eighteen centuries ago, but which went everywhere with him. Out of this intuitive reception of Christ, and from this ceaseless silence of meditation which makes the blessedness of great love, there grew up in him a deep comprehension of the whole, as well as a minute sympathy with all the delicate details of the character of Christ. Day by day, with passionate imitation, he followed his Master, musing on every action, revolving in thought the interdependence of all that Christ had said or done, weaving into the fibres of his heart the principles of the Life he worshipped, till he had received into his being the very impression and image of that unique Personality. His very doctrines were the Life of Christ expressed in words. The Incarnation, Atonement, and Resurrection of Christ were not dogmas to him. In himself he was daily realising them. They were in him a life, a power, a light. This was his Christian consciousness.

Stopford A. Brooke, said of Frederick W. Robertson, in, *Life and Letters of Frederick W. Robertson*, volume II, edited by Stopford A. Brooke, Smith, Elder and Co, 1865, page 168

INNER LIFE

'Inner Life'—interior, internal, man's soul or mind, spirit.

When I was an undergraduate at Balliol, and had taken a step of faith, I began to keep a 'quiet time' each day. In the evening, just before going to bed, I would read a passage of scripture, and think it through with the aid of a pen and paper. When I went to Wycliffe Hall (a theological college in Oxford) we had an official 'quiet time' after the early morning service, before breakfast. In recent months there had been a development in my inner life. I had been collecting short phrases from the Bible and elsewhere, and had stored these away in a card index system. I used these phrases for reflection. If the weather was fine, I would leave my room and go for a walk in the University Parks nearby, armed with one of these cards. I would take a phrase, such as 'Be still, and know that I am God', and spend a few minutes mulling over this phrase, so that it became a part of my inner life. I would then take another phrase and repeat the process until it was time for breakfast.

In retrospect this practice was invaluable and formed the basis of my inner life. Later on I collected material on a larger scale, and this eventually led to the publication of *Visions of Faith*. The contents of this book are mainly about the inner life. With the practice of reflection, *Visions of Faith* can be used to foster the 'quiet time' and so promote the growth of the inner life—soul, mind, or spirit.

Behold, thou desirest truth in the inward being; therefore teach me wisdom in my secret heart.

Psalm 51:6

You shall eat, but not be satisfied, and there shall be hunger in your inward parts.

Micah 6:14

So we do not lose heart. Though our outer nature is wasting away, our inner nature is being renewed every day.

2 Corinthians 4:16

... that according to the riches of his glory he may grant you to be strengthened with might through his Spirit in the inner man, and that Christ may dwell in your hearts through faith.

Ephesians 3:16

I within did flow
With Seas of Life, like Wine.

Thomas Traherne, 'Wonder', in *The Poetical Works of Thomas Traherne*, edited by Gladys I. Wade, P.J. & A.E. Dobell, 1932, page 5

Justice is like the kingdom of God—it is not without us as a fact, it is within us as a great yearning.

George Eliot, *Romola*, T. Nelson and Sons, 1965, page 543

The important matter was the increase of this inward life, the silent growth of this kingdom of God in the hearts of men, the spread of this invisible Church.

Rufus M. Jones, *Spiritual Reformers in the 16th and 17th Centuries*, Macmillan and Co., 1914, page 85

We must revolutionise this system of life, that is based on *outside* things, money, property, and establish a system of life which is based on *inside* things.

D.H. Lawrence, *The Letters of D.H. Lawrence*, volume II, edited by George T. Zytaruk & James T. Boulton, Cambridge University Press, 1981, page 280

God does not die on the day when we cease to believe in a personal deity, but we die on the day when our lives cease to be illumined by the steady radiance, renewed daily, of a wonder, the source of which is beyond all reason.

Dag Hammarskjöld, *Markings*, translated by Leif Sjöberg and W.H. Auden, Faber and Faber, 1964, page 64

The life of Jesus was a calm. It was a life of marvellous composure. The storms were all about it, tumult and tempest, tempest and tumult, waves breaking over Him all the time... But the inner life was as a sea of glass. It was a life of perfect composure... the great calm is there.

Henry Drummond, *The Greatest Thing in the World*, William Collins Sons and Co., 1978, page 169

The indwelling of God is this—to have God ever in mind, established within us. We thus become temples of God whenever our recollection of Him is not interrupted by earthly thoughts, nor the mind disturbed by unexpected passions, but escaping all these, the lover of God withdraws to Him.

St. Basil the Great, in Margaret Smith, *Studies in Early Mysticism in the Near and Middle East*, Sheldon Press, 1931, page 59

Such practice of inward orientation, of inward worship and listening, is no mere counsel for special religious groups, for small religious orders, for special 'interior souls,' for monks retired in cloisters. This practice is the heart of religion. It is the secret, I am persuaded, of the inner life of the Master of Galilee. He expected this secret to be freshly discovered in everyone who would be his follower.

Thomas Kelly, *A Testament of Devotion*, Hodder and Stoughton, 1943, page 31

He that thus seeks shall find; he shall live in truth, and that shall live in him; it shall be like a stream of living waters issuing out of his own soul; he shall drink of the waters of his own cistern, and be satisfied; he shall every morning find this heavenly manna lying upon the top of his own soul, and be fed with it to eternal life; he will find satisfaction within, feeling himself in conjunction with truth, though all the world should dispute against him.

John Smith the Platonist, *Select Discourses*, Cambridge at the University Press, 1859, page 13

For when the soul reaches the perfection of the Spirit, being completely purified from passion, and is joined and commingled with the Holy Spirit by that secret communion, and being united with the Spirit is deemed worthy to become spirit itself, then it becomes all light, all eye, all spirit, all joy, all rest, all exultation, all heart-felt love, all goodness and loving kindness. Such souls as these are strengthened within themselves by the virtues of the Spirit's power, for ever, being blameless within, and spotless and pure.

St. Macarius of Egypt, in Margaret Smith, *Studies in Early Mysticism in the Near and Middle East*, Sheldon Press, 1931, page 65

The man who lives from the deep centre discovers a new dynamic. He is worked through, in a manner wholly different from 'his previous experience'...

The energy coming from 'the deep centre' is not subject to the law of opposites. It is quiet. This is not to say that the man through whom the energy flows lives a life of placid ease. He has to strive and agonize at the conscious level, more so than before, perhaps; but he does not agonize for nothing. New and creative springs of action arise in the depths; and in the midst of his striving the man finds himself serving as a channel by which they find their way into life.

P.W. Martin, *Experiment in Depth*, Routledge and Kegan Paul, 1967, page 225

The divine mystery of this infinite God is revealed and discovered in the hearts of the sons of men, whom He hath chosen: and He hath given us, to enjoy and possess in us a measure of that fulness that is in Himself, even a measure of the same Love and Life, of the same Mercy and Power, and of the same divine Nature... These things ye know, if ye be born from above, and if the immortal birth live in you, and you be constant in the faith, then are you heirs through it, of the everlasting inheritance of eternal life... and all are yours, because you are Christ's, and he is God's, and you have the Father and the Son.

Edward Burroughs, *The Memorable Works of a Son of Thunder and Consolation,* 1672, page 698

The supposed 'inner life' may actually be nothing but a brave and absurd attempt to evade reality altogether. Under the pretext that what is 'within' is in fact real, spiritual, supernatural, etc., one cultivates neglect and contempt for the 'external' as worldly, sensual, material and opposed to grace. This is bad theology and bad asceticism. In fact it is bad in every respect, because instead of accepting reality as it is, we reject it in order to explore some perfect realm of abstract ideals which in fact is no reality at all. Very often, the inertia and repugnance which characterize the so-called 'spiritual life' of many Christians could perhaps be cured by a simple respect for the concrete realities of every-day life, for nature, for the body, for one's work, one's friends, one's surroundings, etc. A false supernaturalism which imagines that 'the supernatural' is a kind of Platonic realm of abstract essences totally apart from and opposed to the concrete world of nature, offers no real support to a genuine life of meditation and prayer. Meditation has no point and no reality unless it is firmly rooted in *life*.

Thomas Merton, *Contemplative Prayer,* Darton, Longman and Todd, 1973, page 45

God dwells secretly in all souls and is hidden in their substance for, were this not so, they would be unable to exist. But there is a difference between these two manners of dwelling, and a great one. For in some He dwells alone, and in others He dwells not alone; in some He dwells contented and in others He dwells displeased; in some He dwells as in His house, ordering it and ruling everything, while in others He dwells as a stranger in the house of another where He is not allowed to do anything or to give any commands. Where He dwells with the greatest content and most completely alone is in the soul wherein dwell fewest desires and pleasures of its own; here He is in His own house and rules and governs it. And the more completely alone does He dwell in the soul, the more secretly He dwells; and thus in this soul wherein dwells no desire, neither any other image or form or affection of aught that is created, the Beloved dwells most secretly, with more intimate, more interior and closer embrace, according as the soul, as we say, is the more purely and completely withdrawn from all save God.

St. John of the Cross, *Living Flame of Love,* translated and edited by E. Allison Peers, Image Books, Doubleday Company, 1972, page 269

If the prophets did so, and if Jesus did so, we too must go out into the desert from time to time.

It is not a question of transporting oneself there physically. For many of us that could be a luxury. Rather, it implies creating a desert space in one's own life. And to create a desert means to seek solitude, to withdraw from men and things, one of the undisputed principles of mental health.

To create a desert means learning to be self-sufficient, learning to remain undisturbed with one's own thoughts, one's own prayer, one's own destiny.

It means shutting oneself up in one's room, remaining alone in an empty church, setting up a small oratory for oneself in an attic or at the end of a passage in which to localize one's personal contact with God, to draw breath, to recover one's inner peace. It means occasionally devoting a whole day to prayer, it means going off into the loneliness of the mountains, or getting up alone in the night to pray.

When all is said and done, creating a desert means nothing more than obeying God. Because there is a commandment—arguably the most forgotten of all, especially by the 'committed', by militants, by priests, and even bishops—which requires us to interrupt our work, to put aside our daily tasks and seek the refreshing stillness of contemplation.

Carlo Carretto, *In Search of the Beyond,* translated by Sarah Fawcett, Darton, Longman and Todd, 1975, page 18

INTERCESSION

'Intercession'—interceding, especially by prayer.

I was on holiday in Sussex during a summer vacation, staying in a bungalow a friend had lent me. It was mid-afternoon and I went out to sit in the garden. The weather was warm and sunny, and I quietly closed my eyes and thought about the academic year that had just ended. Before long an unhappy memory came to mind and disturbed the peace of the afternoon. Several months previously a student had wilfully disobeyed a house rule, and this still rankled with me. I knew the student in question was now in Israel, so decided to pray about this situation which was still troubling me.

Imagine my surprise several days later to receive a letter out of the blue—from Israel. This had been forwarded to me from London. The letter contained an acknowledgement of the wrong committed, along with an apology. When I examined the original postmark, I discovered the letter had been sent on the day I was out in the garden. Coincidence, or the result of intercession?

I have a theory about intercession which is yet another consequence of the Genesis story of the creation of man. After God fashioned and shaped man in his own image and likeness, he breathed into man and man became a living being. This means we all have a potential of the 'divine' inside us. When this becomes a living reality, and we intercede, the 'divine' in us makes contact with the 'divine' in the other, and then 'things happen'. Several quotations in this section are supportive of this view.

The Lord bless you and keep you: The Lord make his face to shine upon you, and be gracious to you: The Lord lift up his countenance upon you, and give you peace.

Numbers 6:24–26

Moreover as for me, far be it from me that I should sin against the Lord by ceasing to pray for you.

1 Samuel 12:23

Again I say to you, if two of you agree on earth about anything they ask, it will be done for them by my Father in heaven. For where two or three are gathered in my name, there am I in the midst of them.

Matthew 18:19–20

Likewise the Spirit helps us in our weakness; for we do not know how to pray as we ought, but the Spirit himself intercedes for us with sighs too deep for words. And he who searches the hearts of men knows what is the mind of the Spirit, because the Spirit intercedes for the saints according to the will of God.

Romans 8:26–27

Why has our sincere prayer for each other such great power over others? Because of the fact that by cleaving to God during prayer I become one spirit with Him, and unite with myself, by faith and love, those for whom I pray; for the Holy Ghost acting in me also acts at the same time in them, for He accomplishes all things. 'We, being many, are one bread, one body.' 'There is one body and one Spirit.'

John of Cronstadt, in, *A Treasury of Russian Spirituality*, edited by G.P. Fedotov, Sheed and Ward, 1977, page 362

In intercession as a whole we have the simplest example provided by the general religious life, of a vast principle which is yet largely unexplored by us. It is the principle, that man's emergent will and energy can join itself to, and work with, the supernatural forces for the accomplishment of the work of God: sometimes for this purpose even entering into successful conflict with the energies of the 'natural world'.

Evelyn Underhill, *Man and the Supernatural*, Methuen and Co., 1927, page 257

If thou shouldst never see my face again,
Pray for my soul. More things are wrought by prayer
Than this world dreams of. Wherefore, let thy voice
Rise like a fountain for me night and day.
For what are men better than sheep or goats
That nourish a blind life within the brain,
If, knowing God, they lift not hands of prayer
Both for themselves and those who call them friend?
For so the whole round earth is every way
Bound by gold chains about the feet of God.

Alfred, Lord Tennyson, 'The Passing of Arthur' from *The Idylls of the Kings*, in *The Poems of Tennyson*, edited by
Christopher Ricks, Longmans, Green and Co., 1969, page 1753

If a nun withdraws from the world's activities it is only that she may live more intensely at its
heart; and the joys and hopes, the griefs and anxieties of the men and women of the age are
hers.

By the gift of herself to Christ and his growing dominion over her, her sensibilities are
refined, and her womanly qualities of compassion, concern for others and self-sacrificing love
are immeasurably increased.

Uprooted, free, she must, with Mary the Mother of the Lord and his most perfect disciple,
ponder in her heart God's revelation so that the torch of true wisdom, which is the insight of
love, may burn brightly on the earth.

Her vocation is to intercede for mankind not merely by word but by her very being.

Striving to live surrendered and exposed to God she is purified by him, and in profound
impoverishment learns experimentally that 'none is good but God alone' and 'without me you
can do nothing'.

Ruth Burrows, in *The Watchful Heart*, edited by Elizabeth Ruth Obbard, Darton, Longman and Todd, 1988, page 21

The fact that we are present in a situation alters it profoundly because God is then present with
us through our faith. Wherever we are, at home with our family, with friends when a quarrel is
about to begin, at work or even simply in the underground, the street, the train, we can recollect
ourselves and say, 'Lord, I believe in you, come and be among us'. And by this act of faith, in a
contemplative prayer which does not ask to see, we can intercede with God who has promised
his presence when we ask for it. Sometimes we have no words, sometimes we do not know how
to act wisely, but we can always ask God to come and be present. And we shall see how often the
atmosphere changes, quarrels stop, peace comes. This is not a minor mode of intercession,
although it is less spectacular than a great sacrifice. We see in it again how contemplation and
action are inseparable, that christian action is impossible without contemplation. We see also
how such contemplation is not a vision of God alone, but a deep vision of everything enabling
us to see its eternal meaning. Contemplation is a vision not of God alone, but of the world in
God.

Anthony Bloom and George LeFebvre, *Courage to Pray*, translated by Dinah Livingstone, Darton, Longman and Todd,
1973, page 56

Concerning intercession: the Church is called to be a community which speaks to the world in
God's name and speaks to God from the middle of the world's darkness and frustration.

What is called the intercession of Jesus means his ceaseless presence with the Father. He is
with the Father not as begging the Father to be gracious, for from the Father graciousness ever
flows.

To approach the Father through Jesus Christ the intercessor is to approach in awareness of
the cost of our redemption by a sacrifice made once for all and a victory once accomplished, a
sacrifice and victory which are both past history and ever present realities. It is this which both
enables and characterizes our response to God through Jesus Christ.

To intercede is to bear others on the heart in God's presence. Our own wantings have their
place, for it is clear from the teaching of Jesus that God wants us to want and to tell him of our
wants. When however we do this 'in the name of Jesus' we learn to bend our wantings to our

glimpses of the divine will. Intercession thus becomes not the bombardment of God with requests so much as the bringing of our desires within the stream of God's own compassion.

Michael Ramsey, *Be Still and Know*, William Collins Sons and Co.., Fount Paperbacks in association with Faith Press, 1982, pages 13, 54 and 74

The first step in intercession is to make a definite 'act' of union with this stream of God's love and power, which is flowing ceaselessly out of His heart, and back to Him again...

Making a conscious effort to unite our wills and hearts with the ever-flowing river of the love of God will give us a restful energy. As we realize that the love of God is flowing through us and using us as it passes, all merely natural strain will disappear. If suffering comes to us in our time of intercession, we must accept it, and still remain tranquilly surrendered to God for His purpose. If we experience difficulty in 'getting going', it would be well to search our hearts to see whether after all we are praying that God will bless *our* efforts for His glory, rather than seeking to be united with *His* will. 'The greatest works wrought by prayer have been accomplished, not by human effort but by human trust in God's effort.' In prayer of this kind we are united with the very life of God, sharing in His work.

'It is the unseen, unknown part of intercession which makes our part both possible and important. It is the wind of the Holy Ghost blowing through us, it is the tide of God's providence, it is the current of the divine desire which really accomplish the work of intercession and yet the human agent is essential for the accomplishment of the activity. Intercession is the expression of God's love and desire which He has deigned to share with man, and in which He uses man.'...

The essence and heart of intercession is self-offering. The deeper our surrender to God, the more true and powerful will be our intercession. Intercession is indeed a basic principle of human living: it expresses that corporate sense of community which is the real nature of human life and it expresses that instinct to give to the point of sacrifice which is one of the deepest elements in our nature, fulfilled once for all by Christ on the Cross... Thus intercession covers the whole world: all the sins and cruelties and miseries of men; all the horrors of war; the sighing of prisoners and captives; the sufferings of the oppressed and the outcast; the despair of those who are far from God: 'Christian intercession is the completion and expression of self-giving.' We offer our poor imperfect love to God to be a channel of His perfect and redeeming love. We offer ourselves to be a way through which God will reach, and save and bless the whole world.

Olive Wyon, *The School of Prayer*, SCM Press, 1943, page 115

JESUS CHRIST

'Jesus Christ'—the name Jesus refers to the person Jesus of Nazareth
as known from historical research; Christ refers to the 'Messiah', or
'Lord's anointed' of Jewish prophecy, now applied to Jesus as
fulfilling this prophecy; image or picture of Jesus.

Jesus Christ is important to me because he worked out in his person what is meant by man being made in the image and likeness of God. As he went through life he discovered the presence of the Father in himself. At the height of his ministry he was able to say to his disciples: 'He who has seen me has seen the Father... Do you not believe that I am in the Father and the Father in me?' He also discovered attributes of the Father in himself, such as light, leading him to claim: 'I am the light of the world, he who follows me will not walk in darkness, but will have the light of life.' Another attribute was joy, drawing out the further claim: 'These things have I spoken to you, that my joy may be in you, and that your joy may be full.'

In the Epistles, the Apostle Paul wrote not only 'of Christ, in whom are hid all the treasures of wisdom and knowledge,' but also acknowledged him to be 'the image of the invisible God'. In a purple passage he points out 'in him the whole fulness of deity dwells bodily', and states what this means for us 'and you have come to fulness of life in him'. I like J.S. Whale's conclusion; the man Christ Jesus has the decisive place in man's ageless relationship with God. He is what God means by 'Man'. He is what man means by 'God'.

'If you have known me, you would have known my Father also; henceforth you know him and have seen him.' Philip said to him, 'Lord, show us the Father, and we shall be satisfied.' Jesus said to him, 'Have I been with you so long, and yet you do not know me, Philip? He who has seen me has seen the Father; how can you say, "Show us the Father"? Do you not believe that I am in the Father and the Father in me? The words that I say to you I do not speak on my own authority; but the Father who dwells in me does his works. Believe me that I am in the Father and the Father in me; or else believe me for the sake of the works themselves.'

John 14:7–11

Therefore God has highly exalted him and bestowed on him the name which is above every name, that at the name of Jesus every knee should bow, in heaven and on earth and under the earth, and every tongue confess that Jesus Christ is Lord, to the glory of God the Father.

Philippians 2:9–11

For in him the whole fulness of deity dwells bodily, and you have come to fulness of life in him, who is the head of all rule and authority.

Colossians 2:9

Jesus Christ is the same yesterday and today and for ever.

Hebrews 13:8

As Man alone, Jesus could not have saved us; as God alone, he would not; Incarnate, he could and did.

Malcolm Muggeridge, *Jesus, The Man Who Lives*, William Collins Sons and Co., 1981, page 31

He does not say 'No man knoweth God save the Son.' That would be to deny the truth of the Old Testament revelation. What He does say is that He alone has a deeper secret, the essential Fatherhood of the Sovereign Power.

D.S. Cairns, *The Riddle of the World*, SCM Press, 1937, page 321

Jesus astonishes and overpowers sensual people. They cannot unite him to history, or reconcile him with themselves. As they come to revere their intuitions and aspire to live holily, their own piety explains every fact, every word.

Ralph Waldo Emerson, 'History', in *Essays*, Bernhard Tauchnitz, 1915, page 24

When criticism has done its worst, the words and acts of Our Lord which remain are *not* those of 'a good and heroic man,' but of one deliberately claiming unique authority and insight, and conscious of a unique destiny.

Evelyn Underhill, *The Letters of Evelyn Underhill*, edited by Charles Williams, Longmans, Green and Co., 1947, page 217

If we refuse the invitation of Christ, some day our greatest pain will lie, not in the things we suffer, but in the realization of the precious things we have missed, and of which we have cheated ourselves.

William Barclay, *The Gospel of Matthew*, volume II, The Saint Andrew Press, 1975, page 296

If you accept that Jesus is the revelation and manifestation of the Father, then you are a follower of Christ and so a Christian. If you move from that to asking in what sense is Christ God, then I would think you have to come in the end to making that act of faith which is recorded of St. Thomas the Doubtful: 'My Lord and my God.'

Basil Hume, in Gerald Priestland, *Priestland's Progress*, BBC Worldwide, 1982, page 41

Christ was the Son of God. But remember in what sense He ever used this name—Son of God because Son of Man. He claims Sonship in virtue of His Humanity. Now, in the whole previous revelation through the Prophets, &c. one thing was implied—only through man can God be known; only through a perfect man, perfectly revealed. Hence He came, 'the brightness of His Father's Glory, the *express image* of His person.' Christ then must be loved as Son of Man before He can be adored as Son of God. In personal love and adoration of Christ the Christian religion consists, not in correct morality, or in correct doctrines, but in a homage to the King.

F.W. Robertson, in *Life and Letters of Frederick W. Robertson*, volume II, edited by Stopford A. Brooke, Smith, Elder and Co., 1865, page 169

In the days of His earthly ministry, only those could speak to Him who came where He was. If He was in Galilee, men could not find Him in Jerusalem; if He was in Jerusalem, men could not find Him in Galilee. But His Ascension means that He is perfectly united with God; we are with Him wherever we are present to God; and that is everywhere and always. Because He is 'in Heaven' He is everywhere on earth; because He is ascended, He is here now. Our devotion is not to hold us by the empty tomb; it must lift up our hearts to heaven so that we too 'in heart and mind thither ascend and with Him continually dwell'; it must also send us forth into the world to do His will; and these are not two things, but one.

William Temple, *Readings in St. John's Gospel*, First and Second Series, Macmillan and Co., 1947, page 382

That is the secret after all—to get to know and love Christ through love for *all* His brothers and sisters, and not to expect to know Christ first and then begin to think of them. St. Francis learnt first how to love everybody and everything for Christ's sake, before he came really to know Christ Himself... I can see more, in the people in church with me, to put me in a right frame for Communion than I can see in all the little 'aids to devotion' given me at my confirmation... In every person we meet, in whom we see something to love, we are seeing something of Christ. For what we recognize as Christ-like in them is due to the Holy Spirit in them, and the power to recognize it is the Holy Spirit in ourselves. God is Love, and His Spirit is the power to love and attract love. This changes one's whole outlook on life, and then we have a glimpse of heaven.

Edward Wilson, in George Seaver, *The Faith of Edward Wilson*, John Murray, 1949, page 35

Anyone who ventures to look the historical Jesus straight in the face and to listen for what He may have to teach him in His powerful sayings, soon ceases to ask what this strange-seeming Jesus can still be to him. He learns to know Him as One who claims authority over him.

The true understanding of Jesus is the understanding of will acting on will. The true relation to Him is to be taken possession of by Him. Christian piety of any and every sort is valuable only so far as it means the surrender of our will to Him.

Jesus does not require of men to-day that they be able to grasp either in speech or in thought Who He is. He did not think it necessary to give those who actually heard His sayings any insight into the secret of His personality, or to disclose to them the fact that He was that descendant of David who was one day to be revealed as the Messiah. The one thing He did require of them was that they should actively and passively prove themselves men who had been compelled by Him to rise from being as the world to being other than the world, and thereby partakers of His peace.

Albert Schweitzer, in George Seaver, *Albert Schweitzer: Christian Revolutionary*, James Clarke and Co., 1944, page 18

He is always seeking *through* the historical Christ, to find the Eternal Christ—the ever-living, ever-present, personal Self Revelation of God . . . 'I esteem Christ the Word of God above all else, for without Him there is no salvation, and without Him no one can enjoy God.' 'Christ . . . has been called the Image, the Character, the Expression of God, yes, the Glory and Effulgence of His Splendour, the very Impression of His Substance, so that in Him God Himself is seen and heard and known. For it is God Himself whom we see and hear and perceive in Christ. In Him God becomes visible and His nature is revealed. Everything that God is, or knows, or wills or possesses, or can do, is incarnated in Christ and put before our eyes. Everything that can be said of God can as truly be said of Christ.'

But this Christ, who is the very Nature and Character of God made visible and vocal, is, as we have seen, not limited to the historical Person who lived in Galilee and Judea. He is an eternal Logos, a living Word, coming to expression, in some degree, in all times and lands, revealing His Light through the dim lantern of many human lives—a Christ reborn in many souls, raised again in many victorious lives, and endlessly spreading His Kingdom through the ever-widening membership of the invisible Church.

Rufus M. Jones, *Spiritual Reformers in the 16th and 17th Centuries*, Macmillan and Co., 1914, page 61

Unless we know Christ experimentally so that 'He lives within us spiritually, and so that all which is known of Him in the Letter and Historically is truly done and acted in our souls—until we experimentally verify all we read of Him—the Gospel is a mere tale to us.' It is not saving knowledge to know that Christ was born in Bethlehem but to know that He is born in us. It is vastly more important to know experimentally that we are crucified with Christ than to know historically that He died in Jerusalem many years ago, and to feel Jesus Christ risen again within you is far more operative than to have 'a notional knowledge' that He rose on the third day. 'When thou begins to find and know not merely that He was conceived in the womb of a virgin, but that *thou* art that virgin and that He is more truly and spiritually, and yet as really, conceived in thy heart so that thou feelest the Babe beginning to be conceived in thee by the power of the Holy Ghost and the Most High overshadowing thee; when thou feelest Jesus Christ stirring to be born and brought forth in thee; when thou beginnest to see and feel all those mighty, powerful actions done in thee which thou readest that He did in the flesh—here is a Christ indeed, a real Christ who will do thee some good.'

Rufus M. Jones, *Spiritual Reformers in the 16th and 17th Centuries*, Macmillan and Co., 1914, page 244

First of all, Jesus Christ was a Man, in the full and psychological sense, sharing truly and fully in the conditions of our empirical humanity. The fact which confronts us in the New Testament in all the wonder of its perfection is an actual human life, which was at the same time true human life. He was no phantom, archangel or demi-god . . . It is vitally important that we do not in any way jeopardize the truth that Jesus was a Man . . . He not only ate and drank, he knew hunger, thirst and weariness. Consider his bravery, his sense of humour, his severity, his tenderness. To use Pilate's words, 'Behold the Man'—poor, born in an outhouse, working, journeying, praying; tempted as we are tempted . . . Behold him, healing and teaching the pathetic multitudes, touched with the feeling of men's infirmities, himself a Man of sorrows and acquainted with grief. He was human enough to weep over the woes of those whom he was not ashamed to call his brethren. Bearing on his heart the burden and shame of their sin, he nevertheless stood in with them and loved them to the end. Utterly clear-sighted, he was the vigorous debater, ruthlessly exposing and fiercely denouncing the shams of so much conventional religion. Without a trace of self-pity he went deliberately to Jerusalem to die. His was the highest, holiest Manhood which this world has seen or can see, and at the last—we men and women being what we are—he was nailed to a gallows to die with criminals, the innocent victim of fear, bigotry, jealous hatred, political opportunism and legalized murder. He was crucified, dead and buried... Here in this human life we meet the living God. It is God himself, personally present and redeemingly active, who comes to meet men in this Man of Nazareth. Jesus is more than a religious genius, such as George Fox, and more than a holy man, such as the lovable Lama in Kipling's *Kim*. He himself knows that he is more... The Gospel story is a tree rooted in the familiar soil of time and sense; but its roots go down into the Abyss and its branches fill the Heavens; given to us in terms of a country in the Eastern Mediterranean no bigger than Wales, during the Roman Principate of Tiberius Caesar in the first century of our era, its range is universal; it is on the scale of eternity. God's presence and his very Self were made manifest in the words and works of this Man...

In short... the Man Christ Jesus has the decisive place in man's ageless relationship with God. He is what God means by 'Man.' He is what man means by 'God.'

J.S. Whale, *Christian Doctrine*, Cambridge University Press, 1942, page 99

We want to realize very definitely what Christ is to us, how we are to look upon Christ and what it was that induced Him to put on all the weakness and pain that life brings to every one of us.

God is a law to Himself. All good men are a law to themselves; all the best men and women and children are those who live with principles. Principles are the laws of life which each person makes for himself, and the best people are those whose principles are so strong that they resist every temptation to anything lower, yet so pliant that they readily give way to anything higher. Like a cog-wheel with a catch, they can always be screwed a turn higher and never drop to where they were before.

Such should be the law of our lives, one tooth higher in the wheel every day. Such is God's Law of Nature, and such was Christ's Law of Life. So that when Christ as a Jew allowed that He was under the law bound to keep the Sabbath without working, when it came to a question of keeping it and turning a deaf ear to suffering, or breaking it and relieving suffering, He chose to break it—because the Law of Mercy is a tooth higher in the cog-wheel than the Law of keeping the Sabbath. But to neglect your work on Saturday night in order to amuse yourself, and to do your work in consequence on Sunday, this is holding the catch back and letting your cog-wheel slip the wrong way.

'We want to realize very definitely what Christ is to us.'—What was He to Wilson? The divinity of Christ was fundamental to his faith. Yet Christ was for him no ready-made perfection, no *deus ex machina*, but a man like others who, though He were a Son, was made perfect through the discipline of suffering; not the Great Exception, but the Great Example; no half-brother or step-brother to mankind, but Elder Brother, with the blood of the human race in His veins, the first-fruits of every human creature, first born among many brethren; perfect as we are not, healthy as a sick man is not, yet the Norm of perfectability and wholeness for all men, who became like us that we might become like Him.

And equally fundamental to his faith in the divinity of Christ, because indissolubly bound up with it, was his faith in the potential divinity of man; Christ's nature being no different in kind from ours, from the least of His brethren, though immeasurably different in degree... 'Not that he counted himself to have apprehended—very far indeed from that; but he pressed toward the mark, in confidence of the final consummation when all should come in the unity of the same faith, by the power of the same indwelling Spirit, 'unto a perfect man, unto the measure of the stature of the man Christ Jesus.'

This is the central theme which inspired all his thinking, and which he strove so faithfully to weave into the texture of his life; it was his reading of the true meaning of human existence—Christ-likeness, and nothing less than that.

Edward Wilson, in George Seaver, *The Faith of Edward Wilson*, John Murray, 1949, page 27

JUDGMENT

'Judgment'—criticism, critical faculty; judgment of mankind by God.

Tolstoy's *The Death of Ivan Ilyitch* brought me up with a start, giving me a different angle on judgment. Ivan was a member of the Russian upper classes. He went to a school of law, and ended up as a government official in a large town. He married, had a large family, and lived comfortably on an estate with servants. To the outward eye, a successful man.

At the latter end of middle age he became ill and took to his bed. One suspects he had cancer. His whole life is taken over by gnawing, unmitigated, agonizing pain, never ceasing for an instance. He begins to reminisce. At first he consoles himself on his various achievements, but mental pain and anguish take over and there is no respite. He goes into a dreamy reverie and hears an inner voice, the voice of his soul, asking him a searching question: 'When have you been happy?' He thinks carefully and is horrified to discover he has only been happy in childhood. The inner voice continues its relentless probe until Ivan questions himself with: 'Maybe I did not live as I ought to have done.' The searing pain gets worse. In his dying moments he comes to realize he has lived by convention and always fulfilled other peoples' expectations of him. What he has not done since childhood is obey the deepest feelings and convictions of his own soul, and so never known real freedom.

I wonder if Tolstoy is warning us of a judgment which takes place in the here-and-now, as to how we have lived our lives.

For the Lord sees not as man sees; man looks on the outward appearance, but the Lord looks on the heart.

1 Samuel 16:7

Those who plow iniquity and sow trouble reap the same.

Job 4:8

Judge not, that you be not judged. For with the judgment you pronounce you will be judged, and the measure you give will be the measure you get. Why do you see the speck that is in your brother's eye, but do not notice the log that is in your own eye? Or how can you say to your brother, 'Let me take the speck out of your own eye,' when there is a log in your own eye? You hypocrite, first take the log out of your eye, and then you will see clearly to take the speck out of your brother's eye.

Matthew 7:1–5

God is not mocked, for whatever a man sows, that he will also reap.

Galatians 6:7

Those consequences which follow from our actions or characters by the operation of God's laws are His judgements upon us.

William Temple, The Church Looks Forward, Macmillan and Co., 1944, page 176

God casts no soul away, unless it cast itself away. Every soul is its own judgement.

Jacob Boehme, in Selected Mystical Writings of William Law, edited by Stephen Hobhouse, Rockliff, 1948, page 371

At the judgement I shall be asked if I have loved. This will be the touchstone question. If I am not failed on this once and for all, I shall be asked further if I have believed and obeyed, accepted and trusted, prayed and followed as best I could the light that was given me.

Hubert van Zeller, Considerations, Sheed and Ward, 1974, page 116

We tend to think of the Divine Judgement as being the infliction upon us by an irresistible Despot of penalties, not growing out of our characters and deeds, but imposed from without ...

128

The Divine Judgement is the verdict upon us which consists in our reaction to *the light* (3.19) when it is offered us.

William Temple, *Readings in St John's Gospel*, First and Second Series, Macmillan and Co., 1947, page 287

A life devoted to the interests and enjoyments of this world, spent and wasted in the slavery of earthly desires, may be truly called a dream, as having all the shortness, vanity, and delusion of a dream; only with this great difference, that when a dream is over nothing is lost but fiction and fancies; but when the dream of life is ended only by death, all that eternity is lost, for which we were brought into being.

William Law, *Selected Mystical Writings of William Law*, edited by Stephen Hobhouse, Rockliff, 1948, page 67

People often wonder about the end of the world and the consummation of human life. Conscience reminds us of past wrongs, foolish actions and childish ignorances. Scripture and preachers remind us of a judgement to come and some people are unscriptural enough to claim to predict the day and hour. The secret is to see ourselves in the light of God's holiness and love, to acknowledge our need of forgiveness, and to accept God's forgiveness and his grace, so that when death or judgement comes we may be ready, trusting and unafraid.

George Appleton, *Journey for a Soul*, William Collins Sons and Co., 1976, page 227

Damnation is no foreign, separate, or imposed state that is brought in upon us, or adjudged to us by the will of God, but is the inborn, natural, essential state of our own disordered nature, which is absolutely impossible in the nature of the thing to be anything else but our own hell both here and hereafter, unless all sin be separated from us and righteousness be again made our natural state by a birth of itself in us. And all this, not because God will have it so by an arbitrary act of His sovereign will but because He cannot change His own nature or make anything to be happy and blessed, but only that which has its proper righteousness and is of one will and spirit with Himself.

William Law, *Selected Mystical Writings of William Law*, edited by Stephen Hobhouse, Rockliff, 1948, page 171

The Day of Judgement is an idea very familiar, and very dreadful, to Christians. 'In all time of our tribulation, in all time of our wealth, and in the day of judgement, Good Lord deliver us.' If there is any concept which cannot by any conjouring be removed from the teaching of Our Lord, it is that of the great separation; the sheep and the goats, the broad way and the narrow, the wheat and the tares, the winnowing fan, the wise and foolish virgins, the good fish and the refuse, the door closed on the marriage feast, with some inside and some outside in the dark. We may dare to hope—some dare to hope—that this is not the whole story, that, as Julian of Norwich said, 'All will be well and all manner of thing will be well.' But it is no use going to Our Lord's own words for that hope. Something we may get from St Paul: nothing of that kind, from Jesus. It is from His own words that the picture of 'Doomsday' has come into Christianity.

C.S. Lewis, *Christian Reflections*, edited by Walter Hooper, Geoffrey Bles, 1967, page 122

Sooner or later the world must burn, and all things in it—all the books, the cloister together with the brothel, Fra Angelico together with the Lucky Strike ads . . . Sooner or later it will all be consumed by fire and nobody will be left . . .

But love laughs at the end of the world because love is the door to eternity and he who loves God is playing on the doorstep to eternity, and before anything can happen love will have drawn him over the sill and closed the door and he won't bother about the world burning because he will know nothing but love . . .

And I have several times thought how at the Last Day I am likely to be one of the ten most abjectly humiliated sinners in the history of the world, but it will be my joy, and it will fill me with love, and I will fly like an arrow to take a back seat very far in the back where the last shall be first. And perhaps if Saint Francis will pray for me, and Saint John of the Cross, and Saint Mary Magdalene, I'll slide down off my high horse now and begin being the last and least in everything.

Thomas Merton, *The Sign of Jonas*, Burns and Oates, 1961, page 118

In the Old Testament God delegates his function of judge on earth in part to the Messianic prince who is destined to establish the earthly kingdom. When therefore the idea of the Day of the Lord develops, we get parallel with it the idea that the Son of Man will be the judge of all men, so that in the New Testament and in the Creeds of the Church it is roundly declared that Christ 'will come again with glory to judge both the quick and the dead'. There can be little doubt but that this actually was the expectation of the New Testament writers generally, though in John the judgment is associated emphatically with his first coming (John 3.19, 9.39, 12.31, etc.), and there is an equation of the gift of the Holy Spirit with the second coming of Christ. Such sayings as these have encouraged many moderns to think of the judgment of Christ in terms of the automatic working of history, and in the general evolutionary development which it is hoped will one day result in a Utopia. But this is not what the New Testament means by the Second Coming and the great Judgment Day. Nothing less than the end of history is involved, and with it a visible manifestation of Christ on this earth, and a demonstration of his eternal victory in the salvation of those who have faith in him and the destruction of those who persist in rebellion. To what extent such statements as these demand a literal interpretation is a matter for legitimate difference of opinion, but there is no justification for categorically denying any such dramatic finale.

N.H. Snaith, in *A Theological Word Book of the Bible*, edited by Alan Richardson, SCM Press, 1950, page 118

KINGDOM OF GOD

*'Kingdom of God'—the central theme of the teaching of Jesus,
involving an understanding of his own person and work.*

I sometimes wonder if we ought to get back to the central message of Jesus. St Luke draws our attention to some words of Jesus in the early part of His ministry—'I must preach the good news of the kingdom of God to other cities also, for I was sent for this purpose.' Later on in his Gospel, St Luke focuses the place where this kingdom of God is to be found—'the kingdom of God is within you'.

In the process of growing in faith, I have come to discover something of the kingdom of God in the depths of my being. At one level this has come through baptism, with the spiritual rebirth of the Father, the Son, and the Holy Spirit. In the course of prayer one has become aware of the 'presence' of the gifts of the Trinity—love, joy, truth, life, light, grace and glory, and so on. I have also been greatly helped by commentators (and critics) who point out 'the kingdom of God is within you', can also mean 'the kingdom of God is among you'. My experience has been that when the kingdom of God 'within you' becomes a living reality, it is as though scales are removed from your eyes, and you are able to see the kingdom of God 'among you'—in other people, in the processes of nature and creation, in other faiths, in work, and in the international scene as a whole. It is then that a phrase of the Lord's Prayer not only enables us to understand the person and work of Jesus, but calls us, too, to the kingdom of God—'Thy Kingdom come... on earth as it is in heaven.'

But seek first his kingdom and his righteousness, and all these things shall be yours as well.

Matthew 6:33

The time is fulfilled, and the kingdom of God is at hand; repent, and believe in the gospel.

Mark 1:15

Nor will they say, 'Lo, here it is!' or 'There!' for behold, the kingdom of God is within you.

Luke 17:21

Truly, truly, I say to you, unless one is born of water and the Spirit, he cannot enter the kingdom of God.

John 3:5

This life, this kingdom of God, this simplicity of absolute existence, is hard to enter. How hard? As hard as the Master of salvation could find words to express the hardness.

George Macdonald, *Unspoken Sermons*, Second Series, Longmans, Green and Co., 1885, page 38

To keep alive the sense of wonder, to live in unquestioning trust, instinctively to obey, to forgive and to forget—that is the childlike spirit, and that is the passport to the Kingdom of God.

William Barclay, *The Gospel of Luke*, The Saint Andrew Press, 1964, page 236

The outer world, with all its phenomena, is filled with divine splendour, but we must have experienced the divine within ourselves, before we can hope to discover it in our environment.

Rudolf Steiner, *Knowledge of the Higher Worlds*, Rudolf Steiner Press, 1963, page 22

This Kingdom of God is now within us. The Grace of the Holy Spirit likewise shines forth and warms us, distils a multitude of fragrances in the air around us, and pervades our senses with heavenly delight, flooding our hearts with inexpressible joy.

Seraphim of Sarov, in *A Treasury of Russian Spirituality*, edited by G.P. Fedotov, Sheed and Ward, 1977, page 277

The Kingdom is something within you which has the power of growth like a seed; something that you discover almost accidentally; something that you are searching for, and of whose value you become more confident and excited as the search proceeds, and you discover truer, lovelier things which are constantly being surpassed; something for which you have to give everything you have, no less yet no more, including the earlier finds with which you were once so completely delighted.

George Appleton, *Journey for a Soul*, William Collins Sons and Co., 1976, page 160

The Kingdom of God was the main subject of the early preaching of Jesus. He claimed that in himself the Kingdom had drawn near, was in operation, and he called to men to accept this fact in faith and to change their attitudes, behaviour and world view. Many of his parables dealt with the meaning of the Kingdom, as if he were wanting to ensure that those who could not at first understand would remember one vivid human story, and that one day the penny would drop. He wanted everyone to share the treasure that he had brought.

George Appleton, *Journey for a Soul*, William Collins Sons and Co., 1976, page 159

The Kingdom of God is within us. When Christ appears in the clouds He will simply be manifesting a metamorphosis that has been slowly accomplished under His influence in the heart of the mass of mankind. In order to hasten His coming, let us therefore concentrate upon a better understanding of the process by which the Holy Presence is born and grows within us. In order to foster its progress more intelligently, let us observe the birth and growth of the divine *milieu*, first in ourselves and then in the world that begins with us.

Pierre Teilhard de Chardin, *Le Milieu Divin*, William Collins Sons and Co., 1960, page 118

Gentlemen, when a man grows older and sees more deeply into life, he does not find, if he possesses any inner world at all, that he is advanced by the external march of things, by 'the progress of civilisation.' Nay, he feels himself, rather, where he was before, and forced to seek the sources of strength which his forefathers also sought. He is forced to make himself a native of the kingdom of God, the kingdom of the Eternal, the kingdom of Love; and he comes to understand that it was only this kingdom that Jesus Christ desired to speak and to testify, and he is grateful to him for it.

Adolf Harnack, *What is Christianity?* translated by Thomas Bailey Saunders, Ernest Benn, 1958, page 93

Why did the idea of the Kingdom of God have no significance in the early church? It was closely connected with the expectation of the end of the world. And when hope of the coming of the end of the world had faded, the idea of the Kingdom of God lost its force as well. So it came about that the creeds were not at the same time preoccupied with the idea of redemption. Only after the reformation did the idea gradually arise that we men and women in our own age must so understand the religion of Jesus that we endeavour to make the Kingdom of God a reality in this world. It is only through the idea of the Kingdom of God that religion enters into relationship with civilization.

Albert Schweitzer, in *An Anthology*, edited by Charles R. Joy, A. and C. Black, 1955, page 110

Poor Sinner! consider the Treasure thou hast within Thee, the Saviour of the world, the eternal Word of God lies hid in Thee, as a Spark of the Divine Nature, which is to overcome Sin and Death, and Hell within Thee, and generate the Life of Heaven again in thy Soul. Turn to thy Heart, and thy Heart will find its Saviour, its God within itself. Thou seest, hearest, and feelest nothing of God, because thou seekest for Him *abroad* with thy outward Eyes, thou seekest for Him in Books, in Controversies, in the Church, and outward Exercises, but *there* thou wilt not find Him, till thou hast *first* found Him in thy Heart. Seek for Him in thy Heart, and thou wilt never seek in vain, for there He dwells, there is the Seat of his Light and Holy Spirit.

William Law, *The Spirit of Prayer*, edited by Sidney Spencer, James Clarke and Co., 1969, page 43

To discover the Kingdom of God exclusively within oneself is easier than to discover it, not only there, but also in the outer world of minds and things and living creatures. It is easier because the heights within reveal themselves to those who are ready to exclude from their purview all that lies without. And though this exclusion may be a painful and mortificatory process, the fact remains that it is less arduous than the process of inclusion, by which we come to know the fullness as well as the heights of spiritual life. When there is exclusive concentration on the heights within, temptations and distractions are avoided and there is a general denial and suppression. But when the hope is to know God inclusively—to realize the divine Ground in the world as well as in the soul, temptations and distractions must not be avoided, but submitted to and used as opportunities for advance; there must be no suppression of outward-turning activities, but a transformation of them so that they become sacramental. Mortification becomes more searching and more subtle; there is need of unsleeping awareness and, on the levels of thought, feeling and conduct, the constant exercise of something like an artist's tact and taste.

Aldous Huxley, *The Perennial Philosophy*, Chatto and Windus, 1974, page 74

No age has ever seen a more pressing need for world adjustment than the one we live in today. I am not referring, now, only to Europe or America, but my own country, which needs it above all others.

Suppose that we set about making this adjustment; with what sort of standard or intention should we make it? The answer to this initial question is very simple. I say, make a standard of the Kingdom of God that Jesus taught. To start with the intention of the Kingdom of God is the sole way of adjusting today's mismanaged world.

In the Kingdom of God the ideal of Jesus has already taken a concrete shape. Jesus Christ regarded himself as the King of the Kingdom of God. Among the heathen, men who have many employees, or wield authority, or exert the power of mammon are held in esteem; but in the Kingdom of God it is just the opposite. In this realm those are respected who labour, who are oppressed or despised, or who humble themselves to serve others. Here the proud and haughty are weeded out. Many schemes today are presented as infallible programmes for remedying the world's ills. But no promise of social reconstruction is so reliable and thoroughgoing as this.

Toyohiko Kagawa, *Meditations*, number 18, translated by Jiro Takenaka, Harper and Brothers, 1950

Modern faith finds the beginning of the Kingdom of God in Jesus and in the Spirit which came into the world with him. We no longer leave the fate of mankind to be decided at the end of the world. The time in which we live summons us to new faith in the Kingdom of God.

We are no longer content, like the generations before us, to believe in the Kingdom that comes of itself at the end of time. Mankind to-day must either realise the Kingdom of God or perish. The very tragedy of our present situation compels us to devote ourselves in faith to its realisation.

We are at the beginning of the end of the human race. The question before it is whether it will use for beneficial purposes or for purposes of destruction the power which modern science has placed in its hands. So long as its capacity for destruction was limited, it was possible to hope that reason would set a limit to disaster. Such an illusion is impossible to-day, when its power is illimitable. Our only hope is that the Spirit of God will strive with the spirit of the world and will prevail. The last petition of the Lord's Prayer has again its original meaning for us as a prayer for deliverance from the dominion of the evil powers of the world. These are no less real to us as working in men's minds, instead of being embodied in angelic beings opposed to God. The first believers set their hope solely upon the Kingdom of God in expectation of the end of the world; we do so in expectation of the end of the human race.

The Spirit shows us the signs of the time and their meaning. Belief in the Kingdom of God makes the biggest demands of all the articles of the Christian faith. It means believing the seemingly impossible—the conquest of the spirit of the world by the Spirit of God. We look with confidence for the miracle to be wrought through the Spirit.

The miracle must happen in us before it can happen in the world. We dare not set our hope on our own efforts to create the conditions of God's Kingdom in the world. We must indeed labour for its realisation. But there can be no Kingdom of God in the world without the Kingdom of God in our hearts. The starting-point is our determined effort to bring every thought and action under the sway of the Kingdom of God. Nothing can be achieved without inwardness. The Spirit of God will only strive against the spirit of the world when it has won its victory over that spirit in our hearts.

Albert Schweitzer, in 'Epilogue: The Conception of the Kingdom of God in the Transformation of Eschatology,' in E.N. Mozley, *The Theology of Albert Schweitzer*, translated by J.R. Coates, A. & C. Black, 1950, page 106

KNOWLEDGE

'Knowledge'—the sum of what is known, as every branch of knowledge, personal knowledge, knowledge of God.

L ast week I went into All Souls for lunch, and spotted the portrait of one of my heroes—Sir Sarvepalli Radhakrishnan. He had been a Fellow of All Souls, but more importantly was at one time President of India. In this introductory paragraph, I have included a short passage from his book, *Indian Philosophy*, as it has something important to say about knowledge. 'Knowledge,' he wrote, 'is not something to be packed away in some corner of our brain, but what enters into our being, colours our emotion; haunts our soul, and is as close to us as life itself. It is the over-mastering power which through the intellect moulds the whole personality, trains the emotions and disciplines the will.'

Wise words indeed. Nowadays we tend to concentrate on the first phrase of his passage, and pack away the contents of a degree course in some corner of our brain. Academic knowledge is so vast and competition so intense, we pressurize our students to excel in one particular discipline, as exam results are seen to be all important. By and large we ignore that over-mastering power which through the intellect moulds the whole personality, trains the emotions and disciplines the will. Who would see to this in a modern-day university anyway? So, for many students, a university education is a big disappointment and leaves many feeling bored and disillusioned.

... for the Lord is a God of knowledge.

1 Samuel 2:3

Wise men lay up knowledge, but the babbling of a fool brings ruin near.

Proverbs 10:14

O the depth of the riches and wisdom and knowledge of God! How unsearchable are his judgments and how inscrutable his ways! For who has known the mind of the Lord, or who has been his counsellor?

Romans 11:33–34

But if one loves God, one is known by him.

1 Corinthians 8:3

Knowledge is the action of the Soul.

Ben Jonson, 'Explorata: or, Discoveries', in *Ben Jonson*, volume VIII, *The Poems, The Prose Works*, edited by C.H. Herford, Percy and Evelyn Simpson, Oxford at the Clarendon Press, 1947, page 588

Knowledge comes, but wisdom lingers.

Alfred, Lord Tennyson, 'Locksley Hall', in *The Poems of Tennyson*, edited by Christopher Ricks, Longmans, Green and Co., 1969, page 697

By faith we know His existence; in glory we shall know His nature.

Blaise Pascal, *Pensées*, translated by W.F. Trotter, Random House Inc., 1941, page 80

To know is not to prove, nor to explain. It is to accede to vision.

Antoine de Saint-Exupéry, *Flight to Arras*, translated by Lewis Galantière, William Heinemann, 1942, page 33

To *know*, to get into the truth of anything, is ever a mystic act,—of which the best Logics can but babble on the surface.

Thomas Carlyle, 'Lectures on Heroes' in *Sartor Resartus*, Chapman and Hall, 1840, page 227

Knowledge is proud that he has learn'd so much;
Wisdom is humble that he knows no more.

William Cowper, 'The Task', in *The Poetical Works of Cowper*, edited by H.S. Milford, Oxford University Press, 1950, page 221

I arrived at Truth, not by systematic reasoning and accumulation of proofs but by a flash of light which God sent into my soul.

Al-Ghazali, cited by Vaswani, 'The Sufi Spirit', in *The New Orient*, May–June, 1924, page 11

An extensive knowledge is needful to thinking people; it takes away the heat and fever, and helps, by widening speculation, to ease the 'burden of the Mystery.'

John Keats, 'Letter to J.H. Reynolds', in *The Works of John Keats*, volume III, edited by H. Buxton Forman, Reeves & Turner, 1883, page 150

There is therefore knowledge and knowledge. Knowledge that resteth in the bare speculation of things, and knowledge that is accompanied with the Grace of faith and love, which puts a man upon doing even the will of God from the heart.

John Bunyan, *The Pilgrim's Progress*, J.M. Dent and Sons, 1964, page 83

God cannot be imagined or conceived. Knowledge of God emerges from a kind of unknowing, a passing beyond all images and concepts into the darkness of unknowing.

This is the knowing of the heart, not of the intellect. It is therefore the knowledge of love. This love itself flows from God, the source, for there is in God a pure act of self-giving by which he ceaselessly communicates himself.

This love is mirrored in the mystery of the Godhead. The Father knows himself in the Son and the Son in the Father. Father and Son communicate in the love of the Holy Spirit.

Bede Griffiths OSB, in Peter Spink, editor, *The Universal Christ*, Darton, Longman and Todd, 1990, page 49

The Indian mind has never been content to know 'about God'; it has always sought to know God. And here there is no separation between subject and object.

To 'realize' God is to experience his presence, not in the imagination or in the intellect but in the ground of the soul from which all human faculties spring.

This is the knowledge which the Upanishads were intended to impart, the knowledge of the Self, the Knower, which is the subject not the object of thought, the ground alike of being and of thought.

To realize God in this way is to discover one's true self.

Bede Griffiths OSB, in Peter Spink, editor, *The Universal Christ*, Darton, Longman and Todd, 1990, page 44

To know God is to know Goodness. It is to see the beauty of infinite Love: To see it attended with Almighty Power and Eternal Wisdom; and using both those in the magnifying of its object. It is to see the Kingdom of Heaven and Earth take infinite delight in *Giving*... He is not an Object of Terror, but Delight. To know Him therefore as He is, is to frame the most beautiful idea in all Worlds. He delighteth in our happiness more than we: and is of all other the most Lovely Object. An infinite Lord, who having all Riches, Honours, and Pleasures in His own hand, is infinitely willing to give them unto me. Which is the fairest idea that can be devised.

Thomas Traherne, *Centuries*, The Faith Press, 1969, page 8

But the greatest error... is the mistaking or misplacing of the last or furthest end of knowledge. For men have entered into a desire of learning and knowledge, sometimes upon a natural curiosity and inquisitive appetite; sometimes to entertain their minds with variety and delight; sometimes for ornament and reputation; and sometimes to enable them to victory of wit and contradiction; and most times for lucre and profession; and seldom sincerely to give a true account of their gift of reason to the benefit and use of men: as if there were sought in knowledge a couch whereupon to rest a searching and restless spirit; or a terrace for a wandering and variable mind to walk up and down with a fair prospect; or a tower of state, for a proud mind to raise itself upon; or a fort or commanding ground, for strife and contention; or a shop, for profit or sale; and not a rich storehouse for the glory of the Creator and the relief of man's estate.

Francis Bacon, *The Advancement of Learning*, Cassell and Company Limited, 1905, page 38

God is invisibly present to the ground of our being, but he remains hidden from the arrogant gaze of our investigating mind which seeks to capture him and secure permanent possession of him in an act of knowledge...

In seeking to know him we must forget the familiar subject-object relationship which characterizes our ordinary acts of knowing. Instead we know him in so far as we become aware of ourselves as known through and through by him. We 'possess' him in proportion as we realize ourselves to be possessed by him in the inmost depths of our being... The aim of meditation... is to come to know him through the realization that our very being is penetrated with his knowledge and love for us...

We have no other reason for being, except to be loved by him as our Creator and Redeemer, and to love him in return...

The whole purpose of meditation is to deepen the consciousness of this basic relationship of the creature to the Creator, and of the sinner to his Redeemer.

Thomas Merton, *Contemplative Prayer*, Darton, Longman and Todd, 1988, page 103

What then can give rise to a true spirit of peace on earth? Not commandments and not practical experience. Like all human progress, the love of peace must come from knowledge. All living knowledge as opposed to academic knowledge can have but one object. This knowledge may be seen and formulated by thousands in a thousand different ways, but it must always embody one truth. It is the knowledge of the living substance in us, in each of us, in you and me, of the secret magic, the secret godliness that each of us bears within him. It is the knowledge that, starting from this innermost point, we can at all times transcend all pairs of opposites, transforming white into black, evil into good, night into day. The Indians call it 'Atman,' the Chinese 'Tao,'; Christians call it 'grace.' Where that supreme knowledge is present (as in Jesus, Buddha, Plato, or Lao-tzu), a threshold is crossed beyond which miracles begin. There war and enmity cease. We can read of it in the New Testament and in the discourses of Gautama. Anyone who is so inclined can laugh at it and call it 'introverted rubbish,' but to one who has experienced it his enemy becomes his brother, death becomes birth, disgrace honour, calamity good fortune. Each thing on earth discloses itself twofold, as 'of this world' and 'not of this world.' But 'this world' means what is 'outside us.' Everything that is outside us can become enemy, danger, fear and death. The light dawns with the experience that this entire 'outward' world is not only an object of our perception but at the same time the creation of our soul, with the transformation of all outward into inward things, of the world into the self.

Herman Hesse, *If The War Goes On*, translated by Ralph Manheim, Pan Books, 1974, page 54

It takes a long time for the average over-intellectualized person to realize that in this particular sphere of reality he must be prepared to receive illumination from the most unexpected quarters, to learn his lessons in completely unfamiliar terms, to strain his ear to catch overtones to which he previously paid little attention, to abandon some of his most cherished preconceptions, to bare himself to truths which he has not hitherto been prepared to face. Yet only at this price can spiritual be substituted for merely intellectual knowledge...

The point is that the particular kind of awareness which the educated derive from dealing with experience in its more intellectual aspects hardly comes into play at all when it is a question of the deeper laws of life. The attention then becomes concentrated upon a certain type of datum which the unsophisticated person can identify and handle just as effectively as can any other—often more effectively, indeed, than the person who is highly educated. We find ourselves in a region in which the vital issues are brought into focus by such factors as acts of devotion, simplicity of behaviour, humbleness of spirit...

We may draw from this an important conclusion. If anything in the nature of a religious revival ever takes place in this country... we shall be prudent not to expect the educated classes to play any more important a part in it than that which is played by people of quite humble origin and pretensions. Spiritual power, insight, and authority—these things are apt at such an epoch to manifest themselves in the most unexpected places, to the confusion of the orthodox. A tram-driver who has been spiritually quickened in the way in which certain slaves were once quickened at the beginning of the Christian era, or as certain Quakers were quickened in the seventeenth century, is a figure to be reckoned with—particularly in a society which, like our own, is beginning to regard the capacities of its intelligentsia with distrust.

Lawrence Hyde, The Prospects of Humanism, Gerald Howe, 1931, page 139

MAN

'Man'—a human being—male or female, the human race, inner, outer; the spiritual, material parts of man.

We have seen some terrible things on television recently. I am thinking of the carnage in Chechnya, the massacres in Rwanda, and some old film of the horrors of the holocaust. Henry Ward Beecher is close to the truth when he recognizes there is the same fierce, destructive nature in man that there is in the wolf; the same cunning, artful nature that there is in the fox. He added we have not descended from the animals, we are with them yet. Fortunately, however, that is only half the story, and our definition above rightly makes mention of the spiritual side of man. Walt Whitman restores our confidence in 'man' by showing us a way in which we can integrate both sides of our nature, and go forward into the future in hope. In 'Starting from Paumanok' he recommends old fashioned worship.

'I say no man has ever yet been half devout enough,
None has ever yet adored or worship'd half enough,
None has begun to think how divine he himself is, and how certain the future is.'

Many of us will have had bad experiences in our journey through life. We cannot really expect to go the whole distance unscathed. I can remember being threatened in the army with a knife, and was very nearly shot in Nigeria. However, most of us can also expect to come across the better side of human nature—and be strangers to Henry Ward Beecher's wild animals, in ourselves and in other people.

The spirit of God has made me, and the breath of the Almighty gives me life.

Job 33:4

Yet thou hast made him little less than God, and dost crown him with glory and honour. Thou hast given him dominion over the works of thy hands; thou hast put all things under his feet.

Psalm 8:5–6

Pilate said to them, 'Behold the man!'

John 19:5

Thus it is written, 'The first man Adam became a living being'; the last Adam became a life-giving spirit. But it is not the spiritual which is first but the physical, and then the spiritual. The first man was from the earth, a man of dust; the second man is from heaven. As was the man of dust, so are those who are of the dust; and as is the man of heaven, so are those who are of heaven. Just as we have borne the image of the man of dust, we shall also bear the image of the man of heaven.

1 Corinthians 15:45–49

A man is a god in ruins.

Ralph Waldo Emerson, in *The Works of Ralph Waldo Emerson*, volume II, *English Traits: The Conduct of Life: Nature*, edited by George Sampson, George Bell & Sons, Ltd., 1906, page 412

I Am a little world made cunningly
Of Elements, and an Angelike spright.

John Donne, *Divine Poems*, v, in *Poetical Works*, edited by Sir Herbert Grierson, Oxford University Press, 1977, page 295

Man is a Wonder to himself; he can neither *govern*, nor *know* himself.

Benjamin Whichcote, *Moral and Religious Aphorisms*, century II, number 186, 1930, page 23

How poor, how rich, how abject, how august,
How complicate, how wonderful, is man!

Edward Young, *Night Thoughts*, Thomas Nelson, 1841, page 3

We know, and it is our pride to know, that man is by his constitution a religious animal.

Edmund Burke, *Reflections on the Revolution in France*, edited by Conor Cruise O'Brien, Penguin Books, 1969, page 187

For a man is not as God,
But then most Godlike being most a man.

Alfred, Lord Tennyson, 'Love and Duty,' in *The Poems of Tennyson*, edited by Christopher Ricks, Longmans, Green and Co., 1969, page 729

Man found his form and his identity under the action of religious principles and energies; the confusion in which he is losing them cannot be re-ordered by purely human efforts.

Nicolas Berdyaev, *The End of Our Time*, translated by Donald Attwater, Sheed and Ward, 1933, page 56

When we talk of 'spirit' in man, we are pointing to that extra dimension of being that belongs to him and that makes him more than a mere physical organism or a highly complicated animal.

John Macquarrie, *Paths in Spirituality*, SCM Press, second edition, 1992, page 43

Nature tels me I am the Image of God, as well as Scripture; he that understands not thus much, hath not his introduction or first lesson, and is yet to begin the Alphabet of man.

Sir Thomas Browne, *The Works of Sir Thomas Browne*, volume I, *Religio Medici*, edited by Geoffrey Keynes, Cambridge University Press, 1964, page 87

We may pause in sorrow and silence over the depths of darkness that are in man; if we rejoice in the heights of purer vision he has attained to. Such things were and are in man; in all men; in us too.

Thomas Carlyle, 'Lectures on Heroes,' in *Sartor Resartus*, Chapman and Hall, 1840, page 187

I say no man has ever yet been half devout enough,
None has ever yet adored or worship'd half enough,
None has begun to think how divine he himself is, and how certain the future is.

Walt Whitman, *Leaves of Grass*, 'Starting from Paumanok', in *The Complete Poems*, edited by Francis Murphy, Penguin Books, 1982, page 54

What piece of work is a man, how noble in reason, how infinite in faculties, in form and moving how express and admirable, in action how like an angel, in apprehension how like a god: the beauty of the world, the paragon of animals.

William Shakespeare, *Hamlet*, II. ii. 303

Since modern man experiences himself both as the seller and as the commodity to be sold on the market, his self-esteem depends on conditions beyond his control. If he is 'successful,' he is valuable; if he is not, he is worthless.

Erich Fromm, *Man For Himself*, Routledge and Kegan Paul, 1975, page 72

To please God... to be a real ingredient in the divine happiness... to be loved by God, not merely pitied, but delighted in as an artist delights in his work or a father in a son—it seems impossible, a weight or burden of glory which our thoughts can hardly sustain. But so it is.

C.S. Lewis, *Screwtape Proposes a Toast*, William Collins Sons and Co., 1982, page 104

No human being is meant to be a carbon copy, a double, an understudy... a shadow. Each must be his own man, much as this may mean resembling someone else's. This is not egocentricity or independence of the herd. It is the incommunicable response to the particular summons of God.

Hubert van Zeller, *Considerations*, Sheed and Ward, 1974, page 15

Man is a microcosmos and contains all things within himself; but of these only what is distinctly individual and characteristic acquires tangible form. He is, moreover, a being who lives in many dimensions, and I have always been conscious of this within myself.

Nicolas Berdyaev, *Dream and Reality*, translated by Katharine Lampert, Geoffrey Bles, 1950, page 1

Man with all his noble qualities, with sympathy which feels for the most debased, with benevolence which extends not only to other men but to the humblest living creature, with his god-like intellect which has penetrated into the movements and constitution of the solar system—with all these exalted powers—Man still bears in his bodily frame the indelible stamp of his lowly origin.

Charles Darwin, *The Descent of Man*, part 1, C.A. Watts and Co., 1930, page 244

Man is both animal and spiritual. On one side he is the most fully developed of the animals; but if that were all, he would present, and know, no problems. Upon him is stamped the Image of God; he is capable of that communion with God which is eternal life. But here again we find two-sidedness; for the Image of God in man is blurred and distorted. How or why this should be so is a question too large for discussion here. The fact is certain. Man, capable by his nature as God made it of communion with God as the author, centre, and goal of his being, does always in greater or less degree conduct himself as though he were himself his own beginning and end, the centre of his own universe. His 'sin' is not a mere survival or disproportionate development of animal tendencies, or an inadequate development of rational control. It is a perversion of reason itself. His capacity for divine communion is become a usurpation of divine authority. The worst, the most typical sin, from which all other sin flows, is not sensuality, but pride.

William Temple, *Citizen and Churchman*, Cambridge University Press, 1941, page 44

In becoming man, God became not only Jesus Christ but also potentially every man and woman that ever existed. In Christ, God became not only 'this' man, but also in a broader and more mystical sense, yet no less truly, 'every man.'

The presence of God in His world as its Creator depends on no one but Him. His presence in the world as Man depends, in some measure, upon men. Not that we can do anything to change the mystery of the Incarnation in itself: but we are able to decide whether we ourselves, and that portion of the world which is ours, shall become *aware* of His presence, consecrated by it, and transfigured in its light.

We have the choice of two identities: the external mask which seems to be real and which lives by a shadowy autonomy for the brief moment of earthly existence, and the hidden, inner person who seems to us to be nothing, but who can give himself eternally to the truth in whom he subsists. It is this inner self that is taken up into the mystery of Christ, by His love, by his Holy Spirit, so that in secret we live 'in Christ.'

Thomas Merton, *New Seeds of Contemplation*, Burns and Oates, 1962, page 228

Jesus told the parable of the prodigal son with each of us in mind, knowing that each of us would live our individual version of the story.

And he loves us as we are, at whatever stage of our journey. He loves the potentiality in us. The potentiality for conversion, return, love, light.

He loves the Magdalene when she is still a sinner, because he already sees her gradual progress towards the light as something marvellous, as something worth serious attention here on earth.

He loves Zacchaeus the sinner, robber, exploiter, and finds it good that such a man can be capable of reversing his conduct and becoming a friend of the poor.

Yes, God loves what in man is not yet.

What has still to come to birth.

What we love in a man is what already is: virtue, beauty, courage, and hence our love is self-interested and fragile.

God, loving what is not yet and putting his faith in man, continually begets him, since love is what begets.

By giving man confidence, he helps him to be born, since love is what helps us to emerge from our darkness and draws us into the light.

And this is such a fine thing to do that God invites us to do the same.

Carlo Carretto, *Summoned by Love*, translated by Alan Neame, Darton, Longman and Todd, 1977, page 98

I see the marks of God in the heavens and the earth, but how much more in a liberal intellect, in magnanimity, in unconquerable rectitude, in a philanthropy which forgives every wrong, and which never despairs of the cause of Christ and human virtue. I do and I must reverence human nature. Neither the sneers of a worldly scepticism, nor the groans of a gloomy theology, disturb my faith in its godlike powers and tendencies. I know how it is despised, how it has been oppressed, how civil and religious establishments have for ages conspired to crush it. I know its history. I shut my eyes on none of its weaknesses and crimes... But injured, trampled on, and scorned as our nature is, I still turn to it with intense sympathy and strong hope. The signatures of its origin and its end are impressed too deeply to be ever wholly effaced. I bless it for its kind affections, for its strong and tender love. I honour it for its struggles against oppression, for its growth and progress under the weight of so many chains and prejudices, for its achievements in science and art, and still more for its examples of heroic and saintly virtue. These are marks of a divine origin and pledges of a celestial inheritance; and I thank God that my own lot is bound up with that of the human race.

William E. Channing, 'Likeness to God,' in *Complete Works*, Routledge and Sons, 1884, page 235

There are moments when God makes us feel the extreme limits of our powerlessness; then and only then, do we understand our nothingness right down to the depths.

For so many years, for too many years, I have fought against my powerlessness, my weakness. Often I have refused to admit it to myself, preferring to appear in public with a nice mask of self-assurance...

Now I do not fight any more; I try to accept myself. I try to face up to myself without illusions, dreams or fantasies. It's a step forward, I believe. And if I had made the step while I was still learning the catechism, I should have gained forty years...

I seem now to have reached a means of encountering him in a way I have never known before; a togetherness I have never experienced before, an awareness of his love I had never previously felt. Yes, it is really my misery which attracts his power, my wounds which shout after him, my nothingness which makes him throw himself open to me.

And this meeting between God's totality and man's nothingness is the greatest wonder of creation. It is the most beautiful betrothal because its bond is a love which gives itself freely and a love which accepts. Really, it is the truth of God and man. The acceptance of this truth comes from humility, and that is why without humility there is no truth, and without truth no humility.

Carlo Carretto, *Letters from the Desert*, translated by Rose Mary Hancock, Darton, Longman and Todd, 1972, page 133

MEDITATION

'Meditation'—the verb means to plan mentally, design; exercise the mind in contemplation on (upon) a subject, thinking about or reflecting on something spiritual or religious.

When we were on our expedition to Nepal in 1963, we visited a Buddhist temple in Kathmandu valley. We saw one of the monks casually spinning prayer wheels and listened to a group of monks playing musical instruments. When the music was over the monks settled down to meditation. They had before them something akin to scriptures, and silently pondered over the contents. I sometimes wonder if this triggered off my interest in meditation. When I got to theological college some weeks later, I began to collect short verses from the Bible, and silently meditated on them. At first I would close my eyes and quietly repeat the verse to myself. 2 Timothy 1:7 was an early favourite: 'For God did not give us a spirit of timidity but a spirit of power and love and self-control.' The next stage was to make a note of valuable sentences I came across in my theological studies, and collect suitable quotations, and add these to the collection. I still have a large number of extracts from George Seaver's book, *Edward Wilson of the Antarctic*. From this book I picked up the habit of keeping a journal and began to meditate with the help of a pen and paper. I found this a great aid to concentration. Much has happened since then. I am enormously indebted to meditation, even though in common parlance I prefer to call it 'reflection'.

Let the words of my mouth and the meditation of my heart be acceptable in thy sight, O Lord, my rock and my redeemer.

Psalm 19:14

I will meditate on thy precepts, and fix my eyes on thy ways.

Psalm 119:15

Watch and pray that you may not enter into temptation; the spirit indeed is willing, but the flesh is weak.

Matthew 26:41

Pray at all times in the Spirit, with all prayer and supplication. To that end keep alert with all perseverance...

Ephesians 6:18

Meditation is a contented but perfectly conscious dwelling of the mind on something likely to elevate our life.

Ernest Dimnet, *What We Live By*, Jonathan Cape, 1932, page 185

Our duty is not primarily to strive and to brace up our wills, but primarily to fasten our attention upon the divine love, that it may do its own work upon us and within us.

William Temple, *The Preacher's Theme To-day*, SPCK, 1936, page 60

The art of meditation may be exercised at all hours, and in all places; and men of genius, in their walks, at table, and amidst assemblies, turning the eye of the mind inwards, can form an artificial solitude; retired amidst a crowd, calm amidst distraction, and wise amidst folly.

Isaac Disraeli, *Literary Character of Men of Genius*, edited by The Earl of Beaconsfield, Frederick Warne and Co., 1881, page 131

Scarcely is there anything which the understanding can know of God,—only the will can greatly love Him. Let a man imprison himself within his own self, in the centre of his soul, wherein is the image of God, and there let him wait upon Him, as one listens to another speaking from some high tower, or as though he had Him within his heart, and as if in all creation there were no other thing save God and his soul.

St Peter of Alcantara, in E. Allison Peers, *Studies of the Spanish Mystics*, volume II, Sheldon Press, 1930, page 114

People need to discover their own self-identity. Many go to drugs, not to forget the miseries of life, but to discover its secrets, to explore an inner life of identity, liberation and happiness. The mystics tell us that this experience can be gained from some discipline of meditation, entering into silence, stilling the activity of the mind, allowing feelings and intuitions to rise from the depths of our being.

George Appleton, *Journey for a Soul*, William Collins Sons and Co., 1976, page 38

Meditation is a channel for continuous reconstitution of the self, to prepare it that it may move into the new... The entire nervous system and the vital processes rest as in deep sleep, while there is a condition of alert attention in the mind, a listening to the world of being. We are then open to the qualities of the Higher Self, which essentially are peace, love, gentleness, courage and joy.

While these fill the soul, there is simply no room for the negative qualities of the lower self, which include remorse, regret, disappointment, anger, resentment for things past, and fear, anxiety and doubt about the future. These negative emotions cannot enter, any more than darkness can remain in a room when we switch on the light.

George Trevelyan, *A Vision of the Aquarian Age*, Coverture, 1977, page 87

Meditative prayer is not an intellectual exercise in which we reflect about theological propositions. In meditation we are not *thinking* about God at all, nor are we thinking of his Son, Jesus, nor of the Holy Spirit. In meditation we seek to do something immeasurably greater; we seek to *be with* God, to *be with* Jesus, to *be with* his Holy Spirit, not merely to think about them.

It is one thing to know that Jesus is the revelation of the Father; or that he is our way to the Father. But it is quite another thing to experience the presence of Jesus within us, to experience the power of his Spirit within us for it is *in that experience* that we are brought into the presence of his Father and our Father.

Holiness is not fundamentally a moral quality. It is rather the unique experience of Presence.

John Main OSB, in *The Joy of Being*, selected by Clare Hallward, Darton, Longman and Todd, 1989, page 26

Often we consider one or two points and jump to the next, which is wrong since we have just seen that it takes a long time to become recollected, what the Fathers call an attentive person, someone capable of paying attention to an idea so long and so well that nothing of it is lost. The spiritual writers of the past and of the present day will all tell us: take a text, ponder on it hour after hour, day after day, until you have exhausted all your possibilities, intellectual and emotional, and thanks to attentive reading and re-reading of this text, you have come to a new attitude. Quite often meditation consists in nothing but examining the text, turning over these words of God addressed to us, so as to become completely familiar with them, so imbued with them that gradually we and these words become completely one. In this process, even if we think that we have not found any particular intellectual richness, we have changed.

Anthony Bloom, *Living Prayer*, Darton, Longman and Todd, 1966, page 55

Meditation has been described as the direct path to God. Until recent years Western thought has largely recorded the practice of meditation as Eastern, even as non-Christian.

As a result of the influence of Eastern culture on the Western world and the current interest in Indian religion and philosophy many in the West now follow the meditative path.

Meditation consists in learning to focus and to control the mind. When the mind is stilled, then the light of the intellect begins to shine. The mind is ordinarily scattered and dissipated, but gather the mind into one and then the pure light shines in the mirror which is oneself.

Speech is the movement by which we go out of ourselves to communicate to another. Meditation takes us within ourselves. It is a process of inner withdrawal, a centring in the place of inner detachment, a staying of the mind upon God.

Bede Griffiths OSB, in *The Universal Christ*, edited by Peter Spink, Darton, Longman and Todd, 1990, page 16

The purpose of meditation is not to achieve an academic exercise in thinking; it is not meant to be a purely intellectual performance, nor a beautiful piece of thinking without further consequences; it is meant to be a piece of straight thinking under God's guidance and Godwards, and should lead us to draw conclusions about how to live. It is important to realise from the outset that a meditation has been useful when, as a result, it enables us to live more precisely and more concretely in accordance with the gospel... Whatever we take, a verse, a commandment, an event in the life of Christ, we must first of all assess its real objective content. This is extremely important because the purpose of meditation is not to build up a fantastic structure but to understand a truth. The truth is there, given, it is God's truth, and meditation is meant to be a bridge between our lack of understanding and the truth revealed. It is a way in which we can educate our intelligence, and gradually learn to have 'the mind of Christ' as St Paul says (1 Corinthians 2:16).

Anthony Bloom, *Living Prayer*, Darton, Longman and Todd, 1966, page 52

The great grace that all of us have been given is to believe in Jesus Christ, to believe in his presence in our hearts and to believe that he invites each of us to enter into that presence. That is an extraordinary gift to have been given.

We have to learn, because it is a gift of such staggering proportions, to respond to it gradually, gently. When we begin we cannot fully understand the sheer magnificence and wonder of it. Each time we return to meditate we enter into that reality a little more deeply, a little more faithfully.

When we begin we probably find our way to meditation as one among many options that we have been looking at and it takes us time to find that this is *the pearl of great price*.

I do not wish to imply that meditation is the only way, but rather that it is the only way I have found. In my experience it is the way of pure simplicity that enables us to become fully, integrally aware of the Spirit Jesus has sent into our heart. This is the recorded experience of the mainstream of the Christian tradition from apostolic times down to our own day.

John Main OSB, in *The Joy of Being*, selected by Clare Hallward, Darton, Longman and Todd, 1989, page 18

Since I learned how to enter the forest of meditation, I have received sweet dewlike drops from that forest. I have found that the door to meditation is open everywhere and any time, at midnight, or at noonday, at dawn or at dusk. Everywhere, on the street, on the trolley, on the train, in the waiting room, or in the prison cell, I am given a resting place of meditation, wherein I can meditate to my heart's content on the Almighty God who abides in my heart.

It is said that Francis of Assisi meditated and prayed, looking up at the sun in broad daylight. Plato has told how Socrates suddenly would pause and stand erect to meditate for a few minutes while walking with his disciples... Jesus withdrew into the wilderness and meditated forty days and forty nights. Sometimes he was lost in meditation and prayer all night long in the mountains of Galilee. Those who draw water from the wellspring of meditation know that God dwells close to their hearts. For those who wish to discover the quietude of old amid the hustle and bustle of today's machine civilization, there is no way save to rediscover this ancient realm of meditation. Since the loss of my eyesight I have been as delighted as if I had found a new wellspring by having arrived at this sacred precinct.

Toyohiko Kagawa, *Meditations*, translated by Jiro Takenaka, Harper and Brothers, 1950, page 1

There is an act of the mind, natural to the earnest and the wise, impossible only to the sensual and the fool, healthful to all who are sincere, which has small place in modern usage, and which few can now distinguish from vacuity. Those who knew what it was, called it *meditation*. It is not *reading*, in which we apprehend the thoughts of others, and bring them to our critical tribunal. It is not *study*, in which we strive to master the known and prevail over it, till it lies in order beneath our feet. It is not *reasoning*, in which we seek to push forward the empire of our positive conceptions... It is not *deliberation*, which computes the particular problems of action, reckons up the forces that surround our individual lot, and projects accordingly the expedient or the right. It is not *self-scrutiny*, which by itself is only shrewdness or at most science turned within instead of without, and analyzing mental feelings instead of physical facts. Its view is not personal and particular, but universal and immense... It brings, not an intense self-conscious-ness and spiritual egotism, but everything for wonder and for love. It does not suggest indirect demonstration, but furnishes immediate perception of things divine, eye to eye with the saints, spirit to spirit with God, peace to peace with Heaven. In thus being alone with the truth of things, and passing from shows and shadows into communion with the everlasting One, there is nothing at all impossible and out of reach... Let any true man go into silence; lift off thought after thought, passion after passion till he reaches the inmost depth of all... and it will be strange if he does not feel the Eternal Presence as close upon his soul, as the breeze upon his brow; if he does not say, 'O Lord, art Thou ever near as this, and have I not known Thee?'

James Martineau, *Endeavours after the Christian Life*, Longmans, Green, Reader and Dyer, 1876, page 186

MIRACLES

'Miracles'—marvellous events due to some supernatural agency;
remarkable occurrence; remarkable specimen (of ingenuity,
impudence, etc).

At the age of ten I knew there was one job I would never do, namely, be a clergyman. The reason for this was as follows. I spent an afternoon with my twin sister at a Girl Guide camp. One of the curates from the parish church was giving instructions on how to cook over a campfire. I remember looking at him, and thinking how stupid he looked in his dog-collar. An instant decision was made. This was definitely not for me. That was the last time I went to the campsite, and instead I became a golf addict.

The impossible happened fifteen years later, and I was forced to eat my words (though I still loath wearing a dog-collar). What brought about the change? I can only equate it in terms of the miraculous. In my early twenties I had an experience of the Holy Spirit whilst reading the book *Margaret*, by James Davidson Ross. This was my equivalent to the Damascus road. When I eventually closed that book, I was utterly convinced of the importance of the spiritual dimension, and knew I had to devote my life to it. This might seem illusory to an outsider, but I was cured of golf addiction, and thirty years later I am still on course. Within the space of a few days the course of my life changed dramatically through what I still take to be God's intervention, and I'm grateful to Him for it.

They forgot what he had done, and the miracles that he had shown them.

Psalm 78:11

Remember the wonderful works that he has done, his miracles, and the judgments he uttered.

Psalm 105:5

Now there was a man of the Pharisees, named Nicodemus, a ruler of the Jews. This man came to Jesus by night and said to him, 'Rabbi, we know that you are a teacher come from God; for no one can do these signs that you do, unless God is with him.'

John 3:1–2

To each is given the manifestation of the Spirit for the common good. To one is given through the Spirit... the working of miracles.

1 Corinthians 12:7–8, 10

Love... is always in the mood of believing in miracles.

John Cowper Powys, *The Meaning of Culture*, Jonathan Cape, 1932, page 170

Miracles happen only to those who believe in them.

French Proverb

A portent (miracle), therefore, does not occur contrary to nature, but contrary to what is known of nature.

St. Augustine, *City of God*, translated by Henry Bettenson, edited by David Knowles, Penguin Books, 1972, page 980

The miracles of Jesus were the ordinary works of his Father, wrought small and swift that we might take them in.

George Macdonald, *Unspoken Sermons*, Second Series, Longmans, Green and Co., 1885, page 52

The divine art of miracle is not an art of suspending the pattern to which events conform but of feeding new events into that pattern.

C.S. Lewis, *Miracles*, William Collins Sons and Co., 1974, page 64

Men talk about Bible miracles because there is no miracle in their lives. Cease to gnaw that crust. There is ripe fruit over your head.

Henry David Thoreau, *The Journal of Henry D. Thoreau*, volume II, edited by Bradford Torrey and Francis H. Allen, 1949, Houghton Mifflin Company, Boston, The Riverside Press, page 33

It is Christ Himself, rather than any of the things which He did, who is the supreme miracle and the chief attestation of the truth of the biblical revelation.

Alan Richardson, *Christian Apologetics*, SCM Press, 1947, page 156

Disbelief in the miracles is usually the result of disbelief in the biblical conception of God as the source of all power or in Christ as the veritable incarnation of the *dunamis* of God.

Alan Richardson, in *A Theological Word Book of the Bible*, edited by Alan Richardson, SCM Press, 1969, page 152

The essence of Jesus' religion is not its miraculous character. Miracles themselves did not constitute the religion of Jesus. It is a gross mistake to take his miracles for the essence of Christianity.

Jesus never made his miracle the central point of his teaching. He simply used this power as a means of manifesting his personality.

The salient feature of Jesus' religion is neither his virgin birth nor his resurrection. The gist of his religion is the uplift of conscience wrought through God and Christ. This implies that, recovering our benumbed divine sense, we enter into that sacred precinct where God and man are united, and there revel in the love of our Heavenly Father. This is the religion of Jesus.

The Miracles were only an addendum, an afterthought.

Christianity would continue unimpaired even if all the miracles were to be completely eliminated from it. Nevertheless, it is a certainty that Jesus Christ could perform miracles, and did perform them. The only question for criticism to decide is how far we are to depend upon their acceptance.

Toyohiko Kagawa, *Meditations*, translated by Jiro Takenaka, Harper and Brothers, 1950, number 36

It is not necessary to go far afield in search for miracles. I am myself a miracle. My physical birth and my soul's existence are miracles. First and foremost the fact that I was ever born is a miracle. The fact that I am still alive despite my shadow- like, weakened body battling a host of devils of disease is a miracle.

Yet the greatest miracle of all is the reality of my soul. That I should be made victorious in temptations, be the object of God's care in a ruined world, be given assurance to go forward into the world of the devout, this is to me a master miracle. At times the storms of passion shake my soul to its depths, but a purer power, stronger a thousand times, has possession of my being and holds sway over me. When I think of this state of my soul it appears, even to me, a miracle.

To my heart value immediately takes on reality, and prayer ere long is reproduced in realization. In the depths of my soul I am daily conscious of the miracle of creation. The miracle of the resurrection becomes not a matter of yesterday, but takes place today in this soul of mine. A virgin conceiving and bearing God in her bosom becomes not an ancient tale in far-off Bethlehem but a present-day fact within me.

Toyohiko Kagawa, in Willima Axling, *Kagawa*, SCM Press, 1946, page 10

But now if all things whatsoever that we look upon are emblems to us of the Highest God, I add that more so than any of them is man such an emblem. You have heard of St. Chrysostom's celebrated saying, in reference to the Shekinah, or Ark of Testimony, visible Revelation of God, among the Hebrews: 'The true Shekinah is Man!' Yes, it is even so: this is no vain phrase; it is veritably so. The essence of our being, the mystery in us that calls itself 'I,'—ah, what words have we for such things?—is a breath of Heaven; the Highest Being reveals himself in man. This body, these faculties, this life of ours, is it not all as a vesture for that Unnamed? 'There is but one temple in the Universe,' says the devout Novalis, 'and that is the Body of Man. Nothing is holier than that high form. Bending before men is a reverence done to this Revelation in the Flesh. We touch Heaven when we lay our hand on a human body!' This sounds like a mere flourish of rhetoric; but it is not so. If well meditated, it will turn out to be a scientific fact; the expression, in such words as can be had, of the actual truth of the thing. *We* are the miracle of miracles.

Thomas Carlyle, 'Lectures on Heroes,' in *Sartor Resartus*, Chapman & Hall, 1840, page 192

Why, who makes much of a miracle?
As to me I know of nothing else but miracles,
Whether I walk the streets of Manhattan,
Or dart my sight over the roofs of houses toward the sky,
Or wade with naked feet along the beach just in the edge of the water,
Or stand under trees in the woods,
Or talk by day with any one I love, or sleep in the bed at night with any one I love,
Or sit at table with the rest,
Or look at strangers opposite me riding in the car,
Or watch honey-bees busy around the hive of a summer forenoon,
Or animals feeding in the fields,
Or birds, or the wonderfulness of insects in the air,
Or the wonderfulness of the sundown, or of stars shining so quiet and bright,
Or the exquisite delicate thin curve of the new moon in spring;
These with the rest, one and all, are to me miracles,
The whole referring, yet each distinct and in its place,
To me every hour of the light and dark is a miracle,
Every cubic inch of space is a miracle,
Every square yard of the surface of the earth is spread with the same,
Every foot of the interior swarms with the same.
To me the sea is a continual miracle,
The fishes that swim—the rocks—the motion of the waves—the ships with men in them,
What stranger miracles are there?

Walt Whitman, 'Miracles', in *The Complete Poems*, edited by Francis Murphy, Penguin Books, 1982, page 409

MISSION

'Mission'—body sent by religious community to convert heathen; field of missionary activity; missionary post; organization in a district for the conversion of people.

When I was in Nigeria in 1968, standing in for the regular priest who was on six months' leave in the UK, the committee of All Saints Church, Jericho, felt they ought to have a missionary outreach. After deliberation, I was sent out to preach in a church in a little village outside Ibadan—well off the beaten track. I went out there one Sunday afternoon, along with an interpreter, a Nigerian canon (a character), who was fluent in Yoruba. We left the metalled road a few miles outside Ibadan, and struggled along a dirt track pitted with holes, eventually reaching our destination intact. The 'church' was a crude open-sided hut in the middle of the village. Word soon got round of our arrival, and in the next hour members of the village gradually assembled in and around the hut, including the animals (considered as valid members of the community). I began the missionary address with an opening sentence, and the Nigerian canon interpreted this in Yoruba, the local tongue. Three minutes later I came out with my next sentence, and the canon repeated the process. The missionary address was designed to last fifteen minutes. An hour and a half later I came out with my final sentence. I don't think we had any 'converts' that day, but my canon colleague beamed and said it was the most brilliant sermon he had ever heard. No one has ever said that of my preaching. I later learnt he was an outstanding preacher.

This day is a day of good news.

2 Kings 7:9

Sing to the Lord, all the earth! Tell of his salvation from day to day. Declare his glory among the nations, his marvelous works among all the peoples!

1 Chronicles 16:23–24

Then he said to his disciples, 'The harvest is plentiful, but the laborers are few; pray therefore the Lord of the harvest to send out laborers into his harvest.'

Matthew 9:37–38

'Peace be with you. As the Father has sent me, even so I send you.' And when he had said this, he breathed on them, and said to them, 'Receive the Holy Spirit.'

John 20:21–22

Kindness has converted more sinners than either zeal, eloquence, or learning.

F.W. Faber, *Spiritual Conferences*, Thomas Richardson and Son, 1859, page 6

Every life is a profession of faith, and exercises an inevitable and silent propaganda.

Henri Frédéric Amiel, *Amiel's Journal*, translated by Mrs Humphry Ward, Macmillan and Co., 1918, page 24

The appeal of Christ to us is not so much to consider how we will be punished as it is to see what we miss, if we will not take his way of things.

William Barclay, *The Gospel of Matthew*, volume II, The Saint Andrew Press, 1975, page 296

There is no expeditious road,
To pack and label men for God,
And save them by the barrel-load.

Francis Thompson, Epilogue to 'A Judgement in Heaven', in *The Works of Francis Thompson*, volume I, Burns and Oates, 1913, page 190

The members of the Church are impelled to engage in this activity because of the charity with which they love God and by which they desire to share with all men in the spiritual goods of this life and the life to come.

Vatican Council II, *The Conciliar and Post Conciliar Documents*, general editor, Austin Flannery, O.P., Fowler Wright Books, 1981, page 821

When a man genuinely and humbly feels he has discovered the buried treasure of the gospel he naturally wants to spread the good news to others and so to bring them closer to God. He must be on guard, however, not to let them stop short of himself.

Hubert van Zeller, *Considerations*, Sheed and Ward, 1974, page 15

I would spend my best efforts to make them follow him whose first servants were the fishermen of Galilee, for with all my heart I believe that that Man holds the secret of life, and that only the man who obeys him can ever come to know the God who is the root and crown of our being, and whom to know is freedom and bliss.

George Macdonald, *The Marquis of Lossie*, Everett and Co., 1912, page 269

I often ask myself why a 'Christian instinct' often draws me more to the religionless people than to the religious, by which I do not in the least mean with any evangelizing intention, but, I might almost say, 'in brotherhood.' While I am often reluctant to mention God by name to religious people—because that name somehow seems to me here not to ring true, and I feel myself to be slightly dishonest (it is particularly bad when others start to talk in religious jargon; I then dry up almost completely and feel awkward and uncomfortable)—to people with no religion I can on occasion mention him by name quite calmly and as a matter of course.

Dietrich Bonhoeffer, *Letters and Papers from Prison*, second revised edition, edited by Eberhard Bethge, SCM Press, 1971, page 154

The principal criticism one might have of contemporary Christians is that we are and have been so slow to understand the full, present magnificence of the invitation to be wholly open to Christ.

Writing of this invitation to life St Paul says, 'It is God himself who has called you to share in the life of his Son Jesus Christ our Lord; and God keeps faith' (1 Corinthians 1:9).

Our mission as modern Christians is to resensitize our contemporaries to the presence of a spirit within themselves. It is not the tradition handed on to us from the past that gives meaning to the Presence. Instead, it is the Presence that fills the tradition with meaning.

The Church witnesses in every generation not to a system of dry doctrines but to the Presence of the living Christ in its midst and its principal message is that this living Presence is a wholly contemporary reality.

John Main OSB, in *The Joy of Being*, selected by Clare Hallward, Darton, Longman and Todd, 1989, page 5

Yet all the time there is, for us whose hearts God has touched, the supreme task to bring home to the people of God himself, in his majesty, his compassion, his claim upon mankind, his astounding gift of his very self in Jesus the Word-made-Flesh. We cannot fulfil the task for this country unless we are striving to fulfil it towards the whole of the world. It therefore demands the service of men and women who will go anywhere in the world in Christ's obedience, who will witness to Christ's love in the insistence that races, black and white, are brothers of equal worth. Here at home our mission means for the Church a constant involvement in the community; we shall strive to penetrate the world of industry, of science, of art and literature, of sight and sound, and in this penetration, we must approach as learners as well as teachers. We need to be learning not only many new techniques, but also what God is saying to us through the new and exciting circumstances of our time. Yet because it is God to whom we witness, we need no less a constant detachment, a will to go apart and wait upon God in quiet, in silence, lest by our very busyness we should rob ourselves and rob others of the realization of God's presence: 'Be still and know that I am God.' Would that everyone whose heart God has touched would guard times of quietness amid our noisy, bustling life, to let God touch the heart again.

Michael Ramsey, *Canterbury Essays and Addresses*, SPCK, page 167

Some say that it is pure presumption to urge repentance upon people and proclaim a gospel of salvation. They insist that only he who is out of step with the times indulges in such arrogant conduct. Among those who argue in this fashion, the wayward, the egoist, the wilful, and those who press for their own selfish way abound.

Others, again, contend that it is wrong to urge repentance upon one's fellows and attempts to save them, because such action issues from a sense of superiority.

Were it possible for men to live an isolated, sundered life, repentance and salvation might not be necessary. In that case the individual might be left to settle his own affairs. But where the syphilitic disease of a debauchee poisons his descendants even to the fourth generation, and where the alcohol which men drink smites with a curse even to the tenth generation, one cannot but implore people to repent.

Even more imperative is the necessity of urging repentance upon moneyed men who, because of their unawakened state, tyrannize over tens of thousands of toilers and treat them as wage-slaves.

From this individualistic standpoint there may be no need to press for repentance and preach salvation, but where life takes on a social aspect, these two moral activities become imperative.

For the individualist in whose consciousness society is still unborn, a world where self-gratification is the norm may seem right, but society will never come to its own on that basis. Because the building of a moral social order known as the Kingdom of God was explicit and inherent in the teachings of Jesus, His religion and the way of the present-day proponents of individualism naturally clash. He who calls evangelism antiquated is a novice as regards life. When the destiny of mankind as a whole is considered, we must acknowledge that Christ made no mistake in His passionate effort to save.

Toyohiko Kagawa, in William Axling, *Kagawa*, SCM Press, 1946, page 128

The dismissal (at the end of a service) means this: You have been on the Mount of Transfiguration, you have seen the glory of God, you have been on the road to Damascus, you have faced the living God, you have been in the upper chamber, you have been here and there in Galilee and Judaea, all the mysterious places where one meets God, and now having spent several days with him, he says now that so much has been given—go, your joy will never abandon you. What you have acquired, you will never lose as long as you remain faithful. Go now, and if truly you have discovered joy, how can you not give joy to others? If truly you have come nearer to truth, how can you keep it for yourself? If truly something has been kindled in you which is life, are you going to allow anyone not to have a spark of this life? It does not mean go round and tell everyone specifically religious things or use clerical phrases. It means that you should go into the world which is yours with a radiance, with a joy, with an intensity that will make everyone look at you and say 'He has something he hadn't before. Is it that truly God has come near? He has something he never had before and which I do not possess—joy, life, certainty, a new courage, a new daring, a vision, where can I get it?'

People will also say to you, 'Mad you are.' I answer in those cases, and there are many, I say 'I am mad, but one thing I find strange. You who are wise call to the mad man, and the mad man is happy, alive and you feel dead; let us share my folly, it is God's folly.'

You are now going to start. With God you go now, with him on all the ways, on all the roads; you can dance on the Mount of Transfiguration, you can bring concreteness of life for others. May God bless you in it with joy. I don't know any other words than 'with joy'—go with joy, bring joy, and then you will have brought everything else, because God is joy, he is life, he is intensity.

Anthony Bloom, *God and Man*, Darton, Longman and Todd, 1971, page 124

MORALS

'Morals'—concerned with the distinction between right and wrong.

We had a visit from an American professor who was an expert in business ethics. Recently he had been taking a seminar in the States with a group of postgraduate students. He began his seminar by outlining the difficulties of business ethics, and raised the fundamental question: how do we decide what is right and what is wrong in a business setting? The corporate answer was: 'Look around, see what the majority of people are doing, and do that; the majority must be right. What's the problem?'

In one of our reflection groups on 'morals' we reached a very different conclusion. To be fair, the situation was more general, and the material put before the group very different. We also had a participant who always selected what he considered to be the most helpful quotation of all, and put that before the group. On this occasion he chose a passage written by William Temple: 'The standard of morals is the mind of Christ; that is our great principle if we are Christian. It will not help you at once to solve each particular problem; it will give you a touch-stone. As you seek to live in the constant companionship of Christ, you will find yourself knowing ever more fully what your duty is in accordance with His mind. Your moral authority is not a principle, but a Person. It is the mind of Christ.'

Here are two very different outlooks. What is our distinction between right and wrong? Do we go by what we feel, or by what we think, or by a subtle combination of both?

The righteous flourish like the palm tree, and grow like a cedar in Lebanon. They are planted in the house of the Lord, they flourish in the courts of our God. They still bring forth fruit in old age, they are ever full of sap and green, to show that the Lord is upright; he is my rock, and there is no unrighteousness in him.

Psalm 92:12–15

He who pursues righteousness and kindness will find life and honour.

Proverbs 21:21

Blessed are those who hunger and thirst after righteousness, for they shall be satisfied.

Matthew 5:6

See that none of you repays evil for evil, but always seek to do good to one another and to all.

1 Thessalonians 5:15

Men are great in proportion as they are moral.

Henry David Thoreau, *The Journal of Henry D. Thoreau*, volume IV, edited by Bradford Torrey and Francis H. Allen, 1949, Houghton Mifflin Company, Boston, The Riverside Press, page 128

Morality, when vigorously alive, sees farther than intellect.

J.A. Froude, *Short Stories on Great Subjects*, volume IV, Longmans, Green and Co., 1907, page 265

If your morals make you dreary, depend upon it they are wrong.

Robert Louis Stevenson, *Across the Plains*, T. Nelson and Sons, 1892, page 276

Conduct is three-fourths of our life and its largest concern.

Matthew Arnold, 'Literature and Dogma', in *The Complete Prose Works of Matthew Arnold*, volume VI, *Dissent and Dogma*, edited by R.H. Super, The University of Michigan Press, 1968, page 180

His [Jesus'] system of morality was the most benevolent and sublime probably that has been ever taught.

Thomas Jefferson, *The Writings of Thomas Jefferson*, Taylor & Maury, 1854, volume IV, page 476

To make our idea of morality centre on forbitten acts is to defile the imagination and to introduce into our judgements of our fellow-men a secret element of gusto.

Robert Louis Stevenson, *Across the Plains*, T. Nelson & Sons, 1892, page 272

Morality, said Jesus, is kindness to the weak; morality, said Nietzsche, is the bravery of the strong; morality, says Plato, is the effective harmony of the whole. Probably all three doctrines must be combined to find a perfect ethic; but can we doubt which of the elements is fundamental?

Will Durant, *The Story of Philosophy*, Ernest Benn, 1946, page 55

It is not strange if we are tempted to despair of good. We ask too much. Our religions and moralities have been trimmed to flatter us, till they are all emasculate and sentimentalized, and only please and weaken. Truth is of a rougher strain. In the harsh face of life, faith can read a bracing gospel.

Robert Louis Stevenson, *Across the Plains*, T. Nelson and Sons, 1892, page 259

The great secret of morals is love; or a going out of our own nature, and an identification of ourselves with the beautiful which exists in thought, action, or person, not our own. A man, to be greatly good, must imagine intensely and comprehensively; he must put himself in the place of another and of many others; the pains and pleasures of his species must become his own.

Percy Bysshe Shelley, 'A Defence of Poetry', in *The Prose Works of Percy Bysshe Shelley*, volume III, edited by H. Buxton Forman, Reeves and Turner, 1880, page 111

The standard of morals is the mind of Christ; that is our great principle if we are Christian. It will not help you at once to solve each particular problem; it will give you a touch-stone. As you seek to live in the constant companionship of Christ, you will find yourself knowing ever more fully what your duty is in accordance with His mind. Your moral authority is not a principle, but a Person. It is the mind of Christ.

William Temple, *Christian Faith and Life*, SCM Press, 1931, reissued 1963, page 60

No society has yet solved the problem of how to teach morality without religion. So the law must base itself on Christian morals and to the limit of its ability enforce them, not simply because they are the morals of most of us, nor simply because they are the morals which are taught by the established Church—on these points the law recognizes the right to dissent—but for the compelling reason that without the help of Christian teaching the law will fail.

Patrick Devlin, *The Enforcement of Morals*, Oxford University Press, 1970, page 25

The things that will destroy us are:
Politics without principle;
Pleasure without conscience;
Wealth without work;
Knowledge without character;
Business without morality;
Science without humanity,
and Worship without sacrifice.

Anon.

Morality is character and conduct, such as is required by the circle or community in which the man's life happens to be placed. It shews how much good *men* require of us. Religion is the endeavour of a man with all his mind, and heart, and soul, to form his life and his character upon the true elements of love and submission to God, and love and good will to man. A spiritual Christian is like a man who learns the principles of music, and then goes on to the practice. A moralist is like a man who learns nothing of the principles, but only a few airs by rote, and is satisfied to know as many tunes as common people do. Morality is good, and is accepted of God, as far as it goes but the difficulty is, it does not go far enough. 'Is not my fifty fathom cable as good as your hundred fathom one?' says the sailor. Yes, as far as it goes; but in water a hundred fathoms deep, if it does not go within fifty fathoms of anchorage, of what use will it be in a storm?

Henry Ward Beecher, *Life Thoughts*, Alexander Strahan and Co., 1859, page 145

If the evil-doing of men should arouse your indignation and uncontrollable grief, even to make you wish to revenge yourself upon the evil-doers, fear most of all that feeling; go at once and seek suffering for yourself just as if you were yourself guilty of that villainy. Accept that suffering and bear it, and your heart will be appeased, and you will understand that you, too, are guilty, for you might have given light to the evil-doers, even as the one man without sin and you have not given them light. If you had, you would have lighted a path for them too, and he who had committed the felony would not have committed it if you had shown him a light. And even if you showed a light but saw that men are not saved even by your light, you must remain steadfast and doubt not the power of the heavenly light; believe that if they were not saved now, they will be saved afterwards. And if they are not saved afterwards, their sons will be saved, for your light will not die, though you were to die yourself. The righteous man departs, but his light remains. People are always saved after the death of him who came to save them. Men do not accept their prophets and slay them, but they love their martyrs and worship those whom they have tortured to death. You are working for the whole, you are acting for the future. Never seek reward, for your reward on earth is great as it is: your spiritual joy which only the righteous find ... Love all men, love everything, seek that rapture and ecstasy. Water the earth with the tears of your joy and love those tears. Be not ashamed of that ecstasy, prize it, for it is a gift of God, a great gift, and it is not given to many, but only to the chosen ones.

Fyodor Dostoyevsky, *The Brothers Karamazov*, volume I, translated by David Magarshack, Penguin Books, 1963, page 379

MYSTICS & MYSTICISM

'Mystics, Mysticism'—a type of religion which puts the emphasis on immediate awareness of relation with God, on direct and immediate awareness of divine presence; religion in its most acute, intense and living stage.

I have a feel for mystics and mysticism. I prefer a type of religion which puts an emphasis on immediate awareness of relation with God. This explains why I am not particularly interested in the external trappings of religion and ecclesiastical chicanery. I feel much more at home in the simple beauty of our small college chapel, with the sun streaming through the windows during the day, and the candlelit atmosphere in the darkness of the night.

The essence of my faith is on direct and immediate consciousness of the divine presence, apprehended traditionally as Father, Son, Holy Spirit, with an additional awareness of the presence of divine attributes such as life, light, truth, joy and love. I feel comfortable in reflection groups, where religion is experienced in its most acute, intense and living stage (I wonder if something similar was the communal experience of Jesus and the disciples). In the silence of a reflection group we open ourselves to God's grace and respond with heart, mind, soul and strength, i.e. with the whole of our beings. We then share and cross-fertilize thoughts, feelings and ideas. I also believe in reflection, meditation and contemplation. These three forms of silent prayer are channels of God's grace. We have much to learn from mystics and mysticism.

The secret things belong to the Lord our God; but the things that are revealed belong to us and to our children for ever, that we may do all the words of this law.

Deuteronomy 29:29

The friendship of the Lord is for those who fear him, and he makes known to them his covenant.

Psalm 25:14

When you read this you can perceive my insight into the mystery of Christ, which was not made known to the sons of men in other generations as it has now been revealed to his holy apostles and prophets by the Spirit; that is, how the Gentiles are fellow heirs, members of the same body, and partakers of the promise in Christ Jesus through the gospel.

Ephesians 3:4–6

... of which I became a minister according to the divine office which was given to me for you, to make the word of God fully known, the mystery hidden for ages and generations but now made manifest to his saints.

Colossians 1:25–26

The mystics are not only themselves an incarnation of beauty, but they reflect beauty on all who with understanding approach them.

Havelock Ellis, *Selected Essays*, J.M. Dent and Sons, 1936, page 186

If you can enjoy the sun and flowers and music where there is nothing except darkness and silence you have then proved the mystic sense.

Helen Keller, *My Religion*, Hodder and Stoughton, 1927, frontispiece

Mystic. One who seeks by contemplation and self-surrender to obtain union with or absorption into the Deity, or who believes in spiritual apprehensions of truths beyond the understanding.

The Concise Oxford Dictionary

... by love, by the willing loss of self, we realize our true nature and become partakers in the being of God. The ego may be said to represent a stage in a spiritual process. By breaking out of its shell we can be born again, into a boundless freedom. That is the doctrine implied in all mystical philosophy.

Gerald Bullett, *The English Mystics*, Michael Joseph, 1950, page 17

The highest thought... is ineffable; it must be felt from one person to another but cannot be articulated. All the most essential and thinking part of thought is done without words. It is not till doubt and consciousness enter that words become possible. Our profoundest and most important convictions are unspeakable.

Samuel Butler, in Gerald Bullett, *The English Mystics*, Michael Joseph, 1950, page 227

We are always in presence of mysticism when we find a human being looking upon the division between earthly and super-earthly, temporal and eternal, as transcended, and feeling himself, while still externally amid the earthly and temporal, to belong to the super-earthly and eternal.

Albert Schweitzer, *The Mysticism of Paul the Apostle*, translated by William Montgomery, A. & C. Black, 1931, page 1

'In the time of the philosophers,' he [Al-Ghazzali] writes, 'as at every other period, there existed some of these fervent mystics. God does not deprive this world of them, for they are its sustainers.' It is they who, dying to themselves, become capable of perpetual inspiration and so are made the instruments through which divine grace is mediated to those whose unregenerate nature is impervious to the delicate touches of the Spirit.

Aldous Huxley, *The Perennial Philosophy*, Chatto and Windus, 1974, page 345

As we grow into Christian maturity we may find ourselves drawn beyond all images and concepts of God into what has been called 'the cloud of unknowing'. Here we find ourselves at the centre of a paradox, for intellectually we do not know, yet ultimately we know that which cannot be grasped by the intellect.

This has been the experience of all the mystics. Today the 'unknowing' is entered into by many who, divided by concepts, images and symbols, nevertheless are feeling a unity in God.

Bede Griffiths OSB, in *The Universal Christ*, edited by Peter Spink, Darton, Longman and Todd, 1990, page 20

The most beautiful and most profound emotion we can experience is the sensation of the mystical. It is the sower of all true science. He to whom this emotion is a stranger, who can no longer wonder and stand wrapt in awe, is as good as dead. To know that what is impenetrable to us really exists, manifesting itself as the highest wisdom and the most radiant beauty which our dull faculties can comprehend only in their most primitive forms—this knowledge, this feeling is at the centre of true religiousness.

Albert Einstein, in Lincoln Barnett, *The Universe and Dr. Einstein*, Victor Gollancz, 1949, page 95

It is a central idea of mysticism that there is a way to God through the human soul. The gate to Heaven is thus kept, not by St. Peter or by any other saint of the calendar; it is kept by each individual person himself as he opens or closes within himself the spiritual circuit of connection with God. The door into the Eternal swings within the circle of our own inner life, and all things are ours if we learn how to use the key that opens, for 'to open' and 'to find God' are one and the same thing.

Rufus M. Jones, *Spiritual Reformers in the 16th and 17th Centuries*, Macmillan and Co., 1914, page 133

The mystics—to give them their short, familiar name—are men and women who insist that they know for certain the presence and activity of that which they call the Love of God. They are conscious of that Fact which is there for all, and which is the true subject-matter of religion; but of which the average man remains either unconscious or faintly and occasionally aware. They know a spiritual order, penetrating, and everywhere conditioning though transcending the world of sense. They declare to us a Reality most rich and living, which is not a reality of time and space which is something other than everything we mean by 'nature', and for which no merely pantheistic explanation will suffice.

Evelyn Underhill, *Man and the Supernatural*, Methuen and Co., 1927, page 21

It was the love of the Father that pressed Jesus to die for love of us; his heart was beating with the Father's love. This is what we must long for, this selfless love of Jesus. Jesus crucified is the dark night into which we must enter so as to be one with God. We must allow ourselves to be drawn into mystery.

So the way to God is not by acquisition, not by building ourselves up, not by understanding but by letting go.

God himself will illumine our blindness, and this obscure knowledge is called mystical theology, the secret wisdom of God. We must renounce all clear perceptions of him and rest on faith alone.

Faith alone unites us to God; it is that journey of transcendence which leaves self so as to attain to God.

We have seen in Jesus the form it takes in this mortal life.

Ruth Burrows, in *The Watchful Heart*, edited by Elizabeth Ruth Obbard, Darton, Longman and Todd, 1988, page 39

Mysticism is a spiritual philosophy which demands the concurrent activity of thought, will, and feeling. It assumes from the outset that these three elements of our personality, which in real life are never sundered from each other, point towards the same goal, and if rightly used will conduct us thither. Further, it holds that only by the consecration of these three faculties in the service of the same quest can a man become effectively what he is potentially, a partaker of the Divine nature and a denizen of the spiritual world. There is no special organ for the reception of Divine or spiritual truth, which is simply the knowledge of the world as it really is. Some are better endowed with spiritual gifts than others, and are called to ascend greater heights; but the power which leads us up the pathway to reality and blessedness is, as Plotinus says, one which all possess, though few use it.

W.R. Inge, *The Philosophy of Plotinus*, volume I, Longmans, Green and Co., 1918, page 5

To say God is within us is to say we are transcendent, for God, our being subsisting in him and for him. He is our centre, our term, our completion.

Mystical contemplation is a divine impetus, vivifying, energizing, bringing into realization what is already there, as at the call of spring the seed begins to germinate. This is scriptural teaching. We must be born again of the Spirit.

Without the Spirit we remain flesh which cannot know God.

The evolution of the butterfly is a marvellous image of what is meant here. The caterpillar must be 'born again'; it must receive an impetus to enable it to be transformed into a butterfly, but it has within it, in its caterpillar state, all the potential for this. Nothing new is added, what is there is fully developed.

So it is with us. God is our Beloved in truth now, but will be so even more truly when we can call him that after long and generous efforts and correspondence with his action. Then we are no longer our own but his.

Ruth Burrows, in *The Watchful Heart*, edited by Elizabeth Ruth Obbard, Darton, Longman and Todd, 1988, page 57

At the core of our personality is a spark lighted at the altar of God in heaven—a something too holy ever to consent to evil, an inner light which can illuminate our whole being. To purify the eyes of the understanding by constant discipline, to detach ourselves from hampering worldly or fleshly desires, to accustom ourselves to ascend in heart and mind to the kingdom of the eternal values which are the thoughts and purposes of God—this is the quest of the mystic and the scheme of his progress through its earthly life. It carries with it its own proof and justification, in the increasing clearness and certainty with which the truths of the invisible world are revealed to him who diligently seeks for them. The experience is too intimate, and in a sense too formless, to be imparted to others. Language was not made to express it, and the imagination which recalls the hours of vision after they have passed paints the vision in colours not its own. Remembered revelation always tends to clothe itself in mythical or symbolic form. But the revelation was real and it is here and here only—in the mystical act *par excellence*, the act of prayer—that faith passes for a time into sight. Formless and vague and fleeting as it is, the mystical experience is the bedrock of religious faith.

W.R. Inge, *Outspoken Essays*, second series, Longmans, Green and Co., 1922, page 14

The real fact of the matter is, that the great mystics are religious geniuses. They make their contribution to religion in ways similar to those in which the geniuses in other fields raise the level of human attainments and achievements. They swiftly seize upon and appreciate the specific achievements of the race behind them; they are profoundly sensitive to the aspirations of their time and to the deep-lying currents of their age; they are suggestible in an acute degree, through heightened interest, to certain ideas or truths or principles which they synthesise by such leaps of insight that slow-footed logic seems to be transcended. Then these unifying and intensifying experiences to which they are subject give them irresistible conviction, 'a surge of certainty,' a faith of the mountain-moving order, and an increasing dynamic of life which, in the best cases, is manifest in thoughts and words and deeds. Their mystical experience seldom supplies them with a new intellectual content which they communicate, but their experience enables them rather to *see* what they know, to get possession of themselves, and to fuse their truth with the heat of conviction. The mystical experience is thus a way of heightening life and of increasing its dynamic quality rather than a way to new knowledge.

Rufus M. Jones, *Spiritual Reformers in the 16th and 17th Centuries*, Macmillan and Co., 1914, page xxiv

NEW CREATION

'New Creation'—renewed, fresh; further, additional; one converted to Christianity, put on the 'new man', show conversion by amendment.

Recently I went to stay with a friend, and his wife and family. Towards the end of my stay he was keen for me to go for a walk with him. Although it was late in the day and nearly dark, we set off and walked round a reservoir. It was eerie in the half-light and reminded me of times in the jungle, long ago. Bats were flying overhead and occasionally one flitted in our direction. When we reached a quiet remote spot, he paused and said, 'This is where it happened.' 'What do you mean?' I asked. 'What happened?' He was unable to put this precisely into words but what had happened was some kind of mystical experience. This experience, coming out of the blue, had effected him profoundly. He was curious to know if I understood what he was talking about, and whether I had ever come across it before. I tried to reassure him, and mentioned some of my own experiences which were similar. He then went on to say this experience had raised all sorts of questions—about himself, his work, and the direction of his life. What was really coming out of all this was a beckoning to a 'new creation', a challenge 'to put on the new nature, created after the likeness of God'. Only he could take that step forward, but I did leave a copy of *Visions of Hope* with him as an aid. The invitation to a 'new creation' happens more frequently than we usually imagine.

For behold, I create new heavens and a new earth; and the former things shall not be remembered or come into mind. But be glad and rejoice for ever in that which I create.

Isaish 65:17–18

A new heart I will give you, and a new spirit I will put within you; and I will take out of your flesh the heart of stone and give you a heart of flesh.

Ezekiel 36:26

Put off your old nature which belongs to your former manner of life and is corrupt through deceitful lusts, and be renewed in the spirit of your minds, and put on the new nature, created after the likeness of God in true righteousness and holiness.

Ephesians 4:22–24

Do not lie to one another, seeing that you have put off the old nature with its practices and have put on the new nature, which is being renewed in knowledge after the image of its creator.

Colossians 3:9–10

And ah for a man to arise in me,
That the man I am may cease to be!

Alfred, Lord Tennyson, 'Maud', X. vi. 396, in *The Poems of Tennyson*, edited by Christopher Ricks, Longmans, Green and Co., 1969, page 1060

So long as a man is capable of self-renewal he is a living being... If we are to remain among the living there must be a perpetual revival of youth within us, brought about by inward change and by love.

Henri Frédéric Amiel, *Amiel's Journal*, translated by Mrs. Humphry Ward, Macmillan and Co., 1918, page 186

We will never change men from the outside. New houses, new conditions, better material things only change the surface. It is the task of Christianity to make, not new things, but new men. And once the new men are created the new world will surely follow. That is why the Church is the most important institution in the world, for it is the factory where *men* are produced.

William Barclay, *The Gospel of Luke*, The Saint Andrew Press, 1964, page 187

St. Paul sees in Jesus the coming of a new man, man as God meant him to be. Jesus is not just one lonely individual but the beginning of a new creation, the spearhead of a new humanity. By our participation in the old humanity we share in its mortality incorporated with Christ, we share his deathless life. More than this, Paul sees an eternal purpose, unperceived in past ages, to bring all things and all men into a unity in Christ.

George Appleton, *Journey for a Soul*, William Collins Sons and Co., 1976, page 68

The great conviction of the New Testament is that by giving us his Spirit Jesus has dramatically transformed the fabric of human consciousness. Our redemption by Jesus Christ has opened up for us levels of consciousness that can be described by St Paul only in terms of a totally new creation.

God became man so that man might become God, as the early Fathers of the Church expressed it. It is our destiny to be divinized by becoming one with the Spirit of God. Divinization is utterly beyond our imagination and our own powers of understanding to comprehend. But it is not beyond our capacity to experience it in love.

Staggering as this revelation is and feeble though our capacity may be to receive it, it is worked out through the ordinariness of our humanity and the ordinariness of our human life.

The big problem in Christianity is to *believe* it.

John Main OSB, in *The Joy of Being*, selected by Clare Hallward, Darton, Longman and Todd, 1989, page 11

While we were yet sinners, Christ died for us. So it is written in the epistles to the Romans. This is love. Some people are proud of having given little bits of charity to others, but such meagre doles cannot represent true love.

This love of Christ cannot be understood by those who think only in the moral terms of give and take, who dwell only on the struggle for existence and its amelioration through mutual aid. The love of Christ has little to do with physiological and psychological considerations. It is his intention to restore the moral ruin at the bottom of a soul. Such love must utilize the power with which God originally created light out of darkness. That creative power is required to create a new soul out of the darkness of sin. Why then must sinners be forgiven? Redemption means that the ego is resmelted in the crucible that is Christ and poured forth anew. When this new creation appears, sins are dissolved and banished by this very process.

Toyohiko Kagawa, *Meditations*, translated by Jiro Takenaka, Harper and Brothers, 1950, number 37

To be inspired in our thoughts by divine knowledge, to be moved in our will by the divine purpose, to mould our emotions into harmony with divine bliss, to get at the great self of truth, goodness, and beauty to which we give the name of God as a spiritual presence, to raise our whole being and life to the divine status, is the ultimate purpose and meaning of human living. Some exceptional individuals have achieved this status and harmony. They are the highest types of humanity yet reached and indicate the final shape which humanity has to assume. They are the forerunners of the new race.

These men with wisdom and vitality, constant awareness and unremitting social effort, are not members of limited groups based on blood and soil but citizens of the new race.

Whatever the individual has done, the race, too, may and should eventually succeed in doing. When the incarnation of God is realized, not only in a few individuals but in the whole of humanity, we will have the new creation, the new race of men and women, mankind transformed, redeemed, and reborn, and a world created anew. This is the destiny of the world, the supreme spiritual ideal. It alone can rouse the deepest creative energies, rescue us from cold reason, inspire us with constructive passion, and unite us mentally, morally, and spiritually in a world fellowship.

Sir Sarvepalli Radhakrishnan, *Eastern Religions and Western Thought*, Oxford University Press, 1940, page 57

For neither circumcision counts for anything nor uncircumcision, but a new creation.
Galatians 6:15.

If I were asked to sum up the Christian message for our time in two words, I would say with Paul: It is the message of a 'New Creation.' We have read something of the New Creation in Paul's second letter to the Corinthians. Let me repeat one of his sentences in the words of an exact translation: 'If anyone is in union with Christ he is a new being; the old state of things has passed away; there is a new state of things.' Christianity is the message of the New Creation, the New Being, the New Reality which has appeared with the appearance of Jesus who for this reason, and just for this reason, is called the Christ...

We all live in the old state of things, and the question asked of us by our text is whether we *also* participate in the new state of things... We have known ourselves in our old being, and we shall ask ourselves in this hour whether we also have experienced something of a New Being in ourselves.

What is this New Being? Paul answers first by saying what it is *not*. It is neither circumcision, nor uncircumcision, he says. For Paul and for the readers of his letter this meant something very definite. It meant that neither to be a Jew nor to be a pagan is ultimately important; that only one thing counts, namely, the union with Him in whom the New Reality is present. Circumcision or uncircumcision—what does that mean for *us*? It can also mean something very definite, but at the same time something very universal. It means that no religion as such produces the New Being. Circumcision is a religious rite, observed by the Jews; sacrifices are religious rites, observed by the pagans; baptism is a religious rite, observed by the Christians. All these rites do not matter—only a New Creation. And since these rites stand, in the words of Paul, for the whole religion to which they belong, we can say: No religion matters—only a new state of things... There are the great religions beside Christianity, Hinduism, Buddhism, Islam and the remnants of classical Judaism; they have their myths and their rites—so to speak their 'circumcision'—which gives each of them their distinction. There are the secular movements: Fascism and Communism, Secular Humanism, and Ethical Idealism. They try to avoid myths and rites; they represent, so to speak, uncircumcision. Nevertheless, they also claim ultimate truth and demand complete devotion. How shall Christianity face them? Shall Christianity tell them: Come to us, we are a better religion, our kind of circumcision or uncircumcision is higher than yours? Shall we praise Christianity, our way of life, the religious as well as the secular? Shall we make of the Christian message a success story, and tell them, like advertisers: try it with us, and you will see how important Christianity is for everybody? Some missionaries and some ministers and some Christian laymen use these methods. They show a total misunderstanding of Christianity. The apostle who was a missionary and a minister and a layman all at once says something different. He says: No particular religion matters, neither ours nor yours. But I want to tell you that something has happened that matters, something that judges you and me, your religion and my religion. A New Creation has occurred, a New Being has appeared; and we are all asked to participate in it...

And now we ask again: What is this New Being? The New Being is not something that simply takes the place of the Old Being. But it is a renewal of the Old which has been corrupted, distorted, split and almost destroyed. But not wholly destroyed. Salvation does not destroy creation; but it transforms the Old Creation into a New One. Therefore we can speak of the New in terms of a *re*-newal: The threefold '*re*,' namely, *re*-conciliation, *re*-union, *re*-surrection.

In his letter, Paul combines New Creation with reconciliation. The message of reconciliation is: Be reconciled to God. Cease to be hostile to Him, for He is never hostile to you. The message of reconciliation is not that God needs to be reconciled. How could He be? Since He is the source and power of reconciliatiion, who could reconcile Him? Pagans and Jews and Christians—all of us have tried and are trying to reconcile Him by rites and sacraments, by prayers and services, by moral behaviour and works of charity. But if we try this, if we try to give something to Him, to show good deeds which may appease Him, we fail. It is never enough; we never can satisfy Him because there is an infinite demand upon us. And since we cannot appease Him, we grow hostile toward Him... This cannot be otherwise; for one is hostile, consciously or unconsciously, toward that by whom one feels rejected. Everybody is in this predicament, whether he calls that which rejects him 'God,' or 'nature,' or 'destiny,' or 'social conditions.' Everybody carries a hostility toward the existence into which he has been thrown, toward the hidden powers which determine his life and that of the universe, toward that which

makes him guilty and that threatens him with destruction because he has become guilty...
There are two symptoms which we can hardly avoid noticing: The hostility against ourselves and
the hostility against others. One speaks so often of pride and arrogance and self-certainty and
complacency in people. But this is, in most cases, the superficial level of their being. Below this,
in a deeper level, there is self-rejection, disgust, and even hatred of one's self... And he who
feels rejected by God and who rejects himself feels also rejected by the others. As he grows
hostile toward destiny and hostile toward himself, he also grows hostile toward other men... Be
reconciled with God—that means, at the same time, be reconciled with the others!

But it does *not* mean try to reconcile the others, as it does not mean to try to reconcile
yourselves. Try to reconcile God. You will fail. This is the message: A new reality has appeared in
which you *are* reconciled. To enter the New Being we do not need to show anything. We must
only be open to be grasped by it, although we have nothing to show.

Being reconciled—that is the first mark of the New Reality. And being reunited is its second
mark. Reconciliation makes reunion possible. The New Creation is the reality in which the
separated is reunited. The New Being is manifest in the Christ because in Him the separation
never overcame the unity between Him and God, between Him and mankind, between Him and
Himself. This gives His picture in the Gospels its overwhelming and inexhaustible power. In
Him we look at a human life that maintained the union in spite of everything that drove Him into
separation. He represents and mediates the power of the New Being because He represents and
mediates the power of undisrupted union. Where the New Reality appears, one feels united with
God, the ground and meaning of one's existence. One has what has been called the love of
one's destiny, and what, today, we might call the courage to take upon ourselves our own
anxiety. Then one has the astonishing experience of feeling reunited with one's self, not in pride
and false self-satisfaction, but in a deep self-acceptance. One accepts one's self as something
which is eternally important, eternally loved, eternally accepted. The disgust at one's self, the
hatred of one's self has disappeared. There is a centre, a direction, a meaning for life. All
healing—bodily and mental—creates this reunion of one's self with one's self. Where there is
real healing, *there* is the New Being, the New Creation... And it creates reunion with the others.
Nothing is more distinctive of the Old Being than the separation of man from man. Nothing is
more passionately demanded than social healing, than the New Being within history and human
relationships...

And if the Church which is the assembly of God has an ultimate significance, this is its
significance: That here the reunion of man to man is pronounced and confessed and realized,
even if in fragments and weaknesses and distortions. The Church is the place where the reunion
of man with man is an actual event, though the Church of God is permanently betrayed by the
Christian churches. But, although betrayed and expelled, the New Creation saves and preserves
that by which it is betrayed and expelled: churches, mankind and history.

The Church, like all its members, relapses from the New into the Old Being. Therefore, the
third mark of the New Creation is re-surrection... Resurrection is not an event that might
happen in some remote future, but it is the power of the New Being to create life out of death,
here and now, today and tomorrow. Where there is a New Being, *there* is resurrection, namely,
the creation into eternity out of every moment of time...

Reconciliation, reunion, resurrection—this is the New Creation, the New Being, the New
state of things. Do we participate in it? The message of Christianity is not Christianity, but a New
Reality. A New state of things has appeared, it still appears; it is hidden and visible, it is there and
it is here. Accept it, enter into it, let it grasp you.

Paul Tillich, *The New Being*, SCM Press, 1956, page 15

OTHER FAITHS

'Other Faiths'—the relationship of Christianity to Judaism, Islam, Buddhism, Hinduism, etc.

This is a big challenge for an Oxford college chaplain. Although the chapel is Church of England, the reality of the situation is that many of our undergraduates and postgraduates belong to other faiths. How then can I minister to them realistically in this multi-faith community?

I have wrestled with this problem for twenty-five years, ever since becoming Chaplain to University College, London, and then Chaplain Fellow of University College, Oxford. This is where I stand at the moment. I regard everyone I come across, irrespective of their religious affiliation (or none), as being made in the image and likeness of God. This affects the way I see people. I back this up with silent reflection. This helps to break down inner barriers, and allows me to grow and develop a faith which is deep in outlook and broad in outreach. I have come to terms with the fact that the chapel building has a limited role in college, and is mainly for Church of England and other Christians. I concentrate on running reflection groups which meet in my rooms and are regarded as neutral territory. In term-time, when I'm working flat out, thirty groups meet each week. The emphasis is not on conversion, but recognizing what we hold in common, and learning from each other. We try to stimulate growth and understanding. For me this is an enormous privilege and a great eye-opener, and some regard it as their most valuable hour of the week.

I was sent only to the lost sheep of the house of Israel.

Matthew 15:24

... a woman, whose little daughter was possessed by an unclean spirit, heard of him, and came and fell down at his feet. Now the woman was a Greek, a Syrophoenician by birth.

Mark 7:25–26

And I have other sheep, that are not of this fold.

John 10:16

Now among those who went up to worship at the feast were some Greeks. So these came to Philip, who was from Bethsaida in Galilee, and said to him, 'Sir, we wish to see Jesus.'

John 12:20–21

If we believe in God as Creator we must surely think of him as wanting to make an impact on all, through their history, their experience, their prophets. We believe that he is the source of all truth, goodness and love, so where we see signs of these we must surely believe that he has been active.

George Appleton, *Journey for a Soul*, William Collins Sons and Co., 1976, page 71

After long study and experience I have come to these conclusions that: 1) all religions are true; 2) all religions have some error in them; 3) all religions are almost as dear to me as my own Hinduism. My veneration for other faiths is the same as for my own faith. Consequently, the thought of conversion is impossible ... Our prayer for others ought never to be: 'God! give them the light thou has given to me!' But: 'Give them all the light and truth they need for their highest development!'

Mohandas K. Gandhi, in Jawaharlal Nehru, *Discovery of India*, Meridian Books, 1951, page 340

People of other faiths are our spiritual neighbours in the journey of life and in the search for spiritual dimensions and values. The outgoing Christian mission has made them neighbours and has stimulated them to examine their own religious traditions. The ease of travel and the development of trade brings them to our countries, so they are now physical as well as spiritual neighbours. Their presence makes them our neighbours, as well as their interest in religious questions. We have to interpret the second great commandment in our attitude towards them.

George Appleton, *Journey for a Soul*, William Collins Sons and Co., 1976, page 70

Once some blind men chanced to come near an animal that someone had told them was an elephant. They were asked what the elephant was like. The blind men began to feel its body. One of them said the elephant was like a pillar; he had touched only its leg. Another said it was like a winnowing-fan; he had touched only its ear. In this way the others, having touched its tail or belly, gave their different versions of the elephant. Just so, a man who has seen only one aspect of God limits God to that alone. It is his conviction that God cannot be anything else.

Sri Ramakrisha, *Ramakrisha: Prophet of New India*, translated by Swami Nikhilananda, Rider and Co., 1951, page 163

These people (Indians) will never hear of Christ in my lifetime. What has God been doing in them all these centuries? Is God absent from them? I must recognise God at work in their laughter, in their love, in their coming to terms with their sufferings, in their prayers. Travel suddenly opens the windows of the soul to the reality of God in other people. If the humble Hindu on the Ganges can't be saved unless he becomes C. of E. or Baptist or R.C., then God is not the God *I* want to believe in. Your faith depends literally on where you stand. If you stand in France you are a Catholic. If you stand in Burma you are a Buddhist. If most of the people in Ulster who are vehemently Protestant had been born in the south, they would have been Roman Catholics.

Colin James, in Gerald Priestland, *Priestland's Progress*, BBC Worldwide, 1982, page 95

In Jesus we see mirrored and perfectly revealed the Cosmic Being, the principle of the Godhead active in all history.

The Cosmic Christ may be seen working in and through the Israelites and speaking through the patriarchs and prophets. In like manner the same Cosmic Being may be seen moving in and through all the great religions in every age.

With the great intermingling of the cultures of East and West witnessed during this century, it has become increasingly difficult not to recognize this activity of the universal Christ. For it has become increasingly apparent that nowhere in the world and at no period of history has God left himself without a witness.

Christ is indeed the Alpha and the Omega, the first and the last, the one who embraces all history in meaning and purpose.

Bede Griffiths OSB, in *The Universal Christ*, edited by Peter Spink, Darton, Longman and Todd, 1990, page 10

It is no longer possible today for one religion to live in isolation from other religions. In almost every country people of different religions are meeting with one another and being compelled to face their differences.

More and more the necessity for contact is being realized. Those who attempt to do so are feeling that dialogue when properly understood is not a compromise but a process of enrichment by which each religion opens itself to the truth to be found in the other religion, and the two parties grow together in a common desire for truth.

Each religion has to hold to its own tradition, yet to allow that tradition to grow as it opens itself to other aspects of truth. So we realize that truth is one, but that it has many faces and each religion is an aspect of that face. The one truth is perceived to be manifesting itself under different signs and symbols.

Bede Griffiths OSB, in *The Universal Christ*, edited by Peter Spink, Darton, Longman and Todd, 1990, page 18

The Holy Spirit is at work in all creation and within all humanity, drawing all men and all things to unity in Christ, that is, into his mystical Body.

The realization of this unity begins within ourselves. From the depths of our being we learn with Christ to say 'Abba, Father'. It is there that we touch the source from which all life flows.

At the surface level of the various religions there are great diversity, differences and contradictions. As we touch one another at the deep level so we find ourselves moving from separation to unity, from contradiction to oneness and from diversity to convergence.

In every human being the Holy Spirit is present and at work. Even when ignored or denied the Spirit is moving, and drawing towards unity in Christ. He is drawing all things back to the source until we enter that absolute unity beyond all duality and are one with the Father.

Bede Griffiths OSB, in *The Universal Christ*, edited by Peter Spink, Darton, Longman and Todd, 1990, page 33

Christianity came out of the Semitic world of Jewish culture. Its teaching, definitions and thought were largely formed by Greek culture and philosophy. For nearly two thousand years the movement of the Church has been westwards.

The twentieth century has witnessed a powerful convergence of Western and Eastern cultures and this is profoundly affecting today's Church. Meditation, once thought to be the prerogative of Eastern and non-Christian religions, has thus opened the door into a Christ-centred spirituality for thousands of Westerners.

The immanent or indwelling God always central to Eastern spirituality is now by many seen to be at one with the Pauline doctrine of 'Christ in you, the hope of glory' (Ephesians 3).

God is one. Knowledge of the one God comes to all human beings through the opening of the heart. This is the true ecumenism.

It is the true interior religion of Christ for which today there is a great yearning.

Bede Griffiths OSB, in *The Universal Christ*, edited by Peter Spink, Darton, Longman and Todd, 1990, page 36

I see God as a vast mountain with its top vanishing into the clouds and its circumference disappearing over the horizon. We do not know what its limits are. Each of us stands in a slightly different position in relation to that mountain; each of us gets a somewhat different view of it. The nearest we—as a human race—can hope to get to a conspectus of the mountain is by adding together our different views, not by pretending (what is impossible) that we can all stand on the same spot: for we were not put on the same spot.

Increasingly we have learned, and we are able, to visit one another's points of view. By doing that we can appreciate why some people say the mountain is green and gentle, others that it is fierce and rocky, others again that it is clad with pine forests. It is all the same mountain, seen from different angles; and to deny any of those points of view is to diminish the truth nature of the mountain.

Equally, to endeavour to approach or climb the mountain as if we could tackle all those features simultaneously is to doom ourselves to an ineffectual and possibly disastrous expedition. It is not impossible to move over to a different base-camp, a different route. But fundamentally I believe that each of us has been set an appropriate route to climb and would do best to follow it. (Incidentally, that does not rule out the possibility that some views of the mountain are deceptive and even dangerous). But we can all witness together to the existence, majesty and glory of the mountain.

Most of us, if we are wise, will follow a guide who speaks our language—though there will always be some who insist they can follow their own lonely way. Some of the routes toward that unseen and here-unknowable summit lie adjacent to one another; some may cross or eventually run together. One party may call across to another, help another out of difficulty, donate some provisions, offer advice on the way ahead. One party may find a harder, steeper or loftier route than another; or again, may settle down to picnic idly on a plateau and cease climbing altogether. Most of our expeditions have been climbing for centuries; the climbers are the great-great-great-grandchildren of men and women who set out long ago. How futile it is to criticise each other for not having arrived on precisely the same path together! We cannot turn back (though some are tempted to). We can only do our best from where we are. But we are still on the same mountain.

Gerald Priestland, *Priestland's Progress*, BBC Worldwide, 1982, page 101

PAIN

'Pain'—suffering, distress, of body or mind.

I sometimes get accused of leading a very sheltered life, and, of course, there is an element of truth in this, but I have been exposed to a great deal of pain and suffering in the course of my ministry. I have had dealings with the blind, the deaf and the dumb. As a part-time hospital chaplain I have visited thousands of chronically sick patients (both old and young) suffering from a wide range of ailments. In the course of my work as a college chaplain I have come across students suffering from mental illness, depression, loneliness, various complexes, failure, schizophrenia, alcoholism, diabetes, epilepsy, bereavement, sexual abuse, compulsive gambling and hundreds undergoing the effects of broken relationships, whether from home or at college. The list is endless. That is why I have included a section on pain in *Visions of Faith*. At some stage in life all of us will go through painful experiences, and these can come to us from a wide variety of sources. Any system of education worthy of the name should prepare people to face pain and tackle it creatively. I think this was one benefit of doing two years of national service. One of the side-effects was the development of a certain outlook on life, and the emergence of a spirit of endurance. I now look back on certain painful experiences with feelings of gratitude and affection.

How long must I bear pain in my soul, and have sorrow in my heart all the day?
Psalm 13:2

Why is my pain unceasing, my wound incurable, refusing to be healed? Wilt thou be to me like a deceitful brook, like waters that fail?
Jeremiah 15:18

So his fame spread throughout all Syria, and they brought him all the sick, those afflicted with various diseases and pains, demoniacs, epileptics, and paralytics, and he healed them.
Matthew 4:24

For the moment all discipline seems painful rather than pleasant; later it yields the peaceful fruit of righteousness to those who have been trained by it.
Hebrews 12:11

Those who do not feel pain, seldom think it is felt.
Samuel Johnson, 'The Rambler', in *The Yale Edition of the Works of Samuel Johnson*, volume III, edited by W.J. Bate and Albrecht B. Strauss, Yale University Press, 1969, page 259

He has seen but half the universe who never has been shown the House of Pain.
Ralph Waldo Emerson, 'Miscellaneous Pieces', in *The Works of Ralph Waldo Emerson*, volume IV, edited by George Sampson, George Bell & Sons, 1906, page 189

Pain is no evil
Unless it conquers us.
Charles Kingsley, 'St. Maura', in *The Life and Works of Charles Kingsley*, volume XVI, *Poems*, Macmillan and Co., 1902, page 271

'If God were good, He would wish to make His creatures perfectly happy, and if God were almighty He would be able to do what He wished. But the creatures are not happy. Therefore God lacks either goodness, or power, or both.' This is the problem of pain, in its simplest form. The possibility of answering it depends on showing that the terms 'good' and 'almighty,' and perhaps also the term 'happy' are equivocal: for it must be admitted from the outset that if the popular meanings attached to these words are the best, or the only possible, meanings, then the argument is unanswerable.

C.S. Lewis, The Problem of Pain, The Centenary Press, 1941, page 14

Union with Jesus consists not in sitting in glory but in sharing his cup of shame, opprobrium, dishonour and powerlessness. These are the things in his mind when he offers us his cup, not the physical sufferings of his Passion.

How can we share this cup in our daily life?

By renouncing all power and every desire for it, every manoeuvre to obtain what we want, to prevail over others; by taking an attitude of unimportance and subjection to the community; by sacrificing the image we have of ourselves and which we sensitively want upheld in our own eyes and that of others; renouncing all desire for status and importance.

The cup Jesus wants to share with us is that of selfless love which is its own reward—he offers no other.

We think we know what the chalice contains and express our eagerness to drink it. When it comes to the point of drinking the above bitter ingredients, we turn away with loathing.

Ruth Burrows, in The Watchful Heart, edited by Elizabeth Ruth Obbard, Darton, Longman and Todd, 1988, page 29

What is the meaning of pain? How does it find a place in a world created by a loving God? If we are to face that tormenting question as Christians we must take care that we are not prejudiced by our natural attitude to pain. For we naturally tend to think of it as the first, if not the worst, of evils. In recent discussions of the problem of evil, suffering has bulked larger than sin. But here, at the foot of the Cross, we learn once for all that pain—agonising pain—may find a place in the perfect life. It did have place there. But no sin has any place there—no form of selfishness, whether hatred, lust or greed. The perfect life and death were sinless; they were not painless. On the contrary, the pain directly contributed to the perfection of the life and death. It was the endurance of the pain that the supreme courage was perfected; it was in the selfless endurance of pain that the supreme love was perfected. Take away pain from life, and you take heroism with it: the result is to make life poorer, nor richer. Of course this truth must never be made an excuse for lack of sympathy towards sufferers; we must relieve them if we can; so we shew love—the very best thing in life. But here, paradoxically, is another justification of pain. It is the chief occasion of sympathy. Our hearts are not easily drawn to others by their joy or their laughter, their virtues or their talents; but pain claims sympathy wherever it occurs. It is the great binder of hearts. And sympathy, being a form of love, is so precious that the cost of pain is not worthy to be compared with it.

We see how false our standards are when we reflect how much of our perplexity about pain is due to the suffering of the innocent. The assumption is that pain is at all costs to be avoided and averted unless it comes as a just penalty for wrong-doing. But this ignores the refining power of pain for those who accept it in gentleness and love. Observation shews that pain either purifies or coarsens the character, according to the degree of its development towards selflessness. From a Christian standpoint it is harder to justify the pain that further coarsens a brutal character which has earned it as a punishment, than the pain which comes to an innocent sufferer and is used as the material of spiritual growth. For there is no unselfishness so great as the unselfish endurance of pain; and when it is so used it becomes something for which the sufferer gives thanks.

The world is full of pain to-day; each of us has a share; for some it is but a slight burden, for others it is crushing. But every Christian can turn it into a blessing if he will seek the companionship of Christ in his suffering; then pain becomes a new point of fellowship with Christ; and even our suffering becomes part of the price of the world's redemption as we fill up what is left over of the sufferings of the Christ. Pain does not then cease to be pain; but it ceases to be barren pain; and in fellowship with Christ upon the Cross we find new strength for bearing it and even for making it the means by which our hearts are more fully cleansed of selfishness and grow towards perfect love.

William Temple, *Palm Sunday to Easter*, SCM Press, 1948, page 32

Revelation, the 'object' of Christian conviction, is not a foolproof system of divine answers to human questions. It is not a system at all, but a destiny—the destiny of men with God and of God among men. So we have to take into account that God has revealed to us only as much as we need in order to dare the next step towards him through the darkness, trusting that for us his light will not be extinguished for ever. God has revealed to us everything that will help us to get to heaven—all of it, but no more.

There are many questions to which Revelation gives no answer at all. God quite simply proves his love for us right to the end, to the Cross. This self-sacrificing love is God's uttermost, ultimate openness of being, the revelation, too, of what God has not yet given us as revelation and perhaps never will. Unfortunately the questions not answered by revelation are exactly the ones that most bitterly torment us. Such, for example, is the question of suffering, which is never given theoretical 'treatment' in the Bible. The book of Job is the supreme song of humanity silent in the face of suffering. People often try to provide a rational justification for suffering. For instance, that suffering is as important for life as shadow and darkness, in order to bring out the light. If we had only this lamentable, threadbare and superficial answer to human suffering, we should have good reason to resist it. Anyone who has even once seen a child suffer, a child in mortal pain, a child screaming for help we cannot give, will have understood once and for all that all the beauty of the world, all the joy and all the radiance of creation cannot justify the suffering of this one child. We Christians should not listen to those people who can explain everything, who can give a quick answer precisely when they don't have one. We should do better to admit honestly that we do not understand God, that we cannot conceive why God has created pain, so much howling, senseless pain. We do not understand why, at the end, the eyes of Christ were so filled with sorrow and weeping that he could not recognize even God.

God does not give an answer to human suffering—he takes it upon himself. He lets the ocean of pain that surrounds him burn through to the very centre of his incarnate being. St. Matthew writes: 'He began to be sorrowful and troubled' (Matthew 26:37). St. Mark puts it even more strongly: 'He began to be greatly distressed and troubled' (Mark 14:33). Luke said that Christ was 'in an agony' (Luke 22:44). In Christ's agony in the Garden of Olives his entire physical and mental self shrank from life to such an extent that 'his sweat became like great drops of blood falling down upon the ground' (Luke 22:44).

In the face of this act of God all questioning stops, even though there is no answer. This falling silent is one of the creative experiences of Christian prayer. The most beautiful words, those that give the most genuine help, are often born in a silence filled with suffering. Silence is the glowing furnace of the word, the forge of true speech and sensitivity. The people who have won the right to speak to us at the worst moments of our lives are those who have suffered in silence, before God, with God, and for his sake. God speaks to us through men whom—like his own Son—he has led into the desert, into the loneliness of suffering, of inner hunger and unquenchable yearning, and who have become quite silent there. For them their suffering has become an election and a mission; they feel inwardly linked to all sufferers; God lets them suffer human need in order that they may be able to sit down alongside a stranger, on the dreary bed of his inner prison and say, 'You are not alone.' Such people have the right to bear another's pain and to seek out God in their hesitant prayer. Their words are more than 'true.' They are words of solidarity.

Ladislaus Boros, *In Time of Temptation*, translated by Simon and Erika Young, Burns and Oates, 1968, page 104

PARADISE

'Paradise'—place of exceptional happiness and delight; often used as a synonym for heaven and for the Garden of Eden before the expulsion of Adam and Eve.

Three years ago I tore a cartilage in my knee whilst playing squash. I saw a specialist and arrangements were made to have it removed by keyhole surgery. On the appointed day I reported to the hospital and went off to the operating theatre. I was given a general anaesthetic (by injection) and the next thing I knew was regaining consciousness in the recovery ward. I was really surprised. The whole thing seemed to have taken only a split second. I checked my knee to see if the operation had been done. Yes, a bandage was in place. I then thought about what had happened. The hour or so under anaesthetic was a complete and utter blank, and seemed to be no time at all. Perhaps this is what death is like after all? I'm sure this is one possibility, with literally nothing to fear.

Is there another possibility to be found under 'Paradise?'

I found the most helpful words in the last sentence of Alan Richardson's long quotation. Ultimately I think the answer has to do with the realm of faith in the total revelation in Christ of God as holy love. I'm very fond of some words that might be helpful here, which come from the topic 'Heaven' quoted by Michael Ramsey. 'But how may we think of heaven? . . . In his work *The City of God*, St Augustine told of heaven thus: "We shall rest and we shall see, we shall see and we shall love, we shall love and we shall praise, in the end which is no end." '

And he said, 'Jesus, remember me when you come into your kingdom.' And he said to him, 'Truly, I say to you, today you will be with me in Paradise.'

Luke 23:42–43

I know a man in Christ who fourteen years ago was caught up to the third heaven—whether in the body or out of the body I do not know, God knows. And I know that this man was caught up into Paradise—whether in the body or out of the body I do not know, God knows—and he heard things that cannot be told, which men may not utter. On behalf of this man I will boast, but on my own behalf I will not boast, except of my weaknesses.

2 Corinthians 12:2–5

He who has an ear, let him hear what the Spirit says to the churches. To him who conquers I will grant to eat of the tree of life, which is in the paradise of God.

Revelation 2:7

Too much of words or yet too few! What to thy Godhead easier than One little glimpse of Paradise to ope the eyes and ears of man?

Sir Richard Burton, *The Kasidah of Haji Abdu Al-Vazdi*, H.J. Cook, 1900, page 3

The world is a mirror of infinite beauty, yet no man sees it.

It is a Temple of Majesty, yet no man regards it. It is a region of Light and Peace, did not men disquiet it. It is the Paradise of God.

Thomas Traherne, *Centuries*, The Faith Press, 1969, page 15

The meanest flowret of the vale,
The simplest note that swells the gale,
The common Sun, the air, and skies,
To him are opening Paradise.

Thomas Gray, 'Ode on the Pleasure Arising from Vicissitude', in *Poetry and Prose*, Oxford at the Clarendon Press, 1971

What is Paradise? All things that are; for all are goodly and pleasant, and therefore may fitly be called a Paradise. It is said also, that Paradise is an outer court of Heaven. Even so this world is verily an outer court of the Eternal, or of Eternity, and specially whatever in Time, or any temporal things or creatures, manifesteth or remindeth us of God or Eternity; for the creatures are a guide and a path unto God and Eternity. Thus this world is an outer court of Eternity, and therefore it may well be called a Paradise, for it is such in truth.

Theologia Germanica, translated by Susanna Winkworth, Stuart and Watkins, 1966, page 119

Now I was come up in spirit through the flaming sword into the paradise of God. All things were new, and all the creation gave another smell unto me than before, beyond what words can utter. I knew nothing but pureness, and innocency, and righteousness, being renewed up into the image of God by Jesus Christ, so that I say I was come up to the state of Adam which he was in before he fell. The creation was opened to me, and it was showed me how all things had their names given them according to their nature and virtue.

George Fox, *The Journal of George Fox*, a revised edition by John L. Nickalls, Cambridge University Press, 1952, page 27

'Since I am coming to that Holy roome
Where, with thy Quire of Saints, for evermore
I shall be made thy music; as I come
I tune the instrument here at the door,
And what I must doe then, thinke here before.'

These words by John Donne direct our attention to the very heart of the purpose of our life on this earth. They stir our imagination and provoke what Wordsworth calls 'obstinate questionings.' How are we to set about this tuning of our instrument, here in the ante-room of earth-life, before joining the great orchestra in the next dimension? Donne's powerful poetic imagery sets fire to our imagination. He is suggestive, not dogmatic, and we are left free to speculate and to undertake our own 'adventures in ideas.' Whatever our beliefs or prejudices about survival after physical death may be, we shall probably be familiar with the concept of many different levels of consciousness; and it is in this direction that we may find an interpretation of Donne's poem.

A wise teacher has said that even a little knowledge and understanding of the next sphere (for which we are all bound, whether we like it or not) will be of great value to us. If the next world is indeed largely a thought-world, Donne's words are fraught with a sense of urgency that underlines the spiritual law of cause and effect: as we think now, so shall we *be* when we discard the body. The metaphor of music, implying a vast orchestra in which we all participate, draws our attention to the possibility of unity in diversity, and to the underlying quality of harmony. Any orchestra would be the poorer if all the instruments were playing the same line of music: the secret lies in perfect blending. Implicit in Donne's image is the suggestion that each one of us will contribute a degree of harmony, or lack of it, according to the quality of thought and character built up through a possible succession of lives. 'As a man thinketh in his heart, so is he.'

Belle Valerie Gaunt and George Trevelyan, *A Tent in which to Pass a Summer Night*, Coventure, 1977, page 61

The pleasant abode of the righteous dead was called PARADISE (Luke 23:43, 2 Corinthians 12:4, Revelation 2:7)—originally a Persian word for a nobleman's park or garden; the term contains a reference to the Garden of Eden, in which was situated the tree of life. There seem to have been two Paradises in the thought of the rabbis—one in Sheol (perhaps that of Luke 23:43) and one in heaven (perhaps that of 2 Corinthians 12:4). But the expression as used by Jesus (once only) is merely a conventional way of saying 'after physical death', and should not be held to constitute an endorsement of rabbinic theories. In post-biblical Christian theology the term came to be used interchangeably with 'heaven'. There is no support in the New Testament for rabbinic speculations (or later Christian ones) about Paradise as a place of purgation where souls are purified from sin and fitted for heaven. Jesus' word to the penitent thief must be understood as a striking application of the doctrine of Justification by Faith rather than as a metaphysical declaration about the condition of the departed.

The opposite of Paradise is GEHENNA, that part of Sheol reserved for the wicked. Gehenna was originally 'the Valley of Hinnom' near Jerusalem, where once child-sacrifice had been offered to Moloch by Ahaz (2 Chronicles 28:3) and Manasseh (33:6); it is thought to have become at a later date the city's refuse dump where rubbish was burnt, and so an appropriate symbol of punishment. Jesus seems to have accepted the conventional rabbinic term (Mark 9:43, 45, 47, etc., RV marg.) and emphasized it with great force. There is no need whatever to regard Jesus' use of the word as endorsing rabbinic (or medieval) notions of future punishment as physical torment; but on the other hand it is impossible to soften the severity of Jesus' warning against unrepented sin, and the sentimentalism which seeks to do so is a distortion of the teaching of Jesus and the New Testament as a whole. Whatever may be implied by the symbolism of 'unquenchable fire' (Mark 9:43) or 'eternal fire' (Matthew.18:8; cf. 25:41) or the casting of the wicked into the 'furnace of fire' (Matthew 13:42, 50), we have no right to explain the symbolism away. From the destruction of Sodom and Gomorrah by the fires of judgment (Genesis 19:24) fire has been the biblical symbol of destruction, condemnation and punishment, and so it continues in the New Testament. The New Testament does not answer questions we like to ask about such matters as the nature of punishment after death, eternal retribution, and so on; and it is as much a mistake to erect its symbolic language into metaphysical answers to such questions as it is to ignore the solemnity of the warnings which that language conveys. The New Testament writers do not seek to satisfy our natural curiosity, but to awaken in us a sense of awed responsibility before God the Judge of all. Such tentative answers as we may propose to these questions must not be based on a few texts but on the total revelation in Christ of God as holy love.

Alan Richardson, in *A Theological Word Book of the Bible*, edited by Alan Richardson, SCM Press, 1950, page 107

PENITENCE

'Penitence'—concerned with making a full and sincere confession of sins, declaring sorrow for them, and promising to amend his or her life, and so make restitution to those whom he or she had wronged.

The school chaplain prepared a group of us for confirmation. Just before we were confirmed he gave us some final instructions on the communion service. He suggested we prepare ourselves carefully before receiving communion, and arrive in chapel ten minutes before the service began. In those few minutes we were to kneel down (signifying humility) and go through a period of self-examination, as a form of penitence. We were to start with 'thought' and come clean with all that had gone wrong in our thought life since we had last communicated. The same was true for 'word'—including the bad language we had almost certainly used as sixteen-year-old schoolboys. Next on his list was 'deed' and we had to own up to all the things we had done which we knew to be wrong. Lastly there was 'omission'. We had to admit all the things we had failed to do, including skimped work in his divinity classes. We were to end our penitential period with a silent confession and were then ready to receive God's absolution in the service, and make a fresh start on receiving the body and blood of Christ.

When I obeyed his instructions, the communion service meant much more to me than the times when I slept in and arrived at the last moment—unprepared. Little did I know then that penitence is the work of a lifetime.

Have mercy on me, O God, according to thy steadfast love; according to thy abundant mercy blot out my transgressions. Wash me thoroughly from my iniquity, and cleanse me from my sin!

Psalm 51:1–2

But if a wicked man turns away from all his sins which he has committed and keeps all my statutes and does what is lawful and right, he shall surely live.

Ezekiel 18:21

I will arise and go to my father, and I will say to him, 'Father, I have sinned against heaven and before you; I am no longer worthy to be called your son; treat me as one of your hired servants.'

Luke 15:18–19

If we confess our sins, he is faithful and just, and will forgive our sins and cleanse us from all unrighteousness.

1 John 1:9

It can take less than a minute to commit a sin. It takes not as long to obtain God's forgiveness. Penitence and amendment should take a lifetime.

Hubert van Zeller, *Considerations*, Sheed and Ward, 1974, page 48

He who is truly penitent and really sorry shall receive pardon without doubt or delay. The prayer that is made by a contrite and humble heart is quickly granted, a heart contrite by fear and humbled by sorrow.

Richard of Saint-Victor, *Selected Writings on Contemplation*, translated by Clare Kirchberger, Faber and Faber, 1957, page 87

We have heard that *the way is narrow that leads to life*. This is the way of penance and few find it. 'Narrow' is what it is called, and called rightly; through it the flesh sheds its unlawful things and the worldly comforts; through it the soul is held back from degenerate delights and decadent thoughts; through it the soul is totally given over to love of the divine. Yet it is not often found among men, because scarcely any have taste for the things of God, but look for earthly joys, and find their pleasure there. So they have recourse to sensual lusts, and neglect the mental: they detest any way that would lead to spiritual well-being, and reject it as narrow and rough, and to their lust intolerable.

Richard Rolle, *The Fire of Love*, translated by Clifton Wolters, Penguin Books, 1981, page 103

It is penitence which creates intimacy with Our Lord. No one can know Him intimately who has not realised the sickness of his own soul and obtained healing from the physician of souls. Our virtues do not bring us near to Christ—the gulf between them and His holiness remains unbridgeable. Our science does not bring us near Him, nor our art. Our pain may give us a taste of fellowship with Him, but it is only a taste unless the great creator of intimacy—penitence—is also there. For in my virtue, my art, my knowledge, there is sure to be some pride—probably, indeed, a great deal of pride. But I cannot be proud of sin which is really admitted to be sin. I can be proud of my dare-devilry; oh, yes, and of anything I do to shock respectability. But then I am not admitting to myself that it is sin—only that other people think it so. When I find something in myself of which I really am ashamed, I cannot at the time be proud of that—though, alas I may be proud of my shame at it, and so make this, too, worthless. In straightforward shame at my own meanness there is no pride and no expectation of forgiveness except through trust in the love of Him who forgives. So it is penitence which brings me in all simplicity to appeal to the sheer goodness and love of God. And we can turn our very sins into blessings if we will let them empty us of pride and cast ourselves upon the generosity of God. 'We receive the due reward of our sins: Jesus, remember me.'

'To-day shalt thou be with me in Paradise.' To-day. We do not have to wait for 'some far-off divine event.' When true penitence opens our hearts to the love of God, forthwith He enters there to reign. Because His Kingdom is spiritual, the sovereignty of His love over hearts that are open to its claim and its appeal, we do not have to wait for Him to come in His kingdom. No doubt its perfection, when all hearts are open and respond, is in the future. But the power of His Kingdom is focussed in His Cross. He reigns from the Tree. Let us come with hearts ready to respond to that shining forth of the Love of God. Let us see how we look in that Presence. Then let us acknowledge our unfitness to be near Him, and hear Him say in answer: 'To-day shalt thou be with Me.'

William Temple, *Palm Sunday to Easter*, Pamphlet, SCM Press, 1948, page 20

Penance—The word derives from the Latin *paenitentia*, meaning penitence or repentance. In Christian history it has variously designated an inner turning to God or a public returning to the church, any of a series of ecclesiastical disciplines designed to facilitate such inward or outward reconversion, and the various works that had to be performed as part of such disciplines. In the Middle Ages the standard *sacramentum paenitentiae* was private confession, which in English came to be known as the sacrament of penance. Today in the Roman Catholic Church it is also called the sacrament of reconciliation.

There is scriptural evidence that early Christians continued the Jewish practice of 'binding and loosing', i.e. restricting recalcitrant members from full participation in the community, and then later releasing them from such restrictions when they mended their ways (cf. 1 Corinthians 5:1–13; 2 Corinthians 2:5–11; Matthew 18:15–18). All Christians, of course, had been enjoined by Jesus to forgive one another, but it was not until the second century that their leaders began publicly to readmit to the church those who had once renounced their faith (cf. *The Shepherd of Hermas*, Mandate 4).

From this simple beginning, the practice of public repentance and reconciliation with the church, not only for apostasy and heresy but also in cases of serious sin such as murder and adultery, grew during the early patristic period into a fully-fledged penitential discipline. The penances imposed sometimes lasted for years, and they culminated in a ritual of reconciliation with the church, represented by the bishop. The length and severity of the discipline, however, combined with the fact that canon law allowed such ecclesiastical reconciliation to be received only once in a lifetime, eventually led to a practice of deathbed repentance. It must be remembered, however, that during these centuries the vast majority of Christians were never directly involved in public penitence.

During the sixth century Irish missionaries introduced the monastic practice of private, repeated confession, made to a priest rather than a bishop, to the European mainland. After some initial resistance from the hierarchy, the new penitential practice grew in popularity and eventually replaced the older form, and during the course of the centuries the harsh penances originally imposed by the monks were supplanted by prayers and other such spiritual works. Also, by the twelfth century, the priest's prayer for the forgiveness of the penitent had evolved into a pronouncement of absolution for sins, and it was in this form that the ritual became one of the seven ecclesiastical sacraments of mediaeval Christendom.

Most of the scholastic theories of penance were concerned to explain how the forgiveness of God came to individuals through the ministry of the priest, but Luther and other Reformers in the sixteenth century insisted that God's grace was immediately available to Christians. This, combined with the conclusion that justification is not dependent on the performance of good works, led them to repudiate the medieval practice and its theological rationale. Some allowed, however, that confession could be beneficial in certain circumstances. (cf. Luther, *Large Catechism*, 'A Short Exhortation to Confession'; Calvin, *Institutes of the Christian Religion*, 111, 4, 12–14). Nevertheless, confession as a general practice eventually disappeared from most churches of the Reformation, including the Anglican, which retains it as one of the five, non-dominical sacraments.

Both the Roman Catholic and Orthodox churches retain the sacrament and regard it as instituted by Christ, although the rites and the theologies behind them are somewhat different in each case. The official Roman rite was revised in 1973, and both before and since that revision the Catholic understanding of the meaning and nature of ecclesiastical reconciliation has been shifting away from the scholastic and somewhat legalistic interpretation of the late mediaeval period, and towards a more biblical and pastoral interpretation of the sacrament.

J. Martos, in *A New Dictionary of Christian Theology*, edited by Alan Richardson and John Bowden, SCM Press, 1983, page 435

PHILOSOPHY

*'Philosophy'—love of wisdom or knowledge, especially that which
deals with ultimate reality, or with the most general causes—
principles of things, study of principles of human action or conduct;
system of conduct of life.*

As far back as I can remember I have always had an interest in philosophy, especially that which deals with ultimate reality. Imagine my delight on spotting a verse of scripture which spoke of 'Christ in whom are hid all the treasures of wisdom and knowledge.' I sometimes wonder if the Church of today has completely lost sight of this verse.

Someone whose writings have impressed me is Nicolas Berdyaev. He was born in Kiev in 1874 and spent his early years in Russia. In 1933 he settled down in Paris where he did most of his writing, and died there in 1948. He has been described as one of the greatest philosophers and prophets of our time. That is why there are a number of his passages in *Visions of Faith*. One of these is included in this section. It goes as follows: 'Philosophical knowledge is a spiritual act, where not only the intellect is active, but the whole of man's spiritual power, his emotions and his will.'

The practice of reflection enables people to think, and for some is a gateway to philosophical knowledge. But, as Berdyaev points out, the pursuit of philosophical knowledge is a spiritual activity as well. In this activity the gifts of the Spirit are brought into play, along with the intellect, the emotions and the will. This is one way to wholeness of life.

Can you find out the deep things of God? Can you find out the limit of the Almighty?

Job 11:7

It is the glory of God to conceal things, but the glory of kings is to search things out. As the heavens for height, and the earth for depth, so the mind of kings is unsearchable.

Proverbs 25:1–3

For Christ did not send me to baptize but to preach the gospel, and not with eloquent wisdom, lest the cross of Christ be emptied of its power. For the word of the cross is folly to those who are perishing, but to us who are being saved it is the power of God. For it is written, 'I will destroy the wisdom of the wise, and the cleverness of the clever I will thwart.'

1 Corinthians 1:17–19

See to it that no one makes a prey of you by philosophy and empty deceit, according to human tradition, according to the elemental spirits of the universe, and not according to Christ.

Colossians 2:8

That untaught innate philosophy.

Lord Byron, 'Childe Harold's Pilgrimage', in *The Complete Poetical Works*, volume II, edited by Jerome J. McCann, Oxford at the Clarendon Press, 1980, page 90

The example of good men is visible philosophy.

English Proverb

Philosophy makes us wiser, but Christianity makes us better men.

Henry Fielding, *The History of Tom Jones*, volume I, J.M. Dent and Sons, 1957, page 377

Any genuine philosophy leads to action and from action back again to wonder, to the enduring fact of mystery.

Henry Miller, *The Wisdom of the Heart*, New Directions Books, 1941, page 93

The object of studying philosophy is to know one's mind, not other people's. Philosophy means thinking things out for oneself.

W.R. Inge, *Outspoken Essays*, Second Series, Longmans, Green and Co., 1922, page 1

Every philosophy is tinged with the colouring of some secret imaginative background, which never emerges explicitly into its trains of reasoning.

Alfred North Whitehead, *Science and the Modern World*, Cambridge University Press, 1932, page 9

Philosophical knowledge is a spiritual act, where not only the intellect is active, but the whole of man's spiritual power, his emotions and his will.

Nicolas Berdyaev, *Christian Existentialism*, selected and translated by Donald A. Lowrie, George Allen and Unwin, 1965, page 119

To be a philosopher is not merely to have subtle thoughts, nor even to found a school, but so to love wisdom as to live according to its dictates, a life of simplicity, independence, magnanimity, and trust.

Henry David Thoreau, *Walden*, The New American Library of World Literature, Inc., 1960, page 15

'Come unto me ... and I will give you rest'; it is not Philosophy that can estimate the right of the Speaker to issue that invitation or to make that promise; that right can be proved or disproved only by the experiment of life.

William Temple, *Nature, Man and God*, Macmillan and Co., 1934, page 520

A Christian cannot live by philosophy. Only the light of Christian revelation gives the end as well as the means of life. It is the same for you as for me and the man in the street. If one has more learning, another has more grace, it is all one.

John Chapman, *The Spiritual Letters of Dom John Chapman*, Sheed and Ward, 1946, page 205

Pretend what we may, the whole man within us is at work when we form our philosophical opinions. Intellect, will, taste, and passion co-operate just as they do in practical affairs; and lucky it is if the passion be not something as petty as a love of personal conquest over the philosopher across the way.

William James, *The Will To Believe*, Longmans, Green and Co., 1904, page 92

The philosophy which is so important in each of us is not a technical matter; it is our more or less dumb sense of what life honestly and deeply means. It is only partly got from books; it is our individual way of just seeing and feeling the total push and pressure of the cosmos.

William James, *Pragmatism*, Longmans, Green and Co., 1943, page 4

The highest triumphs of philosophy are possible only to those who have achieved in themselves a purity of soul. This purity is based upon a profound acceptance of experience, realised only when some point of hidden strength within man, from which he can not only inspect but comprehend life, is found. From this inner source the philosopher reveals to us the truth of life, a truth which mere intellect is unable to discover. The vision is produced almost as naturally as a fruit from a flower out of the mysterious centre, where all experience is reconciled.

Sir Sarvepalli Radhakrishnan, *Indian Philosophy*, volume I, George Allen and Unwin, 1923, page 44

The Challenge of Death is the summary challenge addressed by the universe to man. It is the spear-point of the Challenge of Life, not to be evaded on any terms, as the fashion now is with many to evade it. To find a good in life which is worth achieving in spite of the fact, consciously realized, that this visible scene on which we operate, and we, the visible agents who operate, will presently be gathered to the dark death-kingdoms and enfolded in the everlasting Silence—that is the spear-point of the Challenge, the acid test of philosophy, the point where philosophy must either pass into religion or retire, beaten, from the field. The philosopher may be unaware of this, often is, or will even go out of his way to repudiate all interest in the matter but in the audience that gathers round his feet there is always a vague hope, and sometimes a poignant one, that he will come at last to the critical point where Life and Death stand confronting one another in a 'fell incensed opposition,' that he will let fall the word of wisdom which is to end that conflict and release the mind from the tension it involves—perhaps by teaching content-ment with annihilation, perhaps by an argument for *carpe diem*, perhaps by proving personal immortality. Without that motive, subtly operating in all our curiosities about 'mind and matter,' 'good and evil,' 'reality and appearance,' there would be no market for the philosopher's goods; his performance would be offered to an empty house.

L.P. Jacks, *The Faith of a Worker*, Hodder and Stoughton, 1925, page 24

He thought that to be a Philosopher, a Christian, and a Divine, was to be one of the most illustrious creatures in the world and that no man was a man in act, but only in capacity, that was not one of these, or rather all. For either of these three include the other two. A Divine includes a Philosopher and a Christian; a Christian includes a Divine and a Philosopher; a Philosopher includes a Christian and a Divine. Since no man therefore can be a man unless he be a Philosopher, nor a true Philosopher unless he be a Christian, nor a perfect Christian unless he be a Divine, every man ought to spend his time in studying diligently Divine Philosophy.

This last principle needs a little explication. Not only because Philosophy is condemned for vain, but because it is superfluous among inferior Christians, and impossible, as some think, unto them. We must distinguish therefore of philosophy and of Christians also. Some philosophy, as Saint Paul says, is vain. But then it is vain philosophy. But there is also a Divine Philosophy, of which no books in the world are more full than his own. That we are naturally the Sons of God (I speak of primitive and upright nature,) that the Son of God is the first beginning of every creature, that we are to be changed from glory to glory into the same Image, that we are spiritual Kings, that Christ is the express Image of His Father's person, that by Him all things are made whether they are visible or invisible, is the highest Philosophy in the world; and so it is also to treat, as he does, of the nature of virtues and Divine Laws. Yet no man, I suppose, will account these superfluous, or vain, for in the right knowledge of these Eternal Life consisteth. And till we see into the beauty and blessedness of God's Laws, the glory of His works, the excellency of our soul, &c. we are but children of darkness, at least but ignorant and imperfect: neither able to rejoice in God as we ought, nor to live in communion with Him. Rather we should remember that Jesus Christ is the Wisdom of the Father, and that since our life is hid with Christ in God, we should spend our days in studying Wisdom, that we might be like unto Him that the treasures of Heaven are the treasures of Wisdom, and that they are hid in Christ. As it is written, *in Him are hid all the treasures of Wisdom and Knowledge.*

Thomas Traherne, *Centuries*, The Faith Press, 1969, page 167

POLITICS

'Politics'—science and art of government, political affairs of life, political principles.

Politics, in the sense of the science and art of government, has become so complex, that it has rapidly become the province of the professional politician. How, then, can the man in the street contribute in these circumstances? There is at least one thing he can do: keep a sharp eye on politicians, and expose abuses of power.

A helpful insight in this section comes from the pen of William Temple, a former Archbishop of Canterbury—often regarded as a politically conscious churchman. In his book *The Kingdom of God*, he states the official Church position on politics. He starts off with a warning, and recommends the Church and the official representatives must keep themselves free from the entanglements of party politics. There will come times when they should support or resist a specific measure; but they should not take any share in the strife of parties. He goes on to state that their business is something far more important—the formation of that mind and temper of the whole community which will lead to wholesome legislation by any party and all parties.

To this I would add an insight of John Fenton and Michael Hare Duke. In a joint publication, *Good News*, published twenty years ago, they wrote that the changed circumstances of our present situation make it urgent to take seriously the politics of a kingdom of heaven as a way of handling a technologically conditioned world.

This is a huge task, and needs to be tackled.

Beware lest you say in your heart. 'My power and the might of my hand have gotten me this wealth.' You shall remember the Lord your God, for it is he who gives you power to get wealth.

Deuteronomy 8:17–18

Thine, O Lord, is the greatness, and the power, and the glory, and the victory, and the majesty; for all that is in the heavens and in the earth is thine; thine is the kingdom, O Lord, and thou art exalted as head above all. Both riches and honour come from thee, and thou rulest over all. In thy hand are power and might; and in thy hand it is to make great and to give strength to all. And now we thank thee, our God, and praise thy glorious name.

1 Chronicles 29:11–13

... teaching them to observe all that I have commanded you; and lo, I am with you always, to the close of the age.

Matthew 28:20

Let every person be subject to the governing authorities. For there is no authority except from God, and those that exist have been instituted by God.

Romans 13:1

Everything begins in mysticism and ends in politics.

Charles Péguy, *Basic Verities*, translated by Ann and Julian Green, Kegan Paul, Trench, Trubner and Co., 1943, page 107

Those who say that religion has nothing to do with politics do not know what religion means.

Mohandas K. Gandhi, *The Story of My Experience with Truth, An Autobiography*, translated by Mahadur Desai, Phoenix Press, 1949, page 420

No society can be run on the basis that its members are saints. Any state has to take into account that it has to govern sinners, which means there are going to be tensions between one group and another—but it's better to work that out than have bloody revolution.

Harry Williams, in Gerald Priestland, *Priestland's Progress*, BBC Worldwide, 1982, page 55

The issue of Church involvement in politics hinges on the fact that *we* are concerned with people as politics are concerned with people; you can't divide people up into secular and religious. Whenever the poor are afflicted, or whenever human dignity and freedom is not respected, then the Church has a duty to sound a prophetic note; and it must be prepared to be unpopular on matters which concern politicians as well.

Basil Hume, in Gerald Priestland, *Priestland's Progress*, BBC Worldwide, 1982, page 55

Examining our own position—whatever it may be—from the Christian point of view we must come to the conclusion... that, quite apart from our own personal interests, we hold our accomplishments in trust from God to offer them in His service, and that service on earth is, as Christ taught us so thoroughly, to bring happiness and well-being to our fellow-men—to make our best contribution.

Sir Stafford Cripps, *God in our Work*, Thomas Nelson and Sons, 1949, page 4

I can't see any future for a church that in God's world doesn't accept that it must be involved in that part of it which is political and economic. A church which claims that the world is for Christ must be up to its neck in politics. I don't say party politics—that is more complex. But very often, when people say, 'Let's keep the Church out of politics,' they mean, 'Let's keep it out of left-wing politics.'

Lord Soper, in Gerald Priestland, *Priestland's Progress*, BBC Worldwide, 1982, page 54

But the Church and the official representatives must keep themselves free from the entanglements of party politics. There will come times when they should support or resist a specific measure; but they should not take any share in the strife of parties. Their business is something far more fundamental and important; it is the formation of that mind and temper in the whole community which will lead to wholesome legislation by any party and all parties.

William Temple, *The Kingdom of God*, Macmillan and Co., 1912, page 89

Christianity insists that man is an end because he is a child of God, made in God's image. Man is more than a producing animal guided by economic forces; for he is a being of spirit, crowned with glory and honour, endowed with the gift of freedom. The ultimate weakness of Communism is that it robs man of that quality which makes him man. Man, says Paul Tillich, is man because he is free. This freedom is expressed through man's capacity to deliberate, decide, and respond. Under Communism, the individual soul is shackled by the chains of conformity; his spirit is bound by the manacles of party allegiance. He is stripped of both conscience and reason.

Martin Luther King, *Strength to Love*, William Collins Sons and Co., 1980, page 98

I feel we are here to complement the political parties and knock their heads together occasionally. I think the ministry of Christ is basically reconciliation, and there are times when we can't afford party politics. Our movement is political, but it's non-party-political. We want to get rid of this Red Clydeside image and present the image of a reasonable community trying to work together. If man is made in God's image, he's got to share in God's creative power—not just for his own benefit, but for the benefit of all mankind and for the glory of God. He's got to develop his talents or he's not fully human. Now if he's unemployed, what are we going to do about this? He's going to become not an image but a caricature of God.

James McShane, in Gerald Priestland, *Priestland's Progress*, BBC Worldwide, 1982, page 56

Prayer and politics, far from being alternative modes of discipleship or even opposites, are necessary to each other. If they are divided, the result is either a superficial 'Christian radicalism' which stresses action and service at the expense of awe and vision, or a pietism which reduces spirituality to the private sector.

At the turn of the century Nicolas Berdyaev observes that Christian piety had all too often become a withdrawal from the world and from men, an unwillingness to share human suffering. The world has risen in protest against this form of piety, this indifference to the world's sorrow. Yet against this protest Berdyaev insisted, only a reborn piety can stand. The choice is not between spirituality and action, but between true spirituality and false.

Christian prayer is rooted in a revolutionary vision, it is Kingdom-directed prayer. It is therefore marked by a sense of fulfilment, of yearning, of stretching out into the future and tasting the powers of the age to come. It is never the prayer of security, ease, and the smug certainty. It is a crying out for the Kingdom that is coming. Prayer and politics meet at the point at which this vision of the new age comes into collision, as it must, with political structures based upon a different view of man and of human life. At the heart of our Gospel and our prayer there lies an inescapable core of conflict. This core of conflict is central to the Kingdom which must be the motive force and the visionary cumulus for Christian action.

Christian prayer is rooted also in the materiality of creation, incarnation, resurrection, and eucharist. It has a materialistic basis. Gnostic spirituality, so popular at present in the West, offers a way of living and praying which bypasses or despises the created order, and sees matter as an obstacle to the spiritual life. Christian prayer takes place within the framework of an incarnational theology which sees all matter as the potential vehicle of grace. This materialistic basis for prayer is of the greatest importance if we are to rescue Christian spirituality from the harmful influences of Neo-Platonism and other forms of dualism. The principle that grace comes through the flesh is central to orthodox Christianity. The centrality of the Eucharist in

Christian worship involves the rejection of the false dichotomy between spirit and matter. Christian spirituality is a spirituality of broken bread and outpoured wine, an earthly, common spirituality. Christian prayer is concerned with insight. A central element in prayer is listening, waiting on God in silence, gazing on God, striving to see more clearly. This dimension of clarity and insight contrasts sharply with the blurring of vision and the obscuring of reality which comes through what the fourteenth-century mystic Ruysbroeck called 'false vacancy.' This sense of seeing more clearly is one of the essential criteria in discernment of true prayer from false.

Finally, Christian prayer is concerned with transformation. Many Christians accept that, at a personal level, grace changes and transforms us, that in Christ there is a new creation. But people do not exist in a vacuum, nor is the relationship between personal change and socio-political change a simple one of cause and effect. The Christian virtues of love, forgiveness, gentleness and so on are public virtues. The fruits of the Spirit cannot be insulated in a private realm cut off from the world of political reality.

There is then an inescapable link between prayer and politics, between the mystical and the prophetic dimensions of faith. The renewal to which we are being called today is basically concerned with the restoration of that lost unity. It is very probable that the decay of a genuine mystical life in the Western church has not been unconnected with the decay of prophetic witness. While many see these two traditions as poles apart, they are in fact very close. For without clear vision there can be no authentic struggle. The hands raised in prayer and the hands raised in revolt are often the same hands. Out of prayer comes the spirit of resistance. Karl Barth puts it well. 'To clasp the hands in prayer is the beginning of an uprising against the disorder of the world.'

Kenneth Leech, 'The Meaning of Prayer and Politics', article in *The Times*, Saturday 13 February, 1982

POWER

'Power'—ability to do or act; particular faculty of body or mind,
vigour, energy, influential person, body or thing.

Power is a gift of the Holy Spirit. In theory we receive a seed of power when we are born—for this is a consequence of being made in the image and likeness of God. In baptism (and confirmation) this seed of power is catalysed, or triggered off, by water and the laying on of hands. At the end of the service there is prayer that we may daily increase in the gifts of the Holy Spirit. One of the gifts of the Holy Spirit is power. By this we mean 'energy' and 'vigour', as in the definition above, but also qualities such as 'dynamism' and 'vitality'. But whatever has happened to this 'power'? Is it not true that paradoxically 'impotence' now reigns supreme?

I wonder if we ought to take another look at the communion service. At one level we receive bread and wine. At another level we receive the body and blood of Christ. At a deeper level we receive something of the Father, something of the Holy Spirit, and divine attributes such as life, light, truth, joy, love—and also power. Seen this way, what a powerful sacrament this is. Add to this the practice of a silent and receptive prayer—as in reflection, meditation and contemplation—and it won't be long (if we are genuine in our quest) before we experience 'the immeasurable greatness of his power ... according to the working of his great might.'

The voice of the Lord is powerful, the voice of the Lord is full of majesty.

Psalm 29:4

... he gives power and strength to his people.

Psalm 68:35

But you shall receive power when the Holy Spirit has come upon you.

Acts 1:8

May you be strengthened with all power, according to his glorious might, for all endurance and patience with joy, giving thanks to the Father, who has qualified us to share in the inheritance of the saints in light.

Colossians 1:11–12

Energy is Eternal Delight.

William Blake, 'The voice of the Devil', in The Marriage of Heaven and Hell, Plate 4, in The Complete Writings of William Blake, edited by Geoffrey Keynes, Oxford University Press, 1974, page 149

Patience and Gentleness is Power.

Leigh Hunt, 'Sonnet: On a lock of Milton's hair', in The Poetical Works of Leigh Hunt, edited by H.S. Milford, Oxford University Press, 1923, page 247

The strongest man in the world is the man who stands alone.

Henrik Ibsen, An Enemy of the People, volume VI, translated and edited by James Walter McFarlane, Oxford University Press, 1960, page 126

Right and Truth are greater than any *Power*; and all Power is limited by Right.

Benjamin Whichcote, Moral and Religious Aphorisms, number 34, Elkin, Mathews and Marrot, 1930, page 5

From the summit of power men no longer turn their eyes upward, but begin to look about them.

J.R. Lowell, 'New England Two Centuries Ago', in Among My Books, J.M. Dent and Sons, 1914, page 182

Life engenders life. Energy creates energy. It is by spending oneself that one becomes rich.

Sarah Bernhardt, in Cornelia Otis Skinner, Madam Sarah, Michael Joseph Ltd., 1967, page xvi

Concentration is the secret of strength in politics, in war, in trade, in short, in all management of human affairs.

Ralph Waldo Emerson, The Conduct of Life, Nature and Other Essays, J.M. Dent and Sons, 1911, page 186

Self-reverence, self-knowledge, self-control, These three alone lead life to sovereign power.

Alfred, Lord Tennyson, 'Oenone', in The Poems of Tennyson, edited by Christopher Ricks, Longmans, Green and Co., 1969, page 392

To know the pains of power, we must go to those who have it; to know its pleasures, we must go to those who are seeking it: the pains of power are real, its pleasures imaginary.

C.C. Colton, Lacon, William Tegg, 1866, page 243

We are the wire, God is the current. Our only power is to let the current pass through us. Of course, we have the power to interrupt it and say 'no.' But nothing more.

Carlo Carretto, Letters from the Desert, translated by Rose Mary Hancock, Darton, Longman and Todd., 1972, page 19

A non-violent revolution is not a programme of 'seizure of power.' It is a programme of transformation of relationships ending in a peaceful transfer of power.

Mohandas K. Gandhi, Non-Violence in Peace & War, volume II, Navajivan Publishing House, 1949, page 8

Justice without might is helpless; might without justice is tyrannical... We must then combine justice and might, and for this end make what is just strong, or what is strong just.

Blaise Pascal, Pensées, translated by W.F. Trotter, Random House Inc., 1941, page 103

He (Christ) stimulates us, as other great men stimulate us, but we find a power coming from Him into our lives that enables us to respond. That is the experience that proves Him to be the universal Spirit. It does not happen with others.

William Temple, Christian Faith and Life, SCM Press, 1931, reissued 1963, page 45

You have lost the knack of drawing strength from God, and vain strivings after communion of the *solitude à deux* will do nothing for you at this point. Seek contact with Him now in the goodness and splendour which is in other people, in *all* people, for those who have the art to find it.

Evelyn Underhill, *The Letters of Evelyn Underhill*, edited by Charles Williams, Longmans, Green and Co., 1947, page 98

Give me the strength lightly to bear my joys and sorrows.
Give me the strength to make my love fruitful in service.
Give me the strength never to disown the poor or bend my knees before insolent might.
Give me the strength to raise my mind high above daily trifles.
And give me the strength to surrender my strength to thy will with love.

Rabindranath Tagore, *Gitanjali*, Macmillan and Co., 1971, page 28

Be still and cool in thy own mind and spirit from thy own thought, and then thou wilt feel the principle of God to turn thy mind to the Lord God, whereby thou wilt receive his strength and power from whence life comes, to allay all tempests, against blusterings and storms. That is it which moulds up into patience, into innocency, into soberness, into stillness, into stayedness, into quietness, up to God, with his power.

George Fox, *The Journal of George Fox*, a revised edition by John L. Nickalls, Cambridge University Press, 1952, page 346

At the highest point of his inner self, his soul, man is more God than creature: however much he is the same as creature in his nature, in mind he is like God more than any creature. To the soul at rest in God in her potential, her essential, intellectual nature, everything comes natural as though she were created not at the will of something else but solely at her own. In this point creatures are her subjects, all submitting to her as though they were her handiwork. It was in this power the birds obeyed St. Francis and listened to his preaching. And Daniel took refuge in this power, trusting himself to God alone, when he sat among the lions. Moreover, in this power it has been the custom of the saints to offer up their sufferings which, in the greatness of their love, are to them no suffering.

Meister Eckhart, in Franz Pfeiffer, *Meister Eckhart*, volume I, translated by C. de B. Evans, John M. Watkins, 1956, page 290

What then does Pentecost represent? What change is effected by the outpourings of the Spirit?

The change lies in the relation of the Holy Spirit to the human spirit. This relation was made quite new. Previously the Holy Spirit had acted on men from without, like an external force; as the prophet Ezekiel describes it, 'the hand of the Lord was upon me.' But now the Holy Spirit acts from within. He is in man (Jn xvi.7). It was the union of the divine and human natures in the person of Jesus Christ which first made it possible for the divine Spirit to dwell in a human personality. When the Word was made flesh, the Holy Ghost became the Spirit of the man Jesus; and now that Jesus was glorified the Spirit of Jesus was become the Spirit of consummated humanity, and through the channel of that humanity he could be poured out upon the brethren of Jesus. This new presence of the Spirit has also a corresponding effect on human society. Being the Spirit of the Son of Man, the church which his indwelling creates is a universal church: no longer the church of a small select race but the church of humanity. On earth then the day of Pentecost marks the beginning of this new relation. It is the beginning of the new spiritual life of the church—its second birth. And the characteristic of this life is Power. A transformation takes place, the apostles are new men, all fear of the Jews is gone. Peter, but now afraid of a servant girl, stands up boldly before all the people. The apostles' tongues are loosed and three thousand are converted. The work of the church begins.

R.B. Rackham, *The Acts of the Apostles*, Methuen and Co., 1901, page 14

PRAYER

*'Prayer'—solemn request to God or object of worship; formula
used in praying, practice of praying; entreaty to a person;
thing prayed for.*

One of my friends spent some time in Africa working on a mission station. He told me of an extraordinary journey he had undertaken with an elderly lady missionary. The vehicle, like the missionary, was old and rickety. When they were miles from anywhere the engine played up, and smoke ominously appeared from under the bonnet. Suddenly there was a loud bang and the engine packed up altogether. My friend sat motionless in the vehicle, not knowing what to do next. Not so the missionary. She instantly went into action. 'Get out boy, and get on your knees. Let's pray about it.' She knelt by the bonnet and offered up earnest prayer. She then stood up and said to my friend, 'Right, come on. Get back in, and let's be off.' She turned on the ignition, and the engine spluttered into life. My friend was amazed, but she didn't bat an eyelid. The journey was duly completed.

I have to admit my experience of prayer has not always been like that though there have been some surprises. In the outcome of prayer I have found an insight of William Barclay helpful: 'God will always answer our prayers; *but He will answer them in His way*, and His way will be the way of perfect wisdom and of perfect love. Often if He answered our prayers as we at the moment desire, it would be the worst thing possible for us, for in our ignorance we often ask for gifts which would be our ruin.' I am grateful to God for answering my prayers in His way—not mine.

Give ear, O Lord, to my prayer; hearken to my cry of supplication. In the day of my trouble I call on thee, for thou dost answer me.

Psalm 86:6–7

He fulfils the desire of all who fear him, he also hears their cry, and saves them.

Psalm 145:19

But when you pray, go into your room and shut the door and pray to your Father who is in secret.

Matthew 6:6

And in the morning, a great while before day, he rose and went out to a lonely place, and there he prayed.

Mark 1:35

Prayer is the nearest approach to God, and the highest enjoyment of Him, that we are capable of in this life.

William Law, *A Serious Call to a Devout and Holy Life*, J.M. Dent & Co., 1898, page 78

Prayer is not an old woman's idle amusement. Properly understood and applied, it is the most potent instrument of action.

Mohandas K. Gandhi, *Non-Violence in Peace & War*, volume II, Navajivan Publishing House, 1949, page 77

You pray in your distress and in your need; would that you might pray also in the fullness of your joy and in your days of abundance.

Kahlil Gibran, *The Prophet*, William Heinemann, 1970, page 78

Prayer, crystallised in words, assigns a permanent wavelength on which the dialogue has to be continued, even when our mind is occupied with other matters.

Dag Hammarskjöld, *Markings*, translated by Leif Sjöberg and W.H. Auden, Faber and Faber, 1964, page 97

Lift up your heart to Him, sometimes even at your meals and when you are in company; the least little remembrance will always be acceptable to Him. You need not cry very loud; He is nearer to us than we are aware of.

Brother Lawrence, *The Practice of the Presence of God*, A.R. Mowbray and Co., 1977, page 47

In our Lord's teaching about petitionary prayer there are three main principles. The first is confidence, the second is perseverance and the third, for lack of a better word, I will call correspondence with Christ.

William Temple, *Christian Faith and Life*, SCM Press, 1931, reissued 1963, page 115

He prayeth best, who loveth best
All things both great and small;
For the dear God who loveth us,
He made and loveth all.

Samuel Taylor Coleridge, 'The Ancient Mariner', in *Coleridge, Poetry & Prose*, edited by Stephen Potter, The Nonesuch Press, page 57

The Lord's prayer is the prayer above all prayers, a prayer which the most high Master taught us, wherein are comprehended all spiritual and temporal blessings, and the strongest comforts in all trials, temptations, and troubles, even in the hour of death.

Martin Luther, *Table-Talk*, translated and edited by William Hazlitt, George Bell and Sons, 1895, page 125.

Believe and trust that as it is easy for you to breathe the air and live by it, or to eat and drink, so it is easy and even still easier for your faith to receive all spiritual gifts from the Lord. Prayer is the breathing of the soul; prayer is our spiritual food and drink.

John of Cronstadt, in *A Treasury of Russian Spirituality*, edited by G.P. Fedotov, Sheed and Ward, 1977, page 354

Prayer is a fundamental style of thinking, passionate and compassionate, responsible and thankful, that is deeply rooted in our humanity and that manifests itself not only among believers but also among serious-minded people who do not profess any religious faith.

John Macquarrie, *Paths in Spirituality*, SCM Press, second edition, 1992, page 30

The word 'prayer' is applied to at least four distinct procedures—petition, intercession, adoration, contemplation. Petition is the asking of something for ourselves. Intercession is the asking of something for other people. Adoration is the use of intellect, feeling, will and imagination in making acts of devotion directed towards God in his personal aspect or as incarnated in human form. Contemplation is that condition of alert passivity in which the soul lays itself open to the divine Ground within and without, the immanent and transcendent Godhead.

Aldous Huxley, *The Perennial Philosophy*, Chatto and Windus, 1974, page 251

'Ask and it shall be given' (Matthew 7:7). These words are a thorn in the Christian conscious-ness, they can be neither accepted nor rejected. To reject them would mean a refusal of God's infinite kindness, but we are not yet Christian enough to accept them. We know that the father would not give a stone instead of bread (Matthew 7:9), but we do not think of ourselves as children who are unconscious of their real needs and what is good or bad for them. Yet there lies the explanation of so many unanswered prayers. It can also be found in the words of St John Chrysostom: 'Do not be distressed if you do not receive at once what you ask for: God wants to do you more good through your perseverance in prayer.'

Anthony Bloom, *Living Prayer*, Darton, Longman and Todd, 1966, page 80

He knows what we want before we ask it. Then why ask? Why, because there may be blessings which only are effectively blessings to those who are in the right condition of mind; just as there is wholesome food which is actually wholesome only to those who are healthy in body. If you give the best beef to somebody in typhoid fever, you do him great harm. The worst of all diseases of the soul is forgetfulness of God; and if everything that we need came to us while we forgot God, we should only be confirmed in our forgetfulness of Him, in our sense of independence of Him ... Over and over again, it will happen that, whether or not God can give the blessing which, in His love, He desires to give, will depend on whether or not we recognise the source from which it comes. The way to recognise that He is the source of the blessings, and that we need them, is to ask.

William Temple, *Christian Faith and Life*, SCM Press, 1931, reissued 1963, page 111

To pray is to enter consciously into communion with God or the Source.

At its highest peak prayer becomes contemplation. Here it is wordless. It is a merging of human consciousness with the Divine.

At the centre of the prayerful state is the stilling of the mind. 'Be still, and know that I am God', says the psalmist (Psalm 46:10).

Prayerfulness opens up the channel between the soul and God. So there is intercommunion between the human and the Divine. Prayer stems from meditation, for the latter is preparing the ground for the former.

Prayer may be conceived of as a descent into the depths of the heart and as a rising towards the Godhead. In the opened heart is the prayer that does not cease.

Bede Griffiths OSB, in *The Universal Christ*, edited by Peter Spink, Darton, Longman and Todd, 1990, page 54

Prayer is faith in action, the well-spring of hope, the conversation of love. There is no substitute when we truly want to possess eternal life, when we really become conscious of God.

Anyone who does not pray cannot know God's intimate life (which in theology is called charity). He can only know Him from the outside, as a symbol, as an idea, as a philosophy, as a science, as a number, as space, as eternity.

It is not enough to study theology or advanced exegesis to know God.

God's intimate life is unknowable to man.

He is 'veiled' to man.

He only makes Himself knowable, He only unveils Himself, when we come before Him in an attitude of love, not in an attitude of curiosity.

Prayer, true prayer, is precisely the attitude in which man must present himself before God in order to enter His intimate life, which is the life of the Trinity.

Carlo Carretto, *The God Who Comes*, translated by Rose Mary Hancock, Darton, Longman and Todd, 1974, page 127

If you pray, if you pray seriously, if you pray in truth, it will be God Himself who will send you out, with greater strength, with greater love, towards your brothers, so that you may love them more gratuitously and serve them more delicately.

Well then, you will say, why, why in the past have too many Christians scandalised me with their indifference, with the hardness of their bigoted hearts, with the hermetic sealing of themselves against every problem of justice and liberation of the people?

Yet they were praying, they were contemplating!

No, if they were praying, their prayer was just a bit of rhetoric. If they were contemplating, they were contemplating ... nothing.

They were deceiving you, and they were deceiving the Church.

It is impossible to pray to a personal God—that is, love a personal God—and remain indifferent to your suffering brethren.

It is impossible.

Anyone who prays without suffering for his suffering brothers is praying to a pole, a shadow, not to the living God.

Because if you pray to the living God, you who are living, He, the Living One, sends you to your living brothers.

Carlo Carretto, *The God Who Comes*, translated by Rose Mary Hancock, Darton, Longman and Todd, 1974, page 178

If we ask of the saints how they achieved spiritual effectiveness, they are only able to reply that, in so far as they did it themselves, they did it by love and prayer. A love that is very humble and homely; a prayer that is full of adoration and of confidence. Love and prayer, on their lips, are not mere nice words; they are the names of tremendous powers, able to transform in a literal sense human personality and make it more and more that which it is meant to be—the agent of the Holy Spirit in the world. Plainly then, it is essential to give time or to get time somehow for self-training in this love and this prayer. It is true that in their essence they are 'given,' but the gift is only fully made our own by a patient and generous effort of the soul. Spiritual achievement costs much, though never as much as it is worth. It means at the very least the painful development and persevering, steady exercise of a faculty that most of us have allowed to get slack. It means an inward if not an outward asceticism: a virtual if not an actual mysticism.

People talk about mysticism as if it were something quite separate from practical religion; whereas, as a matter of fact, it is the intense heart of all practical religion, and no-one without some touch of it is contagious and able to win souls.

What *is* mysticism? It is in its widest sense the reaching out of the soul to contact with those eternal realities which are the subject matter of religion. And the mystical life is the complete life of love and prayer which transmutes those objects of belief into living realities.

Evelyn Underhill, *Concerning the Inner Life*, Methuen and Co., 1926, page 31

I had spent some weeks or months without saying any prayers because I had come to consider them a useless waste of time. But everything else seemed to be becoming also a useless waste of time, excepting always the seeing of beauty in nature and the attempt to fix something of it on paper. But it seemed a funny thing that this should be the object for which life was given to us, and I began to wonder how one could find out what one was really put here for; and then it struck me that in the New Testament, and especially in the teaching of Christ, one might be able to write down in one's own words once and for all whatever definite directions one could make out from His teaching. Then, whatever the disciples gave us. So I started a book, and wrote down Christ's directions for life, and then the apostles' and disciples', word for word when the meaning was clear, and my own reading of whatever wasn't clear. Well, I have done this off and on now for a year, and my insight into the meaning of the Gospels has increased enormously, and though there are many directions which are definite and many which are contradictory, it seems to me that across every page may be written as a summary of its teaching—*Love one another* in Truth and Purity, as children, impulsively and uncalculatingly, not with reasoning and quibbling over what is the best way under the circumstances, but as though I were alone with God in everyone I met, not influenced therefore by any human law or convention, but faithfully offering them a true love in act and example, and at all costs to myself. Offer them the best, let them take it or leave it, never the second best or half best or best under the circumstances, but the best always.

Edward Wilson, in George Seaver, *The Faith of Edward Wilson*, John Murray, 1949, page 16

PREACHING

'Preaching'—deliver sermon or religious address, deliver (sermon); give moral advice in obtrusive way; proclaim, expound, (The Gospel, Christ etc.) in public discourse; advocate, inculcate (quality, conduct, principle, etc).

When I was ordained, I had to write out a sermon in full, and read it to the Provost of Bradford Cathedral, for vetting, before unleashing it in the cathedral. This was a good discipline, though a painful one. He used to tell the story of a previous fellow-sufferer who had come to read out his sermon to him, and then asked anxiously—'Will it do?' The Provost's flippant response was—'Do what, do you suppose?' Although he was teasing, his response does raise a fundamental question. What are we trying to do in our preaching?

Various suggestions can be made. Some would say the first preaching of all was a proclamation of Christ's resurrection, and would find support for this in all the preaching recorded in the Acts of the Apostles. Others would point out Jesus originally came preaching the gospel of the kingdom of God. They would find support for this in the four Gospels, and point out most of Jesus' teaching, the Sermon on the Mount, for instance, is about the kingdom of God. Perhaps a subtle combination of the two lies at the heart of preaching. As someone who has struggled in this area for many years, I have a certain affinity with William Barclay: 'The design of preaching is to lead men into the experience of eternal life, to bring them into contact with the promised life of God.' This seems to me fundamental.

But Moses said to the Lord, 'Oh, my Lord, I am not eloquent, either heretofore or since thou hast spoken to thy servant; but I am slow of speech and of tongue.' Then the Lord said to him, 'Who has made man's mouth? Who makes him dumb, or deaf, or seeing, or blind? Is it not I, the Lord? Now therefore go, and I will be with your mouth and teach you what you shall speak.'

Exodus 4:10–12

I have told the glad news of deliverance in the great congregation; lo, I have not restrained my lips, as thou knowest, O Lord. I have not hid thy saving help within my heart, I have spoken of thy faithfulness and thy salvation; I have not concealed thy steadfast love and thy faithfulness from the great congregation.

Psalm 40:9–10

For I will not venture to speak of anything except what Christ has wrought through me.

Romans 15:18

Preach the word, be urgent in season and out of season, convince, rebuke, and exhort, be unfailing in patience and in teaching.

2 Timothy 4:2

A good honest and painful sermon.
Samuel Pepys, The Diary of Samuel Pepys, volume II, 1661, edited by Robert Latham and William Matthews, G. Bell and Sons, 1970, page 55

I like the silent church before the service begins, better than any preaching.
Ralph Waldo Emerson, 'Self-Reliance', in Essays, Bernhard Tauchnitz, 1915, page 52

Every man is a priest, even involuntarily; his conduct is an unspoken sermon, which is for ever preaching to others.
Henri Frédéric Amiel, Amiel's Journal, translated by Mrs Humphry Ward, Macmillan and Co., 1918, page 25

The best preaching is a fruit of constant pastoral visiting; it springs out of the relationship between pastor and people.
William Temple, Readings in St. John's Gospel, First and Second Series, Macmillan and Co., 1947, page 167

The pencil of the Holy Ghost hath laboured more in describing the afflictions of Job than the felicities of Solomon.
Francis Bacon, The Moral and Historical Works of Francis Bacon, Henry G. Bohn, 1852, page 14

It is very important to live your faith by confessing it, and one of the best ways to confess it is to preach it.
Thomas Merton, The Sign of Jonas, Burns and Oates, 1961, page 266

The design of preaching is to lead men into the experience of eternal life, to bring them into contact with the promised life of God.
William Barclay, The Plain Man Looks at the Apostles' Creed, William Collins Sons and Co., 1967, page 376

One may sometimes attend Church for a year, and hear excellent discourses on international peace, on industrial justice, on civil liberties, sex relations, social ethics in every phase; but rarely or never a word to help one's poor little old soul in its effort to enter into commerce with the Eternal.
Vida D. Scudder, The Privilege of Age, J.M. Dent and Sons, 1939, page 216

He only is able to declare with spirit and power any truths or bear a faithful testimony of the reality of them who preaches nothing but what he has first seen and felt and found to be true by a living sensibility and true experience of their reality and power in his own soul. All other preaching, whether from art, hearsay, books, or education, is, at best, but playing with words and mere trifling with sacred things.

William Law, *Selected Mystical Writings of William Law*, edited by Stephen Hobhouse, Rockliff, 1948, page 118

The preacher possesses no magical efficacy. His only power lies in his spiritual experience, his clarified vision, and his organic connection with Christ the Head of the Church and the source of its energy. If his life is spiritually poor and weak and thin, if it lacks moral passion and insight, his ministry will be correspondingly ineffective and futile, for the dynamic spiritual impact of a life is in proportion to its personal experience and its mortal capacity to transmit divine power.

Rufus M. Jones, *Spiritual Reformers in the 16th and 17th Centuries*, Macmillan and Co., 1914, page 79

His (John Everard) new way of preaching—vivid, concrete, touched with subtle humour, grounded in experience and filling old texts with new meaning—appealed powerfully to the common people and to an elect few of the more highly privileged who had won a large enough freedom of spirit to go with him into new paths ... he poured out the best he had in his treasury to any, even the simplest and most ordinary, who cared to hear of this 'spiritual, practical experiment of life.'

Rufus M. Jones, *Spiritual Reformers in the 16th and 17th Centuries*, Macmillan and Co., 1914, page 240

When you preach, you must lead men out of the desire to know everything to the knowledge of the one thing that is needful, to the desire to be in God, and thus no more to conform to the world but to rise above all mysteries as those who are redeemed from the world. 'If only I have Thee, I care nothing for heaven and earth.' (Ps.lxxiii, 25, Luther). 'All things work together for good to them that love God.' Point men to these words as to the peaks of Ararat, where they may take refuge when the flood of the inexplicable overwhelms all around.

Albert Schweitzer, *Christianity and the Religions of the World*, translated by J. Powers, George Allen and Unwin, 1923, page 81

Preaching the Gospel in foreign lands to-day we are the advance-guard of an army that has suffered a defeat and needs to be made fit again. Let us be courageous advance-guards. The truth which the Gospel of Jesus carries within itself cannot be impaired by men's errors nor by their lack of faithfulness. And if only our lives, in genuine nonconformity to the world, reveal something of what it means to be apprehended by the living, ethical God, then something of the truth of Jesus goes out from us.

A word of Scripture which resounds with special meaning for us is the following, written by Paul the apostle of the Gentiles: 'The Kingdom of God is not in words but in power.' That word makes us humble and at the same time fills our hearts with joy.

Albert Schweitzer, *Christianity and the Religions of the World*, translated by J. Powers, George Allen and Unwin, 1923, page 85

There is an old story of a boy who joined the Franciscan Order longing to become a friar preacher. He was put to work in the kitchen for the first months and got more and more restive and impatient to get on with learning to preach. Finally Francis himself drew him by the arm one day and asked him if he would like to go into the village with him to preach. The boy's heart was full as they set out. They stopped on the way to see a man whose son needed work in the town, then to call on an old woman who was sick and lonely, and to visit with a peasant at work in the fields. In the town, they saw a merchant about a post for the son, they begged some food for the brothers at home, they talked with some people in the market place, and then Francis turned to the boy and gaily proposed that they return to the friary. 'But when are we going to preach?' asked the boy in an anguish of concern. Francis slipped his arm about him and said, 'Why, my brother, we've been preaching all the time.'

Douglas Steere, *Where Words Come From*, Swarthmore Lecture, George Allen and Unwin, page 47, 1955

PRIDE

*'Pride'—overweening opinion of one's own qualities, merits, etc;
arrogant bearing or conduct; exalted position, consciousness of this,
arrogance; also proper pride—a sense of what befits one's position,
preventing one from doing an unworthy thing.*

P ride took a blow in the army. After a few weeks I was sent on a WOSB (War Office Selection
Board) and recommended for training to be an Officer. I returned to my unit, still a private
soldier. Word got round, particularly amongst the corporals and sergeants. In the next four days
I was put on six charges, and given the task of cleaning out fifty toilets a day before breakfast.
This proved to be a valuable learning experience and a great antidote to pride.

In theological circles we are concerned with a different form of pride, with more serious
consequences. We have seen in the Genesis story of the creation of man, the divine
inbreathing, giving man an enormous potential of life through God's gift of himself. We have
also seen another truth in this story, namely, that which was fashioned and shaped in the
image and likeness of God, was taken from the dust of the earth. This means we also have an
earthy and creaturely side to our nature. Sadly we have tended to centre ourselves on this side
of our nature, rather than on 'the God within'. Herein lies the essence of pride, leading to a
drastic curtailment of life. There is, however, a proper sense of pride which centres itself on
'the God within', and also accepts the earthy and creaturely side of our nature as a valuable
source of energy and dynamism, to be used creatively.

Talk no more so very proudly, let not arrogance come from your mouth.
1 Samuel 2:3

The beginning of human pride is to desert the Lord, and to turn one's heart away from one's
maker.
Since the beginning of pride is sin, whoever clings to it will pour forth filth.
Ecclesiasticus 10:12–13 (JB)

For from within, out of the heart of man, come evil thoughts, fornication, theft, murder,
adultery, coveting, wickedness, deceit, licentiousness, envy, slander, pride, foolishness. All
these evil things come from within, and they defile a man.
Mark 7:21–23

For every one who exalts himself will be humbled, and he who humbles himself will be exalted.
Luke 14:11

A *Proud* man hath no *God.*
Benjamin Whichcote, *Morals and Religious Aphorisms*, number 801, 1930, Elkin Mathews and Marrot, page 90

The whole trouble is that we won't let God help us.
George Macdonald, *The Marquis of Lossie*, Everett and Co., 1912, page 91

Pride is over-estimation of oneself by reason of self-love.
Spinoza, *Spinoza's Ethics and De Intellectus Emendatione*, J.M. Dent and Sons, 1955, page 134

Evil can have no beginning, but from pride; nor any end, but from humility.
William Law, *Selected Mystical Writings of William Law*, edited by Stephen Hobhouse, Rockliff, 1948, page 107

Pride is therefore pleasure arising from a man's thinking too highly of himself.
Spinoza, *Spinoza's Ethics and De Intellectus Emendatione*, J.M. Dent and Sons, 1955, page 102

There are two states or conditions of pride. The first is one of self-approval, the second one of self-contempt. Pride is seen probably at its purest in the last.

Henri Frédéric Amiel, *Amiel's Journal*, translated by Mrs Humphry Ward, Macmillan and Co., 1918, page 45

Every good thought that we have, every good action that we do, lays us open to pride, and exposes us to the assaults of vanity and self-satisfaction.

William Law, *A Serious Call to a Devout and Holy Life*, J.M. Dent and Co., 1898, page 246

He that is proud eats up himself: pride is his own glass, his own trumpet, his own chronicle and whatever praises itself, but in the deed, devours the deed in the praise.

William Shakespeare, *Troilus and Cressida*, Act II. sc.iii. l.156

Of all the Causes which conspire to blind
Man's erring Judgement, and misguide the Mind,
What the weak Head with strongest Byass rules,
Is *Pride*, the *never-failing Vice of Fools.*

Alexander Pope, 'An Essay on Criticism,' in *The Poems of Alexander Pope*, volume I, *Pastoral Poetry and An Essay on Criticism*, edited by E. Audra and Aubrey Williams, Methuen and Co., 1961, page 263

Nothing hath separated us from God but our own will, or rather our own will is our separation from God... The fall of man brought forth the kingdom of this world; sin in all shapes is nothing else but the will of man driving on in a state of self-motion and self-government, following the workings of a nature broken off from its dependency upon, and union with, the divine will. All the evil and misery in the creation arises only and solely from this one cause.

William Law, *Selected Mystical Writings of William Law*, edited by Stephen Hobhouse, Rockliff, 1948, pages 25 and 29

Almost always God's greatest gifts are wrapped up in the sacking of painful self-knowledge. When we 'got on well' in prayer, when there was satisfaction in the Mass and sacraments, when we could talk inspiringly of spiritual things and others showed respect for our wisdom, we had no idea of the true state of affairs.

Humility is the acceptance of the truth about ourselves, not an effort to work up humble sentiments in spite of our obvious excellence! It is seeing and accepting the truth that we are not noble, good and spiritual.

This acceptance of lowliness means more to God than all our good works and fine intentions. What seems like loss and deprivation of blessings proves the very opposite.

God gives himself not in what exalts our ego, flatters our pride and self-conceit, but in what humbles us.

When God, All-Love, love that in its human expression sheds its last drop of blood for us, draws close... the ego is then shown up for what it is in all its distortion and ugliness.

Ruth Burrows, in *The Watchful Heart*, edited by Elizabeth Ruth Obbard, Darton, Longman and Todd, 1988, page 35

The sin of Adam which robbed him and us of Paradise was due to a false confidence, a confidence which deliberately willed to make the option and experiment of believing in a lie. There was nothing in Adam's perfect peace that warranted this playing with unreality. There was no difficulty in the precept that had to be kept, to avoid falling into illusion. There was no weakness, no passion in his flesh, that drove him to an irrational fulfilment in spite of his better judgment. All these things would only be the consequence of his preferences for what 'was not.' Even the natural and healthy self-love by which Adam's nature rejoiced in its own full realization could gain nothing by adding unreality to the real. On the contrary, he could only become less himself by being other than what he already was.

All this can be summed up in the one word: pride. For pride is a stubborn insistence on being what we are not and never were intended to be. Pride is a deep, insatiable need for unreality, an exorbitant demand that others believe the lie we have made ourselves believe about ourselves.

Thomas Merton, *The New Man*, Burns and Oates, 1962, page 70

There is one vice of which no man in the world is free; which every one in the world loathes when he sees it in someone else; and of which hardly any people, except Christians, ever imagine that they are guilty themselves...

The essential vice, the utmost evil, is Pride. Unchastity, anger, greed, drunkenness, and all that, are mere fleabites in comparison: it was through Pride that the devil became the devil: Pride leads to every other vice: it is the complete anti-God state of mind...

If I am a proud man, then, as long as there is one man in the whole world more powerful, or richer, or cleverer than I, he is my rival and my enemy...

As long as you are proud you cannot know God. A proud man is always looking down on things and people: and, of course, as long as you are looking down, you cannot see something that is above you...

The real test of being in the presence of God is that you either forget about yourself altogether or see yourself as a small, dirty object. It is better to forget about yourself altogether.

C.S. Lewis, *Mere Christianity*, William Collins Sons and Co., 1961, page 106

Does the world as a whole possess the value and meaning that we constantly attribute to certain parts of it (such as human beings and their works) and, if so, what is the nature of that value and meaning? This is a question which, a few years ago, I should not even have posed. For, like so many of my contemporaries, I took it for granted that there was no meaning. This was partly due to the fact that I shared the common belief that the scientific picture of an abstraction from reality was a true picture of reality as a whole; partly also to other, non-intellectual reasons. I had motives for not wanting the world to have a meaning; consequently assumed that it had none, and was able without any difficulty to find satisfying reasons for this assumption.

Most ignorance is vincible ignorance. We don't know because we don't want to know. It is our will that decides how and upon what subjects we shall use our intelligence. Those who detect no meaning in the world generally do so because, for one reason or another, it suits their books that the world should be meaningless...

For myself, as, no doubt, for most of my contemporaries, the philosophy of meaninglessness was essentially an instrument of liberation. The liberation we desired was simultaneously liberation from a certain political and economic system and liberation from a certain system of morality. We objected to the morality because it interfered with our sexual freedom.

Aldous Huxley, *Ends and Means*, Chatto and Windus, 1965, page 269

PROPHETS

'Prophets'—inspired teachers, revealers or interpreters of God's will.

Inspiration is a key word in understanding the nature of the prophet. It means—'drawing in of breath; divine influence.' This brings us back to the underlying vision of this anthology— the divine inbreathing of the Genesis story of the creation of man. If we want to see this fully worked out in a life, we look to the Gospels, to the life of Jesus Christ. Here we see man made in the image and likeness of God. At the same time we see *the prophet*—the inspired teacher, the revealer or interpreter of God's will. No one saw this more clearly than Ralph Waldo Emerson. In a brilliant passage he wrote: 'Jesus Christ belonged to the true race of prophets. He saw with open eye the mystery of the soul. Drawn by its severe harmony, ravished with its beauty, he lived in it, and had his being there. Alone in all history, he estimated the greatness of man. One man was true to what is in you and me. He saw that God incarnates himself in man, and evermore goes forth anew to take possession of his world. He said, in this jubilee of sublime emotion, "I am divine. Through me, God acts; through me, speaks. Would you see God, see me; or see thee, when thou also thinkest as I now think." '

That last phrase is particularly important. Unravelled it means that what Christ experienced, we can also in some measure experience. Take that one stage further, and it means we too can be prophets; but where is the spirit of prophecy today?

Would that all the Lord's people were prophets, that the Lord would put his spirit upon them!

Numbers 11:29

If there is a prophet among you, I the Lord make myself known to him in a vision, I will speak with him in a dream.

Numbers 12:6

Make love your aim, and earnestly desire the spiritual gifts, especially that you may prophesy.

1 Corinthians 14:1

First of all you must understand this, that no prophecy of scripture is a matter of one's own interpretation, because no prophecy ever came by the impulse of man, but men moved by the Holy Spirit spoke from God.

2 Peter 1:20–21

Prophecy consists in catching the best of God's thoughts and telling them.

Charles H. Parkhurst, *The Pattern in the Mount and Other Sermons*, R.D. Dickinson, 1890, page 14

Every honest man is a Prophet; he utters his opinion both of private & public matters. Thus: If you go on So, the result is So. He nevers says, such a thing shall happen let you do what you will. A Prophet is a seer, not an Arbitrary Dictator.

William Blake, 'Annotations to Watson', in *The Complete Writings of William Blake*, edited by Geoffrey Keynes, Oxford University Press, 1974, page 392

The prophet is primarily the man, not to whom God has communicated certain divine thoughts, but whose mind is illuminated by the divine spirit to interpret aright the divine acts; and the act is primary.

William Temple, *The Preacher's Theme*, SPCK, 1936, page 21

The prophets were not Gifford Lecturers with the advantage of some special 'guidance'. They were men faced with practical problems of political, moral and spiritual life... As the prophet faces some actual human need, that truth of God which bears upon it irradiates his mind and he proclaims it in words that thrill our hearts today.

William Temple, *Nature, Man and God*, Macmillan and Co., 1934, page 340

It is just because the prophets and apostles are so indwelt by the Spirit of God that they are so robustly, freely, independently, and concretely human. The incoming of God's Spirit does not eliminate their human qualities so that they become mere puppets of God, but in the fullest sense it makes them *men of God.*

James D. Smart, *The Interpretation of Scripture*, The Westminster Press, 1961, page 196

No pronouncement of a prophet is ever his own; he is an interpreter prompted by Another in all his utterances, when knowing not what he does, he is filled with inspiration, as the reason withdraws and surrenders the citadel of the soul to a new visitor and tenant, the Divine Spirit which plays upon the vocal organism and raises sounds from it, which clearly express its prophetic message.

Philo, in *Three Jewish Philosophers*, edited by Hans Lewy, Harper and Row, Publishers, 1945, page 75

Prophetic religion is based on confident faith; it is life-affirming; it values faith and confidence rather than ecstatic experiences; it is naïve rather than reflective, spontaneous rather than ascetic, masculine rather than feminine. It conceives of God as living, active, and merciful, revealing himself and bringing salvation in the midst of history. For it revelation is an objective, historical fact; the great biblical personalities are bearers of the revelation, and prophetic religion combines respect for the authority of revelation with personal freedom. Sin is breach of the God-ordained order of moral values; salvation is restoration of the broken fellowship; righteous action is itself fellowship with God. Prophets are called to act positively, to proclaim God's will, and to work for his kingdom; they build up fellowship. They take a positive view of human culture but look forward to a new heaven and a new earth. They embody dramatic dualistic tensions; they do not lose sight of the distance between God and man.

Accordingly prophetic prayer arises spontaneously from need and crisis. It includes complaints, questions, petitions and intercessions, not only for individuals but for the coming of the kingdom. It uses various ways of appealing to God's goodness, such as the recollection of his former benefits and the assertion of one's own piety; it expresses dependence, confesses sinfulness and includes trust, submission, thanksgiving and praise. It is often hostile to fixed forms. People of prophetic prayer know themselves to be children and friends of God, who is ever present to hear them.

A. Raymond George, in *A Dictionary of Christian Spirituality*, edited by Gordon S. Wakefield, SCM Press, 1983, page 317

Unlike the priest, pagan or Christian, the prophet is always alone; he always experiences a phase of sharp separation from the religious collective, from the milieu of the people among whom he lives. By his spiritual type, the prophet is always the bearer of the subjective element in religious life, as compared with the objective element whose bearer is the religious collective. And only later those spiritual elements, first expressed by the prophetic individual, take on objective significance, and religious life enters the objective stage. Religious life is born in propheticism and is precipitated in the priesthood... Always oriented to the future, the prophet is always dissatisfied with the present, denounces the evil in the life about him, and awaits the future triumph of higher spiritual elements which are revealed to him in prophetic visions... The prophet breathes the air of freedom, he smothers in the hardened world about him, but in his own spiritual world he breathes freely. He always visions a free spiritual world and awaits its penetration into this stifling world. The prophet foresees the fate of man and of the world, and through contemplation of the spiritual he unriddles the events of the empirical world. The prophetic gnosis is always a philosophy of history, and a philosophy of history is possible only as free prophecy. Unlike the saint, the prophet is submerged in the life of the world and of his own people; he shares the fate of both. But he renounces and denounces the life of the world and of his people he foretells its ruin... The prophet belongs to the human hierarchy, he is a man inspired by God. The prophet does not strive for personal perfection, saintliness or salvation, although he may rise to the highest degree of spiritual perfection, he may or may not be a saint... The prophetic is always a spiritually explosive psychology. The prophet does not calm men's spirits, or bring peace to their souls. Hence the prophetic cannot be the sole or even the predominant element in religious life. The world could not bear the ardent and consuming spirit of prophecy and it must guard itself against such domination. But without the spirit of prophecy, spiritual life would die out in this world...

A Christian renaissance will require not only a consecrated, priestly spirit of the sanctification of life, but a prophetic spirit as well, a spirit of transfiguration, the real alteration of life. The Christian movement proceeds not only from the popular collective, but also from the prophetic individuals of various hierarchical ranks. The priestly hierarchy is the necessary foundation of Christianity, but it must not dominate completely and throttle prophecy. Orientation to the Coming Christ is the prophetic side of Christianity, and cannot be eliminated from it. Through centuries of objectivization, Christianity has become so congealed into a racial, national, collective religion that the spirit of prophecy has dried up and has come to be considered almost as heresy...

At the summit of the spiritual life of humanity are two figures: the image of the prophet and that of the saint. Man has never risen higher than these two images. And both are needed for God's work in the world, for the coming of the Kingdom of God. Both these spiritual ways, the way of sanctity and that of prophecy, are part of the final appearance of Divine-humanity, both are part of the integral life of the Church, of the Church's fulfilment and completion. For the time being, in the mysterious plan of God, prophecy is active outside the visible body of the Church. But the time will come when the prophetic spirit will be recognized as the spirit of the Church, as proceeding out of the Church's depths. So man's religious fate is accomplished in tragedy, in apparent separation, in tormenting conflict. But mankind moves toward fulfilment, toward deification, toward the Kingdom of God... Christian prophecies are not optimistic; they do not justify the theory of progress; they denounce severely the evil coming into this world. But they are not pessimistic; they are above human pessimism and optimism. They await the coming of Christ in power and glory.

Nicolas Berdyaev, *Christian Existentialism*, selected and translated by Donald A. Lowrie, George Allen and Unwin, 1965, page 228

PROVIDENCE

'Providence'—beneficent care of God or nature.

When I was in Nigeria, I was invited out to dinner by a church member called 'King Cashew'. This was not his real name, but a nickname. He was, in fact, the world's expert on cashew nuts and worked for the United Nations. He lived on the other side of Ibadan, five miles away, in an area I had never been to before. I found his house easily enough in the daylight but on the return journey got hopelessly lost. Unbeknown to me I was heading straight for the military governor's house. An enormous scream suddenly rent the air, and sensing something wrong, I brought the car to an immediate halt. This was just as well. I was about to crash through a military check-point. Angry voices in the darkness ahead ordered me out of the car and I was required to put my hands above my head and walk towards the check-point in the beam of the headlights. As I gingerly made my way forward, I heard a safety-catch being released. This made me extremely frightened, and the hairs of the back of my head began to rise. I thought I was about to be shot. However, providence smiled on me that night. The sentries merely wanted to know who I was; what I was doing here; and did I have any cigarettes for them?

The doctrine of providence is not mainstream, but to live with a trust in the beneficent care of God or nature, helps us to lead wholesome lives. Jesus' advice to his disciples was twofold: be wise as serpents and innocent as doves.

Thou visitest the earth and waterest it, thou greatly enrichest it; the river of God is full of water, thou providest their grain, for so thou hast prepared it.

Psalm 65:9

O Lord, thou hast searched me and known me! Thou knowest when I sit down and when I rise up; thou discernest my thoughts from afar. Thou searchest out my path and my lying down, and art acquainted with all my ways. Even before a word is on my tongue, lo, O Lord, thou knowest it altogether. Thou dost beset me behind and before, and layest thy hand upon me. Such knowledge is too wonderful for me; it is high, I cannot attain it. Whither shall I go from thy Spirit? Or whither shall I flee from thy presence? If I ascend to heaven, thou art there! If I make my bed in Sheol, thou art there! If I take the wings of the morning and dwell in the uttermost parts of the sea, even there thy hand shall lead me, and thy right hand shall hold me. If I say, 'Let only darkness cover me, and the light about me be night,' even the darkness is not dark to thee, the night is bright as the day; for the darkness is as light with thee.

Psalm 139:1–12

Therefore do not be anxious about tomorrow, for tomorrow will be anxious for itself. Let the day's own trouble be sufficient for the day.

Matthew 6:34

And God is able to provide you with every blessing in abundance, so that you may always have enough of everything and may provide in abundance for every good work. As it is written, 'He scatters abroad, he gives to the poor; his righteousness endures for ever.' He who supplies seed to the sower and bread for food will supply and multiply your resources and increase the harvest of your righteousness.

2 Corinthians 9:8–10

Accept the place the divine providence has found for you, the society of your contemporaries, the connection of events.

Ralph Waldo Emerson, 'Self-Reliance', *Essays*, Bernhard Tauchnitz, 1915, page 36

What in me is dark
Illumine, what is low raise and support;
That to the height of this great Argument
I may assert Eternal Providence,
And justify the ways of God to men.

John Milton, *Paradise Lost*, i. 22, in *The Poetical Works of John Milton*, edited by the Rev. H.C. Beeching, Oxford at the Clarendon Press, 1900, page 182

We ought to live with the gods. This is done by him who always exhibits a soul contented with the appointments of Providence, and obeys the orders of that divinity which is his deputy and ruler, and the offspring of God. Now this divine authority is neither more nor less than that soul and reason which every man possesses.

Marcus Aurelius, *The Meditations of Marcus Aurelius*, translated by Jeremy Collier, Walter Scott, page 78

Providence has a thousand means to raise the fallen and support the prostrate. Sometimes our fate resembles a fruit tree in winter. Who would think at beholding so sad a sight that these rigid branches, these jagged twigs, would turn green again in the spring and blossom and bear fruit? But we hope it, we know it!

Johann Wolfgang von Goethe, *Wisdom and Experience*, selections by Ludwig Curtius, translated and edited by Hermann J. Weigand, Routledge and Kegan Paul, 1949, page 166

It is a perfectly correct view of things—and strictly consonant with the Gospel—to regard Providence across the ages as brooding over the world in ceaseless effort to spare that world its bitter wounds and to bind up its hurts. Most certainly it is God Himself who, in the course of the centuries, awakens the great benefactors of humankind, and the great physicians, in ways that agree with the general rhythm of progress. He it is who inspires, even among those furthest from acknowledging His existence, the quest for every means of comfort and every means of healing.

Pierre Teilhard de Chardin, *Le Milieu Divin*, William Collins Sons and Co., 1960, page 63

Providence: This is not a biblical word at all, since in the Old Testament and New Testament it occurs only on the lips of a heathen orator (Tertullus) as a conventional flattery of a Roman procurator (Felix) (Acts 24:2, where it means 'foresight'). The idea of divine providence was a Stoic commonplace, and we may surmise Stoic influence behind the use of the word in Wisdom 14:3. Later Christian usage has applied the word to the Fatherly love and care of God, his beneficent providential control of all that happens. This, of course, is an essentially biblical conception, and it is prominent in the teaching of Jesus himself (cf. Matthew 5:45, 6:25–34, 10:29–31). There is dominical authority for the view that the laws of nature reveal to God's children the loving purpose of their heavenly Father 'whose never-failing providence ordereth all things both in heaven and earth' (BCP, Collect for Trinity VIII; cf. also Collect for Trinity II).

Alan Richardson, in *A Theological Word Book of the Bible*, edited by Alan Richardson, SCM Press, 1950, page 182

The manifest world and whatever is moved in any sort take their causes, order and forms from the stability of the divine Mind. This hath determined manifold ways for doing things; which ways being considered in the purity of God's understanding are named Providence; but being referred to those things which He moveth and disposeth are called Fate... Providence is the very divine Reason itself, which disposeth all things. But Fate is a disposition inherent in changeable things, by which Providence connecteth all things in their due order. For Providence equally embraceth all things together, though diverse, though infinite; but Fate puts into motion all things, distributed by places, forms and times; so that the unfolding of the temporal order, being united in the foresight of the divine Mind, is Providence, and the same uniting, being digested and unfolded in time, is called Fate.

... As a workman conceiving the form of anything in his mind, taketh his work in hand and executeth by order of time that which he had simply and in a moment foreseen, so God by his Providence disposeth whatever is to be done with simplicity and stability, and by Fate effecteth by manifold ways and in the order of time those very things which He disposeth... All that is under Fate is also subject to Providence. But some things which are under Providence are above the course of Fate. For they are those things which, being stably fixed in virtue of their nearness to the first divinity, exceed the order of Fate's mobility.

Boethius, in The Perennial Philosophy, Aldous Huxley, Chatto and Windus, 1947, page 213

What, then, is the nature of that spiritual law of life under the direction of which, as he saw it, man should order his life if he would truly live?—It was his steadfast and unalterable conviction that for a man who has wrapped his will in God's will, put his life consciously in the stream of the divine life, freed his soul from all personal ambitions, taken his life on trust as a divine gift—that for such a man there is an overruling Providence which guards and guides him in every incident of his life, from the greatest to the least. He held that all annoyances, frustrations, disappointments, mishaps, discomforts, hardships, sorrows, pains, and even finally disaster itself, are simply God's ways of teaching us lessons that we could never else learn. That circumstances do not matter, are nothing; but that the response of the spirit that meets them is everything; that there is no situation in human life, however apparently adverse, nor any human relationship, however apparently uncongenial, that cannot be made, if God be in the heart, into a thing of perfect joy; that in order to attain this ultimate perfection, one must accept every experience and learn to love all persons; that the love particular should lead up to the love universal; that the worth of life is not to be measured by its results in achievement or success, but solely by the motive of one's heart and the effort of one's will; that the value of experience depends not so much upon its variety or duration as upon its intensity; and that by one single concentrated effort a brief life might attain a level that ages of ordinary development would fall short of, so that a man who lives his life thus 'having become perfect in a little while fulfils long years.'

George Seaver, said of Edward Wilson, in The Faith of Edward Wilson, John Murray, 1949, page 10

PURPOSE

'Purpose'—object, thing intended; fact, faculty, of resolving on something; design or intention.

A lexis Carrel wrote in his book, *Reflections on Life*, that the end of life is not profit, amusement, philosophy, science or religion. It is not even happiness: it is life itself. He added, life consists in the plenitude of all the organic and mental activities of the body.

Some of our undergraduates feel their main purpose in life is to make money; be successful in their careers; marry and have a family; and above all, enjoy themselves. Others take a less materialistic view and prefer to go on to do research, in philosophy (or other art subjects), and in the various sciences. Many go to the professions, though nowadays only a minority to religion. Some take a year out after university, hoping to find a purpose in life. High on the agenda for all—is a pursuit of happiness.

I prefer Alexis Carrel's conclusion, with a belief in life itself. I remember trying to work out what our main purpose in life is, and was greatly helped by observing a rose. I began to see that if the rose unfolded, blossomed, bloomed and died, nobody would be particularly troubled for the flower had actually achieved what it set out to do—namely to be. From this perspective I began to wonder if our main purpose in life is to grow a character, a personality, a soul, which is us at our highest level of development and expression. This is only another way of articulating Alexis Carrel's 'plenitude of all the organic and mental activities of the body', but with the addition of the spiritual dimension.

And if you be unwilling to serve the Lord, choose this day whom you will serve, whether the gods your fathers served in the region beyond the River, or the gods of the Amorites in whose land you dwell; but as for me and my house, we will serve the Lord.

Joshua 24:15

Commit your work to the Lord, and your plans will be established. The Lord has made everything for its purpose, even the wicked for the day of trouble.

Proverbs 16:3–4

I must preach the good news of the kingdom of God to the other cities also; for I was sent for this purpose.

Luke 4:43

Of this gospel I was made a minister according to the gift of God's grace which was given me by the working of his power. To me, though I am the very least of all the saints, this grace was given, to preach to the Gentiles the unsearchable riches of Christ, and to make all men see what is the plan of the mystery hidden for ages in God who created all things; that through the church the manifold wisdom of God might now be made known to the principalities and powers in the heavenly places. This was according to the eternal purpose which he has realized in Christ Jesus our Lord, in whom we have boldness and confidence of access through our faith in him.

Ephesians 3:7–12

What makes life dreary is the want of motive.

George Eliot, *Daniel Deronda*, volume II, J.M. Dent and Sons, 1964, page 580

Purpose is what gives life a meaning... A drifting boat always drifts down-stream.

Charles H. Parkhurst, *The Pattern in the Mount and Other Sermons*, R.D. Dickinson, 1890, page 8

To those who worship Thee; to see Thee is our end,
Who art our source and maker, lord and path and goal.

Boethius, *De Consolatione Philosophiae*, translated by V.E. Watts, Penguin Books, 1969, page 98

Continuity of purpose is one of the most essential ingredients of happiness in the long run, and for most men this comes chiefly through their work.

Bertrand Russell, *The Conquest of Happiness*, George Allen and Unwin, 1984, page 48

The man who consecrates his hours
By vig'rous effort and honest aim,
At once he draws the sting of life and death.

Edward Young, *Night Thoughts*, Thomas Nelson, 1841, page 17

How could there be any question of acquiring or possesssing, when the one thing needful for a man is to *become*—to *be* at last, and to die in the fullness of his being.

Antoine de Saint-Exupéry, *The Wisdom of the Sands*, translated by Stuart Gilbert, Hollis and Carter, 1952, page 127

Many persons have a wrong idea of what constitutes true happiness. It is not attained through self-gratification but through fidelity to a worthy purpose.

Helen Keller, *Helen Keller's Journal*, Michael Joseph, 1938, page 64

The need for devotion to something outside ourselves is even more profound than the need for companionship. If we are not to go to pieces or wither away, we all must have some purpose in life; for no man can live for himself alone.

Ross Parmenter, *The Plant in My Window*, Geoffrey Bles, 1951, page 39

Obstacles cannot bend me,
Every obstacle yields to effort.
Not to leave the furrow.
He who fixes his course by a star changes not.

Leonardo da Vinci, *The Notebooks of Leonardo da Vinci*, volume I, edited by Edward McCurdy, Jonathan Cape, 1977, page 89

The object of life... is the discovery... by a deepening of the self, of the centre of the self that constitutes our unique and personal essence, and which we always run the risk of missing so long as we remain on the surface of things, and think only of self-aggrandisement.

Louis Lavelle, in Paul Foulquié, *Existentialism*, translated by Kathleen Raine, Dennis Dobson, 1947, page 118

What is the meaning of human life, or, for that matter, of the life of any creature? To know an answer to this question means to be religious. You ask: Does it make any sense, then, to pose this question? I answer: The man who regards his own life and that of his fellow creatures as meaningless is not merely unhappy but hardly fit for life.

Albert Einstein, *Ideas and Opinions*, Souvenir Press (Educational & Academic), 1973, page 11

Life does not need comfort, when it can be offered meaning, nor pleasure, when it can be shown purpose. Reveal what is the purpose of existence and how he may attain it—the steps he must take—and man will go forward again hardily, happily, knowing that he has found what he must have—intentional living—and knowing that an effort, which takes all his energy because it is worth his full and constant concentration, is the only life deserving the devotion, satisfying the nature and developing the potentialities of a self-conscious being.

Anon.

What is the course of the life
Of mortal men on the earth?
Most men eddy about
Here and there—eat and drink,
Chatter and love and hate,
Gather and squander, are raised
Aloft, are hurled in the dust,
Striving blindly, achieving Nothing;
and then they die—
Perish; and no one asks
Who or what they have been.

Matthew Arnold, 'Rugby Chapel', in *The Poems of Matthew Arnold*, edited by Kenneth Allott, Longmans, Green and Co., 1965, page 447

Scientists tell us that matter has been in existence for over a thousand million years. Throughout that near eternal age of time God has been at work with unfailing wisdom and patience, taming the recalcitrance of matter, enabling each species of life to find its own goal of beauty and usefulness, training men in mind and spirit, drawing them together in unity, and in Jesus Christ showing them the prototype of human maturity as well as the image of divine love. We know from his revelation of himself that his purpose is good, loving, wise, the most effective thing to be done in every situation, and that his creative and redemptive work will continue until his eternal purpose is achieved.

George Appleton, *Journey for a Soul*, William Collins Sons and Co., 1976, page 233

One thing above all is important: the 'return to the Father.' The Son came into the world and died for us, rose and ascended to the Father; sent us His Spirit, that in Him and with Him we might return to the Father.

That we might pass clean out of the midst of all that is transitory and inconclusive: return to the Immense, the Primordial, the Source, the Unknown, to Him Who loves and knows, to the Silent, to the Merciful, to the Holy, to Him Who is All.

To seek anything, to be concerned with anything but this is only madness and sickness, for this is the whole meaning and heart of all existence, and in this all the affairs of life, all the needs of the world and of men, take on their right significance...

To 'return to the Father' is not to 'go back' in time, to roll up the scroll of history, or to reverse anything. It is a going forward, a going beyond...

Our destiny is to go on beyond everything, to leave everything, to press forward to the End and find in the End our Beginning, the ever-new Beginning that has no end.

Thomas Merton, *Conjectures of a Guilty Bystander*, Burns and Oates, 1968, page 168

Realization of the Supreme 'Player' whose 'play' is manifested in the million-formed inexhaustible richness of beings and events is what gives us the key to the meaning of life. Once we live in awareness of the cosmic dance and move in time with the Dancer, our life attains its true dimension. It is at once more serious and less serious than the life of one who does not sense this inner cosmic dynamism. To live without this illuminated consciousness is to live as a beast of burden, carrying one's life with tragic seriousness as a huge, incomprehensible weight... The weight of the burden is the seriousness with which one takes one's own individual and separate self. To live with the true consciousness of life centred in Another is to lose one's self-important seriousness and thus to live life as 'play' in union with a Cosmic Player.

It is He alone that one takes seriously. But to take Him seriously is to find joy and spontaneity in everything, for everything is gift and grace. In other words, to live selfishly is to bear life as an intolerable burden. To live selflessly is to live in joy.

Thomas Merton, *The Asian Journal*, Sheldon Press, 1974, page 350

After experience had taught me that all things which frequently take place in ordinary life are vain and futile; when I saw that all the things I feared and which feared me had nothing good or bad in them in so far as the mind was affected by them, I determined at last to inquire whether there might be anything which might be truly good and able to communicate its goodness, and by which the mind might be affected to the exclusion of all other things: I determined, I say, to inquire whether I might discover and acquire the faculty of enjoying throughout eternity continual supreme happiness.

I say 'I determined at last,' for at the first sight it seemed ill advised to lose what was certain in the hope of attaining what was uncertain. I could see the many advantages acquired from honour and riches, and that I should be debarred from acquiring these things if I wished seriously to investigate a new matter, and if perchance supreme happiness was in one of these I should lose it; if, on the other hand, it were not placed in them and I gave them the whole of my attention, then also I should be wanting in it.

I therefore turned over in my mind whether it might be possible to arrive at this new principle, or at least at the certainty of its existence, without changing the order and common plan of my life: a thing which I had often attempted in vain. For the things which most often happen in life and are esteemed as the greatest good of all, as may be gathered from their works, can be reduced to these three headings: to wit, Riches, Fame, and Pleasure. With these three the mind is so engrossed that it cannot scarcely think of any other good. As for pleasure, the mind is so engrossed in it that it remains in a state of quiescence as if it had attained supreme good, and this prevents it from thinking of anything else. But after that enjoyment follows pain, which, if it does not hold the mind suspended, disturbs and dullens it. The pursuit of fame and riches also distracts the mind not a little, more especially when they are sought for their own sake, inasmuch as they are thought to be the greatest good. By fame the mind is far more distracted, for it is supposed to be always good in itself, and as an ultimate aim to which all things must be directed...

But the love towards a thing eternal and infinite alone feeds the mind with pleasure, and it is free from all pain so it is much to be desired and to be sought out with all our might... although I could perceive all this quite clearly in my mind, I could not lay aside at once all greed, pleasure, and honour...

One thing I could see, and that was that as long as the mind was employed with these thoughts, it turned away from its former subjects of thought and meditated seriously on this new plan: which was a great comfort to me. For I saw that those evils were not of such a state that they could not be cured by remedies. And although at the commencement these intervals were rare and lasted for a very short space of time, yet afterwards the true good became more apparent to me, and these intervals more frequent and of longer duration.

Spinoza, *Spinoza's Ethics and De Intellectus Emendatione*, J.M. Dent and Sons, 1955, page 227

RECONCILIATION

*'Reconciliation'—a healing, a restoration of relationships,
a re-establishment of friendship.*

In 1962 we saw the meeting of Vatican Council II. This gave an added impetus towards the movement for Christian unity. In 1963, when I went to Wycliffe Hall, a theological college in Oxford, I was invited to join a rugby team called *the Mongrels*. The members of this team were made up of ordinands from various theological colleges in and around Oxford. We had several players from Ripon Hall, Cuddesdon, St Stephen's House and Wycliffe Hall—all Church of England Colleges—each representing different traditions. Other players came from Roman Catholic orders; the Dominicans from Blackfriars; the Benedictines from St Benet's Hall; and the Jesuits from Campion Hall, each also representing different traditions. All in all the Mongrels were a very mixed bunch.

One of our 'characters' owned an old fire engine. The members of our team would foregather, clamber on board, and speed off to the ground. We developed a good *esprit de corps* and established a reputation for tough (though not always clean) rugby. Friendships grew and before long we organized an arena for dialogue when we talked through our differences. The Mongrels proved to be a valuable instrument of relationships as well as a re-establishment of friendships. Out of this reconciliation came a deeper experience of Christian unity.

Agree with God, and be at peace; thereby good will come to you.

Job 22:21

A fool is too arrogant to make amends; upright men know what reconciliation means.

Proverbs 14:9 (NEB)

You have heard that it was said, 'An eye for an eye and a tooth for a tooth.' But I say to you, Do not resist one who is evil. But if any one strikes you on the right cheek, turn to him the other also.

Matthew 5:38–39

All this is from God, who through Christ reconciled us to himself and gave us the ministry of reconciliation; that is, in Christ God was reconciling the world to himself, not counting their trespasses against them, and entrusting to us the message of reconciliation. So we are ambassadors for Christ, God making his appeal through us. We beseech you on behalf of Christ, be reconciled to God.

2 Corinthians 5:18–20

He can never therefore be reconciled to your sin, because sin itself is incapable of being altered: but He may be reconciled to your person, because that may be restored: and, which is an infinite wonder, to greater beauty and splendour than before.

Thomas Traherne, *Centuries*, The Faith Press, 1969, page 72

It is certain that, at the moment of His death, He (Christ) was likewise forsaken and, as it were, annihilated in His soul, and was deprived of any relief and consolation, since His Father left Him in the most intense aridity, according to the lower part of His nature. Wherefore He had perforce to cry out, saying: 'My God! My God! Why hast Thou forsaken Me?' This was the greatest desolation, with respect to sense, that He had suffered in His life. And thus He wrought herein the greatest work that He had ever wrought, whether in miracles or in mighty works, during the whole of His life, either upon earth or in Heaven, which was the reconciliation and union of mankind, through grace, with God.

St John of the Cross, *Ascent of Mount Carmel*, translated and edited by E. Allison Peers, Image Books, Doubleday Company, 1958, page 193

The particular aspect of our Lord's coming to us as a healer of our sinfulness is 'held' for us in a sacrament, a special 'moment'. As always with a sacrament there is a wedding of the human and the divine. Our part is to take our act of sorrow, paltry and inadequate as it is, to that heart which alone has gauged sin, taken its full weight.

Our poor sorrow is taken up, transformed into, the perfect reparation of Jesus.

When we run to our Father's arms in this sacrament we take the whole sinful but dearly-loved world with us. We hear the certain assurance: 'I forgive.' All our wrongs by him are righted. The Church is built up again, her broken walls restored in full.

Many of us, I think, were we to analyse our attitude to confession, would find our lack of zeal regarding it due to the sheer poverty of the rite. We are aware of the utter paltriness of our confession and sorrow. But that is just the point. It is Jesus' atoning love, his sorrow, that are going to matter.

Ruth Burrows, in *The Watchful Heart*, edited by Elizabeth Ruth Obbard, Darton, Longman and Todd, 1988, page 31

'Blessed are the peacemakers: for they shall be called the children of God.' The followers of Jesus have been called to peace. When he called them they found their peace, for he is their peace. But now they are told that they must not only *have* peace but *make* it. And to that end they renounce all violence and tumult. In the cause of Christ nothing is to be gained by such methods. His kingdom is one of peace, and the mutual greeting of His flock is the kiss of peace. His disciples keep the peace by choosing to endure suffering themselves rather than inflict it on others. They maintain fellowship where others would break it off. They renounce all self-assertion, and preserve a dignified silence on the face of hatred and wrong. In so doing they overcome evil with good, and establish the peace of God in the midst of a world of war and hate. But nowhere will that peace be more manifest than where they meet the wicked in peace and are ready to suffer at their hands. The peacemakers will carry the cross with their Lord, for it was on the cross that peace was made. Now that they are partners in Christ's work of reconciliation, they are called the sons of God as He is the Son of God.

Dietrich Bonhoeffer, *The Cost of Discipleship*, SCM Press, 1948, page 102

The Church is called to a ministry of reconciliation which involves breaking down such impersonal problems as 'race' or 'delinquency' into people. There is, first, a preventative task. By the quality of its life-together the Church has the power to reconcile men across racial and other barriers. Joost de Blank at his enthronement service in Cape Town said: 'I suffer from an incurable disease: I am colour blind.' And Alec Fraser of Achimota said: 'I have yet to meet the man for whom Christ did not die.'

Secondly, it is a task of healing the wounds which hatred and prejudice have inflicted on people in mind and heart. We have spoken above of this work in the church-community and in groups of Christians. Reconciliation ... is a work which has power to heal, not only relationships, but also broken hearts, minds and bodies.

In the Church of today we are faced with denominational divisions which greatly weaken our power to reconcile different races. So the Church is broken. But her ministry of reconciliation is even now going on in East Harlem and Notting Hill, just as when Paul wrote to admonish the Corinthians for their party factions, the work of reconciling Jew and Gentile, master and slave, was continuing. The world is in the Church dividing Christians from one another but the Church is also in the world, suffering, healing and reconciling men to each other.

Michael Wilson, *The Church is Healing*, SCM Press, 1966, page 47

REDEMPTION

'Redemption'—redeeming or being redeemed, thing that redeems,
purchase the freedom of another, oneself.

There was a knock on the door of my rooms in college. Tony, a nineteen-year-old apprentice chef, and his girl-friend Marie, were wanting to see me. He had just been told he had terminal cancer, with only a few weeks to live. Could he come and see me about it? I ushered them in and gave them a cup of tea. We then had a three-way conversation and worked out how to make the most of the next few weeks. I asked them if they wanted to get married? The answer was 'no'. Their relationship was just as they wanted it, and there were fears marriage might spoil things. What about a holiday? They had thought about this too and had decided 'no'. What Tony really wanted to do was qualify as a chef, and he wondered if Marie (also an apprentice chef) could be transferred to his shift so that they could work together? This was arranged. Was there anything else? Yes, he would love to do a parachute jump. We later spent a day at an RAF station but weather conditions were against us.

Tony's values in life changed. One day when he came to see me, he was extremely excited—'Do you know,' he said, 'I've just seen the sun for the very first time.' 'No, no,' I retorted, 'you must have seen it hundreds of times.' 'No,' he smiled, 'I *really saw it today*. It is dazzlingly beautiful.' He spoke in similar terms of a blackbird he spotted, and of other people and then back to himself. He died in a most courageous way. He had learnt the secret of 'redeeming' the time.

For I know that my Redeemer lives, and at last he will stand upon the earth, and after my skin has been thus destroyed, then from my flesh I shall see God, whom I shall see on my side, and my eyes shall behold, and not another.

Job 19:25–27

Arise, shine; for your light has come, and the glory of the Lord has risen upon you. For behold, darkness shall cover the earth, and thick darkness the peoples; but the Lord will arise upon you, and his glory will be seen upon you. And nations shall come to your light, and kings to the brightness of your rising.

Isaiah 60:1–3

For the Son of man also came not to be served but to serve, and to give his life as a ransom for many.

Mark 10:45

For the grace of God has appeared for the salvation of all men, training us to renounce irreligion and worldly passions, and to live sober, upright, and godly lives in this world, awaiting our blessed hope, the appearing of the glory of our great God and Saviour Jesus Christ, who gave himself for us to redeem us from all iniquity and to purify for himself a people of his own who are zealous for good deeds.

Titus 2:11–14

Man cannot meet his own deepest need, nor find for himself release from his profoundest trouble. What he needs is not progress, but redemption. If the Kingdom of God is to come on earth, it must be because God first comes on earth himself.

William Temple, *Nature, Man and God*, Macmillan and Co., 1934, page 513

Christianity, however, is not consistent. In the bedrock of its pessimism there are optimistic veins, for it is not only the religion of redemption but of the Kingdom of God. Therefore, it wishes and hopes for a transformation of the world.

Albert Schweitzer, *Christianity and the Religions of the World*, translated by J. Powers, Allen and Unwin, 1923, page 27

Christ lifted up in our heart will redeem our feelings, emotions and passions by the love, grace, and understanding of the Son of God. Inharmony has no hold on us, passion no place in us, hatred nor misunderstanding no expression through us when Christ is lifted up in our heart.

Anon.

Remember that Christianity is not just another religion of individual salvation, differing only in having a different plan of salvation to offer. It is the one and only religion of world-redemption. We are members of the family of God; when we come to Him in Christ, it must always be in the company of our brothers and sisters.

William Temple, *Christian Faith and Life*, SCM Press, 1931, reissued 1963, page 45

By His suffering, our Lord did make it possible for us to avoid suffering continual alienation from God and the consequences of this; and therefore, in a sense, His suffering is substituted for ours; but it is not a transferred penalty: it is something in the nature of a price paid; it is something which He gave, by means of which we are set free. It is a real redemption; but what He is concerned with all the time is delivering us, not from the consequences of sin, but from sin; and the centre of sin is self. So He is delivering us out of self-centredness into a life that finds its centre in God.

William Temple, *Christian Faith and Life*, SCM Press, 1931, reissued 1963, page 86

Thou hast redeemed me,
And therefore with hallelujahs
Do I praise thy Name,
Recounting the ancient glories
Which thou createdst in my soul,
And confessing
That infinitely more is left unsaid.
   O my God,
Sanctify me by thy Spirit,
Make me a temple of the Holy Ghost,
A willing person in the day of thy power.

Thomas Traherne, in *Landscapes of Glory*, edited by A.M. Allchin, Darton, Longman and Todd, 1989, page 18

The redemption it preaches, a redemption to be realised through a merging into spirituality has something grand about it. This idea, so complete in itself, attracts thoughtful men in an almost uncanny way. We, however, have a longing for another kind of union with God. We desire our union with God to result in living ethical spirituality, in activity in the power of God. Such a redemption from the world is the only kind of redemption that can satisfy the longing of the heart. Thus, although we know the charm of the logical religion, we stand by Christianity with all its simplicity and all its antinomies. It is indeed true and valuable, for its answers to the deepest stirrings of our inner will to live.

Albert Schweitzer, *Christianity and the Religions of the World*, translated by J. Powers, Allen and Unwin, 1923, page 52

The word 'redemption' and its cognate forms, like most of the important words of the Bible, is not derived from abstract philosophical thought, but is based upon the distinctive Hebraic way of thinking in concrete terms. It is derived from the practice of buying back something which formerly belonged to the purchaser, but has for some reason passed out of his possession (as in redeeming a pledge from pawn) or of paying the price required to secure a benefit (the money paid for acquiring or freeing a slave) and comes from the same root as the word ransom. When used figuratively in the Bible, it emphasizes the fact that in the saving activity of God, supremely manifested in Christ, something of decisive import has been done for the salvation of mankind.

F.J. Taylor, in *A Theological Word Book of the Bible*, edited by Alan Richardson, SCM Press, 1975, page 185

The great weakness of all doctrines of redemption since the Primitive Christian is that they represent a man as wholly concerned with his own individual redemption, and not equally with the coming of the Kingdom of God. The one thing needful is that we should work for the establishment of a Christianity, which does not permit those who allow their lives to be determined by Christ to be 'of little faith' in regard to the future of the world. However much circumstances may suggest to them this want of faith, Christianity must compel them to realise that to be a Christian means to be possessed and dominated by a hope of the Kingdom of God, and a will to work for it, which bids defiance to external reality. Until this comes about Christianity will stand before the world like a wood in the barrenness of winter.

Albert Schweitzer, *The Mysticism of Paul the Apostle*, translated by William Montgomery, A. and C. Black, 1931, page 384

The entire work of redemption is, thus, to restore man to himself, to bring him once more to the Tree of Life, to enable him to discover the glory all about him, to reveal to him the real values of things, and to bring to birth within him an immortal love. The true healing of the soul is always through the birth of love. Before a soul loves, it lives only to itself; as soon as love is born it lives beyond itself and finds its life in the object of its love. It is Christ who first reveals the full measure of love, who makes us see the one adequate Object of love and who forges within our human spirits the invisible bonds of a love that binds us forever to Him who *so* loved us. Here in him—'a Man loving to all the world, a God dying for mankind' we see that we are infinitely prone to love, and that true love spares nothing for the sake of what it loves—'O miraculous and eternal Godhead suffering on a Cross for me!' 'That Cross is a tree set on fire with invisible flame which illuminateth all the world. The flame is love: the love in His Bosom that died upon it.'

But there is no salvation for us in the Cross until it kindles the same flame of love in us, until that immeasurable love of His becomes an irresistible power in us, so that we henceforth live unto Him that loved us. It must, if it is to be efficacious, shift all our values and set us to loving as He loved—'He who would not in the same cases do the same things Jesus Christ hath done can never be saved,' for love is never timorous. The love of Christ is to dwell within us and every man is to be the object of it. God and we are to become one spirit, that is, one in will and one in desire. Christ must live within us. We must be filled with the Holy Ghost, which is the God of Love; we must be of the same mind with Christ Jesus and led by His Spirit, and we must henceforth treat every man in respect to the greatness of Christ's love—this is salvation in Traherne's conception of it, and holiness and happiness are the same thing. The Cross has not done its complete work for us until we can say: 'O Christ, I see thy crown of thorns in every eye; thy bleeding, naked, wounded body in every soul; thy death liveth in every memory; thy crucified person is embalmed in every affection; thy pierced feet are bathed in every one's tears and it is my privilege to enter with thee into every soul.'

Rufus M. Jones, *Spiritual Reformers in the 16th and 17th Centuries*, Macmillan and Co., 1914, page 332

RELIGION

'Religion'—monastic condition; practice of sacred rites; one of the prevalent systems of faith and worship; human recognition of superhuman controlling power and especially of a personal God entitled to obedience, effect of such recognition on conduct and mental attitude.

Edward Wilson, the doctor on Scott's expedition to the Antarctic, felt the main thing in religion is whether a person has the Spirit of God in him. I have a great sympathy for his viewpoint, and want to go further and indicate what is meant by 'the Spirit of God in him'.

First and foremost an inner presence of the Holy Spirit as experienced by the Apostles, incorporating the Spirit of the Father and the Spirit of the Son. Furthermore this includes an experience of the inner presence of the Spirit of life, the Spirit of light, the Spirit of joy, the

Spirit of grace, the Spirit of power, the Spirit of truth and the Spirit of love, and so on. All these attributes are included in the concept of the Spirit of God in a person. They point to a greater wealth than the jackpot of the National Lottery; to an absolute wealth; to the pearl of great price—to be found in a person.

How then is the Spirit of God to be found in a person? The traditional answer is baptism (and confirmation), but some might feel this initiation sacrament has become emasculated, and for them no longer valid. If so, why not try reflection? A valid starting point might well be the topic 'Finding God' in this anthology. The practice of reflection has already been known to trigger off something of the Spirit of God in man, and to an experience of the very essence of 'religion'.

> I perceive that in every way you are very religious.
>
> Acts 17:22

> Great indeed, we confess, is the mystery of our religion: He was manifested in the flesh, vindicated in the Spirit, seen by angels, preached among the nations, believed on in the world, taken up in glory.
>
> 1 Timothy 3:16

> For men will be lovers of self, lovers of money, proud, arrogant, abusive, disobedient to their parents, ungrateful, unholy, inhuman, implacable, slanderers, profligates, fierce, haters of good, treacherous, reckless, swollen with conceit, lovers of pleasure rather than lovers of God, holding the form of religion but denying the power of it.
>
> 2 Timothy 3:2–5

> If any one thinks he is religious, and does not bridle his tongue but deceives his heart, this man's religion is vain. Religion that is pure and undefiled before God and the Father is this: to visit orphans and widows in their affliction, and to keep oneself unstained from the world.
>
> James 1:26–27

> Religion, that voice of the deepest human experience.
>
> Matthew Arnold, 'Sweetness and Light', in *The Complete Prose Works of Matthew Arnold*, volume V, *Culture and Anarchy*, edited by R.H. Super, The University of Michigan Press, 1965, page 93

> For [Edward] Wilson... religion was a divine life, not a divine science; and embodied personalities and examples, not philosophical systems and doctrinal formulas.
>
> Dr H.S. Pennington in George Seaver, *The Faith of Edward Wilson*, John Murray, 1949, page 5

> True religion is the establishment by man of such a relation to the Infinite Life around him, as, while connecting his life with this Infinitude and directing his conduct, is also in agreement with his reason and with human knowledge.
>
> Leo Tolstoy, *What is Religion?*, The Free Age Press, 1902, page 16

> Religion is something infinitely simple, simple-souled. It is not knowledge, not the content feeling... it is not duty and not renunciation, it is not a limitation: but, within the perfect amplitudes of the universe it is—a direction of the heart.
>
> Rainer Maria Rilke, *Selected Letters of Rainer Maria Rilke*, translated by R.F.C. Hull, Macmillan and Co., 1946, page 336

> It is not religious experiences, but religious experience as a whole, that is of chief concern... For the religious man is not only religious when he prays; his work is religiously done, his recreation religiously enjoyed, his food and drink religiously received; the last he often emphasises by the custom of 'grace before meat.'
>
> William Temple, *Nature, Man and God*, Macmillan and Co., 1934, page 334

> Religion is not a test to judge by, but an immense aid for those who use it to live by. The main thing is whether a person has the Spirit of God in him, which to my mind means simply the

power to love and be kind and unselfish; and many people have this in a very perfect form without professing any religious belief at all, or using any religious practices to keep it.

Edward Wilson, in George Seaver, *The Faith of Edward Wilson*, John Murray, 1949, page 19

Religion, wherever it exists as a concrete and spiritually effective force, requires the exercise of the faculty of intuitive perception, the leap of the mind across and beyond all the data and methods of rational and logical analysis to grasp directly and in concrete experience some element in the nature of things which reason cannot describe or identify. Faith is the substance of things hoped for, the evidence of things not seen.

Anon.

It is well to have specifically holy places, and things, and days, for, without these focal points or reminders, the belief that all is holy and 'big with God' will soon dwindle into a mere sentiment. But if these holy places, things, and days cease to remind us, if they obliterate our awareness that all ground is holy and every bush (could we but perceive it) a Burning Bush, then the hallows begin to do harm. Hence both the necessity, and the perennial danger, of 'religion.'

C.S. Lewis, *Letters to Malcolm*, Geoffrey Bles, 1964, page 100

It is well said, in every sense, that a man's religion is the chief fact with regard to him... By religion I do not mean here the church-creed which he professes... This is not what I call religion... But the thing a man does practically believe;... the thing a man does practically lay to heart, and know for certain, concerning his vital relations to this mysterious Universe, and his duty and destiny there,... That is his *religion.*

Thomas Carlyle, 'Lectures on Heroes', in *Sartor Resartus*, Chapman and Hall, 1840, page 186

Some people say that social and religious movements are two different things. This, however, is said by those who fail to think of religion as an art concerned with the whole of life. If the material and the spiritual are separate entities, and if there is no relation between God and the world, this contention may be true. To him, however, who makes life the realization of the supremest good it is impossible to separate social and religious effort. If religion is the whole of life in action, how can social movements alone exist apart from religion? It is only the timid who interpret God and the world as a dualism. Until even the Stock Exchange is filled to saturation with God there is little hope for genuine religion.

Toyohiko Kagawa, in William Axling, *Kagawa*, SCM Press, 1946, page 56

It is no good asking for a simple religion. After all, real things are not simple. They look simple, but they are not. The table I am sitting at looks simple: but ask a scientist to tell you what it is really made of—all about the atoms and how the light waves rebound from them and hit my eye and what they do to the optic nerve and what it does to my brain—and, of course, you find that what we call 'seeing a table' lands you in mysteries and complications which you can hardly get to the end of. A child saying a child's prayer looks simple. And if you are content to stop there, well and good. But if you are not—and the modern world usually is not—if you want to go on and ask what is really happening—then you must be prepared for something difficult. If we ask for something more than simplicity, it is silly then to complain that the something more is not simple.

C.S. Lewis, *Mere Christianity*, William Collins Sons and Co., 1961, page 42

As our society becomes increasingly less religious its need for the authentically spiritual intensifies.

Religion is the sacred expression of the spiritual but if the spiritual experience is lacking then the religious form becomes hollow and superficial and self-important. *Religion does yield high dividends, but only to the man whose resources are within him* (1 Timothy 6:6).

How often does the violence with which men assert or defend their beliefs betray an attempt to convince themselves that they do really believe or that their beliefs are authentic? The spectre of our actual unbelief can be so frightening that we can be plunged into extreme, self-contradictory ways of imposing our beliefs on others rather than simply, peacefully, living them ourselves.

When religion begins to bully or to insinuate, it has become unspiritual because the first gift of the Spirit, creatively moving in man's nature, is freedom and frankness.

John Main OSB, in *The Joy of Being*, selected by Clare Hallward, Darton, Longman and Todd, 1989, page 4

True religion is always inward and spiritual, is directly initiated within the soul, is independent of form and letter, is concerned solely with the eternal and invisible, and verifies itself by producing within man a nature like that of God as He is seen in Christ. The 'law' of true religion is a new and divinely formed disposition towards goodness—a law written in the heart; its temple is not of stone or wood, but is a living and spiritual temple, its worship consists entirely of spiritual activities, i.e., the offering of genuine praise from appreciative hearts, the sacrifice of the self to God, and the partaking of divine food and drink through living communion with Christ the Life. Religion, of this true and saving sort, never comes through hearsay knowledge, or along the channels of tradition, or by a head knowledge of texts of the written word. It comes only with inward experience of the Word of God, and it grows and deepens as the will of man lives by the Will of God, and as the kingdom of God comes, not in some faraway Jerusalem, or in some remote realm above the sky, but *in a man's own heart.*

Rufus M. Jones, *Spiritual Reformers in the 16th and 17th Centuries*, Macmillan and Co., 1914, page 109

I am convinced that moral standards can only be raised by a revival of religion. The proliferation of 'isms' in our own times proves that no intellectual panacea can command general support. A group of clever people produce a theory of society which they are convinced will result in an earthly paradise, but it is impossible to build a dream society with violent, selfish people. Their theories are bitterly attacked by other groups, and conflict and hatred result.

Religion alone can persuade men to abandon their immediate, short-term selfishness and to dedicate themselves to the common good in complete self-oblivion. By religion, I mean the conviction that this life is not the end; that there is a spiritual world which, though invisible, penetrates all creation, and which can strike a sympathetic note in every human heart.

To accept the existence of this vast spiritual world immensely enlarges our horizon and enables us to see the pettiness of our quarrels and our attempts to grab for ourselves. It can result in a gradual transformation of our characters. But, more often than not, pride in our own cleverness closes our minds to the spiritual world which everywhere surrounds and envelopes us.

Sir John Glubb, *The Fate of Empires and Search for Survival*, William Blackwood and Sons, 1978, page 44

Religion, this feeling of contact with a Greater Power beyond the self, seems to be some fundamental feature in the natural history of man. As one travels through the English country-side, taking the lesser by-ways rather than the great, one cannot, if one goes slowly and is prepared to stop, but be struck by the beauty of the old parish churches and be made to marvel that such glories could be built by such small groups of people, just as one marvels at the great medieval cathedrals in towns which, at the time of their building, must have had only moderate populations. If one goes inside such an old country church one cannot help feeling that here is something fashioned with real love and reverence; elements of superstition there may well be, but in spite of this, surely here is something created not just by an ignorant craving for magic, but by something of profound depth. A naturalist coming from another planet, if his space-ship had the ability to drift across the countryside like a balloon, could not but be struck by the prominence of these buildings in each small community. Amidst the little groups of houses their spires and towers stand up like the sporangia of some organism and he might well be excused for first thinking them to have the importance of some such reproductive process. Indeed they had an equal importance in the past when devotion to God was as real to the population as was that of sexuality. They hardly have the same significance today and some, alas, stand forsaken like fossil skeletons of the past; this, however, may only be a temporary phase due to the accelerated growth of a physical science, whose findings are difficult to reconcile with many of the old doctrinal dogmas. I say temporary because I believe the dogmas on both sides may be revised as theology becomes more natural and science's mechanistic interpretation of life is shown not to be the whole truth. Religion indeed seems to be some fundamental feature in Man's make-up: something which can be as powerful as any other urge. Few can doubt that the wars of religion or of rival ideologies are more bitter than those fought for just economic ends; and we must not forget that those on the two sides of a conflict may well, through the lack of a generally accepted scientific theology, be propelled by different ideas of God that they both, in their prejudice, passionately feel to be right. It would not surprise me if the roots of religion went much deeper down into biological history than is generally conceded, and that it *is* part of the very nature of the living stream.

Sir Alistair Hardy, *The Living Stream*, William Collins Sons and Co., 1965, page 274

RENUNCIATION

'Renunciation'—renouncing, self-denial, giving up of things.

We have in college at the present time an oarsman who has recently rowed against Cambridge in one of the University crews. Prior to the Boat Race he trained six hours a day for several months in order to excel in this sport. Moreover he is engaged in research for a D Phil (Doctor of Philosophy) which requires a similar commitment. At the beginning of the academic year he thought out his strategy and renounced many activities in order to dedicate himself to these two undertakings. Any sportsman or academic worthy of the name has to exercise a similar form of renunciation and self-denial. This is true too, of the dedicated artist and musician.

The same practice applies to the life of faith. In the first instance many things have to be renounced to make way for the presence of God. This is true of all forms of selfishness, self-centredness and egoism. Self-denial here is both searching and costly. In the second instance, time is needed for prayer, whether reflection, meditation or contemplation. Many things, harmless in themselves, have to be given up to make time for prayer. In the third instance, any faith worthy of the name issues in service, and the demands for service are many and manifold. Again certain activities have to be pruned to make time for service. Overall, renunciation is the *sine qua non* of a life of faith. When I first set out on this journey I naïvely thought renunciation was a single act, done once and for all. I now know self-denial has to be practised on a daily basis, but the 'prize' is well worth the cost.

Why does the wicked renounce God, and say in his heart, 'Thou wilt not call to account?'

Psalm 10:13

Thou hast renounced the covenant with thy servant; thou hast defiled his crown in the dust.

Psalm 89:39

We have renounced disgraceful, underhanded ways; we refuse to practice cunning or to tamper with God's word, but by the open statement of the truth we would commend ourselves to every man's conscience in the sight of God.

2 Corinthians 4:2

If we have died with him, we shall also live with him; if we endure, we shall also reign with him.

2 Timothy 2:11–12

I shrink to give up my life, and thus do not plunge into the great waters of life.

Rabindranath Tagore, *Gitanjali*, Macmillan and Co., 1971, page 72

Wherefore forsake all things for God, and then God will be truly given unto you in all things.

John Tauler, *The History and Life of the Reverend Doctor John Tauler*, translated by Susanna Winkworth, Smith, Elder and Co., 1857, page 311

My son, you cannot have complete freedom unless you deny your own claims entirely... Hold on to the brief saying that sums this up—Leave everything and you will find everything.

Thomas à Kempis, *The Imitation of Christ*, translated by Betty I. Knott, William Collins Sons and Co., 1979, page 161

The only value which Christianity sees in voluntary renunciation is that which relates it to love. True renunciation renounces that which is opposed to love, and embraces that which leads to it.

Hubert van Zeller, *Considerations*, Sheed and Ward, 1974, page 69

I know that for the right practice of it the heart must be empty of all other things, because GOD will possess the heart *alone;* and as He cannot possess it *alone*, without emptying it of all besides, so neither can He act *there*, and do in it what He pleases, unless it be left vacant to Him.

Brother Lawrence, *The Practice of the Presence of God*, A.R. Mowbray and Co., 1977, page 42

For anyone who is on a spiritual path, that is, the path to God, there must be an element of renunciation in this life.

In India renunciation is seen as an essential part of spiritual growth and awakening. A man may leave his family at a certain stage of his life and go into the forest, there to find God within his soul. He gives up the comforts of life for a greater good. We do not need to follow this practice literally in order to find our 'true selves', but we must be prepared to sacrifice legitimate things in order that we may find the space in which the spiritual life can blossom.

This is the way of the cross which leads to a kind of death and resurrection.

Bede Griffiths OSB, in *The Universal Christ*, edited by Peter Spink, Darton, Longman and Todd, 1990, page 40

This pearl of eternity is the peace and joy of God within thee, but can only be found by the manifestation of the life and power of Jesus Christ in thy soul. But Christ cannot be thy power and thy life till, in obedience to His call, thou deniest thyself, takest up thy daily cross and followest Him in the regeneration. This is peremptory, it admits of no reserve or evasion, it is the one way to Christ and eternal life. But be where thou wilt, either here or at Rome or Geneva, if self is undenied, if thou livest to thine own will, to the pleasures of thy natural lust and appetites, senses, and passions, and in conformity to the vain customs and spirit of this world, thou art dead whilst thou livest... a stranger to all that is holy and heavenly within thee and utterly incapable of finding the peace and joy of God in thy soul.

William Law, *Selected Mystical Writings of William Law*, edited by Stephen Hobhouse, Rockliff, 1948, page 90

Therefore if a heart is to be ready for him, it must be emptied out to nothingness, the condition of its maximum capacity. So, too, a disinterested heart, reduced to nothingness, is the optimum, the condition of maximum sensitivity.

Take an illustration from nature. If I wish to write on a white tablet, then no matter how fine the matter already written on it, it will confuse me and prevent me from writing down (my thoughts) so that, if I still wish to use the tablet, I must first erase all that is written on it, but it will never serve me as well as for writing as when it is clean. Similarly, if God is to write his message about the highest matters on my heart, everything to be referred to as 'this or that' must first come out and I must be disinterested. God is free to do his will on his own level when my heart, being disinterested, is bent on neither this nor that.

Meister Eckhart, *Meister Eckhart*, translated by Raymond B. Blakney, Harper and Row, Publishers, 1941, page 88

It is by losing the egocentric life that we save the hitherto latent and undiscovered life which, in the spiritual part of our being, we share with the Divine Ground. This new-found life is 'more abundant' than the other, and of a different and higher kind. Its possession is liberation into the eternal, and liberation is beatitude. Necessarily so; for the Brahman, who is one with the Atman, is not only Being and Knowledge, but also Bliss, and, after Love and Peace, the final fruit of the Spirit is Joy. Mortification is painful, but that pain is one of the pre-conditions of blessedness. This fact of spiritual experience is sometimes obscured by the language in which it is described. Thus, when Christ says that the Kingdom of Heaven cannot be entered except by those who are as little children, we are apt to forget (so touching are the images evoked by the simple phrase) that a man cannot become childlike unless he chooses to undertake the most strenuous and searching course of self-denial. In practice the command to become as little children is identical with the command to lose one's life.

Aldous Huxley, *The Perennial Philosophy*, Chatto and Windus, 1974, page 124

To die—for this into the world you came.
Yes, to abandon more than you ever conceived as possible:
All ideals, plans—even the very best and most unselfish—all hopes and desires,
All formulas of morality, all reputation for virtue or consistency or good sense; all cherished theories, doctrines, systems of knowledge,
Modes of life, habits, predilections, preferences, superiorities, weaknesses, indulgences,
Good health, wholeness of limb and brain, youth, manhood, age—nay life itself—in one word: To die—
For this into the world you came.
All to be abandoned, and when they have been finally abandoned,
Then to return to be used—and then only to be rightly used, to be free and open for ever.

Edward Carpenter, *Towards Democracy*, George Allen and Unwin, 1931, page 353

Recollection is awareness of the unconditional. *Prayer* then means yearning for the simple presence of God... Our desire and our prayer should be summed up in St Augustine's words: 'May I know you, may I know myself'.

We wish to gain a true evaluation of ourselves and of the world so as to understand the meaning of our life as children of God redeemed from sin and death. We wish to gain a true loving knowledge of God, our Father and Redeemer. We wish to lose ourselves in his love and rest in him. We wish to hear his word and respond to it with our whole being. We wish to know his merciful will and submit to it in its totality...

All prayer, reading, meditation and all the activities of the monastic life are aimed at *purity of heart*, an unconditional and totally humble surrender to God, a total acceptance of ourselves and of our situation as willed by him. It means the renunciation of all deluded images of ourselves, all exaggerated estimates of our own capacities, in order to obey God's will as it comes to us in the difficult demands of life in its exacting truth.

Thomas Merton, *Contemplative Prayer*, Darton, Longman and Todd, 1973, page 82

To every man comes, sooner or later, the great renunciation. For the young, there is nothing unattainable; a good thing desired with the whole force of a passionate will, and yet impossible, is to them not credible. Yet, by death, by illness, by poverty, or by the voice of duty, we must learn, each one of us, that the world was not made for us, and that, however beautiful may be the things we crave, Fate may nevertheless forbid them. It is the part of courage, when misfortune comes, to bear without repining the ruin of our hopes, to turn away our thoughts from vain regrets. This degree of submission to Power is not only just and right: it is the very gate of wisdom.

But passive renunciation is not the whole of wisdom; for not by renunciation alone can we build a temple for the worship of our own ideals. Haunting foreshadowings of the temple appear in the realm of imagination, in music, in architecture, in the untroubled kingdom of reason, and in the golden sunset magic of lyrics, where beauty shines and glows, remote from the touch of sorrow, remote from the fear of change, remote from the failures and disenchantments of the world of fact. In the contemplation of these things the vision of heaven will shape itself in our hearts, giving at once a touchstone to judge the world about us, and an inspiration by which to fashion to our needs whatever is not incapable of serving as a stone in the sacred temple.

Except for those rare spirits that are born without sin, there is a cavern of darkness to be traversed before that temple can be entered. The gate of the cavern is despair, and its floor is paved with the gravestones of abandoned hopes. There Self must die; there the eagerness, the greed of untamed desire must be slain, for only so can the soul be freed from the empire of Fate. But out of the cavern the Gate of Renunciation leads again to the daylight of wisdom, by whose radiance a new insight, a new joy, a new tenderness, shine forth to gladden the pilgrim's heart.

Bertrand Russell, *Mysticism and Logic, and Other Essays*, Longmans, Green and Co., 1919, page 52

REPENTANCE

*'Repentance'—a change of heart and mind; sometimes brought
about by regret, remorse, sorrow and contrition; a turning round
involving a change of priorities.*

One of our new intake had a drink problem. On a number of occasions she ended up paralytically drunk. I remember one night staying up with her into the early hours of the morning, to make sure nothing untoward happened. Her friends were naturally concerned, as were her tutors.

One day, about half-way through the first term, she appeared at my door and asked if she could come in and have a chat. Something dramatic had happened, some form of religious experience, and she now wanted to be baptized. Initially I was reluctant to go ahead, as her background was that of a different faith. However she persisted, and two or three weeks later she was baptized in the college chapel.

After a few months she asked me if I would prepare her for confirmation. The preparation duly went ahead and the following year she was confirmed—also in the college chapel. She then became a regular member of a reflection group, and ended up having a remarkably successful career at 'Univ'.

What I had witnessed was a 'repentance', a change of heart and mind, a 'turning round' involving a change of priorities. I cannot claim any credit for this. In retrospect I put it down to her, and her response to God's grace. What I saw was the emergence of a delightful person.

Then the spirit of the Lord will come mightily upon you, and you shall prophesy with them and be turned into another man.

1 Samuel 10:6

When I think of thy ways, I turn my feet to thy testimonies.

Psalm 119:59

And Peter said to them, 'Repent, and be baptized every one of you in the name of Jesus Christ for the forgiveness of your sins; and you shall receive the gift of the Holy Spirit.'

Acts 2:38

Repent therefore, and turn again, that your sins may be blotted out, that times of refreshing may come from the presence of the Lord.

Acts 3:19

'But how can God bring this about in me?'—Let him do it, and perhaps you will know.

George Macdonald, *Unspoken Sermons*, Third Series, Longmans, Green and Co., 1889, page 226

Often we shall have to change the direction of our thinking and our wishing and our striving. That is what repentance really means—taking our bearings afresh and trying a new road.

Harry Williams, *The True Wilderness*, Constable and Company, 1965, page 27

If you have behaved badly, repent, make what amends you can and address yourself to the task of behaving better next time. On no account brood over your wrongdoing. Rolling in the muck is not the best way of getting clean.

Aldous Huxley, *Brave New World*, Chatto and Windus, 1970, page vii

Repentance is but a kind of table-talk, till we see so much of the deformity of our inward nature as to be in some degree frightened and terrified at the sight of it. There must be some kind of an earthquake within us, something that must rend and shake us to the bottom, before we can be enough sensible either of the state of death we are in or enough desirous of that Saviour, who alone can raise us from it . . . Sooner or later repentance must have a broken and a contrite heart;

we must with our blessed Lord go over the brook Cedron, and with Him sweat great drops of sorrow before He can say for us, as He said for Himself: 'It is finished.'

William Law, *Selected Mystical Writings of William Law*, edited by Stephen Hobhouse, Rockliff, 1948, page 13

To repent is to adopt God's viewpoint in place of your own. There need not be any sorrow about it. In itself, far from being sorrowful, it is the most joyful thing in the world, because when you have done it you have adopted the viewpoint of truth itself, and you are in fellowship with God. It means a complete revaluation of all things we are inclined to think good. The world, as we live in it, is like a shop window in which some mischievous person has got in overnight and shifted all the price-labels round so that the cheap things have the high price labels on them, and the really precious things are priced low. We let ourselves be taken in. Repentance means getting those price-labels back in the right place.

William Temple, *Christian Faith and Life*, SCM Press, 1931, reissued 1963, page 74

Repentance must not be mistaken for remorse, it does not consist in feeling terribly sorry that things went wrong in the past; it is an active, positive attitude which consists in moving in the right direction. It is made very clear in the parable of the two sons (Matthew 21:28) who were commanded by their father to go to work at his vineyard. The one said, 'I am going', but did not go. The other said, 'I am not going', and then felt ashamed and went to work. This was real repentance, and we should never lure ourselves into imagining that to lament one's past is an act of repentance. It is part of it of course, but repentance remains unreal and barren as long as it has not led us to doing the will of the father. We have a tendency to think that it should result in fine emotions and we are quite often satisfied with emotions instead of real, deep changes.

Anthony Bloom, *Living Prayer*, Darton, Longman and Todd, 1966, page 65

The soul in its nature loves God and longs to be at one with Him in the noble love of a daughter for a noble father; but coming to human birth and lured by the courtships of this sphere, she takes up with another love, a mortal, leaves her father and falls. But one day coming to hate her shame, she puts away the evil of earth, once more seeks her father, and finds her peace...

The soul takes another life as it approaches God; thus restored it feels that the dispenser of true life is There to see, that now we have nothing to look for but, far otherwise, that we must put aside all else and rest in This alone, This become...

Thus we have all the vision that may be of Him and of ourselves; but it is of a self wrought to splendour, brimmed with the Intellectual light, become that very light, pure, buoyant, unburdened, raised to Godhood or, better, knowing its Godhood, all aflame.

Plotinus, *The Enneads*, translated by Stephen MacKenna, Faber and Faber, 1956, page 623

Above all things beware of taking this desire of repentance to be the effect of thy own natural sense and reason, for in so doing thou losest the key of all the heavenly treasure that is in thee, thou shuttest the door against God, turnest away from Him, and thy repentance (if thou hast any) will be only a vain, unprofitable work of thy own hands, that will do thee no more good than a well that is without water... When, therefore, the first spark of a desire after God arises in thy soul, cherish it with all thy care, give all thy heart into it, it is nothing less than a touch of the divine loadstone that is to draw thee out of the vanity of time into the riches of eternity. Get up, therefore, and follow it as gladly as the Wise Men of the East followed the star from Heaven that appeared to them. It will do for thee as the star did for them: it will lead thee to the birth of Jesus, not in a stable at Bethlehem in Judea, but to the birth of Jesus in the dark centre of thy own fallen soul.

William Law, *Selected Mystical Writings of William Law*, edited by Stephen Hobhouse, Rockliff, 1948, pages 91 and 103

We have shown that every soul, though it may be burdened with sins, caught in the net of evil habits, taken captive by the allurements of sinful pleasures; though it be as a captive in exile, confined in the body as in a prison, submerged and fixed fast in mud and clay, closely bound to its members, weighed down by cares, absorbed in business, saddened by fears, afflicted by sorrows, led astray by errors, anxious because of forebodings, uneasy through suspicions, and, lastly, an alien on the earth, in which it finds so many enemies, and, according to the saying of a prophet, defiled with the dead and counted with them that go down into hell (Baruch 3:11); although a soul, I say, be thus under condemnation and thus despairing, yet, as I have shown, it is able to find in itself, not only reason for breathing freely in the hope of mercy and forgiveness, but also for daring to aspire to the heavenly nuptials of the Word; nor does it fear to enter into alliance with God, and to bear the sweet yoke of love with Him who is the King of Angels. For why should it not venture to come confidently into the presence of Him by whose image and likeness it sees and knows that it is still honoured and ennobled? Why should even a Majesty so great be a cause of distrust to a being to whom its own origin gives a ground for confidence? All that it has to do is to preserve with care the original purity of its nature by a pure and honourable life; or, rather, to study to adorn and embellish by good and virtuous thoughts and actions, as by rich colours, that illustrious image which has been impressed upon the depths of its nature at its creation.

St. Bernard, *Life and Works of Saint Bernard*, volume IV, edited by Dom John Mabillon, translated and edited by Samuel J. Eales, John Hodges, 1896, page 507

RESURRECTION

'Resurrection'—rising from the dead, especially the resurrection of Christ; rising again of men at the last day; revival from disuse or inactivity.

At one time I was curious to know what St Paul meant by the expression—'that I may know him and the power of his resurrection'. I was first helped by the account of the two disciples who came across the risen Christ on the road to Emmaus. After he had disappeared from their sight, they said to each other, 'Did not our hearts burn within us while he talked to us on the road, while he opened to us the scriptures?' I think at that point they experienced something of the power of the resurrection.

I have had at least two experiences in which something similar happened to me. The first happened whilst listening to Archbishop Anthony Bloom. At the time he was conducting a teaching week in London University. I was immediately struck by his bright shining eyes, but more so by his words which 'burned within me' as he expounded the scriptures. I was convinced I was in the presence of someone living in the power of the resurrection. The second happened whilst listening to Jean Vanier leading a university mission in Oxford, with Sheila Cassidy. Not only did I feel to be in the presence of the most Christ-like person I have ever encountered but again became aware of this inner sensation. Having had these two brief experiences of living in the power of the resurrection, I find it a little easier to believe Christ did indeed rise from the dead.

Thy dead shall live, their bodies shall rise. O dwellers in the dust, awake and sing for joy!
Isaiah 26:19

And many of those who sleep in the dust of the earth shall awake, some to everlasting life, and some to shame and everlasting contempt.
Daniel 12:2

That I may know him and the power of his resurrection, and may share his sufferings, becoming like him in his death, that if possible I may attain the resurrection from the dead.
Philippians 3:10–11

If then you have been raised with Christ, seek the things that are above, where Christ is, seated at the right hand of God. Set your minds on things that are above, not on things that are on earth.
Colossians 3:1–2

Christian theology has never suggested that the 'fact' of Christ's resurrection could be known apart from faith.

Alan Richardson, *History Sacred and Profane*, SCM Press, 1964, page 206

It has never at any time been possible to fit the resurrection of Jesus into any world view except a world view of which it is the basis.

Lesslie Newbigin, *Honest Religion for Secular Man*, SCM Press, 1966, page 53

You believe in the resurrection, not because it is reported by the apostles but because the resurrected One himself encounters you in a living way as he who unites you with God, as the living Mediator. Now you yourself know it: he lives, he, the Reconciler and Redeemer.

Emil Brunner, *I Believe in the Living God*, translated and edited by John Holden, Lutterworth Press, 1961, page 93

The New Testament promises us that our physical body shall be transmuted into a spiritualized body, like the body of the risen Christ, released from the domination of the material, the spatial and the temporal. Yet in some mysterious way it will be recognizable perhaps with its most significant features, as the nail-marks and the spear-wound on our Lord's resurrection body. We may think of the body as a life-long comrade, who will survive death and in some spiritualized form be our comrade still.

George Appleton, *Journey for a Soul*, William Collins Sons and Co., 1976, page 16

Jesus revealed God to them and became so utterly the central form that they were clinging to Him. But that could not go on for ever. They had to make a painful transition to a new relationship in which they clung to Him as something within their own lives, and not just as a nostalgic kind of thing. The great story that marks this transition is that of Jesus saying to Mary Magdalen on the Resurrection Day: 'Do not cling to Me, as in the past. It really is Me, but you and my other followers are passing on to a new relationship of a very tremendous kind.'

Michael Ramsey, in Gerald Priestland, *Priestland's Progress*, BBC Worldwide, 1982, page 111

Christ has conquered death, not only by suppressing its evil effects, but by reversing its sting. By virtue of Christ's rising again, nothing any longer kills inevitably but everything is capable of becoming the blessed touch of the divine hands, the blessed influence of the will of God upon our lives. However marred by our faults, or however desperate in its circumstances, our position may be, we can, by a total re-ordering, completely correct the world that surrounds us, and resume our lives in a favourable sense. 'To those who love God all things are turned to God.' That is the fact which dominates all explanation and all discussion.

Pierre Teilhard de Chardin, *Le Milieu Divin*, William Collins Sons and Co., 1960, page 61

At the resurrection Jesus becomes the 'head' of the cosmic whole, and the whole creation becomes his Body. This Body of creation redeemed from the forces of sin and division is what constitutes the Church. 'He has put all things under his feet', says St Paul (1 Corinthians 15:27), 'and made him the head over all things for the Church, which is his body, the fullness of him who fills all in all.'

The Church is the fullness, the consummation of all things, the term of the whole evolutionary process. The Divine has taken possession of nature and filled men with his presence. In other words nature has been wholly penetrated with consciousness, and man and nature have become one with the eternal Spirit.

What was accomplished in Jesus through his sacrificial death and his rebirth to eternal life is what is destined to happen in all men and in all creation.

Each of us is called to pass beyond sin and suffering into the new life of the resurrection.

Bede Griffiths OSB, in *The Universal Christ*, edited by Peter Spink, Darton, Longman and Todd, 1990, page 42

The resurrection of Jesus had a far deeper significance than what happened to the flesh. It meant the resurrection of spirit beyond the needs of any carnal body. Therefore, it was not necessary for the disciples to see the resurrected Jesus, nor for the tomb-keepers to observe him. The Roman soldiers guarded the sepulcher least his body should be stolen away, but they were not able to testify to his resurrection either. Much less were casual passers-by.

The first person to discover the resurrection of Jesus that morning was Mary Magdalene whose soul had once been possessed with seven devils. The resurrection of Jesus was a resurrection for such miserable persons as she, for ruined souls. To those who cannot grasp this meaning, resurrection remains an insoluble enigma, an empty falsehood, a prick of doubt. It is an ever-lasting secret. Not a few of us seem inclined to deny this miracle. If we are reluctant to accept sinners as friends, it means that we belong to the sceptics who deny the fact of resurrection. Let us, therefore, remember that the first witness who saw the figure of Jesus the morning of his resurrection had been a prostitute.

Toyohiko Kagawa, *Meditations*, number 35, translated by Jiro Takenaka, Harper and Brothers, 1950

The joy of the Resurrection is something which we, too, must learn to experience, but we can experience it only if we first learn the tragedy of the Cross. To rise again we must die. Die to our hampering selfishness, die to our fears, die to everything which makes the world so narrow, so cold, so poor, so cruel. Die so that our souls may live, may rejoice, may discover the spring of life. If we do this then the Resurrection of Christ will have come down to us also. But without the death on the Cross there is no Resurrection, the Resurrection which is joy, the joy of life recovered, the joy of the life that no-one can take away from us anymore! The joy of a life which is superabundant, which like a stream runs down the hills, carrying with it heaven itself reflected in its sparkling waters. The Resurrection of Christ is reality in history as his death on the Cross was real, and it is because it belongs to history that we believe in it. It is not only with our hearts but with the totality of our experience that we know the risen Christ. We can know him day after day as the Apostles knew him. Not the Christ of the flesh, not Christ as he was seen in bewilderment by people who surrounded him in the days of his earthly life, but the ever-living Christ. The Christ of the spirit of whom St Paul speaks, the risen Christ who belongs to time and eternity because he died once upon the Cross but lives for ever.

Anthony Bloom, *Meditations on a Theme*, A.R. Mowbray and Co., 1972, page 119

If my mind can't quite take certain things—such as the physical Resurrection—does it matter, so long as it doesn't get in the way of belief in Christ as master and saviour and helper, to be sought and served? I know it mattered to the early church, and was perhaps the only way in which they could be convinced—but should one try to force or persuade one's mind to it, if one feels one doesn't need it? You say 'we cannot be expected to do more than yield to God the minds which we actually possess,' so I suppose God takes them and does what he can with them. And of course in time they might develop new powers of faith; as you say, it depends on what happens to make connections. He keeps showing us new things, new lights on the past, new roads for the future, and one hopes for new powers. But what moors, fens, crags and torrents lie all about...

It seems almost better... that God should have sent his Incarnation on earth in form fully human, with human birth and death. I would almost *rather* think He was born like us and died like us, and that it was His spirit only that lived after death, taking the form His friends would recognise. But of course this is no argument at all, and I don't try to make up my mind about it. I don't feel either way that it could make any difference to what I value more and more—the relationship that one tries to keep. But I will keep my mind open about it, and try to think it out. I felt, at the Easter mass, that here was Christ risen and with us, and I didn't care how.

Rose Macaulay, *Letters to a Friend*, edited by Constance Babington Smith, William Collins Sons and Co., 1961, pages 74 and 107

In the earliest days of Christianity an 'apostle' was first and foremost a man who claimed to be an eye-witness of the Resurrection. Only a few days after the Crucifixion when two candidates were nominated for the vacancy created by the treachery of Judas, their qualification was that they had known Jesus personally both before and after His death and could offer first-hand evidence of the Resurrection in addressing the outer world (Acts 1:22)...

The Resurrection is the central theme in every Christian sermon reported in the Acts. The Resurrection, and its consequences, were the 'gospel' or good news which the Christians brought: what we call the 'gospels,' the narratives of Our Lord's life and death, were composed later for the benefit of those who had already accepted the *gospel*. They were in no sense the basis of Christianity: they were written for those already converted. The miracle of the Resurrection, and the theology of that miracle, comes first: the biography comes later as a comment on it...

When modern writers talk of the Resurrection they usually mean one particular moment—the discovery of the Empty Tomb and the appearance of Jesus a few yards away from it. The story of that moment is what Christian apologists now chiefly try to support and sceptics chiefly try to impugn. But this almost exclusive concentration on the first five minutes or so of the Resurrection would have astonished the earliest Christian teachers. In claiming to have seen the Resurrection they were not necessarily claiming to have seen *that*. Some of them had, some of them had not. It had no more importance than any of the other appearances of the risen Jesus—apart from the poetic and dramatic importance which the beginning of things must always have. What they were claiming was that they had all, at one time or another, met Jesus during the six or seven weeks that followed His death. Sometimes they seem to have been alone when they did so, but on one occasion twelve of them saw Him together, and on another occasion about five hundred of them. St. Paul says that the majority of the five hundred were still alive when he wrote the *First Letter to the Corinthians*, i.e. in about AD 55.

C.S. Lewis, Miracles, William Collins Sons and Co., 1974, page 147

In writing in this way about Jesus we must not distort the fact that he was a man, born of human parents. He undoubtedly made a tremendous impact on many people, some of whom found relief from physical illness as a result of their trust in him. In their desire to emphasise his supreme value to them, some of his followers in later years described his life and activities in miraculous terms. Whether we accept this explanation is not important; what matters is the greatness of his personality and his spiritual insight. Because his teaching and way of life ran counter to the convictions and practices of the religious leaders of his time, they, with the consent of the populace, engineered his trial and execution. Men do not like goodness if it challenges their moral failure, or loyalty to truth that calls for a revolutionary change of mind. They killed Jesus because they were afraid of him.

As in his life, so in his approach to death Jesus never faltered in his trust in love, and forgave those who rejected him. By this creative attitude Jesus radically changed a most heinous act of human wickedness into an event that has released love and forgiveness into a dark world. For ever after people know that such love can overcome evil, and in this knowledge have found freedom to live.

Many Friends are sceptical about the New Testament accounts of the physical resurrection of Jesus, although for some this is a crucial element in their faith. Most would agree that the essential meaning behind the story of the first Easter is that death could not destroy all that was of real value in the earthly life of Jesus. The love experienced by his disciples could not be taken from them by his death, because they recognised that it was of an infinite and eternal quality. In fact, it was only after his death that they came to understand and to appreciate fully the deep meaning of his life and to be set free by it.

George H. Gorman, Introducing Quakers, Friends Home Service Committee, 1981, page 19

REVELATION

'Revelation'—disclosing of knowledge, to man by divine or
supernatural agency; knowledge so disclosed.

I like Blaise Pascal's approach to revelation, because it is so positive. In his *Pensées* he wrote that instead of complaining that God had hidden himself, you will give him thanks for having revealed so much of himself. Think, for a moment, of the revelation of God in scripture, culminating in the Gospels in the person of Jesus Christ. Think also of the revelation of the divine in creation. The Psalmist was well aware of this source of revelation when he wrote the heavens are telling the glory of God; and the firmament proclaims his handiwork. A modern writer, Kenneth Leech reminds us in his book *True Prayer* that the saint is essentially someone who communicates and radiates the character of God, his love, his joy, his peace. Think, for a moment, of all those people whose lives have revealed to us something of the divine. Think also of the revelation of God which comes to us in worship, in prayer, and in the joys and tribulations of life. Think too, of the revelation of God which comes to us in unexpected moments and places. For instance, it was while St Ignatius sat by a stream and watched the running water, that the mystery of the nature of God was suddenly revealed to him.

Is there anything we can do to experience this revelation? I think we need to remember revelation lies essentially in God's hands, but we can at least put ourselves in a position where this revelation is likely to happen.

The heavens are telling the glory of God; and the firmament proclaims his handiwork. Day to day pours forth speech, and night to night declares knowledge. There is no speech, nor are there words; their voice is not heard; yet their voice goes out through all the earth, and their words to the end of the world.

Psalm 19:1–4

And the glory of the Lord shall be revealed, and all flesh shall see it together, for the mouth of the Lord has spoken.

Isaiah 40:5

I have raised you up for the very purpose of showing my power in you.

Romans 9:17

But when he who had set me apart before I was born, and had called me through his grace, was pleased to reveal his Son in me.

Galatians 1:15–16

If you only say, you have a Revelation from God; I must have a Revelation from God too, before I can believe you.

Benjamin Whichcote, *Moral and Religious Aphorisms*, number 443, Elkin Mathews and Marrot, 1930, page 51

The one obvious, unmistakable manifestation of the Deity is the law of good and evil disclosed to men by revelation.

Leo Tolstoy, *Anna Karenin*, translated by Rosemary Edmonds, Penguin Books, 1983, page 851

Instead of complaining that God had hidden Himself, you will give Him thanks for having revealed so much of Himself.

Blaise Pascal, *Pensées*, translated by W.F. Trotter, Random House, 1941, page 98

For each truth revealed by grace, and received with inward delight and joy, is a secret murmur of God in the ear of a pure soul.

Walter Hilton, *The Ladder of Perfection*, translated by Leo Sherley-Price, Penguin Books, 1957, page 252

The first and most important fact that we can know about God is ever this: *we* know nothing of Him, except what He Himself has revealed to us.

Emil Brunner, *Our Faith*, translated by John W. Rilling, Charles Scribner's Sons, 1936, page 11

That which we really know about God, is not what we have been clever enough to find out, but what the Divine Charity has secretly revealed.

Evelyn Underhill, *The School of Charity*, Longmans, Green and Co., 1956, page 12

My own mind is the direct revelation which I have from God and far least liable to mistake in telling his will of any revelation.

Ralph Waldo Emerson, *The Heart of Emerson's Journals*, edited by Bliss Perry, Constable and Co., 1927, page 53

The knowledge of man is as the waters, some descending from above, and some springing from beneath: the one informed by the light of nature, the other inspired by divine revelation.

Francis Bacon, *The Advancement of Learning*, Cassell and Company, 1905, page 81

God is revealed as the God of love, and henceforth every morally good act, that is, every act formed by charity, is a revelation of God. Every word of truth and love, every hand extended in kindness, echoes the inner life of the Trinity.

Gabriel Moran, FSC, *Theology of Revelation*, Burns and Oates, 1967, page 127

To see a World in a Grain of Sand
And a Heaven in a Wild Flower,
Hold Infinity in the palm of your hand
And Eternity in an hour.

William Blake, 'Auguries of Innocence,' in *The Complete Writings of William Blake*, edited by Geoffrey Keynes, Oxford University Press, 1974, page 431

In nature we find God; we do not only infer from Nature what God must be like, but when we see Nature truly, we see God self-manifested in and through it. Yet the self-revelation so given is incomplete and inadequate. Personality can only reveal itself in persons. Consequently it is specially in Human Nature—in men and women—that we see God.

William Temple, *Nature, Man and God*, Macmillan and Co., 1934, page 266

Love, whether in its most exalted form as the love between husband and wife, or in the less ardent experience of affection and sympathy, unlocks the doors of our prison-house and reveals to us something of the breadth and length and depth and height of the spiritual world which surrounds us. In various degrees, all cordial human intercourse is a liberation and an enhancement of our personality; it is a channel of revelation.

W.R. Inge, *Personal Religion and the Life of Devotion*, Longmans, Green and Co., 1924, page 16

For two reasons the event in which the fullness of revelation is given must be the life of a Person: the first is that the revelation is to persons who can fully understand only what is personal; the second is that the revelation is of a personal Being, who accordingly cannot be adequately revealed in anything other than personality. Moreover, if the Person who is Himself the revelation is to be truly adequate to that function, He must be one in essence with the Being whom He reveals.

William Temple, *Nature, Man and God*, Macmillan and Co., 1934, page 319

In order that the revelation may effectively reveal or disclose the Divine Purpose there must be men attuned to it so as to discern and in part to understand it. The Apostles were necessary to the effectual disclosure of the Divine Nature which the Incarnation was designed to offer. If none had 'beheld His glory' it would still have been there; the Life and the Death and the Resurrection are in themselves the manifestation of God in the flesh. But though the manifestation would have occurred, it would have been sterile unless some could apprehend it. So it had been with the prophets. If none had been able to interpret the mighty acts of God as what they were, they would have been wrought partly in vain. The essential condition of effectual revelation is the coincidence of a divinely controlled event and minds divinely illumined to read it aright.

William Temple, in *Revelation*, edited by John Baillie and Hugh Martin, Faber and Faber, 1937, page 107

In the ultimate reality there is revealed not merely an identity but a communion. The Christian revelation is that the Godhead itself, the ultimate reality, is a commitment of persons, a communion of powers in love. This gives a further dimension to our understanding of reality.

There cannot be love without two. In the Christian concept the Godhead itself is love, a communion of love. There is a distinction within the Godhead itself, a distinction beyond our comprehension which we endeavour to express theologically in terms of persons and relations. These are human terms pointing to the reality. The reality is that God is love, that there is something which corresponds to personal communion in love in the Godhead and we are called to share in that communion of love.

In the mystical Body of Christ which embraces all redeemed humanity, we do not disappear in the Godhead but we discover a personal relationship of love. Each person is fulfilled and is open to the other person; it is an intercommunion of love in which each embraces the other and all are embraced in God.

Bede Griffiths OSB, in *The Universal Christ*, edited by Peter Spink, Darton, Longman and Todd, 1990, page 23

In former times God used various ways to enlighten us, but now he has spoken once for all by his Son. All other modes of communication are abolished. Formerly God could not make himself understood; there was no one of sufficient transparency to receive him. Now there is. Jesus is the definitive revelation of God; God has nothing more to reveal.

You crave to know, be reassured, have a guarantee? Jesus will satisfy it. You look within at your own subjective feelings, but what do they tell you? They can give no certitude. You have all the guarantee you need in Jesus.

See what he has shown us of the Father's steadfast love, of his will to give us everything. See how he reveals the Father as total forgiveness. What need have you to further reassurance? You seek to know how to please God in all you do—then look to Jesus.

There is scarcely anyone who does not depart from the way of pure faith and seek some subjective revelation or assurance. There is no greater security, consolation or happiness than to lean absolutely on Jesus the Man.

Ruth Burrows, in *The Watchful Heart*, edited by Elizabeth Ruth Obbard, Darton, Longman and Todd, 1988, page 10

By divine revelation is meant the entrance of truth into the depth of living. As long as the truth does not hold sway over the whole of life, cognition and life are two separate entities, God and man are living apart from each other. When the truth penetrates into the whole warp and woof of life, then for the first time God becomes man's motive power and the guiding spirit of all his ways.

Therefore, he who seeks for the divine revelation will not find God through the theory of cognition. First of all let him endeavour to create values. Let him liberate those who are oppressed, feed those who are in want, give sight to the blind, find a way to enrich the poor. Then will he be able to see divine revelations every day.

This is the truth. The emancipators see God daily. God whispers to them. They stand in His presence. While the religionists of the study are seeking for divine revelation through cognition the God of life reveals Himself in the midst of life itself. The divine revelation is not closed. False scholars and false religious teachers are setting it at naught.

Toyohiko Kagawa, in William Axling, *Kagawa*, SCM Press, 1946, page 144

In the infant period of the race, both among the Hebrews and the Gentile peoples, God has used, like a wise Teacher, the symbol and picture-book method. He has disciplined them with external laws and with ceremonies which would move their child-minded imaginations; but all this method was used only because they were not ripe and ready for the true and higher form of goodness. 'They used the face of Moses until they could come to the full Light of the truth and righteousness of God, for which all the time their spirits really hungered and thirsted.' The supreme instance of the divine pictorial method was the sending of Christ to reveal God visibly. Before seeing God in Christ men falsely thought of Him as hostile, stern, and wrathful; now they may see Him in this unveiling of Himself as He actually is, eternally loving, patiently forgiving, and seeking only to draw the world into His love and peace: 'When the Abba-crying spirit of Christ awakens in our hearts we commune with God in peace and love.' But no one must content himself with Christ after the flesh, Christ historically known. That is to make an idol of Him. We can be saved through Him only when by His help we discover the essential nature of God and when He moves us to go on living in the spirit and power as Christ Himself lived. His death as an outward, historical fact does not save us; it is the supreme expression of His limitless love and the complete dedication of His spirit in self-giving, and it is effective for our salvation only when it draws us into a similar way of living, unites us in spirit with Him and makes us in reality partakers of His blood spiritually apprehended. Christ is our Mediator in that He reveals the love of God towards us and moves our will to appreciate it.

Every step of human progress and of spiritual advance is marked by a passage from the dominion of the external to the sway and power of inward experience. God is training us for a time when images, figures, and picture-book methods will be no longer needed, but all men will live by the inward Word and have the witness—'the Abba-crying voice'—in their own hearts.

Rufus M. Jones, *Spiritual Reformers in the 16th and 17th Centuries,* Macmillan and Co., 1914, page 37

SAINTS

'Saints'—the holy people of God.

In the long vacation the Oxford Summer School of Religious Studies takes place in University College. One of the lecturers is Sister Benedicta Ward, SLG. Last year I had the privilege of attending her series of lectures on 'Solitude and Service in the Early Church'. In *A New Dictionary of Christian Theology* she wrote that the holiness of the saints is the restored image of God in them. I wonder if I might use an analogy here to bring out the meaning of her words. I read somewhere of an artist who was asked to restore an icon to its original beauty. At first he gave it a good clean and a layer of dust and candle-smoke was removed. He then discovered someone had superimposed another icon over the original, so he carefully and painstakingly removed it. In turn he discovered another superimposition and slowly and patiently removed that one also. This process was repeated several times. Eventually be got back to the original and found it to be exquisitely beautiful and awe-inspiring. Once more the icon could be used to foster a spirit of devotion and worship.

The holiness of the saints depends on getting back to the restored image of God in them. This mainly comes through prayer and contemplation balanced by a costly spirit of service. As Kenneth Leech says in his book *True Prayer*, to pray is to open oneself to the possibility of sainthood, to the possibility of becoming set on fire by the Spirit.

Precious in the sight of the Lord is the death of his saints.

Psalm 116:15

But the saints of the Most High shall receive the kingdom, and possess the kingdom for ever, for ever and ever.

Daniel 7:18

... called to be saints.

Romans 1:7

I do not cease to give thanks for you, remembering you in my prayers, that the God of our Lord Jesus Christ, the Father of glory, may give you a spirit of wisdom and of revelation in the knowledge of him, having the eyes of your hearts enlightened, that you may know what is the hope to which he has called you, what are the riches of his glorious inheritance in the saints, and what is the immeasurable greatness of his power in us who believe, according to the working of his great might.

Ephesians 1:16–19

Grace is indeed needed to turn a man into a saint; and he who doubts it does not know what a saint or a man is.

Blaise Pascal, *Pensées*, translated by W.F. Trotter, Random House Inc., 1941, page 165

God creates out of *nothing*, wonderful, you say: yes, to be sure, but he does what is still more wonderful: he makes saints out of sinners.

Søren Kierkegaard, *The Journals of Søren Kierkegaard*, edited and translated by Alexander Dru, Oxford University Press, 1938, page 59

They may have had their trials too—failing health, declining years, the ingratitude of men—but they have endured as seeing Him who is invisible.

Benjamin Jowett, *College Sermons*, edited by W.H. Fremantle, John Murray, 1895, page 317

The power of the Soul for good is in proportion to the strength of its passions. Sanctity is not the negation of passion but its order... Hence great Saints have often been great sinners.

Coventry Patmore, 'Aurea Dicta', in *The Rod, the Root and the Flower*, Grey Walls Press, 1950, page 51

They were men of intense religious faith, of marked mystical type, characterized by interior depth of experience, but at the same time they were men of scholarship, breadth and balance.

Rufus M. Jones, *Spiritual Reformers in the 16th and 17th Centuries*, Macmillan and Co., 1914, page 336

This man is known by five signs. First, he never complains. Next, he never makes excuses: when accused, he leaves the facts to vindicate him. Thirdly, there is nothing he wants in earth or heaven but what God wills himself. Fourthly, he is not moved in time. Fifthly, he is never rejoiced: he is joy itself.

Meister Eckhart, in Franz Pfeiffer, *Meister Eckhart*, volume I, translated by C. de B. Evans, John M. Watkins, 1956, page 327

I have met in my life two persons, one a man, the other a woman, who convinced me that they were persons of sanctity. Utterly different in character, upbringing and interests as they were, their effect on me was the same. In their presence I felt myself to be ten times as nice, ten times as intelligent, ten times as good-looking as I really am.

W.H. Auden, *A Certain World*, Faber and Faber, 1971, page 331

A saint is not so much a man who realizes that he possesses virtues and sanctity as one who is overwhelmed by the sanctity of God. God is holiness. And therefore things are holy in proportion as they share what He is. All creatures are holy insofar as they share in His being, but men are called to be holy, in a far superior way—by somehow sharing His transcendence and rising above the level of everything that is not God.

Thomas Merton, *The Sign of Jonas*, Sheldon Press, 1976, page 262

The saints are men and women of prayer to whom we owe our deepest revelations of the Supernatural—those who give us real news about God—are never untrained amateurs or prodigies. Such men and women as Paul, Augustine, Catherine, Julian, Ruysbroeck, are genuine artists of eternal life. They have accepted and not scorned the teachings of tradition: and humbly trained and disciplined their God-given genius for ultimates.

Evelyn Underhill, *Man and the Supernatural*, Methuen and Co., 1927, page 211

There is after all something in Christian saintliness which eludes analysis. For saintliness is the partial expression, the reflection in the external life, of the hidden man of the heart, who is not fully known even by the saint himself; and it is always imperfect, because it is always going on to perfection. I will not have my portrait painted, said a holy man; for which man do you want to paint? One of them is not worth painting, and the other is not finished yet.

W.R. Inge, *Types of Christian Saintliness*, Longmans, Green and Co., 1915, page 92

What is a Saint? A particular individual completely redeemed from self-occupation; who, because of this, is able to embody and radiate a measure of Eternal Life. His whole life, personal, social, intellectual, mystical, is lived in supernatural regard. What is he for? To help, save, and enlighten by his loving actions and contemplations; to oppose in one way or another, by suffering, prayer and work upon heroic levels of love and self-oblation, the mysterious downward drag within the world, which we call sin.

Evelyn Underhill, *Man and the Supernatural*, Methuen and Co., 1927, page 237

Saints are people who have had an encounter with God, however they name him, and have had their lives changed as a consequence. This can be seen significantly in the call of the first disciples, their training by Jesus and their sending out to serve the world in witness and love.

None of them were men of wisdom by human standards, none of them from the noblest families or in positions of power. But because of their devotion and faithfulness to our Lord they made their contribution to God's purpose of love. This is repeated in every generation by faithful followers who live for Jesus, if necessary die for him and whatever be the manner of their death die in him.

George Appleton, *Journey for a Soul,* William Collins Sons and Co., 1976, page 190

Praise be unto God, Who hath consumed the hearts of His saints in the fire of His love and hath taken captive their desires and their spirits by the longing to meet with Him and to look upon Him and hath fixed their sight and their insight upon the vision of the Beauty of His Presence, until by the inbreathing of the spirit of Union, they have become rapt beyond themselves and their hearts have become distraught by the contemplation of the splendours of the Divine Glory, so that they see naught but Him in this world or the world to come, and they remember none in heaven or earth save Him alone... Their grief is only in Him and their longing is only for that which is to be found in his Presence, they are aroused only for Him, and their going to and fro is round about Him alone.

For from Him is all that they hear and it is to Him that they give heed, since He hath closed their eyes to all but Himself and hath made them deaf to all words save His. These are they whom God hath called to be His saints, having claimed them for Himself from among His chosen and His elect.

Al-Ghazali, Margaret Smith, *Al-Ghazali, The Mystic,* Luzac and Co., 1944, page 196

Ours is an age of violence and disbelief. But in spite of that, or perhaps because of it, the earth's interest in virtuous accomplishment is stronger now than it has been at any time since the Age of Reason began ousting religion from its seat of authority. God may be dead insofar as theological concepts no longer direct political and economic affairs. But His heroes still interest the race. They are quoted by columnists, cited by historians, their names taken not always in vain by novelists, biographers, and agnostic tractarians. Thomas More was not long ago the protagonist of a noble play, a notable film as was Becket twice in a decade. Joan of Arc never fails the playwright. Not long ago in the sober *New York Times* an editorial recommended that in our dealings with nature we try, for the sake of conservation, to become more like Francis of Assisi who considered all living creatures his brothers.

In times of crisis we need saints and we often breed them, too. They appeared by hundreds in the first centuries of Christianity when Europe was struggling out of nearly universal darkness into what then passed for the light of civilization. They flourished during the Reformation on both sides of the conflict. Wherever and whenever an evil has existed, from slave-trading to the miseries of famine and war, saints have sprung up to mitigate those evils. They may well be rising among us now, preparing to lead us out of the onrushing night which so threateningly descends. As a matter of fact, I think I number two or three among my acquaintance. One of them spends himself among impoverished Negroes of the South, one wears himself out in Northern slums, the third (completely without personal possessions) by some sleight of hand and heart feeds and lodges hundreds of Bowery derelicts each week.

Phyllis McGinley, *Saint-Watching,* William Collins Sons and Co., 1970, pages 15 and 28

SALVATION

'Salvation'—the saving of the soul; deliverance from sin and its consequences and admission to heaven brought about by Christ; acquisition of wholeness.

At theological college we had to specialize in one particular Epistle as part of our training. For several weeks I carefully studied the text of 1 Peter and examined the contents in some depth. One of my favourite verses comes from the second chapter and reads as follows:

'For you were straying like sheep, but have now returned to the Shepherd and Guardian of your souls.' I liked this verse because it spoke to my condition. In adolescence I had been straying like a sheep, trying to find satisfaction here and there. In this I had not been particularly wicked, but lacked a guiding principle, and was searching to find a sense of purpose and meaning in life. I was vaguely looking to the law for a career. My father was a solicitor and there was a vacancy in the family firm. I read law at university, but discovered my heart was not in jurisprudence. Furthermore my motives for joining the family firm were found to be wanting. Whilst in this state and frame of mind, a friend invited me to go and listen to a sermon preached by the then Bishop of Coventry, Cuthbert Bardsley. I was greatly impressed by the dynamism and vitality of the bishop, and much to my surprise responded to his appeal to take a step of faith. This was my first real encounter with the person of Jesus Christ, who was to become the shepherd and guardian of my soul.

Deliver us, O God of our salvation, and gather and save us from among the nations, that we may give thanks to thy holy name, and glory in thy praise.

1 Chronicles 16:35

Surely his salvation is at hand for those who fear him, that glory may dwell in our land.

Psalm 85:9

Work out your own salvation with fear and trembling; for God is at work in you, both to will and to work for his good pleasure.

Philippians 2:12–13

For you were straying like sheep, but have now returned to the Shepherd and Guardian of your souls.

1 Peter 2:25

What is most contrary to salvation is not sin but habit.

Charles Péguy, *Basic Verities*, translated by Ann and Julian Green, Kegan Paul, Trench, Trubner and Co., 1943, page 181

The notion that the salvation of Jesus is a salvation from the consequences of our sins is a false mean, low notion ... Jesus did not die to save us from punishment; He was called Jesus because he should save his people from their sins.

George Macdonald, *Unspoken Sermons*, Third Series, Longmans, Green and Co., 1889, page 132

Christ died to save us, not from suffering, but from ourselves; not from injustice, far less from justice, but from being unjust. He died that we might live—but live as he lives, by dying as he died who died to himself that he might live unto God.

George Macdonald, *Unspoken Sermons*, Third Series, Longmans, Green and Co., 1889, page 96

There is but one salvation for all mankind, and that is the life of God in the soul. God has but one design or intent towards all mankind and that is to introduce or generate His own life, light, and Spirit in them, that all may be as so many images, temples and habitations of the Holy Trinity ... There is not one for the Jew, another for a Christian, and a third for the heathen. No; God is one, human nature is one, salvation is one, and the way to it is one; and that is, the desire of the soul turned to God.

William Law, *Selected Mystical Writings of William Law*, edited by Stephen Hobhouse, Rockliff, 1948, page 102

The true aim of the soul is not its own salvation; to make that the chief aim is to ensure its perdition ('Whosoever would save his soul shall lose it.'—St. Matthew 16:25); for it is to fix the soul on itself as centre. The true aim of the soul is to glorify God; in pursuing that aim it will attain to salvation unawares. No one who is convinced of his own salvation is as yet even safe, let alone 'saved.' Salvation is the state of him who has ceased to be interested whether he is saved or not, provided that what takes the place of that supreme self-interest is not a lower form of self-interest but the glory of God.

William Temple, *Nature, Nan and God*, Macmillan and Co., 1934, page 390

Consider yourself a refractory pupil for whom you are responsible as mentor and tutor. To sanctify sinful nature, by bringing it gradually under control of the angel within us, by the help of a holy God, is really the whole of Christian pedagogy and of religious morals. Our work—my work—consists in taming, subduing, evangelising and *angelising* the evil self and in restoring harmony with the good self. Salvation lies in abandoning the evil self in principle, and in taking refuge with the other, the divine self,—in accepting with courage and prayer the task of living with one's own demon, and making it into a less and less rebellious instrument of good. The Abel in us must labour for the salvation of the Cain. To undertake it is to be converted, and this conversion must be repeated day by day. Abel only redeems and touches Cain by exercising him constantly in good works. To do right is in one sense an act of violence: it is suffering, expiation, a cross, for it means the conquest and enslavement of self. In another sense it is the apprenticeship to heavenly things, sweet and secret joy, contentment and peace.

Henri Frédéric Amiel, *Amiel's Journal*, translated by Mrs Humphry Ward, Macmillan and Co., 1918, page 70

Who are you who go about to save them that are lost?
Are you saved yourself?
Do you not know that who would save his own life must lose it? Are you then one of the 'lost'?
Be sure, very sure, that each one of these can teach you as much as, probably more than, you can teach them.
Have you then sat humbly at their feet, and waited on their lips that they should be the first to speak—and been reverent before these children—whom you so little understand?
Have you dropped into the bottomless pit from between yourself and them all hallucination of superiority, all flatulence of knowledge, every shred of abhorrence and loathing?
Is it equal, is it free as the wind between you?
Could you be happy receiving favours from one of the most despised of these?
Could you be yourself one of the lost? Arise, then, and become a saviour.

Edward Carpenter, *Towards Democracy*, George Allen and Unwin, 1931, page 180

Ultimately the only way that I can be myself is to become identified with Him in whom is hidden the reason and fulfilment of my existence.
Therefore there is only one problem on which all my existence, my peace and my happiness depend: to discover myself in discovering God. If I find Him I will find myself and if I find my true self I will find Him.
That is something that no man can ever do alone.
Nor can all the men and all the created things in the universe help him in this work.
The only One who can teach me to find God is God, Himself, Alone.
God utters me like a word containing a partial thought of Himself...
But if I am true to the concept that God utters in me, if I am true to the thought of Him I was meant to embody, I shall be full of His actuality and find Him everywhere in myself, and find myself nowhere.
To be 'lost' is to be left to the arbitrariness and pretences of the contingent ego, the smoke-self that must inevitably vanish. To be 'saved' is to return to one's inviolate and eternal reality and to live in God.

Thomas Merton, *New Seeds of Contemplation*, Burns and Oates, 1962, page 28

The future (of mankind) will be dependant on a saving group, embodied in one nation or crossing through all nations. There is saving power in mankind, but there is also the hidden will to self-destruction. It depends on every one of us which side will prevail. There is no divine promise that humanity will survive this or next year. But it may depend on the saving power effective in you or me, whether it will survive. (It may depend on the amount of healing and liberating grace which works through any of us with respect to social justice, racial equality, and political wisdom.) Unless many of us say to ourselves: Through the saving power working in me, mankind may be saved or lost—it will be lost.
But in order to be the bearers of saving power, we must be saved ourselves; the wall separating us from eternal life must be broken through. And here is one thing which strength-

ens the wall and keeps us sick and enslaved. It is our estrangement and guilt which are the impediments which keep us from reaching eternal life here and now. The judgement against us which we confirm in our conscience is the sickness unto death, the despair of life, from which we must be halted in order to say *yes* to life. Healed life is new life, delivered from the bondage of the evil one. Here the last two petitions of our Lord's Prayer become one petition: forgive our trespasses, and deliver us from the evil one—this is one and the same thing. And if we call Jesus, the Christ, our saviour, then we mean that in him we see the power which heals us by accepting us and which liberates us by showing us in his being a new being—a being in which there is reconciliation with ourselves, with our world, and with the divine ground of our world and ourselves.

And now the last question: Who shall be saved, liberated, healed? The fourth gospel says: The world! The reunion with the eternal from which we come, from which we are separated, to which we shall return, is promised to everything that is.

We are saved not as individuals but in unity with all others and with the universe. Our own liberation does not leave the enslaved ones alone, our own healing is a part of the great healing of the world. Therefore, two other petitions of our Lord's Prayer also ask the same: Save us from the evil one, and thy Kingdom come! This Kingdom is his creation, liberated and healed. This is what we hope for when we look from time to eternity. Deliver us—heal us—that is the cry of everything that is; of each of us in unity with all mankind and in unity with the whole universe. The divine answer is: I shall return to me what is separated from me because it belongs to me. I am liberating you today as I did before and will do in the future. Today, when you hear these words, 'I am liberating you, I am healing you', do not resist!

Paul Tillich, *The Eternal Now*, SCM Press, 1963, page 101

SANCTIFICATION

'Sanctification'—holiness of life, saintliness, being made productive or conducive to holiness.

How do we grow in holiness? I found a clue in the opening chapters of St John's Gospel. When John the Baptist saw Jesus his reaction to him was: 'He must increase, but I must decrease.' I thought about this and wondered how to put this into practice. The outcome was the keeping of a journal (or spiritual diary) as an aid to prayer. A start was made at theological college, and for the last thirty years has been invaluable.

Before long I developed a simple form of meditation. I would choose a verse from the Bible and write it down in my journal. I then put into practice the opening words of the Collect for the Second Sunday in Advent, namely: 'Blessed Lord, who hast caused all Holy Scriptures to be written for our learning: Grant that we may in such wise hear them, read, mark, learn, and inwardly digest them.' I would spend an hour on the verse, inwardly digesting the contents, and would record the findings in my journal. This was my first step on the road to holiness, or sanctification. Later on I began collecting suitable material from other sources, such as *A Year of Grace*, and *From Darkness to Light*, both by Victor Gollancz. *The Perennial Philosophy*, by Aldous Huxley, also contained good resource material, as did my favourite book, *The Choice is Always Ours*. I am still trying to put John the Baptist's words into practice, and am continuing to learn what he meant by: 'He must increase, but I must decrease.' Sanctification is costly.

Consecrate yourselves therefore, and be holy; for I am the Lord your God. Keep my statutes, and do them; I am the Lord who sanctify you.

Leviticus 20:7–8

Sanctify yourselves; for tomorrow the Lord will do wonders among you.

Joshua 3:5

Sanctify them in the truth; thy word is truth. As thou didst send me into the world, so I have sent them into the world. And for their sake I consecrate myself, that they also may be consecrated in truth.

John 17:17–19

For this is the will of God, your sanctification.

1 Thessalonians 4:3

Sanctity is not getting noticeably nicer as you go along. It is a revolution. It is continuous conversion.

Hubert van Zeller, *Considerations*, Sheed and Ward, 1974, page 32

All that should be sought for in the exercise of prayer is conformity of our will with the Divine Will; assuredly in this consists the highest perfection.

St. Teresa of Avila, in *On Conformity with the Will of God*, translated by the Rev. James Jones, Catholic Truth Society, 1892, page 8

Even when the marks of it are patently obvious to other people, holiness is not something which the saint sees in himself. It is something he sees by. His prayer and charity give him the right perspectives.

Hubert van Zeller, *Considerations*, Sheed and Ward, 1974, page 31

There is nothing that so sanctifies the heart of man, that keeps us in such habitual love, prayer, and delight in God; nothing that so kills all the roots of evil in our nature, that so renews and perfects all our virtues, that fills us with so much love, goodness, and good wishes to every creature as this faith that God is always present in us with His light and Holy Spirit.

William Law, *Selected Mystical Writings of William Law*, edited by Stephen Hobhouse, Rockliff, 1948, page 32

Every heroic devotion to beauty, truth, goodness, every ungrudging sacrifice, is a crucifixion of self-interest, and thus lies in the direction of sanctity; and wherever we find sanctity we find the transforming act of God, of supernature, upon the creature, irrespective of that creature's dogmatic belief. All Saints, that 'glorious touching Company,' will doubtless include many whom the world classed among its irreligious men.

Evelyn Underhill, *Man and the Supernatural*, Methuen and Co., 1927, page 237

Everything in India has a sacred character. It meets one on every side—they are living in a sacred world. Here in the West we live in a profane world. For the last three centuries we have tried to reduce everything from the sphere of the sacred, the sphere of God.

Science tries to eliminate the sacred; the moon is not something sacred. It has become simply a chemical formation about which we seek to learn all we can. The same is true of the earth and the other planets. So we have eliminated two dimensions of reality, the psychological and the spiritual. We begin to think that the world is one-dimensional, that it is only material. We forget the sacred character of the whole creation. The incarnation of Christ is the great historical affirmation that all matter is sacred.

Bede Griffiths OSB, in *The Universal Christ*, edited by Peter Spink, Darton, Longman and Todd, 1990, page 58

For me to be a saint means to be myself. Therefore the problem of sanctity and salvation is in fact the problem of finding out who I am and of discovering my true self.

Trees and animals have no problem. God makes them what they are without consulting them, and they are perfectly satisfied.

With us it is different. God leaves us free to be whatever we like. We can be ourselves or not, as we please. We are at liberty to be real, or to be unreal. We may be true or false, the choice is ours. We may wear now one mask and now another, and never, if we so desire, appear with our own true face...

We are free beings and sons of God... We are called to share with God the work of *creating*

225

the truth of our identity. We can evade this responsibility by playing with masks, and this pleases us because it can appear at times to be a free and *creative way of living*. It is quite easy, it seems to please everyone. But in the long run the cost and the sorrow come very high. To work out our own identity in God... demands close attention to reality at every moment. Unless I desire this identity and work to find it with Him and in Him, the work will never be done.

Thomas Merton, *New Seeds of Contemplation*, Burns and Oates, 1962, page 25

All gardeners know the importance of good root development before we force the leaves and flowers. So our life in God should be deeply rooted and grounded before we presume to expect to produce flowers or fruits; otherwise we risk shooting up into one of those lanky plants which never do without a stick. We are constantly beset by the notion that we ought to perceive ourselves springing up quickly, like the seed on stony ground showing striking signs of spiritual growth. But perhaps we are only required to go on quietly, making root, growing nice and bushy; docile to the great slow rhythm of life. When we see no startling marks of our own religious progress or our usefulness to God, it is well to remember the baby in the stable and the little boy in the streets of Nazareth. The very life was there present, which was to change the whole history of the human race; the rescuing action of God. At that stage there was not much to show for it yet there is perfect continuity between the stable and the Easter garden, and the thread that unites them is the hidden Will of God. The childish prayer of Nazareth was the right preparation for the awful prayer of the Cross. So it is that the life of the Spirit is to unfold gently and steadily within us till at the last the full stature for which God designed us is attained.

Evelyn Underhill, *The School of Charity*, Longmans, Green and Co., 1956, page 48

Lastly: although there was no definite religious sentiment mingled with it, there was a continual perception of Sanctity in the whole of nature, from the slightest thing to the vastest—an instinctive awe, mixed with delight; an indefinable thrill, such as we sometimes imagine to indicate the presence of a disembodied spirit. I could only feel this perfectly when I was alone and then it would often make me shiver from head to foot with the joy and fear of it, when after being some time away from hills, I first got to the shore of a mountain river, where the brown water circled among the pebbles, or when I first saw the swell of distant land against the sunset, or the first low broken wall, covered with mountain moss. I cannot in the least *describe* the feeling; but I do not think this is my fault, nor that of the English language, for I am afraid, no feeling *is* describable. If we had to explain even the sense of bodily hunger to a person who had never felt it, we should be hard put to it for words; and the joy in nature seemed to me to come of a sort of heart-hunger, satisfied with the presence of a Great and Holy Spirit. These feelings remained in their full intensity till I was eighteen or twenty, and then, as the reflective and practical power increased, and the 'cares of this world' gained upon me, faded gradually away, in the manner described by Wordsworth in his Intimations of Immortality.

John Ruskin, *Modern Painters*, volume III, George Allen and Sons, 1910, page 309

SCIENCE AND RELIGION

'Science'—branch of knowledge; organized body of knowledge that has been accumulated on a subject; one dealing with material phenomena and based mainly on observation, experiment, and induction, as chemistry, biology.

Professor Coulson in his book *Science and Christian Belief*, provides us with an introduction to this topic. 'To the question, "what is a primrose?" several valid answers may be given. One person says:

A primrose by the river's brim
A yellow primrose was to him,
And it was nothing more.

'Just that, and no more. Another person, the scientist, says, "a primrose is a delicately balanced biochemical mechanism, requiring potash, phosphates, nitrogen and water in definite proportions." A third person says, "a primrose is God's promise of spring." All three definitions are correct.'

We see from his words three different approaches to truth—that of the poet, scientist and theologian. Add to this some words of William Temple, and we have an understanding of the relationship of science and religion. In *Nature, Man and God*, he wrote 'the theologian who quarrels with science on its own ground is but a presumptuous fool. But the scientist who quarrels with theology on its own ground is no better. If there is mutual respect and common reverence for truth in all its forms there may still be divergence and even what we have called tension; but there will be no quarrel.'

> Great is Truth, and mighty above all things.
>
> 1 Esdras 4:41 (AV)

For he hath given me certain knowledge of the things that are, namely, to know how the world was made, and the operation of the elements: the beginning, ending, and midst of the times: the alterations of the turning of the sun, and the change of seasons: the circuits of years, and the positions of stars: the natures of living creatures, and the furies of wild beasts: the violence of winds, and the reasonings of men: the diversities of plants, and the virtues of roots.

> Wisdom of Solomon 7:17–20 (AV)

The Lord hath created medicines out of the earth; and he that is wise will not abhor them. Was not the water made sweet with wood, that the virtue thereof might be known? And he hath given men skill, that he might be honoured in his marvellous works. With such doth he heal (men,) and taketh away their pains.

> Ecclesiasticus 38:4–7 (AV)

> ... the earth is the Lord's, and everything in it.
>
> 1 Corinthians 10:26

Science may have found a cure for most evils; but it has found no remedy for the worst of them all—the apathy of human beings.

> Helen Keller, *My Religion*, Hodder and Stoughton, 1927, page 162

The means by which we live have outdistanced the ends for which we live. Our scientific power has outrun our spiritual power. We have guided missiles and misguided man.

> Martin Luther King, *Strength to Love*, William Collins Sons and Co., 1980, page 74

Science investigates; religion interprets. Science gives man knowledge which is power; religion gives man wisdom which is control.

> Martin Luther King, *Strength to Love*, William Collins Sons and Co., 1980, page 11

Anybody who has been seriously engaged in scientific work of any kind realizes that over the entrance to the gates of the temple of science are written the words: *Ye must have faith.* It is a quality which the scientist cannot dispense with.

> Max Planck, *Where is Science Going?* translated and edited by James Murphy, George Allen and Unwin, 1933, page 214

The simple and plain fact is that the scientific method wins its success by ignoring parts of reality as given in experience; it is perfectly right to do this for its own purposes; but it must not be permitted by a kind of bluff to create the impression that what it ignores is non-existent.

> William Temple, *Nature, Man and God*, Macmillan and Co., 1934, page 216

The theologian who quarrels with science on its own ground is but a presumptuous fool. But the scientist who quarrels with theology on its own ground is no better. If there is mutual respect and common reverence for truth in all its forms there may still be divergence and even what we have called tension; but there will be no quarrel.

William Temple, *Nature, Man and God*, Macmillan and Co., 1934, page 288

Science cannot solve the ultimate mystery of nature. And that is because, in the last analysis, we ourselves are part of nature and therefore part of the mystery that we are trying to solve. Music and art are, to an extent, also attempts to solve or at least to express the mystery. But to my mind the more we progress with either the more we are brought into harmony with all nature itself. And that is one of the great services of science to the individual.

Max Planck, *Where is Science Going?* translated and edited by James Murphy, George Allen and Unwin, 1933, page 217

You will hardly find one among the profounder sort of scientific minds without a religious feeling of his own... His religious feeling takes the form of a rapturous amazement at the harmony of natural law, which reveals an intelligence of such superiority that, compared with it, all systematic thinking and acting of human beings is an utterly insignificant reflection. This feeling is the guiding principle of his life and work, in so far as he succeeds in keeping himself from the shackles of selfish desire. It is beyond question closely akin to that which has possessed the religious geniuses of all ages.

Albert Einstein, *Ideas and Opinions*, Souvenir Press (Educational & Academic), 1973, page 40

The scientist has a faith... which is reflected in the fact that he would never consider that an experiment begun on a Wednesday would yield entirely different results from one undertaken on a Friday. He believes in the orderliness of the universe. He stakes his shirt on his faith that everything happens in such a reasonable and well-ordered fashion that the same experiment will give the same result... If the contents of our universe did not behave in so regular and predictable a fashion no real scientific research would be possible.

Roger Pilkington, *World Without End*, Macmillan and Co., 1960, page 13

We all know that there are regions of the human spirit untrammelled by the world of physics. In the mystic sense of the creation around us, in the expression of art, in a yearning towards God, the soul grows upward and finds the fulfilment of something implanted in its nature. The sanction for this development is within us, a striving born with our consciousness or an Inner Light proceeding from a greater power than ours. Science can scarcely question this sanction, for the pursuit of science springs from a striving which the mind is impelled to follow, a questioning that will not be suppressed. Whether in the intellectual pursuits of science or in the mystical pursuits of the spirit, the light beckons ahead and the purpose surging in our nature responds.

Arthur S. Eddington, *The Nature of the Physical World*, Cambridge University Press, 1928, page 327

Modern physics is changing our view of the whole structure of the universe. Matter is no longer conceived of as an extended substance in society, extending beyond ourselves. Matter is now perceived as a 'web of interdependent relations' forming an organic whole.

Science is also telling us that the physical world cannot be separated from the psyche, from the consciousness. Instead of a separate extended world and a separate mind, we have a field of energy which is also interdependent with the whole psychological world, the world of consciousness.

The world can no longer be separate from consciousness; so do we see the significance of St Paul's vision of all nature as in travail and waiting for the manifestation of the children of God (Romans 8).

Bede Griffiths OSB, in *The Universal Christ*, edited by Peter Spink, Darton, Longman and Todd, 1990, page 14

It is, I think, of the very essence of the unseen world that the conception of personality should dominate it. Force, energy, dimensions belong to the world of symbols; it is out of such conceptions that we have built up the external world of physics. What other conceptions have we? After exhausting physical methods we returned to the inmost recesses of consciousness, to the voice that proclaims our personality; and from there we entered a new outlook. We have to build the spiritual world out of symbols taken from our own personality, as we build the scientific world out of the symbols of the mathematician. I think therefore we are not wrong in embodying the significance of the spiritual world to ourselves in the feeling of a personal relationship, for our whole approach to it is bound up with those aspects of consciousness in which personality is centred.

Arthur S. Eddington, *Science and the Unseen World*, George Allen and Unwin, 1929, page 50

Today we are on the threshold of a new age. This is true for the Western scientific disciplines, for psychology and also for spirituality.

Physics has discovered that matter is not the solid substance it was previously supposed to be. It is a field of energies and with that field of energies there is consciousness.

Psychologists are discovering that there is such a thing as transpersonal consciousness, where human beings can go beyond previously understood limits and there become open to a transcendental consciousness.

Here we find an opening up of Western thought to that of the East. The previously dismissed so-called pseudo-science of the East is now profoundly affecting Western thought and the boundaries between science, psychology and spirituality are disappearing.

Scientific motivation and centuries of belief in a mechanistic universe are giving way to the perceptions of an organic universe. This understanding has always existed at the levels of Hindu, Buddhist and Taoist philosophy. All this is at the heart of the new age.

Bede Griffiths OSB, in *The Universal Christ*, edited by Peter Spink, Darton, Longman and Todd, 1990, page 51

Every scientific statement in the long run, however complicated it looks, really means something like, 'I pointed the telescope to such and such a part of the sky at 2.20 a.m. on January 15th and saw so-and-so,' or, 'I put some of this stuff in a pot and heated it to such-and-such a temperature and it did so-and-so.' Do not think I am saying anything against science: I am only saying what its job is. And the more scientific a man is, the more (I believe) he would agree with me that this is the job of science—and a very useful and necessary job it is too. But why anything comes to be there at all, and whether there is anything behind the things science observes—something of a different kind—this is not a scientific question. If there is 'Something Behind,' then either it will have to remain altogether unknown to me or else make itself known in some different way. The statement that there is any such thing, and the statement that there is no such thing, are neither of them statements that science can make ... Supposing science ever became complete so that it knew every single thing in the whole universe. Is it not plain that the question, 'Why is there a universe?' 'Why does it go on as it does?' 'Has it any meaning?' would remain just as they were?

C.S. Lewis, *Mere Christianity*, William Collins Sons and Co., 1961, page 30

All science has God as its author and giver. Much is heard of the conflict between science and religion, and of the contrast between sacred and secular. There may be aspects of truth to which religion is the gate, as indeed there are aspects of truth to which particular sciences are the gate. But if there be a Creator, and if truth be one of his attributes, then everything that is true can claim his authorship, and every search for truth can claim his authority.

When science has appeared to be anti-religious it generally has meant that one or two particular sciences were exaggerating their claim to a sort of omnicompetence for reading the whole meaning of the universe, even though one particular science is, of course, not competent to do more than read one particular aspect of the universe. But the more we Christians are ready to see and acknowledge God in the sciences—God in the truly scientific spirit—the more we shall be witnessing to what is true to the presence of God in the world, and the more entitled we shall be to go on to point out that there can indeed be a certain sort of scientifically trained mentality which is narrow and unperceptive, and robbing itself of a real chance of interpreting the universe aright.

Michael Ramsey, *Through the Year with Michael Ramsey*, edited by Margaret Duggan, Hodder and Stoughton, 1975, page 147

What is sometimes called the conflict between religion and science often proves to be not between religion and science as such, but between bad religion making wrong claims and a bad scientific outlook also making false claims.

A narrow kind of religion that can see God only in biblical literalism, and is blind to the presence of God in the sciences (which, if we could learn from them, would help us to understand the Bible itself better)—that sort of narrowness is a positive invitation to the scientific man to take an anti-religious standpoint, because we are taking a less than truly religious standpoint ourselves in our claim.

We may complain that the scientific mind—by which I think we really mean the technological kind of mind—is very often blind to spiritual values because it practises a sort of omnicompetence which so blinds it.

But we are not now talking about certain sorts of scientific mind, but about the sciences themselves. Take a genuine human science practised with skill and knowledge and integrity. Its author is said to be Mr. So-and-so, or Sir Somebody-Somebody, or Lord Somebody the great biologist, the great geologist, the great astronomer—or whatnot. But the real author of any science is God—the divine Spirit, the Spirit of Truth at work.

It is for us Christians to be far more sensitive to the presence of God in the very middle of all human sciences, and to be more ready to acknowledge God there.

If scientists sometimes are not Christians or believers, we do not help by being blind to God in their work. No, we must all the more acknowledge that God is the author and sustainer of the sciences.

Michael Ramsey, *Through the Year with Michael Ramsey*, edited by Margaret Duggan, Hodder and Stoughton, 1975, page 148

SECULAR

'Secular'—concerned with the affairs of this world, worldly; not sacred, not monastic, not ecclesiastical; temporal, profane, lay; sceptical of religious truth or opposed to religious education.

In 1969 I was appointed Chaplain *to* University College, London, by the then Bishop of London, Robert Stopford. For those not aware of this, 'UCL' was founded in 1826, as an alternative to Oxford and Cambridge. At that time only members of the Church of England were eligible to apply to Oxbridge. Atheists, agnostics, humanists, Jews and nonconformists were excluded from these ancient seats of learning. UCL came into being to rectify this situation and provide a centre of academic excellence for those denied access to Oxbridge.

In many ways UCL is a secular institution and proud of it. Now known as 'the godless students of Gower Street', there are still clauses in the constitution of the college to the effect that there will never be a chapel nor a chaplain on the campus. This is still the case today.

Certain good features have come out of all this. UCL, with its major concern for the events of this world, was quick off the mark in scientific education and research. Several science departments at UCL now have worldwide reputations. As a radical institution, UCL was a pioneer in setting up departments in newly recognized academic subjects, for example, Scandanavian studies. UCL was also in the vanguard of women's education.

Righteousness exalts a nation.
Proverbs 14:34

Remove not the ancient landmark which your fathers have set.
Proverbs 22:28

If possible, so far as it depends upon you, live peaceably with all.
Romans 12:18

Pay all of them their dues, taxes to whom taxes are due, revenue to whom revenue is due, respect to whom respect is due, honour to whom honour is due. Owe no one anything, except to love one another.

Romans 13:7–8

Secularism is a form of opinion which concerns itself only with questions the issues of which can be tested by the experience of life.

G.J. Holyoake, *The Origin and Nature of Secularism*, Watts and Co., 1896, page 63

If only we knew how to look at life as God sees it we should realize that nothing is secular in the world, but that everything contributes to the building of the kingdom of God.

Michel Quoist, *Prayers of Life*, translated by Anne Marie de Commaile and Agnes Mitchell Forsyth, Gill and Macmillan, 1963, page 10

St. John saw no temple in his vision of the new Jerusalem. The temple as the symbol of the sacred is no longer needed, because its mission has been accomplished. God is in everything. In one way the eternal city is a secular city; in another way the secular city has been permeated and become sacred.

George Appleton, *Journey for a Soul*, William Collins Sons and Co., 1976, page 146

Secular conformism, presentation of a false image, ambition at the expense of others, emphasis on money and position: these are the marks of 'living in the flesh.' Leaving the disposal of life to God, referring decisions to gospel principles, trying to reflect Christ's life: these are marks of 'living in the spirit.'

Hubert van Zeller, *Considerations*, Sheed and Ward, 1974, page 85

In the Holy Communion service we take the bread and wine—man's industrial and commercial life in symbol—and offer it to God; because we have offered it to Him, He gives it back to us as the means of nurturing us, not in our animal nature alone, but as agents of His purpose, limbs of a body responsive to His will; and as we receive it back from Him, we share it with one another in true fellowship. If we think of the service in this way, it is a perfect picture of what secular society ought to be.

William Temple, *The Hope of a New World*, SCM Press, 1940, page 70

Many religious people are troubled about the secularization of modern life. In one way this is good and right, for values which were once thought of as religious have now passed into the texture of society. Also there are areas of human life which have their own distinctive laws which ought not to be governed by religious views or ecclesiastical direction. On the other hand, Christians must question the assumption that man's relation to the objective world is the whole of life. There is a spiritual dimension of life which people ignore at their peril. The aim for the Christian is to humanize the sacred and to regard the whole of life as good and God-given.

George Appleton, *Journey for a Soul*, William Collins Sons and Co., 1976, page 144

Man today wants above all to be human. Not a superman, but equally not a sub-man. He wants to be completely man in a world as human as possible. Is it not surprising how man has got the measure of the world, has ventured on the leap into outer space just as he had previously ventured on the descent into the depths of his own psyche? Is it not surprising that he has consequently taken under his control much—indeed, almost everything—for which God, superhuman and supramundane powers and spirits were supposed to be responsible, and has truly come of age?

This in fact is what is meant when people speak of a 'secular,' a 'worldly' world. Formerly 'secularization' meant primarily merely the transference—in a legal-political sense—of ecclesiastical property to worldly uses by individuals and states. But today it seems that not only certain items of ecclesiastical property, but more or less all the important spheres of human life—learning, economy, politics, law, state, culture, education, medicine, social welfare—have been withdrawn from the influence of the Churches, of theology and religion, and placed under the direct responsibility and control of man, who has himself thus become 'secular.'

Hans Küng, *On Being a Christian*, William Collins Sons and Co., 1977, page 26

The process by which property, power and prestige passed from religious to lay control is referred to as secularization. The term was first used in reference to the laicization of church lands by the Treaty of Westphalia in 1648, but the concept has since been extended in its application to refer to the general process by which religious agencies have been divested of their economic, political and social influence. The word is used to allude to diverse aspects of social and religious change, including such items as the following: sequestration by political powers of the property and facilities of the church; the transfer to secular control of activities formerly undertaken by religious agents and of social functions which religion previously fulfilled; the decline in the proportion of their time, energy and resources which men allot to religious concerns; the decay of religious institutions—churches, Sunday schools, uniformed organizations and ancillary organizations; the supplanting in matters of behaviour of religious precepts by demands that accord with purely technical criteria; the suppression of specifically religious consciousness by empirical, rational, instrumental and matter-of-fact attitudes; the increased separation of evaluative and emotional dispositions from cognitive orientations; decline in religious observance and the diminution of such practices as rites of passage, genuflexion, saying grace, church attendance and membership. The term secularization is variously employed to embrace all these—and perhaps other—social phenomena, and in its width of application the concept sometimes loses cogency, but the many-sided nature of this broad process does not warrant the abandonment of a concept which denotes, albeit loosely, the way in which religious institutions, actions and consciousness lose their social significance.

Bryan Wilson, in *A New Dictionary of Christian Theology*, edited by Alan Richardson and John Bowden, SCM Press, 1983, page 534

SELFISHNESS

'Selfishness'—deficient in consideration for others, alive chiefly to personal profit or pleasure, actuated by self-interest, that pursuit of pleasure of one kind or another is the ultimate aim of every action.

Our expedition to Nepal in 1963 completed its scientific project well within schedule. We had been collecting blood samples for eight weeks in three main areas of Nepal. This was for the Lister Institute in London—as part of a scheme run by the World Health Organization, on blood groupings. We had also been involved in helping to set up a blood transfusion unit in Kathmandu. The time had now come to explore a part of Nepal, so we set off on a trek in the Annapurna region, where many Gurkhas were recruited. Eventually we pitched camp at an altitude of 10,000 feet, midway between two villages on the slopes of Annapurna. Here we made a film of village life, later to be shown on TV.

We greatly enjoyed our stay here. After a few days we went down into the valley and filmed the *mukhiya*—the headman. Here our enjoyment promptly came to an end. The *mukhiya* turned out to be a selfish man. He posed for us, surrounded by his cash boxes and registers. He claimed most of the villagers were heavily in debt to him. Interest rates were 25 per cent. In this way he managed to keep a strict control over their lives, reminiscent of serfdom and slavery. We were greatly saddened by this and witnessed the scourges of selfishness at work. This seemed to work both ways. We felt in spite of his wealth, he was not the happiest of men.

A covetous man's eye is not satisfied with his portion; and the iniquity of the wicked drieth up his soul.

Ecclesiasticus 14:9 (AV)

And do you seek great things for yourself? Seek them not; for, behold, I am bringing evil upon all flesh, says the Lord.

Jeremiah 45:5

Do nothing from selfishness or conceit, but in humility count others better than yourselves. Let each of you look not only to his own interests; but also the interests of others.

Philippians 2:3–4

Beloved, I beseech you as aliens and exiles to abstain from the passions of the flesh that wage war against your soul. Maintain good conduct among the Gentiles, so that in case they speak against you as wrongdoers, they may see your good deeds and glorify God on the day of visitation.

1 Peter 2:11–12

The selfish heart deserves the pains it feels.

Edward Young, *Night Thoughts*, Thomas Nelson, 1841, page 8

No man is more cheated than the selfish man.

Henry Ward Beecher, *Proverbs from Plymouth Pulpit*, Charles Burnett & Co., 1887, page 191

Man seeks his own good at the whole world's cost.

Robert Browning, *Luria*, Act I, in *The Poetical Works of Robert Browning*, volume I, Smith, Elder and Co., 1899, page 441

The more selfish you are, the more involved life becomes.

Thomas Merton, *The Sign of Jonas*, Sheldon Press, 1976, page 102

Selfish persons are incapable of loving others, but they are not capable of loving themselves either.

Erich Fromm, *Man For Himself*, Routledge and Kegan Paul, 1975, page 131

Selfish men may possess the earth; but it is the meek who inherit it, and enjoy it as an inheritance from their heavenly Father, free from all the defilements and perplexities of unrighteousness.

John Woolman, *The Journal of John Woolman*, Edward Marsh, 1857, page 311

If a man is centred upon himself, the smallest risk is too great for him, because both success and failure can destroy him. If he is centred upon God, then no risk is too great because success is already guaranteed—the successful union of Creator and creature beside which everything else is meaningless.

Morris West, *The Shoes of the Fisherman*, William Heinemann, 1963, page 296

High though his titles, proud his name,
Boundless his wealth as wish can claim;
Despite those titles, power, and pelf,
The wretch, concentrated all in self,
Living, shall forfeit fair renown,
And, doubly dying, shall go down
To the vile dust, from whence he sprung,
Unwept, unhonour'd, and unsung.

Sir Walter Scott, 'The Lay of the Last Minstrel,' in *The Poems and Plays of Sir Walter Scott*, volume I, J.M. Dent and Sons, 1911, page 401

The great evils of society do not result from the startling and appalling wickedness of some few individuals; they are the result of a few million people like ourselves living together; and if anyone wants to see the picture of his sin, let him look at slums, and wars, and the like. These things have their origin in characters like ours, ready, no doubt, to be generous with superfluities, but in the last resort self-centred with alike the defensiveness and aggressiveness that go with that self-centredness.

William Temple, *The Preacher's Theme To-day*, SPCK, 1936, page 52

For the self-centred spirit there can be no eternal life. Even if it should exist for ever, its existence could only be an ever deepening chill of death. Because it seeks its satisfaction in itself, where none is to be found, it must suffer an always intenser pang of spiritual hunger, which cannot be allayed until that spirit turns to another source of satisfaction. In the self which it contemplates there can only be successive states. The self is not sufficient to inspire a dedication such as brings purposive unity into life.

William Temple, *Nature, Man and God*, Macmillan and Co., 1934, page 424

Anyone who from time to time will sit quiet with himself and survey his life and present state will be conscious of failure. He will remember things of which he is now ashamed. He will see his secret selfishness, his carefully controlled ambitions, his secret lusts. He will know the power of temptations—from without and within. He will recognize times of wilful choice of wrong attitudes and deeds. When he compares himself with the perfection of Jesus, he will realize his need of forgiveness, a fresh start and continuing grace.

George Appleton, *Journey for a Soul*, William Collins Sons and Co., 1976, page 121

We have got used to thinking of prayer in terms of 'my prayer' or 'my praise' of God, and it requires a complete rethinking of our attitude to prayer if we are going to come to see it as a way through Jesus, with Jesus, and in Jesus.

The first requirement is that we begin to understand that we must pass beyond egoism, so that 'my' prayer just doesn't become even a possibility. We are summoned to see with the eyes of Christ and to love with the heart of Christ, to respond to this summons we must pass beyond egoism. In practical terms this means learning to be so still and silent that we cease thinking about ourselves. This is of critical importance—we must be open to the Father through Jesus, and when we are at prayer we must become like the eye that can see but that cannot see itself.

The way we set out on this pilgrimage, of 'other-centredness' is to recite a short phrase, a word that is commonly called today a mantra. The mantra is simply a means of turning our attention beyond ourselves—a way of unhooking us from our own thoughts and concerns.

John Main OSB, *Moment of Christ*, Darton, Longman and Todd, 1984, page xii

To be a Christian is to be very closely united to Christ as living Lord, not alone but in the fellowship of the Church. It means an existence in which our self-centredness is constantly challenged and defeated. The more Christ becomes your true centre, the less can your own selfish pride be the centre. The more you are drawn into the fellowship of those who belong to Christ, the less are you entangled in your selfish pride. That is why again and again the Christian life has been called a 'death to self'; it is the growth in us of Christ's own self-giving unto death. The Sacraments depict this: *Baptism* was from the beginning the means whereby the convert *died* to the old life whose centre was the self; and, having been buried symbolically beneath the water, he stepped out into a new life whose centre was Christ in the midst of the Church's fellowship. *Holy Communion* deepens our unity with Christ who, through the media of bread and wine, feeds us with himself. But it is always his self as given to death. It is his broken body, his blood poured and offered.

These are the great realities upon which Christian people have laid hold. Some have grasped them, once, and forgotten them. Some have grasped them only in a conventional and unreal way. Some have grasped them, and courageously try to be true to them amid much conflict with the reassertions of self and of pride. Some have grasped them and have shewn it in lives in which, notwithstanding humiliating failures, Christ really has been apparent. It all happens through Calvary judging us, Calvary bringing forgiveness to us, and Calvary defeating the pride which rules us.

Michael Ramsey, *Introducing the Christian Faith*, SCM Press, 1970, page 53

SERVICE

'Service'—doing of work, or work done, for another or for a community, etc; assistance or benefit given to someone, readiness to perform this.

I have just officiated at a funeral in the college chapel. This was a sad, yet moving occasion. 'Ted' had worked in the college for thirty-six years, mainly in the treasury. Here he did valuable painstaking work with accounts and bills. He probably, at one time or another, came into contact with every single member of college, and in a calm matter-of-fact way quietly served them. He belonged to a tradition of long-serving members of staff whose service has been a crucial factor in college life.

Fifteen months ago he had a major heart bypass operation. Complications set in and Ted struggled for nearly a year to regain his health. We were delighted when he eventually returned to resume his duties in the treasury. This delight, however, was short-lived. Within the space of a few weeks he was back in hospital with a suspected appendicitis. Various tests were carried out to reveal cancer of the colon. The consultant surgeon was hopeful a relatively minor operation would do the trick, and make way for a life expectancy of twenty, possibly thirty years. Sadly this proved not to be the case. Ted was found to be riddled with cancer and died three weeks later. However he courageously faced up to the end with quiet and calm dignity, typical of the way he had carried out his life of service. Such people are the salt of the earth, and well nigh impossible to replace.

And now, Israel, what does the Lord your God require of you, but to fear the Lord your God, to walk in all his ways, to love him, to serve the Lord your God with all your heart and with all your soul, and to keep the commandments and statutes of the Lord, which I command you this day for your good?

Deuteronomy 10:12–13

Who then will offer willingly, consecrating himself today to the Lord?

1 Chronicles 29:5

You shall worship the Lord your God and him only shall you serve.

Matthew 4:10

When you have done all that is commanded you, say, 'We are unworthy servants, we have only done what was our duty.'

Luke 17:10

Be useful where thou livest.

George Herbert, 'The Church Porch', in *The Works of George Herbert*, edited by F.E. Hutchinson, Oxford at the Clarendon Press, 1972, page 19

They also serve who only stand and wait.

John Milton, *Sonnet on his Blindness*

In Jesus the service of God and the service of the least of the brethren were one.

Dietrich Bonhoeffer, *The Cost of Discipleship*, revised and abridged edition, SCM Press, 1959, page 118

You have not done enough, you have never done enough, so long as it is still possible that you have something of value to contribute.

Dag Hammarskjöld, *Markings*, translated by Leif Sjöberg and W.H. Auden, Faber and Faber, 1964, page 135

When a man turns to Him, desiring to serve Him, God directs his attention to the world and its need. It is His will that our service of Him should be expressed as our service to the world, through Him, and for His sake.

Emil Brunner, *The Divine Imperative*, translated by Olive Wyon, Lutterworth Press, 1942, page 189

The giving of self to the service of God is not like making a single offer, handing over a single gift, receiving a single acknowledgement. It is a continued action, renewed all the time.

Hubert van Zeller, *Considerations*, Sheed and Ward, 1974, page 124

A servant with this clause
Makes drudgery divine:
Who sweeps a room, as for thy laws,
Makes that and th' action fine.

George Herbert, 'The Elixir', in *The Works of George Herbert*, edited by F.E. Hutchinson, Oxford at the Clarendon Press, 1972, page 185

Love seeketh not Itself to please,
Nor for itself hath any care,
But for another gives its ease,
And builds a Heaven in Hell's despair.

William Blake, *Songs of Innocence and of Experience*, 'The Clod and the Pebble', in *The Complete Writings of William Blake*, edited by Geoffrey Keynes, Oxford University Press, 1974, page 211

Small service is true service while it lasts:
Of humblest Friends, bright Creature! scorn not one:
The Daisy, by the shadow that it casts,
Protects the lingering dew-drop from the Sun.

William Wordsworth, 'To a Child, written in her Album,' in *The Poetical Works of William Wordsworth*, volume IV, edited by E. de Selincourt and Helen Darbishire, Oxford at the Clarendon Press, 1958, page 178

An act of prayer at the heart of every act of service—a self-offering to His purpose so that the action may be His and not our own. That, in its perfection, is the secret of the saints. *I live—yet not I!* Christ is the boundless source of energy and love.

Evelyn Underhill, *The Light of Christ*, Longmans, Green and Co., 1944, page 94

There came to me, as I awoke, the thought that I must not accept this happiness as a matter of course, but must give something in return for it... I settled with myself before I got up, that I would consider myself justified in living till I was thirty for science and art, in order to devote myself from that time forward to the direct service of humanity.

Albert Schweitzer, *My Life and Thought*, translated by C.T. Campion, George Allen and Unwin, 1933, page 103

Think not that God will be always caressing His children, or shine upon their head, or kindle their hearts, as He does at the first. He does so only to lure us to Himself, as the falconer lures the falcon with its gay hood. Our Lord works with His children so as to teach them afterwards to work themselves; as He bade Moses to make the tables of stone after the pattern of the first which He had made Himself. Thus, after a time, God allows a man to depend upon himself, and no longer enlightens, and stimulates, and rouses him. We must stir up and rouse ourselves, and be content to leave off learning, and no more enjoy feeling and fire, and must now serve the Lord with strenuous industry and at our own cost.

John Tauler, *The History and Life of the Reverend Doctor John Tauler*, translated by Susanna Winkworth, Smith, Elder and Co., 1857, page 280

Acceptable service done for God is that which proceeds from non-attachment. To be detached from oneself, from people, from things and to act with a completely pure motivation is difficult but that is the only true service for God and for humanity.

According to the Gospels, we have to be totally detached even from father and mother and wife and children and lands and all that we have, then we love totally and serve perfectly.

It is equally wrong to be either averted from or attached to somebody or something. When we are totally detached then we are able to see clearly and deal with the situation without reaction, with a calm and peaceful mind and with a true understanding.

Bede Griffiths OSB, in *The Universal Christ*, edited by Peter Spink, Darton, Longman and Todd, 1990, page 5

But it is not said of Jesus that he reached down from on high to pull us up from slavery, but that he became a slave with us. God's compassion is a compassion that reveals itself in servanthood. Jesus became subject to the same powers and influences that dominate us, and suffered our fears, uncertainties, and anxieties with us. Jesus emptied himself. He gave up a privileged position, a position of majesty and power, and assumed fully, and without reservation a condition of total dependency. Paul's hymn of Christ does not ask us to look upward, away from our condition, but to look in our midst and discover God there.

This is not the last word, however. 'Being as we are, he was humbler yet, even to accepting death, death on a cross.' Here the essence of God's compassion is announced. Not only did he taste fully the dependent and fearful condition of being human, but he also experienced the most despicable, and horrifying form of death—death on a cross. Not only did he become human, but he also became human in the most dejected and rejected way. Not only did he know human uncertainties and fears, but he also experienced the agony, the pain, and total degradation of the bloody torture and death of a convicted criminal. In this humiliation, Jesus lived out the full implications of emptying himself to be with us in compassion. He not only suffered our painful human condition in all its concreteness but he also suffered death with us in one of its rawest, ugliest, and most degrading forms. It was a death that we 'normal' human beings would hardly be willing to consider ours.

In the Gospel stories of Jesus' healings, we sense how close God wants to be with those who suffer. But now we see the price God is willing to pay for this intimacy. It is the price of ultimate servanthood, the price of becoming a slave, completely dependent on strange, cruel, alien forces. We spontaneously protest against this road of self-emptying and humiliation. We certainly appreciate people who try to understand us. We are even grateful for people who want to feel with us. But we become suspicious when someone chooses to undergo the pain that we would avoid at all costs. We understand conditional solidarity, but we do not understand solidarity that has no limits.

Henri J.M. Nouwen, *Compassion*, Darton, Longman and Todd, 1982, page 25

SIN

'Sin'—transgression, a transgression against the divine law or principles of morality.

I find a short passage from St Mark's Gospel speaks to a reality of my condition. 'For from within, out of the heart of man, come evil thoughts, fornication, theft, murder, adultery, coveting, wickedness, deceit, licentiousness, envy, slander, pride, foolishness. All these evil things come from within and they defile a man.'

I take this to be a consequence of the Genesis story of the creation of man. In Genesis 2.7 we read 'the Lord God formed man of dust from the ground, and breathed into his nostrils the breath of life; and man became a living being.' I find it helpful to know I am a 'man of dust' and consequently earthy and creaturely. I acknowledge this to be a valuable part of human nature and a vast source of energy and dynamism—to be used creatively. If transgressed, then danger, sin and destruction—as I know to my cost.

I also accept the other truth which comes out in this verse—of God breathing something of his own nature into man. I take this to mean we have something of the divine being in the depths of ourselves, to be experienced as Father, Son, Holy Spirit, and as divine attributes such as life, light, truth, joy and love. Christ in his life, centred himself on the Father and the Holy Spirit, and brought about an inner integration, of the divine and the earthy and creaturely, thereby becoming very God and very man. This 'victory over sin' enables us to follow in his footsteps and enter into our inheritance, and enjoy that more abundant life, free from the domination of sin.

But who can discern his errors? Clear thou me from hidden faults. Keep back thy servant also from presumptuous sins; let them not have dominion over me!

Psalm 19:12–13

Come now, let us reason together, says the Lord: though your sins are like scarlet, they shall be as white as snow; though they are red like crimson, they shall become like wool.

Isaiah 1:18

She will bear a son, and you shall call his name Jesus, for he will save his people from their sins.

Matthew 1:21

Since all have sinned, and fall short of the glory of God, they are justified by his grace as a gift, through the redemption which is in Christ Jesus.

Romans 3:23–24

Poor soul, the centre of my sinful earth.

William Shakespeare, Sonnet 146, l.1

A sinful heart makes feeble hand.

Sir Walter Scott, *Marmion*, in *The Poems and Plays of Sir Walter Scott*, volume I, J.M. Dent and Sons, 1911, page 543

Men may securely sin, but safely never.

Ben Jonson, 'The Forest', in *Ben Jonson*, volume VIII, *The Poems, The Prose Works*, edited by C.H. Herford, Percy and Evelyn Simpson, Oxford at the Clarendon Press, 1947, page 113

You have ordained and so it is with us, that every soul that sins brings its own punishment upon itself.

St. Augustine, *Confessions*, translated by R.S. Pine-Coffin, Penguin Books, 1964, page 33

Sin is something inside our fallen selves trying to come out and be free to hurt. The evil outside ourselves in the fallen world is something which is trying to come in—also to hurt.

Hubert van Zeller, *Considerations*, Sheed and Ward, 1974, page 49

The safest road to Hell is the gradual one—the gentle slope, soft underfoot, without sudden turnings, without milestones, without signposts.

C.S. Lewis, *The Screwtape Letters*, William Collins Sons and Co., 1960, page 65

The worst sin towards our fellow creatures is not to hate them, but to be indifferent to them; that's the essence of inhumanity.

George Bernard Shaw, *The Devil's Disciple*, act II, in *The Complete Plays of Bernard Shaw*, Paul Hamlyn, 1965, page 230

One shall not kill 'the evil impulse,' the passion, in oneself, but one shall serve God *with it*; it is the power which is destined to receive its direction from man.

Martin Buber, *Hasidism*, The Philosophical Library, Inc., 1948, page 71

Sin is a fearful thing, and unrighteousness is the sorest ailment of the soul, secretly sapping its sinews ... a self-chosen evil, the offspring of a man's set purpose of mind.

Cyril of Jerusalem, *The Catechetical Letters of St Cyril*, J.G. and F. Rivington, 1838, page 14

Such harmony is in immortal souls,
But whilst this muddy vesture of decay
Doth grossly close it in, we cannot hear it.

William Shakespeare, *The Merchant of Venice*, Act V. sc.i. l.64

Whenever you fight against the root of sin in general or any sin in particular, hold fast to this desire, and fix your mind upon Jesus Christ for whom you long rather than upon the sin which you are fighting.

Walter Hilton, *The Ladder of Perfection*, translated by Leo Sherley-Price, Penguin Books, 1957, page 109

St. Paul says that the wages of sin is death, not that God condemns us to death for our sins, but that sin kills the life of the spirit. Sin is a sickness that leads to spiritual death unless it is cured by forgiveness and the soul kept healthy by grace.

George Appleton, *Journey for a Soul*, William Collins Sons and Co., 1976, page 122

Over and over again, as we break some rule which seems rather arbitrary and meaningless, we discover the principle which had dictated it. We set in motion the causes and effects from which we understand, for the first time, why there had ever been that prohibition; then it is too late. The discovery is called the Fall of Man.

William Temple, *Christian Faith and Life*, SCM Press, 1931, reissued 1963, page 65

The smallest atom of good realized and applied to life, a single vivid experience of love, will advance us much further, will far more surely protect our souls from evil, than the most arduous *struggle* against sin, than the resistance to sin by the severest ascetic methods of chaining the dark passions within us.

Father Yelchaninov, in *A Treasury of Russian Spirituality*, edited by G.P. Fedotov, Sheed and Ward, 1977, page 461

Sin is the putting of self in the centre where God alone should be. Sin is acting from the self instead of from God. It is falling short of the will and glory of God. Often it is more than that—it is setting one's will against God's will, consciously (where guilt is involved) or unconsciously (when the sinful consequences are equally disastrous).

George Appleton, *Journey for a Soul*, William Collins Sons and Co., 1976, page 122

In the Creation story God says: 'Let us make man in our image, after our likeness' (Genesis 1:26). And sin may well be said to be man's failure to reach the object and the purpose for which he was created. As G.K. Chesterton put it: 'Whatever else is true of man, man is not what he was meant to be.' So, then ... sin is failure ... Sin is the failure to be what we should have been and what we ought to have been, what we could have been and what we might have been.

William Barclay, *The Plain Man Looks at the Apostles' Creed*, William Collins Sons and Co., 1967, page 304

All sins are contained in this one category, that one turns away from things divine and truly enduring, and turns towards those which are mutable and uncertain. And although the latter are rightly placed each in its order, and work out that beauty proper to them it is nevertheless the mark of a perverted and ungoverned mind to be in subjection to them as things to be pursued, when by the divine order and law it is set above them as things to be directed.

St Augustine, in *An Augustine Synthesis*, arranged by Erich Przywara, SJ, Sheed and Ward, 1945, page 124

Eden is on no map, and Adam's fall fits no historical calendar. Moses is not nearer the Fall than we are, because he lived three thousand years before our time. The Fall refers not to some datable aboriginal calamity in the historic past of humanity, but to a dimension of human experience which is always present—namely, that we who have been created for fellowship with God repudiate it continually; and that the whole of mankind does this along with us. Everyman is his own 'Adam,' and all men are solidarily 'Adam.' Thus, Paradise before the Fall, the *status perfectionis*, is not a period of history, but our 'memory' of a divinely intended quality of life, given to us along with our consciousness of guilt.

J.S. Whale, *Christian Doctrine*, Cambridge University Press, 1942, page 52

I think sin is anything which leads to a greater deadening of one's mind, one's personality, one's feelings. God is ultimately interested in my being totally alive: everything that comes from Him is life-giving. I think that my belief in the Devil—call him what you like—sees him as the personification of the inbuilt false promise that goes with a great many experiences—they hold out false hopes of greater vitality. We think: if I do that, I'll get a kick out of it. Well, each time you get less and less of a kick, and it ends up making you deader instead of more alive. Whatever we do that creates deadness is a sin. And in terms of society, if I organise some institution the end result of which is the greater deadening of the human community, then that is a gigantic sin.

John V. Taylor, in Gerald Priestland, Priestland's Progress, BBC Worldwide, 1982, page 70

I'm very much of a Jungian, and I feel Jung's concept of the dark side in all of us is very near the truth. If we equate that dark side with the Devil, we are not far wrong in our understanding of what the Devil is up to. The interesting thing about the dark side, or the Devil, is that he was a fallen angel—he belongs to God really—and our problem is to reconcile the dark side and make use of its energy. It's always recognised that the Devil is walking up and down the earth, full of energy. In education I used to find the apparently wicked boy was full of it. You've got to understand it, come to terms with it and make use of it. In other words, bring the Devil back into God's Kingdom.

Kenneth Barnes, in Gerald Priestland, Priestland's Progress, BBC Worldwide, 1982, page 72

The Fathers of the Church saw that every one of us is more or less like the Prodigal, starving in a distant land, far from our Father's House. This is the common condition of mankind exiled from God and from Paradise by an inordinate preoccupation with perishing things and by a constant inclination to self-gratification and sin. Since this is in fact our position, and since our mental prayer is a journey from time into eternity, from the world to God, it follows that we cannot make a good meditation unless we realize, at least implicitly, the starting point of our journey.

If we admit the truth, we will start out on a basis of humility, recognize the need for effort, and perhaps we will be rewarded with a little of the grace of compunction, which is the most precious of all helps in mental or any other kind of prayer.

Compunction is simply an awareness of our indigence and coldness and of our need for God.

For the man who has a sense of compunction, prayer is a living act which brings him face to face with God in an I-Thou relationship which is not imaginary but real.

Thomas Merton, Spiritual Direction and Meditation, Burns and Oates, 1961, pages 74 and 83

An awareness of our sinfulness is part of holiness; you simply cannot have holiness without it for it is the inevitable effect of God's closeness. This is why true sorrow for sin is never morbid, depressed, for it carries within it the certainty of forgiveness.

The keenest sense of our guilt is thus bound up with the unfailing certainty of pardon; and the deepest contrition excludes all discouragement by renewing childlike trust. We should want compunction like this with all our hearts.

Scripture assures us that Jesus comes to heal our blindness, and blindness in regard to sin is our chief blindness. To a great extent, perhaps wholly, we choose how much we see. We cannot have God unless we are prepared to see ourselves, our lives, our past and present as they are, and half-consciously we know this revelation would be terrible. Therefore we make a choice not to see, or not to see very much.

Come and enlighten us, Sun of Holiness. Show us our sloth, our pride, our shirking of the demands of life, our evasions.

Reveal to us our sinfulness in the light of your mercy, and then we shall be healed and know perfect joy.

Ruth Burrows, in The Watchful Heart, edited by Elizabeth Ruth Obbard, Darton, Longman and Todd, 1988, page 30

The first Light which shined in my Infancy in its primitive and innocent clarity was totally eclipsed: insomuch that I was fain to learn all again. If you ask me how it was eclipsed? Truly by the customs and manners of men, which like contrary winds blew it out: by an innumerable company of other objects, rude, vulgar, and worthless things, that like so many loads of earth and dung did overwhelm and bury it: by the impetuous torrent of wrong desires in all others whom I saw or knew that carried me away and alienated me from it: by a whole sea of other matters and concernments that covered and drowned it: finally by the evil influence of a bad education that did not foster and cherish it. All men's thoughts and words were about other matters. They all prized new things which I did not dream of. I was a stranger and unacquainted with them; I was little and reverenced their authority; I was weak, and easily guided by their example: ambitious also, and desirous to approve myself unto them. And finding no one syllable in any man's mouth of those things, by degrees they vanished, my thoughts (as indeed what is more fleeting than a thought?) were blotted out and at last all the celestial great and stable treasures to which I was born, as wholly forgotten, as if they had never been.

Thomas Traherne, *Centuries*, The Faith Press, 1969, page 114

SOCIETY

*'Society'—social mode of life, the customs and organizations of a
civilized society—any social community.*

Henry Ward Beecher wrote over a hundred years ago 'the great want of society to-day is the habit of adhering to absolute truth and reliable honesty.' I think we have largely lost sight of adhering to these two basic fundamental qualities, and society is found to be wanting as a result. Take, for instance, the whole realm of relationships. Nearly fifty per cent of marriages in this country now break down and end in divorce. A few years ago I did a small research project on suicides and was horrified to discover the large number of people taking their lives—hardly a symptom of a healthy society. I shudder to think of the number of pregnancies terminated by abortion. As regards crime, we are told the figures of reported crime are actually going down, at the very time prison populations continue to expand to record levels. Who can we believe, when it seems the powers that be have also largely abandoned the habit of adhering to absolute truth and reliable honesty? Large pay rises in the private sector and tight pay controls in the public sector smack of injustice, and are deeply demoralizing to the vast majority of people. It really does appear, with one or two laudable exceptions, that an epidemic of financial greed has hit the upper echelons of society in this country with disastrous results. Where, you may ask, is the Established Church in all this? Have we also largely abandoned the habit of absolute truth and reliable honesty?

Am I my brother's keeper?

Genesis 4:9

Honour your father and your mother, that your days may be long in the land which the Lord your God gives you.

Exodus 20:12

... as you wish that men would do to you, do so to them.

Luke 6:31

Remember those who are in prison, as though in prison with them; and those who are ill-treated, since you also are in the body.

Hebrews 13:3

The spirit of truth and the spirit of freedom—*these* are the pillars of society.

Henrik Ibsen, *Pillars of Society*, volume V, act IV, translated and edited by James Walter McFarlane, Oxford University Press, 1961

We know, and what is better we feel inwardly that religion is the basis of civil society, and the source of all good and of all comfort.

Edmund Burke, in Conor Cruise O'Brien, editor, *Reflections on the Revolution in France*, Penguin Books, 1969, page 186

The first duty of society is to give each of its members the possibility of fulfilling his destiny. When it becomes incapable of performing this duty it must be transformed.

Alexis Carrel, *Reflections on Life*, translated by Antonia White, Hamish Hamilton, 1952, page 132

The test of every religious, political, or educational system, is the man which it forms. If a system injures the intelligence it is bad. If it injures the character it is vicious. If it injures the conscience it is criminal.

Henri Frédéric Amiel, *Amiel's Journal*, translated by Mrs Humphry Ward, Macmillan and Co., 1918, page 27

There are large proportions of our fellow citizens for whom the bottom is liable to fall out of life through no action of their own, but simply through the way in which our economic system is worked or works, and it is a shocking evil and we must fight against it.

William Temple, *The Church Looks Forward*, Macmillan and Co., 1944, page 121

All our rational investigation and rational planning of the economic and political and social spheres is without meaning unless it is the means to one end—the living of the personal life of community in joy and freedom. To sacrifice life to its own conditions is the ultimate insincerity and the real denial of God.

John Macmurray, *Reason and Emotion*, Humanities Press International, 1972, page 254

More potent than school, or even than home, as a moral influence, is the whole structure of society, and especially its economic structure. This fixes for all their place in the general scheme; and the way in which they gain and keep that place of necessity determines a great deal of their conduct and profoundly influences their outlook upon life.

William Temple, *The Hope of a New World*, SCM Press, 1940, page 49

If we let the economic aim become predominant, we shall find that it disintegrates our society, that it treats every individual primarily as so much labour power to be used where he most conduces to efficiency of output, irrespective of all his social ties and traditional roots. The economic approach to life atomises society.

William Temple, *The Church Looks Forward*, Macmillan and Co., 1944, page 128

We concentrate on social reform and economic justice and better standards of life, of housing, of health, of education... Will they even work if we ignore our own complete make-up? A recent writer has put it better than I can. 'What do all these promises of material Utopias amount to?' he asks, 'that people can get good results without bothering to be good—that you can build a good society out of bad men.'

R.L. Smith, in *Man's Dilemma and God's Answer*, Broadcast Talks, SCM Press, 1944, page 76

You cannot bring about prosperity by discouraging thrift; you cannot strengthen the weak by weakening the strong; you cannot help the wage-earner by pulling down the wage-payer; you cannot further the brotherhood of man by encouraging class hatred; you cannot help the poor by destroying the rich; you cannot establish sound security on borrowed money; you cannot keep out of trouble by spending more than you earn; you cannot build character and courage by taking away man's initiative and independence; you cannot help men permanently by doing for them what they could and should do for themselves.

Attributed to Abraham Lincoln

Humanity is divided because man is divided in himself. The two great traditions of East and West stand as the two sides of understanding of man. So far these two traditions have grown independently with little relation beyond occasional rivalry. The time has come to integrate them.

In the West today the masculine aspect, the rational, the aggressive power of the mind is dominant, while in the East the feminine aspect, the intuitive aspect of the mind prevails.

The future of the world depends on the 'marriage' of these two minds, the conscious and the unconscious, the rational and the intuitive, the active and the passive. This 'marriage' must take place first within the individual. Then only can external union take place.

Bede Griffiths OSB, in Peter Spink, editor, *The Universal Christ*, Darton, Longman and Todd, 1990, page 1

Happiness lies in the fulfilment of the spirit through the body. Thus humanity has already evolved from an animal life to one more civilized. There can be no complete return to nature, to nudism, desert-islandry: city life is the subtlest ingredient in the human climate. But we have gone wrong over the size of our cities and over the kind of life we lead in them; in the past the clods were the peasants, now the brute mass of ignorance is urban. The village idiot walks in Leicester Square. To live according to nature we should pass a considerable time in cities, for they are the glory of human nature, but they should never contain more than two hundred thousand inhabitants; it is our artificial enslavement to the large city, too sprawling to leave, too enormous for human dignity, which is responsible for half our sickness and misery. Slums may well be breeding-grounds of crime, but middle-class suburbs are incubators of apathy and delirium. No city should be too large for a man to walk out of in a morning.

Cyril Connolly, *The Unquiet Grave*, part I, 'Ecce Gubernator', Hamish Hamilton, 1945, page 26

Our present economic, social and international arrangements are based, in large measure, upon organized lovelessness. We begin by lacking charity towards Nature, so that instead of trying to co-operate with Tao or the Logos on the inanimate and sub-human levels, we try to dominate and exploit, we waste the earth's mineral resources, ruin its soil, ravage its forests, pour filth into its rivers and poisonous fumes into its air. From lovelessness in relation to Nature we advance to lovelessness in relation to art—a lovelessness so extreme that we have effectively killed all the fundamental or useful arts and set up various kinds of mass-production by machines in their place. And of course this lovelessness in regard to art is at the same time a lovelessness in regard to the human beings who have to perform the fool-proof and grace-proof tasks imposed by our mechanical art-surrogates and by the interminable paperwork connected with mass-production and mass-distribution. With mass-production and mass-distribution go mass-financing, and the three have conspired to expropriate ever-increasing numbers of small owners of land and productive equipment, thus reducing the sum of freedom among the majority and increasing the power of a minority to exercise a coercive control over the lives of their fellows. This coercively controlling minority is composed of private capitalists or governmental bureaucrats or of both classes of bosses acting in collaboration—and, of course, the coercive and therefore essentially loveless nature of the control remains the same, whether the bosses call themselves 'company directors' or 'civil servants.' The only difference between these two kinds of oligarchical rulers is that the first derive more of their power from wealth than from position within a conventionally respected hierarchy, while the second derive more power from position than from wealth.

Aldous Huxley, *The Perennial Philosophy*, Chatto and Windus, 1974, page 109

SONS OF GOD

'Sons of God'—a consequence of the Genesis story of the creation of man, fully worked out in the life of our Lord, activated by baptism and nurtured by prayer, grace and sacramental worship.

In my teens I went to the dentist on a regular basis, with my young sister. She always made sure I went to the dentist's chair first, while she sat down and observed proceedings from afar. Each time the dentist discovered a cavity I would hear a little snigger. I think she enjoyed the prospect of me having to undergo the pain of the dentist's drill. One day, when she was not there, I took the liberty of asking him a question that puzzled me. How did he manage to deal with teeth only day after day? What was it that stimulated him? 'Well, William,' he replied, 'I tend to think there's a person behind the teeth.' This answer fitted in well with my experience of him so far. He always seemed to take an interest in me—as he did in my young sister.

Later, when I was ordained, I can remember going to take a funeral, and was sitting in the front seat of the hearse. As we went through the city, I saw a policeman come to attention and salute the hearse. I was impressed by this. Did it mean he had been trained to respect everyone as a potential son of God, to be revered, even in death?

Some of the older generation also raise their hats to clergy as a mark of respect. Is there a hope here that behind the dog-collar lurks a son of God, representing the Son of God? Are we worthy of this kind of respect?

You are gods, sons of the Most High.

Psalm 82:6

For to us a child is born, to us a son is given; and the government will be upon his shoulder, and his name will be called 'Wonderful Counsellor, Mighty God, Everlasting Father, Prince of Peace.'

Isaiah 9:6

And because you are sons, God has sent the Spirit of his Son into our hearts, crying, 'Abba! Father!' So through God you are no longer a slave but a son, and if a son then an heir.

Galatians 4:6–7

See what love the Father has given us, that we should be called children of God; and so we are.

1 John 3:1

He is the Son of God in that sense (among others) in which we say of a man that he is the son of his father, meaning that in him the father's character is reproduced. So supremely is our Lord the Son because in Him we truly see the Father.

William Temple, *Christian Faith and Life*, SCM Press, 1931, reissued 1963, page 35

Our Lord recalls us to our original being, our intimate being.

We are children of God all through our lives, however young, however old, however experienced or disillusioned. We have to return to this original being, assured now of what we first felt in unquestioning intuition or received trustingly from others.

George Appleton, *Journey for a Soul*, William Collins Sons and Co., 1976, page 82

The writers of the New Testament all observe a certain use of language which has deep significance. They often imply that God is the Father of all men but they do not speak of all men as His children; that expression is reserved for those who, by the grace of God, are enabled in some measure to reproduce His character.

William Temple, *Readings in St. John's Gospel*, First and Second Series, Macmillan and Co., 1947, page 12

(Was Jesus the Son of God?) To think it is a clear-cut concept which can be dealt with in that sort of way seems to me to be a total misunderstanding. Anybody who had read scriptural history and so on would know that the phrase 'Son of God' has so many different concepts, indicating one who is in a very special relationship to God, focal for other men's faith towards God. What our book (The Myth of God Incarnate) was feeling after was something which would keep the positive implications of a great deal of the traditional religious language, but free people from thinking it had to be understood in ways which I honestly believe diminish the effective reality of Jesus for our continuing faith.

Maurice Wiles, in Gerald Priestland, *Priestland's Progress*, BBC Worldwide, 1982, page 40

Yes, God is there before you, watching you.

His look is creative, capable of achieving the impossible.

And just as he looked on the chaos at the beginning, hovered over the waters with the smile of his favour, and drew forth the cosmos, so, looking at you with the same favouring smile, he realizes the final purpose of creation: love.

Take courage, then: God loves you.

I know you do not deserve it, so it is useless to go on saying so: the fact is, he loves you.

I know you are tormented by doubts, but do not be afraid. He loves you, and his love is freely given. He does not love you for what you are worth; he loves you because, as God, he cannot help loving you: he is love.

Let yourself go; let him take hold of you.

He accepts you as a son.

Carlo Carretto, *In Search of the Beyond*, translated by Sarah Fawcett, Darton, Longman and Todd, 1975, page 81

I cannot explain the mystery of how someone who is a human being just like I am can also be worshipped. And yet the more real the mystery has become for me, it isn't that Jesus has become more like God, but that all my brothers and sisters have. It is through Him that I recognise God in my neighbour—through Jesus I've discovered the uniqueness of everyone. And there was in Him a quality of willingness to be defeated and destroyed by His enemies, and to go on loving them, that alone made possible a new quality of life afterwards...

But so special that in Him those who loved Him were able to recognise something they had to call God; it was divine. If others have somehow come through this Jesus to share aspects of His holiness, that mysteriously makes us one with God. There is a sense in which every man becomes divine. I would not want to draw hard, dogmatic lines between the rest of humanity and this Jesus.

Paul Oestreicher, in Gerald Priestland, *Priestland's Progress*, BBC Worldwide, 1982, page 43

Here you ask of me nothing else than to be content that I am your Child and your Friend. Which means simply to accept your friendship because it is your friendship, and your Fatherhood because I am your son... You have called me here to be repeatedly born in the Spirit as your son... to speak your name of 'Father' just by being here as 'son' in the Spirit and the Light which you have given, and which are no unearthly light but simply this plain June day, with its shining fields, its tulip tree, the pines, the woods, the clouds, and the flowers everywhere.

To be here with the silence of Sonship in my heart is to be a centre in which all things converge upon you. That is surely enough for the time being.

Therefore, Father, I beg you to keep me in this silence so that I may learn from it the word of your peace and the word of your mercy and the word of your gentleness to the world: and that through me perhaps your word of peace may make itself heard where it has not been possible for anyone to hear it for a long time.

Thomas Merton, *Conjectures of a Guilty Bystander*, Burns and Oates, 1968, page 175

'Then the Lord God formed man out of the dust of the ground and breathed into his nostrils the breath of life, and man became a living being.' (Genesis 2:7).

The life of Adam, that is to say, the 'breath' which was to give actuality and existence and movement to the whole person of man, had mysteriously proceeded from the intimate depths of God's own life. Adam was created not merely as a living and moving animal who obeyed the command and will of God. He was created as a 'son' of God because his life shared something of the reality of God's own breath or Spirit. For 'breath' is the same as 'spirit' (the Latin word *spiritus* is related to *spirare*, to breathe)...

If the expression may be permitted, Adam's very existence was to be a kind of 'inspiration.' God intended not only to conserve and maintain Adam's bodily life. He would also foster and increase, even more directly and intimately, the spiritual life and activity which were the main reason for Adam's existence. Adam, then, was meant from the very first to live and breathe in unison with God, for just as the soul was the life of Adam's body, so the Spirit of God, swelling in Adam, was to be the life of his soul. For him, then, to live would mean to 'be inspired'—to see things as God saw them, to love them as He loved them, to be moved in all things ecstatically by the Spirit of God.

Thomas Merton, *The New Man*, Burns and Oates, 1962, page 36

SOUL

'Soul'—the spiritual or immaterial part of man, often regarded as immortal; the moral or emotional or intellectual nature of a person; the meeting-place of God in man.

One of the proverbs in Henry Ward Beecher's *Proverbs from Plymouth Pulpit* helps us to understand the nature of the soul. This proverb reads as follows: 'There is a direct in-shining, a direct in-breathing, a direct in-reaching of the Divine Soul upon the human soul.'

The life of Jesus revealed an inner relationship with the Father. Beecher's words imply there is in Jesus' life a direct in-shining, a direct in-breathing, a direct in-reaching of the Father. The same could be said of Jesus' life and the Holy Spirit—a direct in-shining, a direct in-breathing, a direct in-reaching of the Holy Spirit. The same too, could be said of love—a direct in-shining, a direct in-breathing, a direct in-reaching of love. We see this clearly in operation in the two great commandments: 'You shall love the Lord your God with all your heart, and with all your soul, and with all your mind, and with all your strength... You shall love your neighbour as yourself.' This experience also applies to other divine attributes, such as life, light, truth, joy and grace. In this way Jesus entered fully into his divine inheritance, and thereby opened a way for our entrance into the same inheritance. Consequently in baptism we experience a rebirth—in the name (nature) of the Father, in the name (nature) of the Son, and in the name (nature) of the Holy Spirit. What could be simpler and yet more profound than this? There is a need for rediscovering the meeting-place of God in man today.

March on, my soul, with might!

Judges 5:21

... the One who shaped him, who breathed an active soul into him, and inspired a living spirit.

Wisdom of Solomon 15:11 (JB)

For what shall it profit a man, if he shall gain the whole world, and lose his own soul? Or what shall a man give in exchange for his soul?

Mark 8:36–37 (AV)

May the God of peace himself sanctify you wholly; and may your spirit and soul and body be kept sound and blameless at the coming of our Lord Jesus Christ.

1 Thessalonians 5:23

I count life just a stuff
To try the soul's strength on.

Robert Browning, 'In A Balcony', in *The Poetical Works of Robert Browning*, volume I, Smith, Elder and Co., 1899, page 559

'I tell you these things, not because you know them not, but because ye know them.' All living instruction is nothing but corroboration of intuitive knowledge.

Coventry Patmore, 'Aurea Dicta', in *The Rod, The Root and the Flower*, The Grey Walls Press, 1950, page 47

By the word soul, or psyche, I mean that inner consciousness which aspires. By prayer I do not mean a request for anything preferred to a deity; I mean intense soul-emotion, intense aspiration.

Richard Jefferies, *The Story of My Heart*, Duckworth and Co., 1923, page 143

And see all sights from pole to pole,
And glance, and nod, and bustle by,
And never once possess our soul
Before we die.

Matthew Arnold, 'A Southern Night', in *The Poems of Matthew Arnold*, edited by Kenneth Allott, Longmans, Green and Co., 1965, page 460

Highly ought we to rejoice that God dwelleth in our soul, and much more highly ought we to rejoice that our soul dwelleth in God. Our soul is *made* to be God's dwelling-place and the dwelling-place of the soul is God, which is *unmade*. And high understanding it is, inwardly to see and know that God, which is our Maker, dwelleth in our soul and an higher understanding it is, inwardly to see and to know that our soul, that is made, dwelleth in God's Substance: of which Substance, God, we are that we are.

Lady Julian of Norwich, *Revelations of Divine Love*, edited by Grace Warrack, Methuen and Co., 1949, page 130

Either we have an immortal soul, or we have not. If we have not, we are beasts; the first and wisest of beasts, it may be; but still true beasts. We shall only differ in degree, and not in kind; just as the elephant differs from the slug. But by the concession of all the materialists of all the schools, or almost all, we are not of the same kind as beasts—and this also we say from our own consciousness. Therefore, methinks, it must be the possession of a soul within us that makes the difference.

Samuel Taylor Coleridge, *Table Talk of Samuel Taylor Coleridge*, George Routledge and Sons, 1884, page 33

It seems to me that what one aims at is to work with one's mind and one's soul *together*. By soul I mean that 'thing' that makes the mind really important. I always picture it like this. My mind is a very complicated, capable instrument. But the interior is dark. It *can* work in the dark and throw off all kinds of things. But behind that instrument like a very steady gentle light is the soul. And it's only when the soul *irradiates* the mind that what one does matters . . . What I *aim* at is that state of mind when I feel my soul and my mind are one. It's awfully, terribly difficult to get at. Only solitude will do it for me.

Katherine Mansfield, *The Letters of Katherine Mansfield*, edited by J. Middleton Murry, Constable and Co., 1928, Volume 11, page 203

Thus the Lord, the spirit, becomes the soul of our souls, becomes spiritually what he always was creatively; and as our spirit informs, gives shape to our bodies, in like manner his soul informs, gives shape to our souls. In this there is nothing unnatural, nothing at conflict with our being. It is but that the deeper soul that willed and wills our souls, rises up, the infinite Life, into the Self we call *I* and *me*, but which lives immediately from him, and is his very own property and nature—unspeakably more his than ours . . . until at length the glory of our existence flashes upon us, we face full to the sun that enlightens what it sent forth, and know ourselves alive with an infinite life, even the life of the Father; know that our existence is not the moonlight of a mere consciousness of being, but the sun-glory of a life justified by having become one with its origin, thinking and feeling with the primal Sun of life, from whom it was dropped away that it might know and bethink itself, and return to circle forever in exultant harmony around him. Then indeed we *are*; then indeed we have life; the life of Jesus has, through light, become life in us; the glory of God in the face of Jesus, mirrored in our hearts, has made us alive; we are one with God for ever and ever.

George Macdonald, *Unspoken Sermons*, Third Series, Longmans, Green and Co., 1889, page 53

I had learned, it seemed, that a spiritual progress was possible to man, by which out of the discordant elements of his being—the desire of the Heart and the knowledge of the Mind—a harmony was created. This harmony was a new kind of being, and it had been called by Jesus and Eckhart and Keats, the Soul. This Soul was at once a new condition of the total human being and a faculty of knowledge. It was aware of the universe as a harmony, and of itself as a part of that harmony; and this awareness was a joyful awareness. This was the ground of the mystical faith that the Soul was consubstantial with God. God, in this mystical sense, was the inseparable counterpart of the Soul; and the Soul, in the process and very moment of becoming aware of its own self-existence, became also aware of the existence of an omnipresent God of which itself was, as it were, a focus of self-knowledge.

This strange and simple process was the 'rebirth' which Jesus had taught, and which was the central mystery of all high religion. It could occur in complete independence of any particular religion; it was the outcome of an internecine conflict between the desire of the Heart and the knowledge of the Mind . . . This conflict between Heart and Mind, between feeling and knowledge, was obviously independent of religion, in any ordinary sense of the word. It was simply incidental to humanity. Man, being man, was bound to endure this conflict. If he did not endure it, he was less than man, in the sense that he was turning away from something which it was his duty as a man to look upon... Some drugged themselves with a religion which assured them that the desires of the Heart would be realized, and that death was only the doorway to life; some sought forgetfulness in busy plans for the amelioration of human circumstance; some sought to live in the moment. But there were always a few on whom the opiates failed to work. By some queer destiny the conflict was forced upon them. Heart and Mind in them insisted each upon its own rights, and the claims could not be reconciled. There was a deadlock in the centre of their being, and they passed steadily into a condition of isolation, inanition, abandonment and despair. Their inward division was complete.

Then came, out of that extreme and absolute division, a sudden unity. A new kind of consciousness was created in them. Mind and Heart, which had been irreconcilable enemies, became united in the Soul, which loved what it knew. The inward division, which had divided the human being also from the universe of his knowledge, was healed; in a single happening, man became one in himself and one with all that was without him. He knew that he was called upon to play his part in the harmony revealed to him.

This was the great secret of religion; but only because it was the great secret of life. Men who learned and obeyed it, became different. They were a new kind of men. They gained no happiness, nothing that the world accounts desirable came to them, their lives burned out in a blaze of sorrow and broken hopes: but an extraordinary beauty was manifest in them.

John Middleton Murry, *God*, Jonathan Cape, 1929, page 69

SUFFERING

'Suffering'—undergoing pain, loss, grief, defeat, disablement, change, punishment, wrong, etc.

I have been thinking about the carnage of the two World Wars recently, and specifically of the holocaust. Most forms of suffering pale into insignificance in comparison, except when we ourselves have suffered directly, or have witnessed suffering in another, close by.

In the small ways I have suffered, I have stopped asking the question, 'Why has this happened to me?' This seems to be the wrong sort of question. The thing has already happened, and that's that. The important question now is: 'How am I going to respond to this suffering, and is it possible to make a creative use of it?'

Whilst out in Singapore doing national service I was extremely active. I had been appointed Cross Country Running Officer, and went out on training runs with the team before breakfast. Running with Gurkhas was no sinecure, especially when there were hills to be negotiated. In the evenings I played hockey for the Battalion XI, and found this equally exhausting. The outcome was a severe dose of prickly heat. The doctor was torn between invaliding me back to England, or putting me on a new, dangerous drug. Fortunately he chose the latter. I was under strict orders to go to bed for several days, be on my back, and to lie down perfectly still. I was bored stiff, but learnt important lessons. My mind took over and sorted out a great deal of dross. I was able to return to duties a wiser man.

But I will sing of thy might; I will sing aloud of thy steadfast love in the morning. For thou hast been to me a fortress and a refuge in the day of my distress.

Psalm 59:16

When you pass through the waters I will be with you; and through the rivers, they shall not overwhelm you; when you walk through fire you shall not be burned, and the flame shall not consume you.

Isaiah 43:2

For because he himself has suffered and been tempted, he is able to help those who are tempted.

Hebrews 2:18

Therefore let those who suffer according to God's will do right and entrust their souls to a faithful Creator.

1 Peter 4:19

He who suffers much will know much.

Greek Proverb

In time of sickness the soul collects itself anew.

Latin Proverb

Although the world is full of suffering, it is full also of the overcoming of it.

Helen Keller, *Optimism*, George G. Harrop, 1903, page 17

Know how sublime a thing it is
To suffer and be strong.

Henry Wadsworth Longfellow, 'The Light of Stars', in *The Poetical Works of Longfellow*, edited by Humphrey Milford, Oxford University Press, 1913, page 4

Understood in its deepest sense, being Christ's follower means suffering that is unendurable to the great majority of mankind.

C.G. Jung, *The Collected Works of C.G. Jung*, volume XII, *Psychology and Alchemy*, translated by R.F.C. Hull, Routledge and Kegan Paul, 1953, page 22

I wonder why we suffer so strangely—to bring out something in us, I try to believe, which can't be brought out in any other way.

A.C. Benson, *Extracts from the Letters of Dr. A.C. Benson to M.E.A.*, Jarrolds Publishers, 1927, page 13

Shut out suffering, and you see only one side of this strange and fearful thing, the life of man. Brightness, and happiness, and rest—that is not life. It is only one side of life: Christ saw both sides.

F.W. Robertson, *Sermons*, Fifth Series, Kegan Paul, Trench, Trubner and Co, 1890, page 17

It *did* come—the day when the grief became small. For what had befallen me and seemed so hard to bear became insignificant in the light of the demands which God was now making. But how difficult it is to feel that this was also, and for that very reason, the day when the joy became great.

Dag Hammarskjöld, *Markings*, translated by Leif Sjöberg and W.H. Auden, Faber and Faber, 1964, page 87

The mark of the spiritually mature man is that he can endure sorrow without bitterness, bewilderment without fuss, loss without envy or recrimination or self-pity. Above all, whatever the set-backs and misunderstandings, public and private, that he maintains a belief in the essential goodness of mankind.

Hubert van Zeller, *Considerations*, Sheed and Ward, 1974, page 122

When trouble hits us we can react to it in a variety of ways. We can let it knock us out, so that we lose all hope and stamina. We can rebel and refuse to accept the rightness or merit of it. We can fill our lives with feverish activity so that we have no time to think about it. Or we can accept it—without defeat, rebellion or evasion—trusting that God will make clear tomorrow what is so difficult to understand today.

George Appleton, *Journey for a Soul*, William Collins Sons and Co., 1976, page 51

Sooner or later suffering, misfortune, trouble come to every life. Some of it comes from our own ignorance, some from our own mistakes, some is a consequence of our own sin. But in almost every life there is a residue which seems inexplicable. Our Christian faith does not completely explain the mystery of suffering. It teaches us how to deal with suffering. It assures us that God does not will suffering, but he is in it, to redeem it and to turn it into good and blessing. Let us also remember that the perfect life was not exempt from suffering.

George Appleton, *Journey for a Soul*, William Collins Sons and Co., 1976, page 50

The logical mind can never cease from questioning the necessity of suffering. It is perhaps the greatest metaphysical mystery of all. But no answer can be given by logic itself. The answer can perhaps be felt in a new state, but the knowing comes with the doing, not before, and then remains incommunicable.

'Who then devised the torment? Love.' What can a man make of that in his ordinary self-willed state? But let him silence the self, the silence will be invaded by love, and for a fraction of a second he might know. A drop of that portion will strengthen him for long years.

Anon *(on T.S. Eliot's Four Quartets)*

Creative suffering—and this alone is real suffering—is positively non-resistant. It is a spiritual act, not a physical or mental reaction. And we cannot truly perform it until we wholly consent to the situation in which we find ourselves, however painful or disconcerting it may be, regarding it as the price we must pay for spiritual growth. By thus consenting to suffer we learn how to live by dying, how to surrender our existence to our being, until it is informed, more and more, by the eternal light of our essence.

To suffer thus is to pass through the defensive warfare of pain and pleasure to the pure joy in which we wholly accept and are accepted by life. And this is, also, to live from moment to moment in peaceful communion with death. For only by thus dying to what is resistant in ourselves can we enjoy the inexhaustible originality of life when it is left free to act in us from its true centre.

Hugh L'Anson Fausset, *Fruits of Silence*, Abelard-Schuman, 1963, page 197

Perhaps the main task of the minister is to prevent people from suffering for the wrong reasons. Many people suffer because of the false supposition on which they have based their lives. That supposition is that there should be no fear or loneliness, no confusion or doubt. But these sufferings can only be dealt with creatively when they are understood as wounds integral to our human condition. Therefore ministry is a very confronting service. It does not allow people to live with illusions or immortality and wholeness. It keeps reminding others that they are mortal and broken, but also that with the recognition of this condition, liberation starts.

A Christian community is therefore a healing community not because wounds are cured and pains are alleviated, but because wounds and pains become openings or occasions for a new vision. Mutual confession then becomes a mutual deepening of hope, and sharing weakness becomes a reminder to one and all of the coming strength.

Henri J.M. Nouwen, *The Wounded Healer*, Doubleday, 1979, page 93

One night a man had a dream. He dreamt he was walking along the beach with his Lord. Across the sky flashed scenes from his life. For each scene he noticed two sets of footprints in the sand, one belonging to him, the other to the Lord. When the last scene in his life flashed before him he looked back at the footprints on the sand. He noticed that many times along the path of his life there was only one set of footprints. He also noticed that it happened at the very lowest and saddest times of his life. This really bothered him, and he questioned the Lord about it. 'Lord, you said that, once I decided to follow you, you would walk with me all the way. But I've noticed that during the most difficult times in my life there is only one set of footprints. I don't understand why, in times when I needed you most, you would leave me.' The Lord replied, 'My precious child, I love you and would never leave you during your trials and sufferings; when you see only one set of footprints, it was then that I carried you.'

Margaret Fishback Powers, 'Footprints'

How can wounds become a source of healing? This is a question which requires careful consideration. For when we want to put our wounded selves in the service of others, we must consider the relationship between our professional and personal lives. On the one hand, no minister can keep his own experience of life hidden from those he wants to help... On the other hand, it would be very easy to misuse the concept of the wounded healer by defending a form of spiritual exhibitionism. A minister who talks in the pulpit about his own personal problems is of no help to his congregation, for no suffering human being is helped by someone who tells him that he has the same problems. Remarks such as, 'Don't worry because I suffer from the same depression, confusion and anxiety as you do,' help no one. This spiritual exhibitionism adds little faith to little faith and creates narrow-mindedness instead of new perspectives. Open wounds stink and do not heal.

Making one's own wounds a source of healing, therefore, does not call for a sharing of superficial personal pains but for a constant willingness to see one's own pain and suffering as rising from the depth of the human condition which all people share.

Henri J.M. Nouwen, *The Wounded Healer*, Doubleday, 1979, page 88

In page after page of the New Testament we are told that in so far as we share in Christ's sufferings we are made partakers here and now of His resurrection. This is the great and glorious paradox of Christian experience: that it is by dying that we live, that it is by sharing with Jesus the horror of His agony that we live with Him reigning indestructibly in peace. Once we are willing to see and feel the desert in which we live, the desert becomes fertile, bringing forth every tree whose fruit shall be for meat, and the leaf thereof for healing. Once we know that we are poor, the Kingdom of Heaven is ours. So when our lot is cast with somebody who is finding his cross, his desert, his poverty overwhelming, we are on holy ground. For it is precisely here that God is present to save, to save us as well as them. So our identification with the other person brings to our lives and to their's the power, the joy, the victory which is already ours and all mankind's in Christ Jesus our Lord.

That, I believe, is the message which our age is waiting to hear—a realistic recognition of suffering and evil in the universe, not trying apologetically to pretend that things are better than they are, together with the first-hand affirmation of this suffering and evil as the place where the Son of Man is glorified and with Him we and all mankind.

Harry Williams, *The True Wilderness*, Constable and Company, 1965, page 102

I should like this to be accepted as my confession.

There is no limit to human suffering. When one thinks: 'Now I have touched the bottom of the sea—now I can go no deeper,' one goes deeper. And so it is for ever. I thought last year in Italy, any shadow more would be death. But this year has been so much more terrible that I think with affection of the Casetta! Suffering is boundless, it is eternity. One pang is eternal torment. Physical suffering is—child's play. To have one's breast crushed by a great stone—one could laugh!

I do not want to die without leaving a record of my belief that suffering can be overcome. For I do believe it. What must one do? There is no question of what is called 'passing beyond it.' This is false.

One must *submit*. Do not resist. Take it. Be overwhelmed. Accept it fully. Make it *part of life*.

Everything in life that we really accept undergoes a change. So suffering must become Love. This is the mystery. This is what I must do. I must pass from personal love to greater love. I must give to the whole of life what I gave to one. The present agony will pass—if it doesn't kill. It won't last. Now I am like a man who has had his heart torn out—bear it—bear it! As in the physical world, so in the spiritual world, pain does not last for ever. It is only so terribly acute now. It is as though a ghastly accident had happened. If I can cease reliving all the shock and horror of it, cease going over it, I will get stronger.

Here, for a strange reason, rises the figure of Doctor Sorapure. He was a good man. He helped me not only to bear pain, but he suggested that perhaps bodily ill-health is necessary, is a repairing process, and he was always telling me to consider how man plays but a part in the history of the world. My simple kindly doctor was pure of heart as Tchehov was pure of heart. But for these ills one is one's own doctor. If 'suffering' is not a repairing process, I will make it so. I will learn the lesson it teaches. These are not idle words. These are not the consolations of the sick.

Life is a mystery. The fearful pain will fade. I must turn to work. I must put my agony into something, change it. 'Sorrow shall be changed into joy.' It is to lose oneself more utterly, to love more deeply, to feel oneself part of life,—not separate.

Oh Life! accept me—make me worthy—teach me.

Katherine Mansfield, *Journal of Katherine Mansfield*, edited by J. Middleton Murry, Constable and Co., 1927, page 163

TEMPTATION

*'Temptation'—tempting or being tempted, incitement especially to
wrongdoing; attractive thing or course of action; archaic putting to
the test.*

Whilst Chaplain *to* University College, London, I went through a testing time and was tempted to leave the ordained ministry. I looked around for openings elsewhere, and was attracted to student counselling, or some form of psychotherapy. Fortunately providence came to my rescue and took me on a three-week choir tour to America, organized by the London University Church of Christ the King. We began with a week in New York. At the first opportunity I nipped off to a certain bookshop, to buy a copy of *The Choice is Always Ours*, by Dorothy Berkley Phillips—a book which had been highly recommended to me. Initially I was doomed to disappointment. The shop had sold all its copies. However, the assistant went to the second-hand department and much to my delight found a copy there. Back at the hotel, I quickly realized I had been looking for this book for ten years. Between choir practices and performances I spent the rest of the tour with my nose in the book. By the time we landed at Gatwick, I was back on course with an outline of a new vision of faith.

The next few months were exciting as the vision unfolded. Altogether it has taken twenty years to work out the vision in depth and breadth. As I look back I value that initial period of testing and temptation. Without that I would never have come across *The Choice is Always Ours* which has changed the whole course of my life.

Vindicate me, O Lord, for I have walked in my integrity, and I have trusted in the Lord without wavering. Prove me, O Lord, and try me; test my heart and my mind. For thy steadfast love is before my eyes, and I walk in faithfulness to thee.

Psalm 26:1–3

For thou, O God, hast tested us; thou hast tried us as silver is tried. Thou didst bring us into the net; thou didst lay affliction on our loins; thou didst let men ride over our heads; we went through fire and through water; yet thou hast brought us forth to a spacious place.

Psalm 66:10–12

Watch and pray that you may not enter into temptation; the spirit indeed is willing, but the flesh is weak.

Mark 14:38

Blessed is the man who endures trial, for when he has stood the test he will receive the crown of life which God has promised to those who love him.

James 1:12

Every evil to which we do not succumb is a benefactor.

Ralph Waldo Emerson, 'Compensation', in *Essays*, Bernhard Tauchnitz, 1915, page 84

Subdue your appetites... and you've conquered human nature.

Charles Dickens, *Nicholas Nickleby*, The Gresham Publishing Company, 1904, page 36

No man is tempted so, but may o'recome,
If that he has a will to Masterdome.

Robert Herrick, 'Temptations', *The Poetical Works of Robert Herrick*, edited by F.W. Moorman, Oxford at the Clarendon Press, 1915, page 389

Ay me, how many perils doe enfold ·
The righteous man, to make him daily fall?
   Were not, that heavenly grace doth him uphold,
And stedfast truth acquit him out of all.

Edmund Spenser, *Spenser's Faerie Queene*, edited by J.C. Smith, Oxford at the Clarendon Press, 1964, page 95

The story of the Temptations is, of course, a parable of His spiritual wrestlings, told by Himself to His disciples. It represents the rejection, under three typical forms, of all existing conceptions of the Messianic task, which was to inaugurate the Kingdom of God.

William Temple, *Readings in St. John's Gospel*, First and Second Series, Macmillan and Co., 1947, page xxvi

In the very overcoming of temptation... we may draw out a hidden spiritual sweetness, as the bees suck honey from the thorn-bushes as well as from all other flowers. He who has not been tempted, knows nothing, nor lives as yet, say the wise man Solomon, and the holy teacher St. Bernard. We find more than a thousand testimonies in Scripture to the great profit of temptation; for it is the special sign of the love of God towards a man for him to be tempted and yet kept from falling; for thus he must and shall of a certainty receive the crown.

John Tauler, *The History and Life of the Reverend Doctor John Tauler*, translated by Susanna Winkworth, Smith, Elder and Company, 1857, page 404

There are but two things that we can do against temptations. The first is to be faithful to the light within us, in avoiding all exposure to temptation, which we are at liberty to avoid. I say, all that we are at liberty to avoid, because it does not always depend upon ourselves, whether we shall escape occasions of sin. Those that belong to the situation in life in which Providence has placed us, are not under our control. The other is to turn our eyes to God in moments of temptation, to throw ourselves immediately upon the protection of heaven, as a child, when in danger, flies to the arms of its parent.
   The habitual conviction of the Presence of God is the sovereign remedy; it supports, it consoles, it calms us. We must not be surprised that we are tempted. We are placed here to be proved by temptations. Everything is temptation to us.

F. de la M. Fénelon, *Letters and Reflections of Fénelon*, edited by B.W. Randolph, A.R. Mowbray and Co., 1906, page 93

The starting-point of all evil temptings lies in inconstancy of mind and small confidence in God. The slack man who abandons his fixed resolve is battered by all kinds of temptation like a ship with no steersman, driven to and fro by the waves.
   Iron is proved in the fire, and the upright man in temptation. We often do not know what we are capable of till temptation reveals what kind of persons we are.
   All the same, when temptation first appears, we must be especially alert, because it is easier to defeat the enemy if we do not allow him to set foot inside the door of the mind but meet him on the step as he knocks. As an ancient writer once said: Resist the beginnings—cure is provided too late. (Ovid, *Remedium Amoris*, l.91). For first of all, a thought simply crosses the mind, then it grows stronger and takes shape; then comes pleasure, an evil impulse, and consent. So our malignant enemy gradually obtains complete entry if we do not resist him at the start. If a man is slow in stirring himself up to resist, he will grow weaker every day, while the enemy forces grow stronger.

Thomas à Kempis, *The Imitation of Christ*, translated by Betty I. Knott, William Collins Sons and Co., 1979, page 54

The possibility of being tempted, of being allured and seduced, belongs to the dignity of the human person endowed with free will and committed to a struggle in a world of good and evil, of light and darkness, of reality and lies. Temptation is not possible where the freedom of the will has been removed by psychic disorder. It is reduced by the force of habit when actions are more and more determined by a habitual giving way to temptation. To be tempted therefore is a human condition. The more a person is truly human the more he or she will be tempted. Christ *par excellence* is the tempted one.

Temptation is not primarily an individual matter. It is primarily social. Humans are social beings and as such are tempted, for it is human society that is the object of temptation. It is human society that has been set on a course and has a history and a future to be aimed at and attained. The Church is above all a tempted society and all the more so as it freely undertakes a faithfulness to its vocation. The experience of Israel, pre-eminently of Christ and of his company, is the privilege of being tempted, of being allured into leaving the path—to go after power, influence, security, status and anything else that would relieve the necessity of the way of the cross, and succumb to the worship of the penultimate, or of plausible lies. Temptation can rightly be perceived in all the tragedy and grandeur of its possible outcome in the light of the primal conflict of good and evil. It is trivialized if it is reduced to the individual's possibility of lapses. Nevertheless, it is in the complexity of the temptation experience of persons that the corporate outcome of the temptations of the people of God and of human society is determined. Temptation assumes the reality of responsibility, personal and corporate.

In the Christian story the two temptations of Adam, who succumbed, and of Christ, who stood firm, are the two primary experiences into which we are drawn for defeat or victory. In each case there is an allurement of self-satisfaction, self-security and the avoidance of the limitation of the human condition. To resist temptation is to maintain direction, to keep to the path, and the more one is concerned with doing so the more one is aware of temptation. Self-justification presents itself with most temptations. As in the classic stories of the original temptation and that of Christ's, there are always at hand excellent reasons why we should give way. They keep their strength even though often they are contradictory...

Much has been said of the moral purpose of temptation as a testing ground for the soul, but an undue emphasis on this aspect can lead to a pursuit of spiritual perfection which obscures the corporate nature of the struggle. Certainly the awareness of the power and subtlety of temptation throws one back on God, and the first stages of dealing with temptation involve an awareness sometimes painfully acute of our own lack of resources and of our defencelessness against the assault. There is also the common condition of leaving ourselves open to being overcome through lack of attention and loss of purpose in unguarded moments.

We are tempted and we can also tempt, both other people and God. To tempt God means to put him to the test by asking for a manifestation of his presence to supply our needs and desires.

This is due to a failure of faith to endure the seeming absence of God, and to trust in God on the basis of past care. It can also take the form, as in the temptation of Christ, of presumptuously acting in the belief that God must always be at hand to save us from our own follies.

Christians find in the experience of temptation the only recourse is to the victory of Christ over temptation and to the belief that 'God will not allow us to be tempted above that which we are able, but will with the temptation provide a means of escape'.

Roland Walls, in *A Dictionary of Pastoral Care*, edited by Alastair V. Campbell, SPCK, 1987, page 277

THANKSGIVING

'Thanksgiving'—expression of gratitude, especially to God.

One of my favourite Biblical verses is 1 Thessalonians 5:18: 'Give thanks in all circumstances.' At the age of ten, when I joined the choir of Huddersfield Parish Church, Frank Woods, the Vicar (who later became Archbishop of Melbourne) taught us to say the General Thanksgiving, and these words have stayed with me ever since. Shortly afterwards I was taught a method of prayer, and thanksgiving became an important part of my prayer life. At night, immediately before going to sleep, I would say my prayers, and these always started on a note of thanksgiving. I would thank God for all the blessings of the day, for food, health, school, shelter, clothing, parents, family, friends, and anything else I could think of for which to give thanks. Often I would fall asleep on a note of thanksgiving, and I'm sure this improved the quality of sleep. As I have gone through life I have become increasingly thankful on a wider scale. For instance, how fortunate we are living in relative peace, when there is so much war and strife in other areas of the world. I am also grateful for many things we tend to take for granted, such as eyesight, hearing, speaking, eating, running and walking. Nowadays I am increasingly grateful for a job of work and an income at a time when there is so much unemployment and redundancy.

I have also learnt to give thanks for certain things which have not come to fruition in life. This has speeded up the process of acceptance and has opened up new areas of life. Such has been my experience of 'giving thanks in all circumstances.'

But I am like a green olive tree in the house of God. I trust in the steadfast love of God for ever and ever. I will thank thee for ever, because thou hast done it. I will proclaim thy name, for it is good, in the presence of the godly.

Psalm 52:8–9

It is good to give thanks to the Lord, to sing praises to thy name, O Most High; to declare thy steadfast love in the morning, and thy faithfulness by night, to the music of the lute and the harp, to the melody of the lyre. For thou, O Lord, hast made me glad by thy work; at the works of thy hands I sing for joy.

Psalm 92:1–4

Thanks be to God for his inexpressible gift!
2 Corinthians 9:15

... be filled with the Spirit... always and for everything giving thanks in the name of our Lord Jesus Christ to God the Father.

Ephesians 5:18, 20

Let us, therefore, be thankful for health and a competence; and above all, for a quiet conscience.

Izaak Walton, *The Complete Angler*, Macmillan and Co., 1906, page 172

To wake at dawn with a winged heart and give thanks for another day of loving.

Kahlil Gibran, *The Prophet*, William Heinemann, 1970, page 15

Gratitude is a fruit of great cultivation; you do not find it among gross people.

Samuel Johnson, *Boswell's Life of Johnson*, volume V, edited by G.B. Hill, revised by L.F. Powell, Oxford at the Clarendon Press, 1950, page 232

Let never day nor night unhallow'd pass,
But still remember what the Lord hath done.

William Shakespeare, *II King Henry VI*, II. i. 85

Cultivate the thankful spirit—it will be to thee a perpetual feast. There is, or ought to be, with us no such things as small mercies. A really thankful heart will extract motive for gratitude from everything, making the most even of scanty blessings.

Anon.

Thank God every morning, when you get up, that you have something to do that day which must be done, whether you like it or not. Being forced to work, and forced to do your best, will breed in you temperance and self-control, diligence and strength of will, cheerfulness and content and a hundred virtues which the idle man never knows.

Charles Kingsley, *Town and Country Sermons*, Macmillan and Co., 1868, page 99

It is probable that in most of us the spiritual life is impoverished and stunted because we give so little place to gratitude. It is more important to thank God for blessings received than to pray for them beforehand. For that forward-looking prayer, though right as an expression of dependence upon God, is still self-centred in part, at least, of its interest; there is something which we hope to gain by our prayer. But the backward-looking act of thanksgiving is quite free from this. In itself it is quite selfless. Thus it is akin to love. All our love to God is in response to His love for us; it never starts on our side. 'We love, because He first loved us.' (1 John 4:19).

William Temple, Readings in St. John's Gospel, First and Second Series, Macmillan and Co., 1947, page 189

Almighty God, Father of all mercies, We thine unworthy servants do give thee most humble and hearty thanks For all thy goodness and loving-kindness To us, and to all men. We bless thee for our creation, preservation, and all the blessings of this life; But above all, for thine inestimable love In the redemption of the world by our Lord Jesus Christ; For the means of grace, And for the hope of glory. And, we beseech thee, give us that due sense of all thy mercies, That our hearts may be unfeignedly thankful, And that we shew forth thy praise, Not only with our lips, but in our lives; By giving up ourselves to thy service, And by walking before thee in holiness and righteousness all our days; through Jesus Christ our Lord, to whom with thee and the Holy Ghost be all honour and glory, world within end. Amen.

The Book of Common Prayer, General Thanksgiving

If any one would tell you the shortest, surest way to all happiness, and all perfection, he must tell you to make a rule to yourself, to thank and praise God for everything that happens to you. For it is certain that whatever seeming calamity happens to you, if you thank and praise God for it, you turn it into a blessing. Could you therefore work miracles, you could not do more for yourself than by this thankful spirit; for it heals with a word speaking, and turns all that it touches into happiness ...

And although this be the highest temper that you can aim at, though it be the noblest sacrifice that the greatest saint can offer unto God, yet is it not tied to any time, or place, or great occasion, but is always in your power, and may be the exercise of every day. For the common events of every day are sufficient to discover and exercise this temper, and may plainly show you how far you are governed in all your actions by this thankful spirit.

William Law, A Serious Call to a Devout and Holy Life, J.M. Dent and Co., 1898, page 232

Only he who gives thanks for little things receives the big things. We prevent God from giving us the great spiritual gifts He has in store for us, because we do not give thanks for daily gifts. We think we dare not be satisfied with the small measure of spiritual knowledge, experience, and love that has been given to us, and that we must constantly be looking forward eagerly for the highest good. Then we deplore the fact that we lack the deep certainty, the strong faith, and the rich experience that God has given to others, and we consider this lament to be pious. We pray for the big things and forget to give thanks for the ordinary, small (and yet really not small) gifts. How can God entrust great things to one who will not thankfully receive from Him the little things? If we do not give thanks daily for the Christian fellowship in which we have been placed, even where there is no great experience, no discoverable riches, but much weakness, small faith, and difficulty; if on the contrary we only keep complaining to God that everything is so paltry and petty, so far from what we expected, then we hinder God from letting our fellowship grow according to the measure and riches which are there for us all in Jesus Christ.

Dietrich Bonhoeffer, Life Together, SCM Press, 1963, page 19

Inward devotion often brings forth gratitude; for none can thank and praise God so well as the inward and devout man. And it is just that we should thank and praise God, because He has created us as reasonable creatures, and has ordained and destined heaven and earth and the angels to our service and because He became man for our sins, and taught us, and lived for our sake, and showed us the way; and because He has ministered to us in humble raiment, and suffered an ignominious death for the love of us, and promised us His eternal kingdom and Himself also for our reward and for our wage. And He has spared us in our sins, and has forgiven us or will forgive us; and has poured His grace and His love into our souls, and will dwell and remain with us, and in us, throughout eternity. And He has visited us and will visit us all the days of our lives with His noble sacraments, according to the need of each, and has left us His Flesh and His Blood for food and drink, according to the desire and the hunger of each; and has set before us nature and the Scriptures and all creatures, as examples, and as a mirror, that therein we may look and learn how we may turn all our deeds to works of virtue; and has given us health and strength and power, and sometimes for our own good has sent us sickness; and in outward need has established inward peace and happiness in us; and has caused us to be called by Christian names and to have been born of Christian parents. For all these things we should thank God here on earth, that hereafter we may thank Him in eternity.

John of Ruysbroeck, *The Adornment of the Spiritual Marriage*, translated by C.A. Wynschenk Dom, edited by Evelyn Underhill, John M. Watkins, 1951, page 64

TIME

'Time'—duration; continued existence; progress of this viewed as affecting person or things, past, present, and future.

There are currently two refrains to be heard in college. One is—'I am too busy'—and the other is—'I don't have the time.' Last night I had a phone call from a former student who is now a general practitioner. His analysis of the situation is half the country is working too hard, and the other half is hardly working at all. How this situation came into being perplexes him. Is the love of money the root of all evil? Or have we lost a vision of eternity and ended up prisoners of time?

I greatly enjoyed working in Nigeria for six months, standing in for the regular priest. After a few days' briefing he returned to England with his wife and family for a period of long leave. As soon as I arrived up-country, in Ibadan, I became conscious of a different concept of time. Friendship was an important feature of everyday life. The quality of family life was on a different plane, where children, parents, grandparents and other members of the extended family were equally valued and respected. There was time for leisure, and I envied the ability of my cook to lie down after lunch and take a nap under a tree, a perfect picture of relaxation.

I received a shock on returning to England the following November. Stress and strain were everywhere visible, along with a noticeable decline in the quality and value of life. A new concept of time is urgently needed for the twenty-first century.

But I trust in thee, O Lord, I say, 'Thou art my God.' My times are in thy hand.

Psalm 31:14–15

For everything there is a season, and a time for every matter under heaven: a time to be born, and a time to die; a time to plant, and a time to pluck up what is planted; a time to kill, and a time to heal; a time to break down, and a time to build up; a time to weep, and a time to laugh; a time to mourn, and a time to dance; a time to cast away stones, and a time to gather stones together; a time to embrace, and a time to refrain from embracing; a time to seek, and a time to lose; a time to keep, and a time to cast away; a time to rend, and a time to sew; a time to keep silence, and a time to speak; a time to love, and a time to hate; a time for war, and a time for peace.

Ecclesiastes 3:1–8

We must work the works of him who sent me, while it is day; night comes, when no one can work. As long as I am in the world, I am the light of the world.

John 9:4–5

… we look not to the things that are seen but to the things that are unseen; for the things that are seen are transient, but the things that are unseen are eternal.

2 Corinthians 4:18

Time is the great physician.

Benjamin Disraeli, *Henrietta Temple*, John Lane, The Bodley Head, 1906, page 430

The more a person is able to direct his life consciously, the more he can use time for constructive benefits.

Rollo May, *Man's Search For Himself*, George Allen and Unwin, 1953, page 259

Both in thought and in feeling, even though time be real, to realise the unimportance of time is the gate of wisdom.

Bertrand Russell, *Mysticism and Logic and Other Essays*, Longmans, Green and Co., 1919, page 21

Dost thou love Life? then do not squander Time;
for that's the Stuff Life is made of.

Benjamin Franklin, *Poor Richard's Almanacks*, Richard Saunders, Paddington Press, 1976, page 132

If time is not to be either hoarded or pressed out of existence it must be spent as possessions are spent; not solely for personal use but for others.

Hubert van Zeller, *Considerations*, Sheed and Ward, 1974, page 60

Time lost is time when we have not lived a full human life, time unenriched by experience, creative endeavour, enjoyment and suffering.

Dietrich Bonhoeffer, *Letters and Papers from Prison*, William Collins Sons and Co., 1963, page 134

Man's greatest disease is the consciousness of transcience. Nothing is so likely to produce despair as the awareness of the contingency and vanity of life. A powerful and time-honoured cure is to seek a perception of eternity.

Peter Munz, *Problems of Religious Knowledge*, SCM Press, 1959, page 129

If the doors of perception were cleansed, every thing would appear to man as it is, infinite.
   For man has closed himself up, till he sees all things thro' narrow chinks of his cavern.

William Blake, *The Marriage of Heaven and Hell*, plate 14, 'A Memorable Fancy', in *The Complete Writings of William Blake*, edited by Geoffrey Keynes, Oxford University Press, 1974, page 154

Time ... is what keeps the light from reaching us. There is no greater obstacle to God than time. He means not time alone but temporalities: not only temporal things but temporal affections; not only temporal affections but the very taint and aroma of time.

Meister Eckhart, in Franz Pfeiffer, *Meister Eckhart*, volume I, translated by C. de B. Evans, John M. Watkins, 1956, page 237

What is Time? The shadow on the dial, the striking of the clock, the running of the sand, day and night, summer and winter, months, years, centuries—these are but arbitrary and outward signs, the measure of Time, not Time itself. Time is the Life of the soul. If not this, then tell me, what is Time?

Henry Wadsworth Longfellow, *Hyperion*, George Routledge and Sons, 1887, page 123

Everything is in the mind; time and beyond time, hell and heaven, death and life. The key to understanding is awareness in the now. But awareness of the moment is not a state that comes naturally to man. Usually, if at all, it comes and goes, elusively, with happiness or suffering; it comes with the creative urge, in abstract thought, through the love of God, or the love of creatures.

Anon. (on T.S. Eliot's Four Quartets)

The happy moments of life have continually escaped my grasp. I could never be reconciled to the fact that time is in a perpetual flux and that each moment is devoured by, and vanishes into, the succeeding one. This terrible aspect of time has caused me intense and unspeakable pain. To part with people, with things, with places, has been a source of agony to me as dreadful as death ...
   The problem of time may well be the fundamental problem of philosophy, especially of the philosophy of existence.

Nicolas Berdyaev, *Dream and Reality*, translated by Katharine Lampert, Geoffrey Bles, 1950, page 29

Once I said: 'They are not always happy who set their hearts on time.'

St. Paul says: 'Rejoice in the Lord always.' St. Augustine says: 'To rejoice always is to find your joy above or beyond time.' One Scripture says that three things there are, that prevent a person from knowing anything about God at all. The first is time, the second, materiality, the third, multiplicity. As long as these three are in me, God is not mine nor is his work being done... All these things must be got rid of before God comes in and then you may have them in a higher and better way, namely, that the many are made one in you.

Meister Eckhart, *Meister Eckhart*, translated by Raymond B. Blakney, Harper and Row, Publishers, 1941, page 151

The word 'time' is used in two ways in the New Testament. The first is in the sense of duration, time by the clock or the calendar, a purely impersonal, chronological idea. The second is judged by rightness, ripeness, achievement of purpose, which is determined by reference to God, in his goodwill, in his love and patience. Those who believe in God try to live their lives in chronological time with ever-deepening understanding of God's purpose, God's timelessness and their own keen eye for opportunity.

George Appleton, *Journey for a Soul*, William Collins Sons and Co., 1976, page 221

Take Time to THINK...
It is the source of power.
Take Time to PLAY...
It is the secret of perpetual youth.
Take Time to READ...
It is the fountain of wisdom.
Take Time to PRAY...
It is the greatest power on earth.
Take Time to LOVE and BE LOVED...
It is a God-given privilege.
Take Time to BE FRIENDLY...
It is the road to happiness.
Take Time to LAUGH...
It is the music of the soul.
Take Time to GIVE...
It is too short to be selfish.
Take Time to WORK...
It is the price of success.
Take Time to DO CHARITY...
It is the key to heaven.

Author unidentified, found on a bookmark

TRANSFORMATION

*'Transformation'—transforming, being transformed, as having
undergone a great transformation, change of character, disposition,
outward appearance.*

I remember visiting a patient in hospital, and before leaving, he asked me to pray for him. I did so, with the laying on of hands. This was repeated again in the following weeks. Soon there was a noticeable change in his features. Healing was taking place and he was being transformed. This is difficult to put into words but it was as though light was emanating through him, and he was becoming more peaceful and serene.

He was discharged from hospital, and after a period at home, took up the threads of life again. A year later his wife rang to say her husband had just died, but there was no need for me to visit her straight away. She went on to explain her husband had a serious haemorrhage, and was readmitted to the hospital. According to the nurses he should have been on pain killers, but declined them and said he was all right. He knew he was going to die, but was not afraid and maintained his peaceful demeanour. When she and her son visited him, both were aware of light radiating through him. When he died she went to her vicar, and asked for a special funeral. She said her husband had died in faith and she wanted the funeral to register this and be a joyful occasion. The vicar complied and the funeral was a celebration. When I saw her shortly afterwards, I was surprised by her appearance. She, too, had been transformed and her face was radiant.

> Look to him, and be radiant.
>
> Psalm 34:5

A man's wisdom makes his face shine, and the hardness of his countenance is changed.

Ecclesiastes 8:1

And after six days Jesus took with him Peter and James and John his brother, and led them up a high mountain apart. And he was transfigured before them, and his face shone like the sun, and his garments became white as light.

Matthew 17:1–2

And gazing at him, all who sat in the council saw that his face was like the face of an angel.

Acts 6:15

The central idea in Christianity is not justification, but transfiguration.

Nicolas Berdyaev, *Christian Existentialism*, selected and translated by Donald A. Lowrie, George Allen and Unwin, 1965, page 248

It is far more important that one's life should be perceived than that it should be transformed; for no sooner has it been perceived, than it transforms itself of its own accord.

Maurice Maeterlinck, *The Treasure of the Humble*, translated by Alfred Sutro, George Allen, 1897, page 185

Life should be a giving birth to the soul, the development of a higher mode of reality. The animal must be humanised: flesh must be made spirit; physiological activity must be transmuted into intellect and conscience, into reason, justice, and generosity, as the torch is transmuted into life and warmth. The blind, greedy selfish nature of man must put on beauty and nobleness. This heavenly alchemy is what justifies our presence on the earth; it is our mission and our glory.

Henri Frédéric Amiel, *Amiel's Journal*, translated by Mrs Humphry Ward, Macmillan and Co., 1918, page 285

The mainspring of life is in the heart. Joy is the vital air of the soul... To make anyone happy, then, is strictly to augment his store of being, to double the intensity of his life, to reveal him to himself, to ennoble him and transfigure him. Happiness does away with ugliness, and even makes the beauty of beauty. The man who doubts it, can never have watched the first gleams of tenderness dawning in the clear eyes of one who loves;—sunrise itself is a lesser marvel... Heroism, ecstasy, prayer, love, enthusiasm, weave a halo round the brow, for they are a setting free of the soul, which through them gains force to make its envelope transparent and shine through upon all around it... intense life and supreme joy can make the most simple mortal dazzlingly beautiful. Man, therefore, is never more truly man, than in these divine states.

Henri Frédéric Amiel, *Amiel's Journal*, translated by Mrs Humphry Ward, Macmillan and Co., 1918, page 104

God does not hurry over things: time is his, not mine. And I, little creature, man, have been called to be transformed into God by sharing his life. And what transforms me is the charity which he pours into my heart.

Love transforms me slowly into God.

But sin is still there, resisting this tranformation, knowing how to, and actually saying 'no' to love.

Living in our selfishness means stopping at human limits and preventing our transformation into Divine Love. And until I am transformed, sharing the life of God, I shall be of 'this earth' and not of 'that heaven.'

Baptism has raised me to the supernatural state, but we must grow in this state, and the purpose of life is that growth. And charity, or rather God's love, is what transforms us.

Carlo Carretto, *Letters from the Desert*, translated by Rose Mary Hancock, Darton, Longman and Todd, 1972, page 9

If the soul is transformed by participation in the divine nature so also must the body be and with the body the whole material universe.

God in Christ becomes what we are in order than we might become his 'body'.

This transformation of man by the divine life begins even now on earth, but it is only completed when man's body is also transformed by the resurrection.

When the resurrection takes place, then the whole universe is transformed together with the body of man. In this sense the whole universe becomes the 'Body of Christ'.

Man and nature will then become wholly penetrated by the divine consciousness and share alike in the bliss of the divine love which is poured out on the whole creation. Then we can say that the whole universe of insentient and sentient beings will become the 'Body of God'.

Bede Griffiths OSB, in *The Universal Christ*, edited by Peter Spink, Darton, Longman and Todd, 1990, page 27

The Transfiguration of Christ stands as a gateway to the saving events of the Gospel, and is as a mirror in which the Christian mystery is seen in its unity.

But the Transfiguration meant the taking of the whole conflict of the Lord's mission, just as it was, into the glory which gave meaning to it all.

Confronted as he is with a universe more than ever terrible in the blindness of its processes and the destructiveness of its potentialities mankind must be led to the Christian faith not as a panacea of progress nor as an other-worldly solution unrelated to history, but as a Gospel of Transfiguration. Such a Gospel both transcends the world and speaks to the immediate here-and-now. He who is transfigured is the Son of Man; and, as He discloses on mount Hermon another world, he reveals that no part of created things and no moment of created time lies outside the power of the Spirit, who is Lord, to change from glory into glory.

Michael Ramsey, *The Glory of God and the Transfiguration of Christ*, Longmans, Green and Co., 1949, pages 144, 146 and 147

The 'Our Father' takes the needs and the agonizing conflicts of mankind and lifts them into the realm of the Kingdom and the Father.

Transfiguration is indeed a central theme of Christianity, the transforming of sufferings and circumstances, of men and women with the vision of Christ before them and the Holy Spirit within them.

The transfiguring of suffering is attested in Christian life. Sometimes a person suffers greatly, and the suffering continues and does not disappear; but through nearness to Christ there is seen a courage, an outgoing love and sympathy, a power of prayer, a Christlikeness of a wonderful kind.

Circumstances are transfigured. Something blocks your path, some fact of life or person or obstacle which is utterly thwarting and frustrating. It seems impossible to remove it or ignore it or surmount it. But when it is seen in a larger context, and that context is Jesus crucified and risen, it is in a new orbit of relationships and while it remains, it remains differently. A phrase of St Paul seems to interpret the experience, when he contrasts our 'light affliction' with the 'exceeding weight of glory', the one belonging to time and the other to eternity. Such is the transforming of circumstances, not by their abolition but by the lifting of them into the orbit of a crucified and risen Jesus.

Michael Ramsey, in *Gateway to God*, edited by Lorna Kendall, Darton, Longman and Todd, 1988, page 56

'Justification is not only forgiveness of sins, but it is more, it is the actual healing and renewing of the inward man.' It must involve a real and radical transformation of man's nature—man must cease from sin and the love of it, he must receive from beyond himself a passion for goodness and a power to enable him to achieve it. The *passion* for goodness... is created through the vision of the God-Man who has suffered and died on the Cross for us, and has been glorified in absolute newness of life; and the *power* for moral holiness is supplied to the soul by the direct inflowing of divine Life-streams from this new Adam, who is henceforth the Head of the spiritual order of humanity, the Life-giving stream of life flowing out from the central divine Light and Fire, which is God Himself, into our hearts, by which we are inflamed with love for God and for our neighbour, and by which we see both what we lack in ourselves and what can abundantly supply our lack, so that we may be made ready for the Kingdom of God and be prepared to become children of God. 'Real faith... that is to say, justifying faith, can come from nothing external. It is a gracious and gratuitous gift of God through the Holy Spirit. It is an emanation from the eternal Life of God, and is of the same essence and substance as God Himself.' It is, in fact, the Eternal Word of God become vocal and vital within the inner region of our own lives.

Rufus M. Jones, *Spiritual Reformers in the 16th and 17th Centuries*, Macmillan and Co., 1914, page 77

TRINITY

'Trinity'—union of three persons (Father, Son, Holy Spirit) in one Godhead, the doctrine of the Trinity.

At theological college we were encouraged to understand the mystery of the Trinity by way of analogy. The analogy given was of a three-leaf clover—one main stem with three minor stems (plus leaves) emanating from it. After theological college, I remember coming across a priest who was convinced he had found a better analogy than this traditional one. He had broken a lightbulb and the filament fell out. He found this consisted of a single piece of wire with three smaller wires attached to it—hence an analogy of the Trinity. I prefer Harry Emerson Fosdick in his choice of a human analogy. He wrote there were three ways in which a man might know Beethoven. One man might know Beethoven the composer and be an expert student of his works. Another man might know Beethoven the performer, hearing him play and rejoicing in his skill. Another man might know Beethoven as an intimate friend, living in his home as a comrade and companion. Beethoven has three 'personae', he reveals himself in three characters—composer, performer, friend. But what if a man could know Beethoven all three ways at once! Then he would indeed know him, and the crown and consummation of that whole experience would be that Beethoven the composer and performer had become his friend. All in all I tend to think of our bodies as being temples of the Trinity. After baptism we should expect to find something of the Father, the Son and the Holy Spirit in the depths of our being, leading to an inner knowledge of the three members of the Trinity, yet still be living in the awe of its mystery.

Go therefore and make disciples of all nations, baptizing them in the name of the Father and of the Son and of the Holy Spirit.

Matthew 28:19

The grace of the Lord Jesus Christ and the love of God and the fellowship of the Holy Spirit.

2 Corinthians 13:14

For there are three that bear record in heaven, the Father, the Word, and the Holy Ghost: and these three are one.

1 John 5:7 (AV)

The three persons in the Godhead are Three in one sense, and One in another. We cannot tell how; and that is the mystery!

Samuel Johnson, *Boswell's Life of Johnson*, volume V, edited by G.B. Hill, revised by L.F. Powell, Oxford at the Clarendon Press, 1950, page 88

The Holy Spirit is the Person in the Trinity with whom we are most constantly in conscious contact.

William Temple, *Christian Faith and Life*, SCM Press, 1931, reissued 1963, page 94

Our doctrine, teaching, experience of the Church, must be, so to speak, in a comatose state, unless there be an active, experimental, loving knowledge of the Name of the Holy Trinity, which is the living power wherewith the Church is bound together by the Holy Ghost.

R.M. Benson, *Further Letters of Richard Meux Benson*, edited by W.H. Longridge, A.R. Mowbray and Co., 1920, page 220

We are enclosed in the Father, and we are enclosed in the Son, and we are enclosed in the Holy Ghost. And the Father is enclosed in us, and the Son is enclosed in us, and the Holy Ghost is enclosed in us; Almightiness, All-Wisdom, All-Goodness: one God, one Lord.

Lady Julian of Norwich, *Revelations of Divine Love*, edited by Grace Warrack, Methuen and Co., 1949, page 131

I believe in the Father, the Son, and the Holy Ghost, as three distinct Persons: but I believe that above our knowledge there is a point of coincidence and unity between them. What it is I do not know. That is the unrevealed part. The revealed part is that the Divine nature stands forth to us as separate, individual Father—separate, individual Son—and separate, individual Spirit; and that in the vast recess of the being of God, which transcends our knowledge, there is a coming together of the three.

Henry Ward Beecher, *Royal Truths*, Alexander Strahan and Co., 1862, page 45

My thoughtless youth was wing'd with vain desires,
My manhood, long misled by wandring fires,
Follow'd false lights; and when their glimps was gone,
My pride struck out new sparkles of her own.
 Such was I, such by nature still I am,
Be thine the glory, and be mine the shame.
 Good life be now my task: my doubts are done,
(What more could fright my faith, than Three in One?)

John Dryden, 'The Hind and the Panther,' in *The Poems of John Dryden*, volume II, edited by James Kinsley, Oxford at the Clarendon Press, 1958, page 452

There is in the Godhead a pure will of love, a pure act of self-giving by which he ceaselessly communicates himself.
 As the Father knows himself in the Son, and the Son in the Father, so Father and Son communicate in the love of the Holy Spirit.
 The Holy Spirit is this expression of love within the Godhead, the relation of love which unites the persons of the Godhead. Yet there is no 'duality' but an identity of nature and consciousness in the bliss of love.
 The bliss of the Godhead is the overflowing love of God, the mysterious communication of love within the Godhead.

Bede Griffiths OSB, in *The Universal Christ*, edited by Peter Spink, Darton, Longman and Todd, 1990, page 52

God is especially present in the hearts of His people, by His Holy Spirit: and indeed the hearts of holy men are temples in the truth of things, and in type and shadow they are heaven itself. For God reigns in the hearts of His servants: there is His Kingdom. The power of grace hath subdued all His enemies: there is His power. They serve Him night and day, and give Him thanks and praise: that is His glory. The temple itself is the heart of man; God dwells in our heart by faith, and Christ by His Spirit, and the Spirit by His purities: so that we are also cabinets of the mysterious Trinity and what is this short of heaven itself, but as infancy is short of manhood and letters of words.

Jeremy Taylor, *Holy Living*, abridged by Anne Lamb, The Langford Press, 1970, page 22

An ordinary simple Christian kneels down to say his prayers. He is trying to get into touch with God. But if he is a Christian he knows that what is prompting him to pray is also God; God, so to speak, inside him. But he also knows that all his real knowledge of God comes through Christ, the Man who was God—that Christ is standing beside him, helping him to pray, praying for him. You see what is happening. God is the thing to which he is—the goal he is trying to reach. God is also the road or bridge along which he is being pushed to that goal. So that the whole three-fold life of the three-personal Being is actually going on in that ordinary little bedroom where an ordinary man is saying his prayers. The man is being caught up into the highest kinds of life—what I call *Zoe* or spiritual life: he is being pulled into God, by God, while still remaining himself.

C.S. Lewis, Mere Christianity, William Collins Sons and Co., 1961, page 138

I am a dwelling-place.
    I am not alone.
    In the secret depths of my poor human substance is the presence of God.
    Not a God who is a solitary, but a God who is Trinity, a God who is love.
    A God who is Father, a God who is Son, a God who is Holy Spirit. But a God made One by love.
    And a God whose love enables me to become one with Him: 'that you may be one / as you, Father, are in me, and I in you; / I pray that they may be one in us / that the world may believe that you sent me' (John 17:21).
    I believe that no moment exists for man which is more important, more beautiful, more dramatic, more decisive, more radical than the moment when he becomes aware of—or, rather, 'lives'—this reality.
    When God reveals Himself in His nature as one and in His actions as three, Pentecost penetrates the depths of man's heart.

Carlo Carretto, The God Who Comes, translated by Rose Mary Hancock, Darton, Longman and Todd, 1974, page 87

God offers himself in three ways: his Spirit, his presence and his revelation of himself. And for these three offers he asks but one thing: 'If a man loves me.'
    The man who offers God his love becomes 'paradise on earth,' the Trinity is a reality within him; he is an instrument of the Spirit and of God's will.
    These three ways of God offering himself to us are possible because of the death and resurrection of Christ, and are a reality because of him.
    It is through prayer that we absorb this reality, for prayer establishes us in the deepest possible relationship with God. By our prayer we share the life of God.
    The Trinity becomes a reality in us as the guest of the soul. Earth becomes heaven. Why go on searching for God beyond the stars when he is so close to us, within us Heaven, this hidden place, is not some lofty vaulting construction, studded with stars. It is a land of intimate closeness, so near that we can speak to God, stay with him, worship him anywhere.
    His Holy Spirit is in us.

Carlo Carretto, Letters from the Desert, translated by Rose Mary Hancock, Darton, Longman and Todd, 1972, page 52

How wonderful is it that God by being Love should prepare a Redeemer to die for us? But how much more wonderful, that by this means Himself should be, and be God by being Love! By this means also he refineth our nature, and enableth us to purge out the poison and the filthy plague of Sin. For love is so amiable and desirable to the Soul that it cannot be resisted. Love is the Spirit of God. In Himself it is the Father, or else the Son, for the Father is in the Son, and the Son is in the Father: In us it is the Holy Ghost. The Love of God being seen, being God in us: Purifying, illuminating, strengthening, and comforting the soul of the seer. For God by shewing communicateth Himself to men and angels. And when he dwelleth in the soul, dwelleth in the sight. And when He dwelleth in the sight achieving all that love can do for such a soul. And thus the world serveth you as it is a mirror wherein you contemplate the Blessed Trinity. For it plainly sheweth that God is Love, and in His being Love you see the unity of the Blessed Trinity, and a glorious Trinity in the Blessed Unity.

Thomas Traherne, Centuries, The Faith Press, 1969, page 78

TRUST

*'Trust'—firm belief in the honesty, veracity, justice, strength, etc., of
a person or thing—as our trust is in God.*

This topic contains another of my favourite biblical verses: 'I send you out as sheep in the midst of wolves; so be wise as serpents and innocent as doves.' This verse reminds me of an experience I had whilst out in what was then known as 'Malaya'. I was driving a Land Rover with three Gurkhas in the back. We were travelling up the main road in a northerly direction. There was very little traffic on the road on that particular day. Ahead we saw what we thought was a mirage, caused by the heat of the day, but it turned out to be a huge snake crossing the road. Shouts of excitement came from the back of the Land Rover. 'Kill it, Saheb,' came a chorus in Gurkhali behind me. Spurred on by this encouragement, I put my foot hard down on the accelerator and aimed for the centre of the snake. As we sped towards it, I braced myself up for the impact. Nothing happened. Suddenly I was aware of a flash by the side window—there was the head of the snake staring in at me. Fortunately we were going too fast for the snake to strike back.

In retrospect the snake had been very cunning. It had waited until the very last moment, and then deftly moved out of the way of the speeding Land Rover, into a retaliatory position.

This story sometimes comes out in a reflection group. Trust is extremely important, but Christ was right when he sent out his disciples 'as sheep in the midst of wolves' with the injunction: 'so be wise as serpents and innocent as doves'.

Into thy hand I commit my spirit; thou hast redeemed me, O Lord, faithful God.

Psalm 31:5

Thou dost keep him in perfect peace, whose mind is stayed on thee, because he trusts in thee.

Isaiah 26:3

I send you out as sheep in the midst of wolves; so be wise as serpents and innocent as doves.

Matthew 10:16

Train yourself in godliness; for while bodily training is of some value, godliness is of value in every way, as it holds promise for the present life and also for the life to come. The saying is sure and worthy of full acceptance. For to this end we toil and strive, because we have set our hope on the living God, who is the Saviour of all men, especially of those who believe.

1 Timothy 4:7–10

God provides for him that trusteth.

George Herbert, 'Outlandish Proverbs,' number 728, in *The Works of George Herbert*, edited by F.E. Hutchinson, Oxford at the Clarendon Press, 1972, page 345

Trust men, and they will be true to you; treat them greatly, and they will show themselves great, though they make an exception in your favour to all their rules of trade.

Ralph Waldo Emerson, in *The Works of Ralph Waldo Emerson*, volume I, *Essays and Representative Men*, edited by George Sampson, George Bell and Sons, 1906, page 128

We can trust Him wholly with His world. We can trust Him with ourselves. We are sure He cares far more to make the best of us, and to do the most through us, than we have ever cared ourselves. He is ever trying to make us understand that He yearns to be to us more than aught in the universe besides. That He really wants us, and needs us, is the wonder and strength of our life.

A.W. Robinson, *The Personal Life of the Clergy*, Longmans, Green and Co., 1902, page 157

Trust, which is always on the way to being love, must be spontaneous or non-existent. It grows of itself within our hearts as we come to appreciate the character and wisdom of someone whose record we know; and it grows most surely when we come to know personally in actual companionship someone who, the more we know him, inspires in us more trust and confidence in his character and wisdom.

William Temple, *The Hope of a New World*, SCM Press, 1940, page 28

What is very startling to the philosopher whose mental habit is controlled by scientific interests is the abundance of testimony given by those who have had intimate experience of men's spiritual life to the conviction that in the early stages prayer receives literal fulfilment with great frequency; that later on this becomes less frequent, until it seems almost to cease, as though God at first gives encouragement of the most obvious kind and later withdraws this in order to evoke a deeper trust.

William Temple, *Nature, Man and God*, Macmillan and Co., 1934, page 297

'Abraham trusted in God' (Gen.xv.6). To trust in God alone and join no other with Him is no easy matter, by reason of our kinship with our yokefellow, mortality, which works upon us to keep our trust placed in riches and repute and office and friends and health and strength and many other things. To purge away each of these, to distrust created being, which in itself is wholly unworthy of trust, to trust in God, and in Him alone, even as He alone is truly worthy of trust—this is a task for a great and celestial understanding which has ceased to be ensnared by aught of the things that surround us.

Philo, in *Three Jewish Philosophers*, edited by Hans Lewy, Harper and Row, Publishers, 1945, page 89

In all your affairs rely wholly on God's Providence... Imitate little children, who, as they with one hand hold fast to their father, with the other gather strawberries or blackberries along the hedges. So too, as you gather and handle the goods of this world with one hand, you must with the other always hold fast the hand of your heavenly Father, turning yourself towards Him from time to time to see if your actions or occupations be pleasing to Him. Above all things, take heed that you never leave His hand and His protection or think to gather more or to gain some advantage. For should He forsake you, you will not be able to go a step further without falling to the ground.

St Francis de Sales, *Introduction to the Devout Life*, translated and edited by John K. Ryan, Longmans, Green and Co., 1962, page 147

If the universe was created by God and human life planned by God, then we should see principles of goodness and wisdom embedded in both. The writer of the book of Genesis pictures God looking at his creation and finding it good. He is emphatic that man is akin to God, made in the divine image. He is conscious of man's ignorance, foolishness and wilfulness, but never does he think of man as being so depraved as not to be able to hear God speaking within himself. There may be a lot of original sin but there is also original goodness to which God and men can appeal. In spite of occasional natural catastrophes, for most of the time we think life is good. So we can trust life, both empirically from experience, and also because we trust the Creator.

George Appleton, *Journey for a Soul*, William Collins Sons and Co., 1976, page 84

The whole world is yours... the whole life, present and future, not parts of it. These important words speak of scientific knowledge and its passion, artistic beauty and its excitement, politics and their use of power, eating and drinking and their joy, sexual love and its ecstasy, family life and its warmth and friendship with its intimacy, justice with its clarity, nature with its might and restfulness, the man-made world above nature, the technical world and its fascination, philosophy with its humility—daring only to call itself love of wisdom—and its profundity— daring to ask ultimate questions. In all of these things is wisdom of this world and power of this world and all these things are ours. They belong to us and we belong to them; we create them and they fulfill us.

Paul Tillich, *The New Being*, SCM Press, 1956, page 111

It would be sentimental folly to expect men to trust one another when they obviously cannot be trusted. But at least they can learn to trust God. They can bring themselves to see that the mysterious power of God can... protect men unaccountably against themselves, and that He can always turn evil into good... If they can trust and love God, who is infinitely wise and who rules the lives of men, permitting them to use their freedom even to the point of almost incredible abuse, they can love men who are evil... If we can love the men we cannot trust... and if we can to some extent share the burden of their sin by identifying ourselves with them, then perhaps there is some hope of a kind of peace on earth, based not on the wisdom and the manipulations of men but on the inscrutable mercy of God.

Thomas Merton, *New Seeds of Contemplation*, Burns and Oates, 1977, page 91

We must submit our whole being to the discipline of the desert and not seek to avoid it. Like the Israelites of old we must press forward along a way we know not, trusting ourselves to God's guidance, relying on him to supply all our needs.

Alas! Like them we can grow weary of the wilderness, but let us not lose hope. Let us leave it to God to give us sufficient pleasure and comfort to sustain us. He will send us manna and make sweet water spring from the rock in due time, when we really need it.

We learn by experience that there is beauty and tenderness even in the desert, but it must be of God's providing. Let us accept with humble love all the comforts both material and spiritual which he provides for us but let us not seek them for ourselves.

Oftentimes the silence and bleakness of the desert seems to penetrate into the depths of our souls, a desert of loneliness and aridity. We must not try to evade this suffering; just trust in God to see us through, putting a seal upon our lips, letting the silent peace of the desert enfold us.

Ruth Burrows, in *The Watchful Heart*, edited by Elizabeth Ruth Obbard, Darton, Longman and Todd, 1988, page 18

TRUTH

'Truth'—quality or state of being true or truthful.

I wonder if I might mention again the Genesis story of the creation of man. In the divine inbreathing we are born with a seed or spark of *truth* in the depths of our being. The consequences of this were fully worked out in the life of our Lord, so much so he became 'truth'—hence his statement: 'I am the truth.' The writer of St John's Gospel acknowledged this when he wrote in the prologue: 'And the Word became flesh and dwelt among us, full of grace and truth.'

Jesus also knew this inner truth was part of man's heritage, and promised his disciples— 'you will know the truth, and the truth will make you free'. Indeed an aspect of his role was to consecrate his disciples in truth. This comes out in his prayer to the Father: 'As thou didst send me into the world, so I have sent them into the world. And for their sake I consecrate myself, that they also may be consecrated in truth.' Furthermore he saw clearly the Holy Spirit had a vital function as regards truth: 'When the Spirit of truth comes, he will guide you into all the truth.'

Paul realized what Christ had experienced, we can all in some measure also experience. Hence he used this intriguing phrase of his own experience: 'As the truth of Christ is in me...' (Romans 11:10). A modern writer, Rufus Jones, concisely sums all this up in these marvellous words: 'To find Truth... we must break through the outward shell of words and phrases which house it, and by *experience and practice* discover the "inward beauty, life and loveliness of Truth."'

Now I know that you are a man of God, and that the word of the Lord in your mouth is truth.

1 Kings 17:24

Consider how I love thy precepts! Preserve my life according to thy steadfast love. The sum of thy word is truth.

Psalm 119:159–160

But he who does what is true comes to the light, that it may be clearly seen that his deeds have been wrought in God.

John 3:21

You will know the truth, and the truth will make you free.

John 8:32

Rather than love, than money, than fame, give me truth.

Henry David Thoreau, *Walden*, The New American Library of World Literature, Inc., 1960, page 219

The friend of Truth obeys not the multitude *but the Truth*.

Rufus M. Jones, *Spiritual Reformers in the 16th and 17th Centuries*, Macmillan and Co., 1914, page 90

Say not, 'I have found the truth,' but rather, 'I have found a truth.'

Kahlil Gibran, *The Prophet*, William Heinemann, 1970, page 66

Truth is given, not to be contemplated, but to be done. Life is an action—not a thought.

F.W. Robertson, *Sermons*, First Series, Kegan Paul, Trench, Trubner and Co., 1893, page 289

But it is not enough to possess a truth; it is essential that the truth should possess us.

Maurice Maeterlinck, *The Treasure of the Humble*, translated by Alfred Sutro, George Allen, 1897, page 187

God offers to every mind its choice between truth and repose. Take which you please—you can never have both.

Ralph Waldo Emerson, 'Intellect', in *Essays*, Bernhard Tauchnitz, 1915, page 198

'I cannot hear what you say for listening to what you are.'
 Teaching and preaching are both 'truth through personality.'

William Barclay, *The Gospel of Luke*, The Saint Andrew Press, 1964, page 79

Truth lies in character. Christ did not simply *speak* truth: He *was* truth: true through and through; for truth is a thing, not of words, but of Life and Being.

F.W. Robertson, *Sermons*, First Series, Kegan Paul, Trench, Trubner and Co., 1893, page 286

The gospel story, whether historically true or not, could still be regarded as a parable: that is, as a working model, cast in fictitious form, of the way things really are.

Sydney Carter, *Dance in the Dark*, William Collins Sons and Co., 1980, page 26

The highest thing a man is capable of is to make an eternal truth true... Did Christ ever undertake to prove some truth or another, or to prove the truth? No, but He made the truth true...

Søren Kierkegaard, *Christian Discourses*, translated by Walter Lowrie, Princeton University Press, 1974, page 104

The inquiry of truth, which is the love-making, or wooing of it, the knowledge of truth, which is the presence of it, and the belief of truth, which is the enjoying of it, is the sovereign good of human nature.

Francis Bacon, *The Moral and Historical Works of Francis Bacon*, Henry G. Bohn, 1852, page 2

When man is, with his whole nature, loving and willing the truth, he is then a live truth. But this he has not originated in himself. He has seen it and striven for it, but not originated it. The one originating, living, visible truth, embracing all truths in all relations, is Jesus Christ. He is true; he is the live Truth.

George Macdonald, *Unspoken Sermons*, Third Series, Longmans, Green and Co., 1889, page 79

When a man is true, if he were in hell he could not be miserable. He is right with himself because right with him whence he came. To be right with God is to be right with the universe; one with the power, the love, the will of the mighty Father, the cherisher of joy, the lord of laughter, whose are all glories, all hopes, who loves everything, and hates nothing but self-ishness.

George Macdonald, *Unspoken Sermons*, Third Series, Longmans, Green and Co., 1889, page 81

Truth is the perfect correlation of mind and reality; and this is actualised in the Lord's Person. If the Gospel is true and God is, as the Bible declares, a Living God, the ultimate truth is not a system of propositions grasped by a perfect intelligence, but is a Personal Being apprehended in the only way in which persons are ever fully apprehended, that is, by love.

William Temple, *Readings in St. John's Gospel*, First and Second Series, Macmillan and Co., 1947, page 230

From my youth I have held the conviction that all religious truth must in the end be capable of being grasped as something that stands to reason. I, therefore, believe that Christianity, in the contest with philosophy and with other religions, should not ask for exceptional treatment, but should be in the thick of the battle of ideas, relying solely on the power of its own inherent truth.

Albert Schweitzer, *Christianity and the Religions of the World*, translated by Joanna Powers, George Allen and Unwin, 1924, page 18

To the question, 'what is a primrose?' several valid answers may be given. One person says:
'A primrose by the river's brim
A yellow primrose was to him,
And it was nothing more.'
Just that, and no more. Another person, the scientist, says 'a primrose is a delicately balanced biochemical mechanism, requiring potash, phosphates, nitrogen and water in definite propor-tions.' A third person says 'a primrose is God's promise of spring.'
All three descriptions are correct.

C.A. Coulson, *Science and Christian Belief*, Oxford University Press, 1955, page 70

There is an Indian saying: 'The bee came to suck the honey, but his feet got stuck in it.' We can only avoid the fate of the bee if we regard our lives as a perpetual search for meaning, an exercise in discrimination between the real and the unreal. In that spirit, we shall welcome all kinds of experience, both pleasant and painful, and it will never harm us. For the Truth lies hidden everywhere, within every experience and every object of the universe. Everything that happens to us, no matter how seemingly trivial, throughout the day, offers some tiny clue which could lead us toward wider spiritual knowledge and eventual liberation.

How to Know God, The Yoga Aphorisms of Patangali, translated by Swami Prabhavananda and Christopher Isherwood, The New American Library, 1969, page 91

The more we try the clearer becomes our insight, and the more we use our thinking faculties the quicker they become in their power of grasping points of Truth. Truths are not things we can pick up without taking trouble to hunt for them. And when we find a truth we really possess it, because it is bound to our heart by the process by which we reached it... through trouble, difficulty, or sorrow... a man binds it into his life. But what is easily come by is easily lost. Every bit of truth that comes into a man's heart burns in him and forces its way out, either in his actions or in his words. Truth is like a lighted lamp in that it cannot be hidden away in the darkness because it carries its own light.

Edward Wilson, in *The Faith of Edward Wilson*, George Seaver, John Murray, 1949, page 17

Truth is within ourselves; it takes no rise
From outward things, whate'er you may believe.
There is an inmost centre in us all,

Where truth abides in fulness; and around,
Wall upon wall, the gross flesh hems it in,
This perfect, clear perception—which is truth.
   A baffling and perverting carnal mesh
Binds it, and makes all error: and to KNOW
Rather consists in opening out a way
Whence the imprisoned splendour may escape,
Than in effecting entry for a light
Supposed to be without.

Robert Browning, *Paracelsus*, I, in *The Poetical Works of Robert Browning*, volume I, Smith, Elder and Co. 1899, page 26

What is the essential truth signified by the organization, doctrine and rituals of the Church?

   It is the presence of the divine life among men, the mystery of being which is the ground of all religion and of all existence manifesting itself in the presence of Jesus Christ.

   In this revelation the mystery of being reveals itself as a mystery of love, of an eternal love ever rising from the depths of being in the Godhead and manifesting itself in the total self-giving of Jesus on the cross.

   The Church has no other purpose than to communicate this love, to create a community of love, to unite all men in the eternal ground of being which is present in the heart of every man.

Bede Griffiths OSB, in *The Universal Christ*, edited by Peter Spink, Darton, Longman and Todd, 1990, page 22

Not only in Jesus Christ does *the Spirit of Truth* touch the hearts of men. He spoke to and through Plato, as the early Christian Fathers fully recognised; and has spoken through many a seer, poet and prophet both within and outside the Canon of Holy Scripture. Wherever there is response in the hearts of men to the manifested glory of God, whether that manifestation be in nature or in history, there the Spirit of Truth is at work. He inspires all Science and all Art, and speaks in the conscience of the heathen child. Yet it is also true that the Son sends Him. For only in the Word made flesh is the glory of God truly displayed. *We beheld his glory* (1.14); that is the condition of receiving the Holy Spirit in His Power. He 'proceedeth from the Father and (or through) the Son.'

William Temple, *Readings in St. John's Gospel*, First and Second Series, Macmillan and Co., 1947, page 275

How do we attain to intimacy with God, or rather, how do we enter into the intimacy offered?

   We must be certain that no wooing is necessary. We do not have to find ways of attracting the divine partner, of getting him to notice us. Here is someone who is love itself and the very fount of our existence, enfolding us, inviting us to receive him, drawing us to his heart.

   Scripture and mystical writers have used the different modes of love and friendship—parent/child, husband/wife, brother, friend—to tell us something of the reality of God's love and desire for us. Each is inadequate. All together they are inadequate.

   It is not easy to speak properly of a deep human relationship; how much more so when one of the partners is God! And even if one were able, through profound experience and intensive thought and effort, to give what seems as close approximation to the truth as possible, its understanding depends on the heart of the recipient.

   Truth must find an echo in the one who hears it if it is to be recognized. Put it another way: a heart must really be listening, really wanting the truth, really wanting God.

Ruth Burrows, in *The Watchful Heart*, edited by Elizabeth Ruth Obbard, Darton, Longman and Todd, 1988, page 4

At every stage of religious development man may rebel, if not without violence to his own nature, yet without absurdity. He can close his spiritual eyes against the Numinous, if he is prepared to part company with half the great poets and prophets of his race, with his own childhood, with the richness and depth of uninhibited experience. He can regard the moral law as an illusion, and so cut himself off from the common ground of humanity. He can refuse to identify the Numinous with the righteous, and remain a barbarian, worshipping sexuality, or the dead, or the life-force, or the future. But the cost is heavy. And when we come to the last step of all, the historical Incarnation, the assurance is strongest of all. The story is strangely like many myths which have haunted religion from the first, and yet it is not like them. It is not transparent to the reason: we could not have invented it ourselves. It has not the suspicious *a priori* lucidity of Pantheism or of Newtonian physics... If any message from the core of reality ever were to reach us, we should expect to find in it just that unexpectedness, that wilful, dramatic anfractuosity which we find in the Christian faith. It has the master touch—the rough, male taste of reality, not made by us, or, indeed, for us, but hitting us in the face.

C.S. Lewis, The Problem of Pain, The Centenary Press, 1941, page 12

UNITY

*'Unity'—oneness, being one or single or individual, being
formed of parts that constitute a whole, due interconnexion
and coherence of parts.*

The church I looked after in Nigeria for six months, whilst the regular priest came back to England on furlough, was called All Saints' Church, Jericho, Ibadan. In the 1960s a scheme was under way in Nigeria to unite the Christian churches. All Saints' Church pioneered the way and came into being as a united church—made up of Anglicans, Methodists and Presbyterians. Unfortunately the scheme for unity broke down at the last minute, and All Saints' Church found itself out on a limb. For six months I had the enormous privilege of being in charge of this unique church.

The committee was impressive. Members included a Nigerian prince, two bank managers, two high ranking civil servants, two headmistresses, two professors, a Lawyer of the Supreme Court, and a lady in charge of Wolsey Hall, Oxford (Ibadan branch). The diversity of background led to a very rich mix and created a dynamic and stimulating atmosphere.

Every Sunday morning we had a service of holy communion (Anglican). This was always an Anglican form of service. At 10.30 a.m. we had a morning service (Methodist) and at 6.00 p.m. an evening service (Presbyterian). With these two services we would ring the changes, so there was always variety.

I experienced 'unity' in those six months, and regard my time at All Saints' Church, Jericho, Ibadan, a vintage period of ministry.

Behold, how good and pleasant it is when brothers dwell in unity!
Psalm 133:1

Come, let us join ourselves to the Lord in an everlasting covenant which will never be forgotten.
Jeremiah 50:5

May the God of steadfastness and encouragement grant you to live in such harmony with one another, in accord with Christ Jesus, that together you may with one voice glorify the God and Father of our Lord Jesus Christ. Welcome one another, therefore, as Christ has welcomed you, for the glory of God.

Romans 15:5–7

There is one body and one Spirit, just as you were called to the one hope that belongs to your call, one Lord, one faith, one baptism, one God and Father of us all, who is above all and through all and in all.

Ephesians 4:4–6

We wait with thine apostles for the Holy Spirit.
O qualify us for his coming by giving us with the apostles unity in ourselves, unity in thy Church, unity with thee, that as unity tied God and man together, so it may unite thy Holy Spirit to us, and make him delight to dwell within us.

Make us to remember that as unity is the best preparation, so division is the greatest opposition to thy Holy Dove's coming upon us.

Thomas Traherne, in *Landscapes of Glory*, edited by A.M. Allchin, Darton, Longman and Todd, 1989, page 34

The unity of Christendom which alone we can desire and rationally seek to promote is not the unity of a world-wide centralised government, but unity of spirit based on a common faith and a common desire to see the Kingdom of God, which is 'righteousness and peace and joy in the Holy Ghost,' established on earth. There will be diversities of gifts, but the same Spirit; differences of ecclesiastical organisation, but the same Lord. We must not expect that India, China, and Japan, if they ever adopt Christianity, will be European Christians. They have their ancient traditions, unlike the Graeco-Roman traditions which formed Catholicism; they must build their national churches upon these, in complete independence.

The sole bond of a spiritually united Christendom is the Person and the Gospel of the Divine Founder.

W.R. Inge, *Lay Thoughts of a Dean*, G.P. Putnam's Sons, 1926, page 300

All our conflicts arise because we stop at a certain level. Christians stop at the Christian religion, Muslims at Islam, and if you are a Hindu you stop at your own symbolism. Each one feels himself separate from the others. Only when you go beyond these distinctions and are open to the reality beyond, can you overcome these conflicts.

The ultimate reality includes all the differences in the world. It does not abolish them. You and I are all contained in the Absolute.

We see everything separated, but if you have the vision of reality you perceive all the differences in that total unity. We have to get beyond limited mental perceptions and even parapsychological perceptions to a pure spiritual wisdom, a vision where the whole universe is seen as a total unity in the Absolute Godhead, and we ourselves as one in this Absolute, each a unique manifestation of the one eternal reality.

Bede Griffiths OSB, in *The Universal Christ*, edited by Peter Spink, Darton, Longman and Todd, 1990, page 50

The time may come—and I hope will come—when the immense majority of English Christians may be content to worship under the same roof; but assuredly we shall not live to see it, and overtures to the Protestant bodies seem to me, I regret to say, quite premature.

Reunion then, in the same sense of fusion with any other Church or Churches, is not a question of practical politics. But let us remember that all good Christians in England are our brethren and have a claim to individual recognition as good Christians. I entirely agree with the words—I forget who uttered them—that the idea of a common Christianity, behind all denominational loyalties, is one which we should steadily hold before ourselves, and encourage by every means in our power. Let us further remember, with a view to hastening the happy healing of our unhappy divisions—which we pray and hope for, but shall not live to see—how very partial, how very external, almost superficial, those divisions are. Has the Church of Christ ever been divided in the chambers where men shut their door and pray to their Father who is in secret? Do we not all pray the same prayers—at least the same prayer of prayers? Has it ever been divided in the service of praise and thanksgiving? How many of us know or care which hymns in 'Ancient and Modern' were written by Roman Catholics, which by Anglicans, and which by Dissenters? Has it ever been divided in the shelves where we keep our books of devotion? The *Imitation of Christ*, Taylor's *Holy Living and Dying*, *The Counsels of Father John Sergieff of Cronstadt*, Penn's *No Cross no Crown* jostle each other near our bedhead, and do not quarrel. The mystics all tell the same tale. They have climbed the same mountain, and their witness agrees together. All ages, denominations, and languages are blended harmoniously on that Jacob's ladder which scales the heavens in far other fashion than is ever dreamed of by the builders of Babel. Has Christendom ever been divided in the world of letters? Do not Biblical scholars, historians, philosophers forget their denominational differences, and work side by side in the cause of truth? Lastly, are we divided in philanthropy and social service? Do we not unite, naturally and spontaneously, in the warfare against vice, crime, and injustice? These are no slight bonds of union. They embrace by far the greater part of our life as children of God and brethren to each other. Is it not much that we already have in common? Let us not magnify the institutional barriers which part us at public worship, but at no other times. If the Church of the future will, we hope, be co-extensive with all who love the Lord Jesus Christ in incorruptness; if this is the goal towards which we are moving, however slowly; if this is the idea of the Church which already exists in the mind of God as a fact; let us press forward thither in heart and mind;

let us anticipate that which will surely come to pass, and which, when it has come to pass, will make what is now the present appear in quite a new light; let us keep that 'ideal of a Christian Church' ever before us, gazing upon it with that eye of faith which gives substance to things hoped for, and conviction to things not seen.

W.R. Inge, *The Church and the Age*, Longmans, Green and Co., 1912, page 63

VOCATION

*'Vocation'—divine call to, or sense of fitness for a career
or occupation; employment, trade, profession.*

There was a porter who worked at the lodge of University College (Oxford) called Richard. In his spare time he played bass guitar in a group which led the worship in a local church. This was a part of his vocation. He loved music and one of his heroes was Buddy Holly. He knew each member of Buddy Holly's group—The Crickets—personally.

Another part of his vocation was his work at University College. He took a great interest in undergraduates and knew them all by name. He was friendly and helpful, with a great capacity for kindness. Above all he was a good listener. Many a quiet hour on the evening shift was spent listening to undergraduates who came to chat and pass the time of day. Tragically he died at the early age of 48—of a heart attack—whilst on duty in the lodge.

The college community was shocked and grief-stricken. His funeral took place in the college chapel. We knew his many friends and acquaintances would come to this service and were concerned as the chapel only seats 120. Arrangements were made for an overflow in the dining hall. Even so, 300 people crammed into the chapel to pay their last respects to Richard. He was given a good send off—to the music of Buddy Holly and The Crickets. Apparently Richard had spent the happiest years of his life at University College. Living out one's vocation can be fun—and fulfilling.

I cry to God Most High, to God who fulfils his purpose for me.

Psalm 57:2

Before I formed you in the womb I knew you, and before you were born I consecrated you; I appointed you a prophet to the nations.

Jeremiah 1:5

You did not choose me, but I chose you and appointed you that you should go and bear fruit and that your fruit should abide.

John 15:16

Forgetting what lies behind and straining forward to what lies ahead, I press on toward the goal for the prize of the upward call of God in Christ Jesus.

Philippians 3:13–14

Do not despise your situation; in it you must act, suffer, and conquer. From every point on earth we are equally near to heaven and to the infinite.

Henri Frédéric Amiel, *Amiel's Journal*, translated by Mrs Humphry Ward, Macmillan and Co., 1918, page 45

Vocation is not the exceptional prerogative of a few specially good or gifted people... All men and women are called to serve God.

F.R. Barry, *Vocation and Ministry*, James Nisbet and Co., 1958, page 8

All things are produced more plentifully and easily and of a better quality when one man does one thing which is natural to him and at the right time, and leaves other things.

Plato, *The Republic of Plato*, translated by B. Jowett, Oxford at the Clarendon Press, 1881, page 49

Each man has his own vocation. The talent is the call. There is one direction in which all space is open to him. He has faculties silently inviting him thither to endless exertion. He is like a ship in a river: he runs against obstructions on every side but one; on that side all obstruction is taken away, and he sweeps serenely over a deepening channel into an infinite sea.

Ralph Waldo Emerson, 'Spiritual Laws', in *Essays*, Bernhard Tauchnitz, 1915, page 120

What are you going to do with your lives? To choose your career for selfish reasons is a worse sin than, let us say, committing adultery, for it is the withdrawal of the greater part of your time and energy from the service of God. Of course you are not going to be turned out of a club for doing it, but you will turn yourself out of the fellowship of Christ by doing it.

William Temple, *Christian Faith and Life*, SCM Press, 1931, reissued 1963, page 44

Whatever the work you do for a living, it must be a form of service of some kind, for no one will pay you for your work if he does not want it done. What makes all the difference is what you are thinking of first and foremost, as you consider the spirit and temper in which you carry out your work. Is it your livelihood or is it God's service? The work in itself is both. But which do you think of first? Nothing would bring nearer the promised day of God than that all Christian people should enter on their profession in the spirit of those who regard it as their chief sphere of serving God.

William Temple, *Christian Faith and Life*, SCM Press, 1931, reissued 1963, page 107

There is a will for career as well as for character. There is a will for *where*—in what place, viz., in this town or another town—I am to become like God, as well as *that* I am to become like God. There is a will for where I am to be, and what I am to be, and what I am to do to-morrow. There is a will for what scheme I am to take up, and what work I am to do for Christ, and what business arrangements to make, and what money to give away. This is God's private will for me, for every step I take, for the path of life along which He points my way: God's will for my *career*.

Henry Drummond, *The Greatest Thing in the World*, William Collins Sons and Co., 1978, page 291

When Christ calls a man, he bids him come and die. It may be a death like that of the first disciples who had to leave home and work to follow him, or it may be a death like Luther's, who had to leave the monastery and go out into the world. But it is the same death every time—death in Jesus Christ, the death of the old man at his call. Jesus' summons to the rich young man was calling him to die, because only the man who is dead to his own will can follow Christ. In fact every command of Jesus is a call to die, with all our affections and lusts. But we do not want to die, and therefore Jesus Christ and his call are necessarily our death as well as our life.

Dietrich Bonhoeffer, *The Cost of Discipleship*, revised and abridged edition, SCM Press, 1959, page 79

But if you are in doubt how you may best lay out your life, and if you are quite clear in your acceptance of Jesus Christ as your Saviour and your God, then the mere circumstances of the time constitute a call to the Church's direct service in its ministry which you must face; for there is no sphere of life in which a man can more certainly lay out all his talents in the service of God. It will call for every capacity; it will bring you into touch with human beings in every conceivable relation. There is no life so rich or so full of all those joys which come from serving people at the point of their greatest need.

William Temple, *Christian Faith and Life*, SCM Press, 1931, reissued 1963, page 139

People ought not to consider so much what they are to do as what they *are;* let them but *be* good and their ways and deeds will shine brightly. If you are just, your actions will be just too. Do not think that saintliness comes from occupation; it depends rather on what one is. The kind of work we do does not make us holy but we may make it holy. However 'sacred' a calling may be, as it is a calling, it has no power to sanctify but rather as we *are* and have the divine being within, we bless each task we do, be it eating, or sleeping, or watching, or any other. Whatever they do, who have not much of (God's) nature, they work in vain.

Meister Eckhart, *Meister Eckhart*, translated by Raymond B. Blakney, Harper and Row, Publishers, 1941, page 6

God's call is mysterious; it comes in the darkness of faith. It is so fine, so subtle, that it is only with the deepest silence within us that we can hear it.

And yet nothing is so decisive and overpowering for a man on this earth, nothing surer or stronger.

This call is uninterrupted: God is always calling us! But there are distinctive moments in this call of his, moments which leave a permanent mark on us—moments which we never forget...

Prayer had become the most important thing. But it was still the hardest part of my daily life. Through my vocation to prayer I learned what is meant by 'carrying other people' in our prayer.

So, after many years I can say that I have remained true to my vocation, and at the same time I am completely convinced that one never wastes one's time by praying; there is no more helpful way of helping those we love.

Carlo Carretto, *Letters from the Desert*, translated by Rose Mary Hancock, Darton, Longman and Todd, 1972, page xv

He that is choice of his time will also be choice of his company, and choice of his actions...

God hath given to man a short time here upon earth, and yet upon this eternity depends...

We must remember that the life of every man may be so ordered, and indeed must, that it may be a perpetual serving of God. For God provides the good things of the world to serve the needs of nature by the labours of the ploughman, the skill and pains of the artisan, and the dangers and traffic of the merchant: these men are, in their calling, the ministers of the Divine Providence, and the stewards of the creation, and servants of a great family of God, the world, in the employment and procuring necessaries for food and clothing, ornament and physic. In their proportions also a king and a priest and a prophet, a judge and an advocate... are doing the work of God. So that no man can complain that his calling takes him off from religion; his calling itself, and his employment in honest trades and offices is a serving of God.

Jeremy Taylor, *Holy Living*, abridged by Anne Lamb, The Langford Press, 1970, page 9

THE WAY

'The Way'—way of life, principles or habits governing one's actions,
a way of faith, a journey of faith—pilgrimage.

'I am the way,' said Jesus, 'Yes, I know that,' I was thinking, 'but I have my way too.' I was at the cross-roads of life, an undergraduate at university, wondering what to do in life. My 'way' was fairly straightforward. I was reading law at university and concentrating on getting my degree. The overall plan was to qualify as a solicitor, join the family firm, become a partner, buy a house, a car and so on, marry, settle down and have a family. This surely must be 'the right way' because this is roughly what most people do in life. With this plan, there was job security, status, a good financial return, the prospect of a comfortable lifestyle—and holidays abroad.

'I am the way,' persisted Jesus.

I began thinking more deeply about 'my way'. Was it not inherently selfish? Was law the most important thing in my life? Why did I want status and money? Was it to attract women and find a good wife? What about working in an office, nine to five, five days a week, for a possible forty years? Was this a good way of life? The self-questioning continued.

'I am the way.' At last the truth of these words came home to me, and I responded, and life became an adventure. Travelling this road has not been easy. Many sacrifices have been made, but at least one has experienced life in all its fulness.

See, I have set before you this day life and good, death and evil. If you obey the commandments of the Lord your God which I command you this day, by loving the Lord your God, by walking in his ways, and by keeping his commandments and his statutes and his ordinances, then you shall live and multiply, and the Lord your God will bless you in the land which you are entering to take possession of it.

Deuteronomy 30:15–16

Commit your way to the Lord; trust in him, and he will act.

Psalm 37:5

I am the way.

John 14:6

But earnestly desire the higher gifts. And I will show you a still more excellent way.

1 Corinthians 12:31

That He would teach men the perfect way. And there has never come, before Him nor after Him, any man who has taught anything divine approaching to this.

Blaise Pascal, *Pensées*, translated by W.F. Trotter, Random House, 1941, page 261

It is easy enough, assuming we have read the gospels, to know what the way stands for. It is less easy to stand for that way ourselves. It is extremely difficult to direct our thinking and living along that way and no other.

Hubert van Zeller, *Considerations*, Sheed and Ward, 1974, page 120

'Thou must thyself be the way. The spiritual understanding must be born in thee.' 'A Christian is a new creature in the ground of the heart.' 'The Kingdom of God is not from without, but it is a new man, who lives in love, in patience, in hope, in faith and in the Cross of Jesus Christ.'

Rufus M. Jones, *Spiritual Reformers in the 16th and 17th Centuries*, Macmillan and Co., 1914, page 171.

Every man and woman has two journeys to make through life. There is the outer journey, with its various incidents, and the milestones of youth, marriage, middle age, and senility. There is also an inner journey, a spiritual Odyssey, with a secret history of its own.

W.R. Inge, *More Lay Thoughts of a Dean*, G.P. Putnam's Sons, 1931, page 69

To be committed to the way which is Christ means being committed to whatever aspects of it he may introduce me to. It will probably involve opposition and frustration and disappointment, it will possibly involve shame and guilt, it will most certainly mean the cross and obedience 'even unto death'.

Hubert van Zeller, *Considerations*, Sheed and Ward, 1974, page 120

The time of meditation might often seem to you to be a complete waste of time, but only remember, Jesus dwells in your heart. Your faith will be tested and so your faith will be strengthened.

And so, make it the Way, the way you follow, leaving self behind and entering fully into the power of Christ's love. Everything else in your life flows from that personal encounter in your meditation because it is there that you find your own conviction.

Each time we meditate we return to the grounding consciousness of Being, and each time we return to the changing pattern of our life more firmly rooted in our being and so more able to perceive life as mystery and to communicate this perception in joy to others.

John Main OSB, in *The Joy of Being*, selected by Clare Hallward, Darton, Longman and Todd, 1989, page 46

I do not feel that the Christian myth has anything left to tell Western man unless he understands it outside-in. He must discover that what seemed to be the far-off edges of time, where God is Alpha and Omega, are the present, and that the pilgrimage from earth to Heaven is not a journey into the future but into the Centre. He must realize that the 'death' through which we must pass before God can be seen does not lie ahead of us in time. 'Death' is the point at which 'I' come to an end, and beyond which lies the unknown, and this point is not 'on' but 'in'. 'The Kingdom of God is within you'. For if I explore myself a little way, I come to a point where I do not understand or recognize myself any more. The 'I was' which I know becomes the 'I am' which I never see. The roots of my consciousness disappear into an unknown region where I am as foreign to myself as to the pulse of my heart and the currents of my nerves. For what is most truly and inwardly myself is ever beyond that small area of knowledge and control which is called the ego. Paradoxically, the most central and fundamental region of my being seems to be most 'other'—like the God of theistic imagery. Thus while I think of the ego as my actual *self*, I am off-centre. I am 'beside myself', so that the coursing of my blood and all the deeper processes of body and mind seem to be the work of someone or something else, giving a sensation of strangeness and 'the creeps' when I feel them.

This basic 'shift' in the position of God from the periphery of the world to the centre requires also a shift of faith. We have to recognize that the totally undefinable and incomprehensible 'something' which is our most inward self is—in all important respects—beyond our control. For the self which knows and controls is never, at the same time, the known and controlled. This is the most important lesson in the world for a civilization which aspires to omnipotence, to the control of *everything*. For every attempt to establish total control on the part of the conscious ego starts a vicious circle. Thus our culture becomes a system of controls in which the solution of each new problem simply multiplies the number of problems to be solved, as in the myth of the Hydra monster who grows seven new heads for each one cut off. The complete control of life is impossible for the reason that we are part of it, and that, in the last analysis, the system is not a thing controlled but a thing controlling.

We are therefore compelled to have faith in something which is at once ourselves, in the most basic sense, and not ourselves, in the sense of the ego, the remembered 'I'. But this faith cannot have any tangible content, such as a system of beliefs, for the simple reason that the fundamental Self cannot be defined. Therefore it is not to be verbalized positively as a believing in or about. It is to be expressed negatively, as a *not* trying to control and to grasp, as a 'letting-go' and not as a 'holding-to'. Furthermore, such 'letting-go' faith must come about not as a positive work to be done, but through the realization that there is really nothing else to do, since it is actually impossible to grasp the inmost Self.

The positive consequences of this faith in terms of love, joy, and illumination are strictly gratuitous. They emerge unpredictably and uncontrollably from the inner depths. The 'letting-go' removes the obstacle to their coming, but the actual coming, the Second Advent, is 'like a thief in the night,' and we 'know not the day nor the hour.' Generally speaking, they follow immediately upon the act of release. The apparent delay is usually due to the fact that one is trying to force their arrival, so that the release is not actually complete. And the mind stops 'forcing' only through the clear conviction of its uselessness.

As soon as one gets used to looking at the Christian images from this outside-in point of view, it becomes obvious that, in this way, they make sense as they never did before. God returns to his temple, the heart, the centre of all things—of man, of time, of space. Heaven is no longer in the place of Hell, the 'outer darkness' of the most distant spaces and far- off times, but appears in the place of the most intense reality—the *now*. Christ actually rises from the dead, and is revealed in *this* moment, and is no more locked up in the tomb of the remote past, in the dead letter of the written Gospels. The Mass is for once effectively sacrificed, for the Body of Christ, the Church, is really willing to be broken, finding no further need to hold itself together with definitions and claims. The Faith becomes actual *faith*, which is self-surrender, as distinct from all anxious clinging to dogmatic rocks and doctrinal idols. The authority of the Church becomes self-evident, which is to say that the Church actually realizes authority, so that there is no more necessity to prove it, to convince itself, by exaggerated proselytism and preposterous claims of spiritual monopoly. The dispensation of the Law, in which virtue is forced, actually gives way to the dispensation of Grace, in which virtue happily 'happens', and is not grotesquely imitated.

So understood, the marvellous symbols of Christianity might still—one is tempted to say, might begin to—have a message for Western man, that anxious and restless eccentric who has 'no time' because he has reduced his present to an abstract dividing line between past and future, and who confuses his very self with a past which is no more and a future which is not yet. He, too, needs to be turned outside-in, to live in the real world which he thinks is abstract, instead of in the abstract world which he takes for reality. And for this he must know that the true place of Bethlehem, Calvary and Olivet is no more in history, and that Death, the Second Advent, and Heaven are not in a time to come. His 'sin,' his missing of the point, can only be forgiven if he repents—turns back—from his past, as from the future which it implies, and returns again to his Creator, the present reality from which he 'ex-ists'. Whereupon the life which had seemed momentary would be found momentous, and that present which had seemed to be no time at all would be found to be eternity.

Alan W. Watts, *Myth and Ritual in Christianity*, Thames and Hudson, 1953, page 232

WHOLENESS

*'Wholeness'—in good health, in sound condition, intact; thing
complete in itself, organic unity, complete system, total make up of
parts.*

A few weeks ago I was leading a morning session on 'Visions and Reflection', and one of the participants asked me what I was trying to do in reflection groups. (For those unfamiliar with reflection groups, there is some information about them in the Introduction of this book.) I said in reply I was trying to bring about some form of wholeness unique to each individual person. The emphasis of *Visions of Faith* is on the 'God within' seen primarily as

Father, Son, Holy Spirit, life, light, joy, truth, love, and so on. Many of the excerpts are about people's experiences of 'God within' as well as thoughts and feelings of the divine in the depths of our being. Reflection is rather like 'practising the presence of God' to quote a phrase used by Brother Lawrence, a seventeenth-century Carmelite lay brother. In silence we open ourselves up to experience something of the presence of God. Some find it helpful to think of reflection as a listening form of prayer, in which great use is made of the mind and heart (feelings), as well as intuition and imagination. Reflection is really about the cure of souls, enabling people to come to wholeness through releasing the divine in them. As D.H. Lawrence wrote in *The Phoenix*: 'To be alive, to be man alive, to be whole man alive: that is the point.'

I give thanks to thee, O Lord my God, with my whole heart, and I will glorify thy name for ever.
Psalm 86:12

The whole head is sick, and the whole heart faint. From the sole of the foot even to the head, there is no soundness in it.
Isaiah 1:5–6

But he who is united to the Lord becomes one spirit with him.
1 Corinthians 6:17

Until we all attain to the unity of the faith and of the knowledge of the Son of God, to mature manhood, to the measure of the stature of the fulness of Christ.
Ephesians 4:13

Knowledge, love, power,—there is the complete life.
Henri Frédéric Amiel, *Amiel's Journal*, translated by Mrs Humphry Ward, Macmillan and Co., 1918, page 42

When we rejoice in our fulness, then we can part with our fruits with joy.
Rabindranath Tagore, *Stray Birds*, Indian Edition, Macmillan and Co., 1941, page 42

I wished for all things that I might enjoy life, and was granted life that I might enjoy all things.
Anon.

Nothing can be sole or whole
That has not been rent.
W.B. Yeats, 'Words for Music Perhaps', in *Collected Poems of W.B. Yeats*, Macmillan and Co., 1973, page 295

The cure for all the illness of life is stored in the inner depth of life itself, the access to which becomes possible when we are alone. This solitude is a world in itself, full of wonders and resources unthought of. It is so absurdly near, yet so unapproachably distant.
Rabindranath Tagore, *Letters to a Friend*, George Allen and Unwin, 1928, page 55

Many of us do not grow an inner health and maturity as we grow in bodily health, mental ability and control over outside things. Few of us devote to the study of God and his will the same time and application that we give to worldly studies and professional training. The writers of the New Testament frequently lament the lack of maturity in the Christians for whom they are writing. That spiritual maturity is essential for inner health, right attitudes and right decisions and is creative for a dimension of life beyond the physical and the material.
George Appleton, *Journey for a Soul*, William Collins Sons and Co., 1976, page 110

Yesterday I met a whole man. It is a rare experience but always an illuminating and ennobling one. It costs so much to be a full human being that there are very few who have the enlightenment or the courage, to pay the price... One has to abandon altogether the search for security, and reach out to the risk of living with both arms. One has to embrace the world like a lover, and yet demand no easy return of love. One has to accept pain as a condition of existence. One has to court doubt and darkness as the cost of knowing. One needs a will stubborn in conflict, but apt always to the total acceptance of every consequence of living and dying.

Morris West, *The Shoes of the Fisherman*, William Heinemann, 1983, page 204

I keep on saying Our Lord was the first psychiatrist, with a penetrating awareness of human beings ten times better than psychological theory. And finally, what He did on the Cross was to take all the human ingredients and transform them into both a human wholeness and a divine wholeness. Only Christ could achieve that. What Our Lord could do was to take the fulness of being divine and transform it in terms which we could understand. He could, on the Cross, express His fear of being abandoned with the certainty that He was not. None of us, as human beings, has that hundred-per-cent certainty of the divine presence. It was only God that could have this awareness of the Father.

Jack Dominion, in Gerald Priestland, *Priestland's Progress*, BBC Worldwide, 1982, page 82

The unknown remains unknown. It is still a mystery, for it cannot cease to be one. The function of faith is not to reduce mystery to rational clarity, but to integrate the unknown and the known together in a living whole, in which we are more and more able to transcend the limitations of our external self...

Faith is not just conformity. It is *life*. It embraces all the realms of life, penetrating into the most mysterious and inaccessible depths not only of our unknown spiritual being but even of God's own hidden essence and love. Faith, then, is the only way of opening up the true depths of reality, even of our own reality. Until a man yields himself to God in the consent of total belief, he must inevitably remain a stranger to himself, an exile from himself, because he is excluded from the most meaningful depths of his own being: those which remain obscure and unknown because they are too simple and too deep to be attained by reason.

Thomas Merton, *New Seeds of Contemplation*, Burns and Oates, 1962, page 106

One of the challenges we all face is to be continually sensitive to the unfolding of God's plan in our lives: to give free and open assent to the destiny his love is shaping for us.

It is so easy to lose that sensitivity. So much of our life is dominated by the mechanical, by the response that is expected or demanded of us, by attempts to predict or anticipate growth, that we are always in danger of losing contact with life as a mystery—and so with life itself.

Any fixed pattern we try to impose on our life falsifies the truth of the mystery that is eternally present and so unpredictable.

Our day-to-day life is of vital importance as the mystery of transformation is worked out in us and through us by the power of Christ. No detail is insignificant because the reassimilation of all creation in Christ is to be complete.

The plan being worked out in the life of each of us is the same as that being realized in all creation, the bringing into unity with Christ of all that is. The first sphere of this great movement into unity is the achievement of wholeness within ourselves.

John Main OSB, in *The Joy of Being*, selected by Clare Hallward, Darton, Longman and Todd, 1989, page 9

The Christian mystical tradition teaches men to find God's presence within... The metaphor which is for me the most satisfying of all is that of the soul's centre as the focus of the divine action. The centre of a circle is equidistant from all the points on the circumference; and to say that God acts upon the soul from the centre suggests that the sweep of his action takes in the whole personality and not merely the narrow area of consciousness. The metaphor also suggests that the experience of God within is an experience of being integrated, centred, made one. But I believe the centre is best understood as a potentiality that needs to be actualised if we are to grow to full maturity. Men tend to be pulled first one way and then another by opposite tendencies, there is the urge to dominate and the urge to submit, to turn outwards to other people and to withdraw into your shell, there is the aspiration for the spiritual and there is the equally strong counter-pull of the flesh. As the centre becomes actualized the opposed tendencies are held in a creative tension and harnessed in the service of the personality as a whole. I regard this centre, once actualized, as both a point of focus to help concentration on God's action within and also the centre through which God guides us. The symbol of the centre can help a man in practice to cooperate with God. God rules us through the whole of what we are, through our conscious thinking and deciding and through the unconscious that balances and corrects our conscious attitudes. As I learn to find God in the centre, this occillation, this pendulum swing, is slowed down. In perplexity I turn to the centre for guidance; in weakness I turn to the centre for strength. I don't mean that God does not guide and strengthen me from outside. He addresses me through my brother, through the community of faith to which I belong, through every soul I meet. He speaks to me through the Scriptures, through the wisdom of the past, through prophets and wise men today. But the wisdom and help that comes from outside are only truly assimilated and made my own when I have referred them to the centre within. It is through the centre, I believe, that the Holy Spirit enlightens the mind, fires the heart, makes firm the will. It is the focus of God's action, the sanctuary where he dwells.

C.R. Bryant, SSJE, 'The Psychology of Prayer' (an unpublished lecture), page 10

Most men have a dual interpretation of themselves—two pictures of their two selves in separate rooms. In one room are hung all the portraits of their virtues, done in bright, splashing, glorious colours, but with no shadows and no balance. In the other room hangs the canvas of self-condemnation ... painted equally as unrealistically with dark and morbid greens, blacks, and no lights or relief.

Instead of keeping these two pictures isolated from one another, we must look at them together and gradually blend them into one. In our exalted moods we are afraid to admit guilt, hatred, and shame as elements of our personality; and in our depressed moods we are afraid to credit ourselves with the goodness and the achievement which really are ours.

We must begin now to draw a new portrait and accept and know ourselves for what we are. We are relative, and not *absolute*, creatures; everything we do is tinged with imperfection. So often people foolishly try to become rivals of God and make demands of themselves which only God could make of Himself—rigid demands of absolute perfection ...

A splendid freedom awaits us when we realize that we need not feel like moral lepers or emotional pariahs because we have some aggressive, hostile thoughts and feelings toward ourselves and others. When we acknowledge these feelings we no longer have to pretend to be that which we are not. It is enough to know what we *are*! We discover that rigid pride is actually the supreme foe of inner victory, while flexible humility, the kind of humility that appears when we do not demand the impossible or the angelic of ourselves is the great ally of psychic peace ...

We should learn to accept this pluralism in ourselves, to rejoice in the truth that we human beings consist of a variety of moods, impulses, traits, and emotions ...

If we become pluralistic in thinking about ourselves, we shall learn to take the depressed mood or the cruel mood or the unco-operative mood for what it is, one of the many, fleeting, not permanent. As pluralists we take ourselves for worse as well as for better, cease demanding a brittle perfection which can lead only to inner despair.

There are facets of failure in every person's make-up and there are elements of success. Both must be accepted while we try to emphasize the latter through self-knowledge. The attainment of proper self-love must become the concern of every wise religion because as long as human beings are enslaved to wrong attitudes toward themselves they cannot help expressing wrong attitudes toward others. If the self is not loved, how can the neighbour be loved as oneself?

Joshua Loth Liebman, *Peace of Mind*, William Heinemann, 1946, page 53

WILL

*'Will'—faculty by which a person decides or conceives himself
as deciding upon and initiating action; power of determining
one's choice of action independently of causation, doing the
will of God, God's will.*

When I was a teenager at school, sometimes I would get up early and go to a communion service in the Lady Chapel. In those days we used the Book of Common Prayer, and one of the offertory sentences which registered with me was: 'Not every one that saith unto me. Lord, Lord, shall enter into the kingdom of heaven; but he that doeth the will of my Father which is in heaven.' When I took a deeper step of commitment in my early twenties these words challenged me even more forcibly, and brought about a determination to do 'the will of my Father' at all costs. I certainly did not want to be labelled a hypocrite. In retrospect this developing attitude of 'all or nothing' influenced me in going forward to ordination. Some of William Barclay's words put over my feelings at the time concisely: 'The one great principle was that in all things a man must seek God's will and that, when he knows it, he must dedicate his whole life to the obeying it.' I was also influenced by those searching words of the Lord's Prayer: 'Thy kingdom come, Thy will be done.'

Well, the step to ordination was taken, but how difficult it has been to do God's will in the succeeding years. Help has been found in these words of Jesus: 'If any man's will is to do his will, he shall know whether the teaching is from God or whether I am speaking on my own authority.'

I delight to do thy will, O my God; thy law is within my heart.

Psalm 40:8

Teach me to do thy will, for thou art my God! Let thy good spirit lead me on a level path!

Psalm 143:10

Not my will, but thine, be done.

Luke 22:42

If any man's will is to do his will, he shall know whether the teaching is from God or whether I am speaking on my own authority.

John 7:17

In His will is our peace.

Dante Alighieri, *The Divine Comedy*, volume I, 'Paradisio', iii. 85, translated by Charles S. Singleton, Princeton University Press, Bollingen Series LXXX, 1977

The unconquerable Will.

John Milton, *Paradise Lost*, book 1, in *The Poetical Works of John Milton*, edited by The Revd H.C. Beeching, Oxford at the Clarendon Press, 1900, page 184

Great things are not done by impulse, but by a series of small things brought together. And great things are not something accidental, but must certainly be *willed.*

Vincent van Gogh, *Dear Theo—An autobiography of Vincent van Gogh*, edited by Irving Stone, Constable and Company, 1937, page 187

He (Christ) hangs all true acquaintance with divinity upon the doing of God's will: 'If any man will do His will, he shall know of the doctrine, whether it be of God.' (John 7:17).

John Smith the Platonist, *Select Discourses*, Cambridge at the University Press, 1859, page 9

He gave man the power to thwart his will, that, by means of that same power, he might come at last to do his will in a higher kind and way than would otherwise have been possible.

George Macdonald, *Unspoken Sermons*, Third Series, Longmans, Green and Co., 1889, page 229

The star of the unconquered will,
He rises in my breast,
Serene, and resolved, and still
And calm, and self-possessed.

Henry Wadsworth Longfellow, 'The Light of Stars,' in *The Poetical Works of Longfellow*, edited by Humphrey Milford, Oxford University Press, 1913, page 4

The one complete cure for the sense of frustration and futility is to know and do the will of God. Everyone to whom this becomes a reality is at once supplied with a purpose in life and one which covers the whole of life.

William Temple, *The Hope of a New World*, SCM Press, 1940, page 114

Remember our great principles: (1) That there is nothing so small or apparently trifling, even the fall of a leaf, that is not ordained or permitted by God; (2) That God is sufficiently wise, good, powerful and merciful to turn the most seemingly disastrous events to the good and profit of those who are capable of adoring and humbly accepting all these manifestations of his divine and adorable will.

Jean Pierre de Caussade, SJ, *Self-Abandonment to Divine Providence*, edited by Father John Joyce, SJ, Burns and Oates, 1962, page 123

God's will is not just goodwill towards men in the sense of a benevolent disposition, though it is certainly that. It is a determined, dynamic force, working to achieve his purpose, ceaselessly opposed to evil, constantly countering the mistaken or sinful moves of men, always ready to guide those who take his will as the purpose of their lives, immediately generous to supply more than abundant grace to carry it out. 'Thy will be done!' is a cry of glad acceptance of the rightness, goodness and love of God. 'Thy will be done' is an equally joyful conviction.

George Appleton, *Journey for a Soul*, William Collins Sons and Co., 1976, page 234

'I will arise and go to my Father,' and so develop in itself the highest *Divine* of which it is capable—the will for the good against the evil—the will to be one with the life whence it has come, and in which it still is—the will to close the round of its procession in its return, so working the perfection of reunion—to shape in its own life the ring of eternity—to live immediately, consciously, and active-willingly from its source, from its own very life—to restore to the beginning the end that comes of that beginning—to be the thing the maker thought of when he willed, ere he began to work its being.

George Macdonald, *Unspoken Sermons*, Second Series, Longmans, Green and Co., 1885, page 168

How am I to know the will of God?

Whatever is demanded by truth, by justice, by mercy, or by love must surely be taken to be willed by God. To consent to His will is, then, to consent to be true, or to speak truth, or at least seek it. To obey Him is to respond to His will expressed in the need of another person, or at least to respect the rights of others. For the right of another man is the expression of God's love and God's will. In demanding that I respect the rights of another God is not merely asking me to conform to some abstract, arbitrary law: He is enabling me to share, as His son, in His own care for my brother. No man who ignores the rights and needs of others can hope to walk in the light of contemplation, because his way has turned aside from truth, from compassion and therefore from God.

Thomas Merton, *New Seeds of Contemplation*, Burns and Oates, 1962, page 15

It is all very well to declare that I exist in order to save my soul and give glory to God by doing so. And it is all very well to say that in order to do this I obey certain commandments and keep certain counsels. Yet knowing this much, and indeed knowing all moral theology and ethics and canon law, I might still go through life conforming myself to certain indications of God's will without ever fully giving myself to God. For that, in the last analysis, is the real meaning of His will. He does not need our sacrifices, He asks for our *selves*.

And if He prescribes certain acts of obedience, it is not because obedience is the beginning and the end of everything. It is only the beginning. Charity, divine union; transformation in Christ: these are the end...

And since no man is an island, since we all depend on one another, I cannot work out God's will in my own life unless I also consciously help other men to work out His will in theirs. His will, then, is our sanctification, our transformation in Christ, our deeper and fuller integration with other men. And this integration results not in the absorption and disappearance of our own personality, but in its affirmation and its perfection.

Thomas Merton, *No Man is an Island*, Hollis and Carter, 1955, page 55

Concentration, whether in meditation or in prayer, can only be achieved by an effort of will. Our spiritual life is based on our faith and determination, and any incidental joys are a gift of God. St Seraphim of Sarov, when asked what it was that made some people remain sinners and never make any progress while others were becoming saints and living in God, answered: 'Only determination.' Our activities must be determined by an act of will, which usually happens to be contrary to what we long for; this will, based on our faith, always clashes with another will, our instinctive one. There are two wills in us, one is the conscious will, possessed to a greater or lesser degree, which consists in the ability to compel ourselves to act in accordance with our convictions. The second one is something else in us, it is the longings, the claims, the desires of all our nature, quite often contrary to the first will. St Paul speaks of the two laws that fight against each other (Romans 7:23). He speaks of the old and new Adam in us, who are at war. We know that one must die in order that the other should live, and as we must realise that our spiritual life, our life as a human being taken as a whole, will never be complete as long as these two wills do not coincide. It is not enough to aim at the victory of the good will against the evil one; the evil one, that is the longings of our fallen nature, must absolutely, though gradually, be transformed into a longing, a craving, for God. The struggle is hard and far-reaching.

Anthony Bloom, *Living Prayer*, Darton, Longman and Todd, 1966, page 63

Men have always wanted to handle their lives as they plan their careers. Money, power, pleasure, women, drink or other enjoyments attract them on earth. Many people would be willing to renounce worldly pleasures if they received convincing proofs that the ultimate rewards would make the deal worthwhile. But if such a deal could be made, it would not be due to love, but to business discernment. The object of the training can only be achieved by a loving donation of ourselves, uncertain of reward. Christ himself put the matter exactly. 'My doctrine,' he said, 'is not mine but his that sent me. If any man will do his will, he shall know of the doctrine whether it be of God.' The abandonment of our own interests and our surrender to his guidance must be the first step. After that, our trust will grow.

Evelyn Underhill has a good illustration of the situation. She supposes someone looking at a great cathedral, a mass of gray stone with the windows showing a dark dusty colour. It does not look very cheerful. But if we push open the doors and go in, we suddenly see that all the windows are really brightly coloured glass, which light up all the walls and, through which the beams of the sun shine with dazzling light, staining the stone floors with brilliant patterns of red, blue, green and gold. You cannot see the glory if you stand outside, asking sneeringly what proof there is that inside is beautiful. You have got to go in yourself.

Sir John Glubb, *The Way of Love*, Hodder and Stoughton, 1974, page 66

WORK

'Work'—expenditure of energy, striving, application of effort to some purpose; task to be undertaken, employment, especially of earning money by labour; laborious occupation.

'Work hard, play hard, pray hard, and then you will be happy.' This was the advice I was given on arriving at school. For the next seven years I put these words into practice, and found I was very happy. My first work experience was in the army, whilst doing national service. As a private soldier the advice I received was somewhat different from school. On the first day we were taught never to volunteer for anything, and the next day received instructions on the gentle art of skiving. In the Gurkhas it was back to the 'work hard, play hard' ethic, but somehow the 'pray hard' bit was missed out. Whilst at university I had some valuable work experience in a bacon factory during a long vacation. The pigs were slaughtered at one end of the production line, and I was at the far end of the production line, stacking sides of bacon into a huge refrigerator, and doing something (I've forgotten precisely what) with the heads of pigs. I was incredibly bored as the job made no demands on my mind whatsoever. After a few weeks I came to the conclusion the secret of work was interest in the job—and enjoyment. This was not the main reason why I became a priest, but I am still very interested in the work I do, and am fortunate in that the greater part of my work is enjoyable, creative and fulfilling.

Six days you shall work, but on the seventh day you shall rest.

Exodus 34:21

Let the favour of the Lord our God be upon us, and establish thou the work of our hands upon us, yea, the work of our hands establish thou it.

Psalm 90:17

This is the work of God, that you believe in him whom he has sent.

John 6:29

Each man's work will become manifest; for the Day will disclose it, because it will be revealed with fire, and the fire will test what sort of work each one has done.

1 Corinthians 3:13

The real essence of work is concentrated energy.

Walter Bagehot, *Biographical Studies*, edited by Richard Holt Hutton, Longmans, Green, and Co., 1907, page 370

A man can be so busy making a living that he forgets to make a life.

William Barclay, *The Gospel of Matthew*, volume II, The Saint Andrew Press, 1976, page 296

I don't like work—no man does—but I like what is in the work,—the chance to find yourself. Your own reality—for yourself, not for others—what no other man can ever know.

Joseph Conrad, *Heart of Darkness*, in *Youth, a Narrative and Two Other Stories*, J.M. Dent and Sons, 1923, page 85

Every citizen should have a voice in the conduct of the business or industry which is carried on by means of his labour, and the satisfaction of knowing that his labour is directed to the well being of the community.

William Temple, *Christianity and the Social Order*, Penguin Books, 1942, page 73

The work of the Church is done, not by ecclesiastical officials nor under the direction of ecclesiastical committees, but by members of the Church who do the ordinary work of the world in the inspiration of Christian faith and in a spirit sustained by Christian prayer and worship.

William Temple, *Citizen and Churchman*, Cambridge University Press, 1941, page 48

Capitalism is an evil thing, because it is based on what is called enlightened self-interest, and that is a baptismal name for selfishness. Poverty is a crime. The Church has been very specific on other matters. It hasn't hesitated to speak arbitrarily on most intimate affairs like sex. I don't see why it should restrict its particularity to those and not extend them to the world of the unemployed.

Lord Soper, in Gerald Priestland, *Priestland's Progress*, BBC Worldwide, 1982, page 54

Commitment does not stop with contemplation. It seeks issue in work. For the God discovered thus is a God at work, reconciling the world to Himself. And those who worship in spirit and truth find themselves called to a ministry of reconciliation. A world unfinished and broken is to be made whole. Ultimately, it is God, not we, who must heal it, but in our small measure, we may be co-labourers with God. That is our calling. Worship sends us out to work. But work in turn, through frustration or consummation, may continually tend again toward worship, wherein illumination and renewal are to be found. Such, in part, is man's way toward God.

Robert Lowry Calhoun, *God and the Common Life*, The Shoe String Press, 1954, page 240

Perhaps if the Churches had had the courage to lay their emphasis where Christ laid it, we might not have come to this present frame of mind in which it is assumed that the value of all work, and the value of all people, is to be assessed in terms of economics. We might not so readily take for granted that the production of anything (no matter how useless or dangerous) is justified so long as it issues in increased profits and wages; that so long as a man is well paid, it does not matter whether his work is worthwhile in itself or good for his soul; that so long as a business deal keeps on the windy side of the law, we need not bother about its ruinous consequences to society or the individual. Or at any rate, now that we have seen the chaos of bloodshed which follows upon economic chaos, we might at least be able to listen with more confidence to the voice of an untainted and undivided Christendom.

Dorothy L. Sayers, *Unpopular Opinions*, Victor Gollancz, 1946, page 11

There is no prospect that machine work will ever make anything like the demand on character from the ordinary worker that the old crafts used to make and some skilled work in some callings makes today; the craftsman who knows something of what beauty is because his own hands bring it into being, the farmer whose work trains him in observation and sympathy, the small trader with his wide range of contacts with people, the sailor, the nurse, the teacher, all get more from their work as well as giving more to it than the modern factory worker ever can... If the factory worker is ever in his life to meet the experiences that call upon his purposiveness, his creative capacity, his sense of perfection, and to be conscious of carrying significant responsibility in society, it must be in his leisure...

This involves a profound re-thinking of the balance of life. We have been accustomed to think that the challenge that develops character is met in work; that work is the adventure in which you find yourself, for the sake of which you have to grow, in which you find the chief interest in life and its paramount duties. This is the Puritan conception of work; it is not true of all periods of history.

Civilisation, in the sense of spiritual achievement, has largely been the creation of human leisure; music, art, philosophy, science, have owed much to men who had time to spare from bread winning. Working-class leisure has already made its not insignificant contributions: peasant communities have developed folk dance, embroidery, wood-carving, and ballad; town-dwellers have their chapels, trade unions, and brass bands... Today we think of leisure as the margin of life that may rightly be spared for relaxation or enjoyment after a good day's work. But for thousands of people there will never be a good day's work to be done, there will only be a lever to be pulled (or the like) for eight or nine or ten hours. If work in the sense of breadwinning means machine minding, work that is the making of a man must be done in leisure from breadwinning. Leisure must become the most truly strenuous part of life, a tonic rather than a sedative.

Constance Reaveley and John Winnington, *Democracy and Industry*, Chatto and Windus, 1947, page 135

We have known an honour of work exactly similar to that which in the Middle Ages ruled hand and heart. The same honour had been preserved, intact underneath. We have known this care carried to perfection, a perfect whole, perfect to the last infinitesimal detail. We have known this devotion to *l'ouvrage bien faite*, to the good job, carried and maintained to its most exacting claims. During all my childhood I saw chairs being caned exactly in the same spirit, with the same hand and heart as those with which this same people fashioned its cathedrals...

Those bygone workmen did not serve, they worked. They had an absolute honour, which is honour proper. A chair rung had to be well made. That was an understood thing. That was the first thing. It wasn't that the chair had to be well made for the salary or on account of the salary. It wasn't that it was well made for the boss, nor for connaisseurs, nor for the boss' clients. It had to be well made itself, in itself, for itself, in its very self. A tradition coming, springing from deep within the race, a history, an absolute, an honour, demanded that this chair rung be well made. Every part of the chair which could not be seen was just as perfectly made as the parts which could be seen. This was the selfsame principle of cathedrals...

There was no question of being seen or of not being seen. It was the innate being of work which needed to be well done... All honours converged towards that honour. A decency and a delicacy of speech. A respect for home. A sense of respects, of all respects, of respect itself. A constant ceremony, as it were. Besides, home was still very often identified with the work-room, and the honour of home and the honour of the work-room were the same honour. It was the honour of the same place. It was the honour of the same hearth. What has become of all this? Everything was a rhythm and a rite and a ceremony from the moment of rising in the early morning. Everything was an event, a sacred event. Everything was a tradition, a lesson, everything was bequeathed, everything was a most saintly habit. Everything was an inner elevation and a prayer. All day long, sleep and wake, work and short rest, bed and board, soup and beef, house and garden, door and street, courtyard and threshold, and the plates on the table.

Laughing, they used to say, and that to annoy the priests, that *to work is to pray*, and little did they know how true that was.

So much of their work was a prayer, and the work-room an oratory.

Charles Péguy, *Basic Verities*, translated by Ann and Julian Green, Kegan Paul, Trench, Trubner and Co., 1943, page 79

WORLDLINESS

'Worldliness'—temporal, earthly, exclusively or preponderantly concerned with or devoted to the affairs of this life, especially the pursuit of wealth or pleasure, prudence in advancing one's own interests.

Some years ago I went to a brilliant concert given by Elizabeth Soderstrom—the Swedish soprano. This took place in the hall of University College, Oxford. After the concert the Master very kindly invited the Fellows (and their spouses) and his guests back to the lodgings for a buffet supper. Here we were given an opportunity to meet Elizabeth Soderstrom informally.

During the meal I found myself chatting to a woman dripping with diamonds. After a while she asked me what I did in college. When I explained to her I was the college chaplain she questioned somewhat frivolously, 'Oh, do they still have a chaplain here?' The implication of this query was that in these enlightened days, there was no longer any need for a chaplain. I proceeded to bore her for the rest of the evening describing the nature of my work in college.

In many ways she typified people who only believe in things they can see, feel and touch. In our conversation, she let slip success and status were extremely important to her. The lavish display of diamonds indicated an obsession with wealth, and her face bore the features of a life devoted to the pursuit of pleasure. In short, she epitomized worldliness.

He will judge the world with righteousness, and the peoples with his truth.
Psalm 96:13

Woe to those who are wise in their own eyes, and shrewd in their own sight!
Isaiah 5:21

What will it profit a man, if he gains the whole world and forfeits his life?
Matthew 16:26

Do not love the world or the things in the world. If any one loves the world, love for the Father is not in him. For all that is in the world, the lust of the flesh and the lust of the eyes and the pride of life, is not of the Father but is of the world. And the world passes away.
1 John 2:15–17

Where wealth and freedom reign contentment fails,
And honour sinks where commerce long prevails.

Oliver Goldsmith, 'The Traveller', in *Collected Works of Oliver Goldsmith*, volume IV, edited by Arthur Friedman, Oxford at the Clarendon Press, 1966, page 252

One belongs to the world as long as one is more ashamed of a *faux pas*, a display of ignorance, a wrong turn of phrase, a misquotation than of an unloving action.

Theodor Haecker, *Journal in the Night*, translated by Alexander Dru, The Harvill Press, 1950, page 39

The world is too much with us; late and soon,
Getting and spending, we lay waste our powers:
Little we see in Nature that is ours;
We have given our hearts away, a sordid boon!

William Wordsworth, 'The World is Too much with us', in *The Poetical Works of William Wordsworth*, volume III, edited by E. de Selincourt and Helen Darbishire, Oxford at the Clarendon Press, 1954, page 16

The world expresses itself in magnificence, the spirit in magnanimity. The one means making big, inflating. The other means greatness (or openness) of mind, heart, soul. It is the difference between false and true generosity.

Hubert van Zeller, *Considerations*, Sheed and Ward, 1974, page 10

The things which most often happen in life and are esteemed as the greatest good of all, as may be gathered from their works, can be reduced to these three headings: to wit, Riches, Fame, and Pleasure. With these three the mind is so engrossed that it cannot scarcely think of any other good.

Spinoza, *Spinoza's Ethics and De Intellectus Emendatione*, J.M. Dent and Sons, 1955, page 227

Most people are kept from a true sense and taste of religion, by a regular kind of sensuality and indulgence, than by gross drunkenness. More men live regardless of the great duties of piety, through too great a concern for worldly goods, than through direct injustice.

William Law, *A Serious Call to a Devout and Holy Life*, J.M. Dent and Co., 1898, page 85

My name is Ozymandias, king of kings:
Look on my works, ye Mighty and despair!
Nothing beside remains. Round the decay
Of that colossal wreck, boundless and bare
The lone and level sands stretch far away.

Percy Bysshe Shelley, 'Ozymandias', in *The Poetical Works of Percy Bysshe Shelley*, volume II, edited by H. Buxton Forman, George Bell and Sons, 1892, page 294

Fathers and teachers, what is a monk? Among the educated this word is nowadays uttered with derision by some people, and some even use it as a term of abuse. And it is getting worse as time goes on. It is true, alas, it is true that there are many parasites, gluttons, voluptuaries and insolent tramps among the monks. Educated men of the world point out: 'You are idlers and useless members of society,' they say, 'You live on the labour of others. You are shameless beggars.' And yet think of the many meek and humble monks there are, monks who long for solitude and fervent prayer in peace and quiet. These attract their attention less and they even pass them over in silence, and how surprised they would be if I told them that the salvation of Russia would perhaps once more come from these meek monks who long for solitary prayer! For they are verily prepared in peace and quiet 'for an hour, and a day, and a month, and a year.' In their solitude they keep the image of Christ pure and undefiled for the time being, in the purity of God's truth, which they received from the Fathers of old, the apostles and martyrs, and when the time comes they will reveal it to the wavering righteousness of the world. That is a great thought. That star will shine forth from the East.

That is what I think of the monk, and is it false, is it arrogant? Look at the worldly and all those who set themselves above God's people on earth, has not God's image and God's truth been distorted in them? They have science, but in science there is nothing but what is subject to the senses. The spiritual world, however, the higher half of man's being, is utterly rejected, dismissed with a sort of triumph, even with hatred. The world has proclaimed freedom, especially in recent times, but what do we see in this freedom of theirs? Nothing but slavery and self-destruction! For the world says: 'You have needs, and therefore satisfy them, for you have the same rights as the most rich and most noble. Do not be afraid of satisfying them, but multiply them even.' That is the modern doctrine of the world. In that they see freedom. And what is the outcome of this right of multiplication of needs? Among the rich *isolation* and spiritual suicide and among the poor envy and murder, for they have been given the rights, but have not been shown the means of satisfying their needs. We are assured that the world is getting more and more united and growing into a brotherly community by the reduction of distances and the transmission of ideas through the air. Alas, put no faith in such a union of peoples. By interpreting freedom as the multiplication and the rapid satisfaction of needs, they do violence to their own nature, for such an interpretation merely gives rise to many senseless and foolish desires, habits and most absurd inventions. They live only for mutual envy, for the satisfaction of their carnal desires and for showing off. To have dinners, horses, carriages, rank, and slaves to wait on them is considered by them a necessity, and to satisfy it they sacrifice life, honour, and love of mankind. Why, they even commit suicide, if they cannot satisfy it. We see the same thing among those who are not rich, while the poor drown their unsatisfied needs and envy in drink. But soon they will drown it in blood instead of in drink—that's where they are being led. I ask you: is such a man free? I knew one 'fighter for an idea,' who told me himself that when he was deprived of tobacco in prison he was so distressed by this privation that he nearly went and betrayed his 'idea' just to get a little tobacco! And it is such a man who says, 'I'm fighting for humanity!' How can such a man fight for anything and what is he fit for? For some rash action, perhaps, for he cannot hold out long. And it is no wonder that instead of gaining freedom, they have fallen into slavery, and instead of serving the cause of brotherly love and the union of humanity, they have, on the contrary, sunk into *separation* and isolation, as my mysterious visitor and teacher said to me in my youth. And that is why the idea of service to humanity, of brotherhood and of the solidarity of men is more and more dying out in the world. Indeed, this idea is even treated with derision, for how can a man give up his habits, where can such a slave go, if he is so used to satisfying his innumerable needs which he has himself created? He lives in isolation, and what does he care for the rest of mankind? And they have now reached the point of having more and more things and less and less joy in life.

The monastic way is different. People even laugh at obedience, fasting and prayer, and yet it is through them that the way lies to real, true freedom: I cut off all superfluous and unnecessary needs, I subdue my proud and ambitious will and chastise it with obedience, and, with God's help, attain freedom of spirit and with it spiritual joy! Which of them is more capable of conceiving a great idea and serving it—the rich man in his isolation or the man *freed* from the tyranny of material things and habits? The monk is reproached for his solitude: 'You have sought solitude to find salvation within the walls of the monastery, but you have forgotten the brotherly service of humanity.' But we shall see which will be more zealous in the cause of brotherly love. For it is they and not we who live in isolation, but they don't see that. In the olden times leaders of men came from our midst, so why cannot it happen again now? The same meek and humble monks, living a life of fasting and silence, will rise again and go forth to work for the great cause. The salvation of Russia comes from the people. And the Russian monastery has from time immemorial been on the side of the people. If the people are isolated, then we too are isolated. The people believe as we do. An unbelieving leader will never achieve anything in Russia, even if he were sincere at heart and a genius in intelligence. Remember that. The people will meet the atheist and overcome him, and Russia will be one and orthodox. Therefore, take care of the people and guard their heart. Educate them quietly. That is your great task as monks, for this people is a Godbearer.

Fyodor Dostoyevsky, *The Brothers Karamazov*, volume 1, translated by David Magarshack, Penguin Books, 1963, page 368

WORSHIP

*'Worship'—reverent homage or service paid to God; acts, rites or
ceremonies of honour and respect, adoration and devotion.*

Over the years I have greatly enjoyed church music, and listening to anthems, feel to be close to the spirit of worship. For the most part I find formal worship difficult, and was greatly helped in my understanding by a stray sentence from J. Neville Ward's book, *Five for Sorrow, Ten for Joy*. In this book he wrote: 'Institutional religion will always exasperate us because it is carried on in the words and deeds of inadequate and sinful human beings.' As mentioned previously Anthony Bloom enabled me to understand another difficulty with formal worship. In *Living Prayer*, he wrote: 'One of the reasons why communal worship or private prayer seems to be so dead or so conventional, is that the act of worship, which takes place in the heart communicating with God, is too often missing. Every expression, either verbal or in action, may help, but they are only expressions of what is essential, namely, a deep silence of communion... if we want to worship God, we must first of all learn to feel happy, being silent together with him.' Jesus brought these two insights together when he said: 'The hour is coming, and now is, when the true worshippers will worship the Father in spirit and truth, for such the Father seeks to worship him. God is spirit, and those who worship him must worship in spirit and truth.' In the silence of reflection we try to worship God in spirit and truth.

Gladden the soul of thy servant, for to thee, O Lord, do I lift up my soul.
Psalm 86:4

Worship the Lord in holy array; tremble before him, all the earth!
Psalm 96:9

... if anyone is a worshipper of God and does his will, God listens to him.
John 9:31

Fear God and give him glory... and worship him who made heaven and earth, the sea and the fountains of water.
Revelation 14:7

God in us worships God.
Ralph Waldo Emerson, *The Heart of Emerson's Journals*, edited by Bliss Perry, Constable and Co., 1927, page 51

Wonder... is the basis of Worship.
Thomas Carlyle, *Sartor Resartus*, Ward, Lock and Co., page 52

We *Worship* God best; when we Resemble Him most.
Benjamin Whichcote, *Moral and Religious Aphorisms*, number 248, Elkin, Mathews and Marrot, 1930

So long as the letter is the servant of the spirit and not its master, the spirit gives life to the letter. Hence public worship. Hence vocal prayer.
Hubert van Zeller, *Considerations*, Sheed and Ward, 1974, page 86

Who worship God shall find him. Humble love,
And not proud reason, keeps the door of heav'n;
Love finds admission, where proud science fails.
Edward Young. *Night Thoughts*, Thomas Nelson, 1841, page 244

When our Lord told the Samaritan woman that worship of the Father should be in spirit and in truth he was not ruling out considerations of place, ceremonial, formulas. He was saying that these factors were useless unless animated by spirit and truth.

Hubert van Zeller, *Considerations*, Sheed and Ward, 1974, page 87

For worship is the submission of all our nature to God. It is the quickening of the conscience by His holiness; the nourishment of mind with His truth; the purifying of imagination by His beauty; the opening of the heart to His love; the surrender of will to His purpose—and all of this gathered up in adoration, the most selfless emotion of which our nature is capable.

William Temple, *Readings in St. John's Gospel*, First and Second Series, Macmillan and Co., 1947, page 68

One of the reasons why communal worship or private prayer seem to be so dead or so conventional is that the act of worship, which takes place in the heart communing with God, is too often missing. Every expression either verbal or in action, may help, but they are only expressions of what is essential, namely, a deep silence of communion ... if we want to worship God, we must first of all learn to feel happy, being silent together with him.

Anthony Bloom, *Living Prayer*, Darton, Longman and Todd, 1966, page vii

All our external religious activities—services, communions, formal devotions, good works— these are either the expressions or the support of this inward life of loving adherence. We must have such outward expressions and supports, because we are not pure spirits but human beings, receiving through our senses the messages of Reality. But all their beauty is from within; and the degree in which we can either exhibit or apprehend that beauty depends on our own inward state.

Evelyn Underhill, *Concerning the Inner Life*, Methuen and Co., 1926, page 32

The word 'worship' comes from an old English word meaning worship—giving to God his true worth as Creator, Redeemer, and indwelling Spirit. Worship is man's response to these divine activites. As we realize the greatness, the goodness and the 'allness' of God, we forget ourselves and our hearts break forth in praise. Yet worship is not just an expression in words or music of feeling, but the outgoing of our hearts and the acceptance of God as the governing reality of our lives. He becomes our chiefest good and our lives are henceforth offered to him in loving obedience.

George Appleton, *Journey for a Soul*, William Collins Sons and Co., 1976, page 215

Outward worship of itself avails nothing. We have to pay attention, apply our minds to God's service: the whole of ourselves must be brought to bear on our loving service of him. This cannot be done without great labour.

Day by day, hour by hour, we must be renewing the offering of ourselves, making sure it is not a matter of words and sentiments, but actuality. Everything we do from morning to night must be truthful, coming from our deepest centre.

How few of us, says St Thérèse, always do our best, never take little holidays, but are *always* attentive to God, present to him, waiting on him, loving him.

This is the living sacrifice, holy and acceptable, the pure spiritual worship which alone matters to him.

Ruth Burrows, in *The Watchful Heart*, edited by Elizabeth Ruth Obbard, Darton, Longman and Todd, 1988, page 24

It is an inestimable joy that I was raised out of nothing to see and enjoy this glorious world: It is a Sacred Gift whereby the children of men are made my treasures, but O Thou who art fairer than the children of men, how great and unconceivable is the joy of thy Love! That I who was lately raised out of the dust, have so great a Friend, that I who in this life am born to mean things according to the world should be called to inherit such glorious things in the way of heaven, such a Lord, so great a Lover, such heavenly mysteries, such doings and such sufferings, with all the benefit and pleasure of them in Thy intelligible kingdom: it amazeth, it transporteth and ravisheth me. I will leave my father's house and come unto Thee; for Thou art my Lord and I will worship Thee.

Thomas Traherne, Centuries, edited by Bertram Dobell, P.J. and A.E. Dobell, 1950, page 67

Here, in the heart and love and life of Nature, and with Christ by my side, I cannot bring myself to go to church, when the whole of creation calls me to worship God in such infinitely more beautiful and inspiring light and colour and form and sound. Not a single thing out here but suggests love and peace and joy and gratitude...

If I didn't feel and know that He was there with me always, natural things—trees, skies, flowers, and animals—would have no fascination for me whatever. But I know that every joy I feel in a wood is understood and felt more perfectly by Christ at my side; I feel always as though He were leading me about and showing me things, and for everything I thank Him—in fact, it's a running conversation all the time. When I am with other people or in a bad temper, I don't feel this; but oh, the joy of getting away alone and getting Him to show you things.

Edward Wilson, in George Seaver, The Faith of Edward Wilson, John Murray, 1949, page 33

The Christian hope of the future is that this, the true meaning and message of the Incarnation, will come to be more deeply understood and the demand on man's worshipping love and total self-offering, will receive a more complete response—a response stretching upward in awe-struck contemplation to share that adoring vision of the Principle which is 'the inheritance of the saints in light,' and downwards and outwards in loving action, to embrace and to transform the whole world. When this happens, Christian sacramental worship will at last disclose its full meaning, and enter into its full heritage. For it will be recognized as the ritual sign of our deepest relation with Reality, and so of the mysterious splendour of our situation and our call; the successive life of man freely offered in oblation, and the abiding life of God in Christ received, not for our own sakes, but in order to achieve that transfiguration of the whole created universe, that shining forth of the splendour of the Holy, in which the aim of worship shall be fulfilled.

Evelyn Underhill, Worship, Nisbet and Co., 1943, page 343

If the Church has emphasized the function of art in her public prayer, it has been because she knew that a true and valid aesthetic formation was necessary for the wholeness of Christian living and worship. The liturgy and the chant and Church art are all supposed to form and spiritualize man's consciousness, to give him a tone and a maturity without which his prayer cannot normally be either very deep or very wide or very pure.

There is only one reason why this is completely true: art is not an end in itself. It introduces the soul into a higher spiritual order, which it expresses and in some sense explains. Music and art and poetry attune the soul to God because they induce a kind of contact with the Creator and Ruler of the Universe. The genius of the artist finds its ways by the affinity of creative sympathy, or connaturality, into the living law that rules the universe. This law is nothing but the secret gravitation that draws all things to God as to their centre. Since all true art lays bare the action of this same law in the depths of our own nature, it makes us alive to the tremendous mystery of being in which we ourselves, together with all other living and existing things, come forth from the depths of God and return again to Him.

Thomas Merton, No Man Is An Island, Burns and Oates, 1974, page 30

Index

A

Addison, Joseph 40, 58, 80
Al-Ansari 71
Al-Ghazali 135, 221
Amiel, Henri Frédéric 44, 71, 75, 78, 81, 90, 96, 148, 157, 184, 187, 223, 242, 261, 276, 282
Appleton, George 24, 47, 52, 60, 67, 75, 81, 82, 100, 116, 129, 132, 142, 158, 161, 162, 195, 212, 220, 231, 234, 239, 244, 249, 250, 260, 267, 282, 286, 294
Arnold, Matthew 33, 93, 105, 151, 195, 203, 246
Auden, W.H. 220
Augustine, St 41, 44, 93, 116, 145, 238-239
Aurelius, Marcus 18, 192

B

Bacon, Francis 21, 26, 27, 35, 69, 136, 184, 216, 269
Bagehot, Walter 288
Barclay, William 75, 125, 131, 148, 158, 184, 239, 269, 288
Barnes, Kenneth 240
Barry, F.R. 46, 87, 276
Basil the Great, St 119
Beard, Rebecca 87
Beecher, Henry Ward 87, 152, 233, 264
Benson, A.C. 249
Benson, R.M. 264
Berdyaev, Nicolas 18, 28, 64, 75, 78, 90, 107, 111, 139-140, 173, 190, 259, 261
Bernanos, George 105
Bernard, St. 210
Bernhardt, Sarah 178
Blake, William 19, 43, 87, 97, 100, 178, 189, 216, 236, 259
Bloom, Anthony 47, 55, 67, 88, 122, 143, 150, 181, 210, 213, 287, 294
Boehme, Jacob 128
Boethius 192, 194
Bonhoeffer, Dietrich 18, 56, 148, 199, 235, 257, 259, 277
Book of Common Prayer 257
Boros, Ladislaus 166
Bowker, John 90
Brooke, Stopford A. 117
Brooks, Phillips 29
Brown, John 22
Browne, Sir Thomas 41, 105, 139
Browning, Robert 22, 69, 92, 233, 246, 270
Brunner, Emil 212, 215, 236

Bryant, C.R. 283
Buber, Martin 238
Bullett, Gerald 153
Bunyan, John 35, 71, 135
Burke, Edmund 22, 41, 77, 139, 242
Burroughs, Edward 120
Burrows, Ruth 16, 23, 30, 38, 49, 62, 88, 122, 155, 165, 187, 199, 217, 240, 268, 271, 294
Burton, Sir Richard 167
Butler, Samuel 154
Butterfield, Herbert 44
Byron, Lord 172

C

Cairns, D.S. 125
Calhoun, Robert Lowry 288
Camus, Jean Pierre 42
Carlyle, Thomas 18, 26, 37, 135, 139, 146, 204, 293
Carpenter, Edward 208, 223
Carrel, Alexis 242
Carretto, Carlo 41, 57, 65, 85, 120, 140, 141, 178, 182, 244, 261, 265, 278
Carter, Sydney 269
Casals, Pablo 58
Caussade, Jean Pierre de 56, 286
Channing, William E. 141
Chapman, John 173
Chardin, Pierre Teilhard de 33, 57, 64, 132, 192, 212
Coburn, John B. 94
Coleridge, Samuel Taylor 27, 52, 181, 247
Collick, Elizabeth 97-98
Colton, C.C. 26, 40, 178
Concise Oxford Dictionary 153
Confucius 96
Connolly, Cyril 243
Conrad, Joseph 77, 288
Cooke, Grace 99
Coulson, C.A. 270
Cowper, William 96-97, 135
Craig, Archibald C. 66
Cripps, Sir Stafford 175
Cyril of Jerusalem 238

D

Dante Alighieri 285
Darwin, Charles 140
Dell, William 43

Devlin, Patrick 152
Dickens, Charles 253
Dimnet, Ernest 142
Disraeli, Benjamin 96, 258
Disraeli, Isaac 142
Dodd, C.H. 94
Dominion, Jack 283
Donne, John 38, 71, 138
Dostoyevsky, Fyodor 152, 291
Drummond, Henry 119, 277
Dryden, John 80, 264
Durant, Will 151

E

Eckhart, Meister 113, 114, 179, 207, 220, 259, 260, 277
Eddington, Arthur S. 228
Egypt, St. Macarius of 119
Einstein, Albert 52, 154, 195, 228
Eliot, George 19, 118, 194
Elizabeth of Dijon 102
Ellis, Havelock 87, 153
Emerson, Ralph Waldo 24, 32, 125, 138, 164, 178, 184, 192, 216, 253, 266, 269, 277, 293
Epictetus 114

F

Faber, F.W. 148
Farmer, Herbert H. 69
Farrar, Frederick W. 102
Fausset, Hugh L'Anson 65, 250
Fénèlon, F. de la M. 254
Ferguson, John 20
Fielding, Henry 172
Fox, George 35, 168, 179
Francis de Sales 267
Franklin, Benjamin 33, 259
Fromm, Erich 38, 64, 69, 96, 139, 233
Froude, J.A. 151
Furlong, Monica 55

G

Gandhi, Mohandas K. 38, 78, 161, 175, 178, 180
Gaunt, Belle Valerie 168
George, A. Raymond 189
Gibran, Kahlil 180, 256, 269
Glubb, Sir John 205, 287
Goethe, Johann Wolfgang von 192

Gogh, Vincent van 285
Goldsmith, Oliver 291
Gollancz, Victor 94
Goodacre, N.W. 100
Gore, Charles 108
Gorman, George H. 214
Gray, Thomas 167
Grenfell, Joyce 92
Griffiths, Bede, OSB 75, 94, 100, 135, 143, 154, 162-163, 182, 207, 212, 216, 225, 228, 229, 236, 242, 262, 264, 271, 274

H

Habgood, John 27
Haecker, Theodor 44, 78, 291
Hallock, Frank H. 107
Hammarskjöld, Dag 18, 33, 64, 82, 87, 119, 180, 235, 249
Hanson, R.P.C. 30
Hardy, Sir Alistair 205
Harnack, Adolf 132
Heard, Gerald 91
Herbert, George 96, 235, 236, 266
Herrick, Robert 254
Hesse, Herman 136
Higham, Florence 19
Hilton, Walter 215, 239
Hodgson, Leonard 87
Holyoake, G.J. 231
Houlden, J.L. 36
Hugel, Friedrich von 75, 116
Hume, Basil 125, 175
Hunt, Leigh 178
Huxley, Aldous 49, 72, 78, 133, 154, 181, 188, 207, 209, 243
Hyde, Lawrence 136

I

Ibsen, Henrik 178, 241
Inge, W.R. 44, 47, 61, 76, 81, 109, 117, 155, 173, 216, 220, 274, 280
Irenaeus, St 116

J

Jacks, L.P. 173
James, Colin 162
James, William 32, 52, 105, 173
Jefferies, Richard 75, 246
Jefferson, Thomas 151

John of Cronstadt 121, 181
John of Ruysbroeck 93, 257
John of the Cross, St 120, 198
Johnson, Samuel 43, 47, 77, 87, 93, 164, 256, 263
Jones, Rufus M. 35, 45, 60, 61, 72, 82, 93, 102, 106, 114, 119, 126, 154, 156, 185, 202, 205, 217, 220, 262, 269, 280
Jonson, Ben 22, 134, 238
Jowett, Benjamin 220
Julian of Norwich 247, 264
Jung, C.G. 16, 64, 90, 249

K

Kagawa, Toyohiko 45, 133, 144, 146, 149, 158, 204, 212, 217
Kant, Immanuel 57
Keats, John 135
Keller, Helen 153, 194, 227, 249
Kelly, Thomas 119
Kempis, Thomas à 22, 35, 44, 72, 81, 84, 207, 254
Kennedy, G.A. Studdert 41
Kierkegaard, Søren 22, 35, 219, 269
King, Martin Luther 78, 176, 227
Kingsley, Charles 164, 256
Küng, Hans 231

L

Lavelle, Louis 195
Law, William 33, 41, 71, 84, 105, 113, 129, 132, 180, 185-187, 207, 209, 210, 222, 225, 257, 291
Lawrence, Brother 181, 207
Lawrence, D.H. 52, 119
Leech, Kenneth 176
LeFebvre, George 122
Lewis, C.S. 23, 27, 61, 72, 80, 129, 139, 145, 165, 188, 204, 213, 229, 238, 265, 271
Liebman, Joshua Loth 284
Longfellow, Henry Wadsworth 22, 100, 249, 259, 286
Lowell, J.R. 81, 178
Luther, Martin 181

M

Macaulay, Rose 213
Macdonald, George 35, 64, 66, 81, 84, 93, 106, 131, 145, 148, 186, 209, 222, 247, 269, 270, 285, 286
Macleod, George F. 61

Macmurray, John 19, 242
Macquarrie, John 107, 139, 181
Maeterlinck, Maurice 77, 261, 269
Main, John, OSB 20, 33, 47, 65, 72, 103, 143, 144, 149, 158, 204, 234, 280, 283
Mann, Thomas 64
Mansfield, Katherine 247, 251
Marcus Aurelius see under Aurelius, Marcus
Maritain, Jacques 27
Martin, P.W. 119
Martineau, James 19, 97, 144
Martos, J. 171
Maugham, W. Somerset 78
May, Rollo 24, 259
McGinley, Phyllis 221
McShane, James 176
Meredith, George 74
Merton, Thomas 20, 34, 45, 55, 70, 79, 111, 120, 129, 136, 140, 184, 187, 195, 196, 208, 220, 223, 225, 233, 240, 245, 268, 283, 286, 295
Miller, Henry 172
Miller, Stuart 93
Milton, John 192, 235, 285
Montefiore, Hugh 60
Moorman, J.R.H. 68
Moran, Gabriel 216
Morris, William 96
Muggeridge, Malcolm 124
Munz, Peter 259
Murry, John Middleton 247

N

Newbigin, Lesslie 212
Niebuhr, Reinhold 38
Nouwen, Henri J.M. 237, 250
Noüy, Lecomte du 90

O

Oestreicher, Paul 245
Oldham, J.H. 27, 48
Osler, Sir William 38, 81

P

Palmer, Samuel 97
Parkhurst, Charles H. 81, 189, 194
Parmenter, Ross 194
Pascal, Blaise 32, 33, 84, 135, 178, 215, 219, 279

Patmore, Coventry   117, 220, 246
Péguy, Charles   19, 175, 222, 289
Penn, William   35, 60
Pennington, Dr H.S.   203
Pepys, Samuel   184
Peter of Alcantara, St   142
Phillips, J.B.   91
Philo   189, 267
Pilkington, Roger   228
Planck, Max   227, 228
Plato   276
Plotinus   210
Pope, Alexander   52, 187
Powys, John Cowper   145
Priestland, Gerald   163
Priestley, J.B.   52
Pringle-Pattison, A.S.   116
Procter, Adelaide Anne   96

Q

Quoist, Michel   60, 231

R

Rackham, R.B.   179
Radhakrishnan, Sir Sarvepalli   114, 158, 173
Ramakrisha, Sri   162
Ramsey, Michael   36, 103, 108, 110, 111, 117, 122, 149, 212, 229, 230, 234, 262
Rashdall, Hastings   60
Reaveley, Constance   289
Reindorp, George   60
Richard of Saint-Victor   170
Richardson, Alan   146, 168, 192, 212
Rilke, Rainer Maria   70, 203
Robertson, F.W.   125, 249, 269
Robinson, A.W.   266
Robinson, Forbes   52, 97
Rolle, Richard   54, 170
Ruskin, John   95, 226
Russell, Bertrand   25, 194, 208, 259

S

Saint-Exupéry, Antoine de   135, 194
Santayana, George   27
Sayers, Dorothy L.   54, 289
Schweitzer, Albert   30, 39, 76, 88, 126, 132, 133, 154, 185, 200, 201, 202, 236, 270

Scott, Sir Walter   22, 233, 238
Scudder, Vida D.   184
Seaver, George   193
Seraphim of Sarov   132
Shakespeare, William   22, 69, 77, 93, 96, 139, 187, 238, 239, 256
Shaw, George Bernard   238
Shelley, Percy Bysshe   38, 151, 291
Silesius, Angelus   116
Smart, James D.   189
Smith, John, the Platonist   104, 119, 285
Smith, R.L.   44, 242
Snaith, N.H.   130
Soper, Lord   175, 288
Southey, Robert   96
Spencer, Herbert   38
Spenser, Edmund   254
Spinoza   74, 186, 196, 291
Steere, Douglas   185
Steiner, Rudolf   131
Sterne, Laurence   87
Stevenson, Robert Louis   151
Stone, Irving   21
Swedenborg, Emanuel   92

T

Tagore, Rabindranath   38, 64, 179, 206, 282
Tatelbaum, Judy   98
Tauler, John   72, 206, 236, 254
Taylor, F.J.   201
Taylor, Jeremy   264, 278
Taylor, John V.   107, 240
Temple, William   26, 27, 29, 33, 44, 45, 47, 54, 57, 61, 64, 66, 67, 75, 81, 87, 88, 103, 107, 109, 110, 125, 128, 140, 142, 151, 165, 170, 173, 176, 178, 181, 184, 189, 200, 201, 203, 210, 216, 222, 227, 231, 233, 234, 239, 242, 244, 254, 256, 264, 266, 267, 270, 271, 277, 286, 288, 294
Tennyson, Alfred, Lord   33, 41, 52, 57, 69, 122, 134, 139, 157, 178
Teresa of Avila, St   225
Theologia Germanica   16, 106, 168
Thompson, Francis   18, 148
Thoreau, Henry David   146, 151, 173, 269
Tillich, Paul   15, 159, 223, 267
Tolstoy, Leo   16, 53, 54, 93, 203, 215
Traherne, Thomas   19, 48, 76, 107, 114, 118, 135, 167, 174, 198, 201, 240, 265, 273, 294
Trench, Richard Chevenix   93
Trevelyan, George   143, 168

U

Underhill, Evelyn   25, 42, 44, 54, 59, 78, 84, 104, 108, 116, 121, 125, 154, 179, 182, 215, 220, 225, 226, 236, 294, 295

V

Vatican Council II   20, 29, 35, 148
Vaughan, Henry   74
Vidler, Alec R.   47
Vinci, Leonardo da   64, 195
Vlastos, Gregory   50

W

Waddams, Herbert   108
Walls, Roland   254
Walton, Izaak   93, 256
Watts, Alan W.   116, 280
Weatherhead, Leslie D.   29
Weil, Simone   72, 85
West, Morris   78, 233, 282
Whale, J.S.   126, 239
Whichcote, Benjamin   26, 81, 139, 178, 186, 215, 293
Whitehead, Alfred North   57, 173

Whiting, Lilian   25
Whitman, Walt   38, 41, 94, 139, 147
Wilde, Oscar   15, 36
Wiles, Maurice   62, 244
Williams, Harry   175, 209, 251
Wilson, Bryan   232
Wilson, Edward   25, 36, 125, 127, 183, 203, 270, 295
Wilson, Michael   199
Winnington, John   289
Wood, H.G.   54
Woolman, John   54, 233
Wordsworth, William   57, 81, 96, 236, 291
Wyon, Olive   123

Y

Yeats, W.B.   282
Yelchaninov, Father   239
Young, Edward   139, 194, 233, 293

Z

Zeller, Hubert van   64, 128, 139, 148, 170, 207, 225, 231, 236, 238, 249, 259, 279, 280, 291, 293, 294

ACKNOWLEDGMENTS

Aldous Huxley, *Ends and Means* and *Brave New World* by permission of Mrs Laura Huxley.

Thomas Merton, *The Sign of Jonas* reprinted by permission of Curtis Brown Ltd. Copyright © 1953 by The Abbey of Our Lady of Gethesemani, renewed by The Trustees of the Merton Legacy Trust.

John Middleton Murray, *God* by permission of The Society of Authors and the Estate of John Middleton Murray.

Henry Miller, *The Wisdom of the Heart* copyright © 1941 by New Directions Pub. Corp. Reprinted by permission of New Directions.

John Cowper Powys, *The Meaning of Culture* by permission of the Estate of John Cowper Powys.